Hitler's Atomic Bomb

Who were the German scientists who worked on atomic bombs during World War II for Hitler's regime? How did they justify themselves afterwards? Examining the global influence of the German uranium project and post-war reactions to the scientists involved, Mark Walker explores the narratives surrounding "Hitler's bomb." The global impacts of this project were cataclysmic. Credible reports of German developments spurred the American Manhattan Project, the nuclear attacks on Hiroshima and Nagasaki, and in turn the Soviet efforts. After the war these scientists' work was overshadowed by the twin shocks of Auschwitz and Hiroshima. *Hitler's Atomic Bomb* sheds light on the postwar criticism and subsequent rehabilitation of the German scientists, including the controversial legend of Werner Heisenberg and Carl Friedrich von Weizsäcker's visit to occupied Copenhagen in 1941. This scientifically accurate but nontechnical history examines the impact of German efforts to harness nuclear fission and the surrounding debates and legends.

MARK WALKER is the John Bigelow Professor of History at Union College, Schenectady, New York. His research interests include twentieth-century science, particularly science and technology under National Socialism. Previous publications include *The Kaiser Wilhelm Society during National Socialism* (Cambridge, 2009) and *The German Physical Society in the Third Reich: Physicists between Autonomy and Accommodation* (Cambridge, 2012).

Hitler's Atomic Bomb

*History, Legend, and the Twin Legacies
of Auschwitz and Hiroshima*

Mark Walker

Union College, New York

Shaftesbury Road, Cambridge CB2 8EA, United Kingdom

One Liberty Plaza, 20th Floor, New York, NY 10006, USA

477 Williamstown Road, Port Melbourne, VIC 3207, Australia

314–321, 3rd Floor, Plot 3, Splendor Forum, Jasola District Centre, New Delhi – 110025, India

103 Penang Road, #05–06/07, Visioncrest Commercial, Singapore 238467

Cambridge University Press is part of Cambridge University Press & Assessment, a department of the University of Cambridge.

We share the University's mission to contribute to society through the pursuit of education, learning and research at the highest international levels of excellence.

www.cambridge.org
Information on this title: www.cambridge.org/9781009479288

DOI: 10.1017/9781009479264

© Mark Walker 2024

This publication is in copyright. Subject to statutory exception and to the provisions of relevant collective licensing agreements, no reproduction of any part may take place without the written permission of Cambridge University Press & Assessment.

First published 2024

Printed in the United Kingdom by CPI Group Ltd, Croydon CR0 4YY

A catalogue record for this publication is available from the British Library

Library of Congress Cataloging-in-Publication Data
Names: Walker, Mark, 1959– author.
Title: Hitler's atomic bomb : history, legend, and the twin legacies of Auschwitz and Hiroshima / Mark Walker, Union College, New York.
Other titles: History, legend, and the twin legacies of Auschwitz and Hiroshima
Description: Cambridge ; New York, NY : Cambridge University Press, 2024. | Includes bibliographical references.
Identifiers: LCCN 2023048700 | ISBN 9781009479288 (hardback) | ISBN 9781009479264 (ebook)
Subjects: LCSH: World War, 1939–1945 – Science. | Atomic bomb – Germany – History – 20th century. | Nuclear physics – Research – Germany – History – 20th century. | Science and state – Germany – History – 20th century. | Arms race – History – 20th century.
Classification: LCC D810.S2 W35 2024 | DDC 940.54/86730943–dc23/eng/20240131
LC record available at https://lccn.loc.gov/2023048700

ISBN 978-1-009-47928-8 Hardback

Cambridge University Press & Assessment has no responsibility for the persistence or accuracy of URLs for external or third-party internet websites referred to in this publication and does not guarantee that any content on such websites is, or will remain, accurate or appropriate.

This book is dedicated to my wife Linda, son Chris, and daughter Kerry.

Contents

List of Figures	*page* viii
Preface	ix
Acknowledgments	x
List of Abbreviations	xi
Introduction	1

Part I The Bomb

1 Farm Hall	5
2 Nuclear Fission	13
3 Lightning War	21
4 Selling Uranium	48
5 Total War	77
6 The War is Lost	109

Part II Living with the Bomb

7 Oversimplifications	147
8 Compromising with Hitler	179
9 Rehabilitation	215
10 Copenhagen	240
Conclusion	268
Epilogue: The Historian as Historical Actor	272
Glossary	275
Notes	276
Archives	327
Bibliography	329
Index	341

Figures

1.1 The House at Farm Hall	*page* 6
3.1 Werner Heisenberg at Farm Hall	22
3.2 Paul Harteck at Farm Hall	23
3.3 Walther Bothe in 1938	27
3.4 Karl Wirtz at Farm Hall	31
3.5 Kurt Diebner at Farm Hall	34
3.6 Otto Hahn at Farm Hall	36
3.7 Carl Friedrich von Weizsäcker at Farm Hall	36
3.8 Schematic diagram of experiments B-I and B-II	38
4.1 Schematic diagram of chain reactions in uranium	57
4.2 Schematic diagram of experiments L-III and L-IV	63
4.3 Lectures in the Harnack House	68
5.1 Schematic diagram of a double ultracentrifuge	80
5.2 Schematic diagram of experiment G-I	93
5.3 Schematic diagram of experiment G-II	96
5.4 Photograph of experiment G-III	100
6.1 Walther Gerlach at Farm Hall	110
6.2 Schematic diagram of experiments B-VI and B-VII	119
6.3 Schematic diagram of experiment B-VIII	122
6.4 Schematic diagram of hollow-point design	125
7.1 Samuel Goudsmit during the Alsos Mission	148
7.2 Hand-drawn diagram of chain reactions in uranium	163

Preface

Historians usually get only one chance to write a history. My Ph.D. dissertation, subsequently published as a book, also examined the German efforts to build atomic bombs during World War II.[1] This book is not an updated version of my earlier work but rather a new history written directly from the sources, many of which were not available when I first researched this topic. These new materials include the Farm Hall transcripts, documents from the Kaiser Wilhelm Institute for Physics retrieved from Russian archives, Niels Bohr's unpublished letters to Werner Heisenberg, Carl Friedrich von Weizsäcker's papers, and the correspondence between Elisabeth and Werner Heisenberg.

I am breaking with historiographic tradition in a few ways. When writing about the Third Reich, as opposed to the postwar period, I use the adjective "National Socialist" or its acronym "NS" instead of "Nazi," except when a historical actor used the latter term. Rather than use Adolf Hitler's title in German, "Führer," I have translated it as "Leader." In both cases I want to help the English-language reader better experience what life was like during National Socialism. During the Third Reich a German would not have often heard or said the more pejorative "Nazi," while using the German word "Führer" in English hides the symbolism, which was very important and clear to Germans, that Hitler led and they were expected to follow.

Although I discuss historiography where appropriate in this book, this will be supplemented by a more thorough discussion of the literature in a forthcoming separate publication.

Acknowledgments

Because I have been wrestling with this topic for all my professional career, my debts of gratitude are many. Historians can only write history when they have access to sources. I am grateful to Helmut Rechenberg at the Max Planck Institute for Physics and the Archives of the German Museum for Science and Technology, including its former archivist Wilhelm Fußl, both in Munich; the Berlin Document Center (now part of the Federal German Archives) and the Archives of the Max Planck Society, both in Berlin; the Niels Bohr Library at the American Institute of Physics in College Park, Maryland; and the Archives and Special Collections of the Rensselaer Polytechnic Institute in Troy, New York and its former archivist John Dojka for making this book possible. My research was greatly facilitated by grants from the German Academic Exchange Service, the Berlin Program of the Social Science Research Council, the Humboldt Foundation, and the Fulbright Program. I was very fortunate to be a visiting researcher in the Max Planck Society Research Program directed by Carola Sachse for the History of the Kaiser Wilhelm Society during National Socialism, the codirector along with Dieter Hoffmann of the Research Project for the History of the German Physical Society in the Third Reich, to teach as a visiting professor at Nikolaus Rupke's institute at the University of Göttingen and as Friedrich Steinle's guest at the Technical University of Berlin, and be the guests of Helmuth Trischler and Ulf Hashagen as a scholar-in-residence at the Research Institute in the German Museum for Science and Technology. I am most grateful to the many colleagues who have helped me grapple with the history of science and technology during National Socialism: Helmuth Albrecht, Ulrich Albrecht, Mitchell Ash, Richard Beyler, Cathryn Carson, David Cassidy, Ute Deichmann, Michael Eckert, Paul Forman, John Guse, Ulf Hashagen, Susanne Heim, Andreas Heinemann-Grüder, Klaus Hentschel, Dieter Hoffmann, Uwe Hoßfeld, Horst Kant, Andreas Kleinert, Hemut Maier, Herbert Mehrtens, Benno Müller-Hill, Michael Neufeld, Gerhard Rammer, Volker Remmert, Monika Renneberg, Volker Roelcke, Carola Sachse, Florian Schmaltz, Reinhard Siegmund-Schultze, Ruth Lewin Sime, Helmuth Trischler, Heike Weber, Burghard Weiss, Sheila Weiss, and Stefan Wolff.

Abbreviations

DAAD	*Deutsche Akademischer Austauschdienst* (German Academic Exchange Service).
DAL	*Deutsche Akademie für Luftfahrtforschung* (German Academy for Aviation Research).
DFG	*Deutsche Forschungsgemeinschaft* (German Research Foundation).
DFR	*Deutscher Forschungsrat* (German Research Council).
DWI	*Deutsches Wissenschaftliches Institut* (German Cultural Institute).
HWA	*Heereswaffenamt* (Army Ordnance).
IDO	*Institut für deutsche Ostarbeit* (German Institute for Eastern Work).
KWG	*Kaiser-Wilhelm-Gesellschaft* (Kaiser Wilhelm Society).
KWIfC	*Kaiser-Wilhelm Institut für Chemie* (Kaiser Wilhelm Institute for Chemistry).
KWIfP	*Kaiser-Wilhelm Institut für Physik* (Kaiser Wilhelm Institute for Physics).
MPG	*Max-Planck-Gesellschaft* (Max Planck Society).
NARA	National Archives and Records Administration.
NATO	North Atlantic Treaty Organization.
NDW	*Notgemeinschaft der Deutschen Wissenschaft* (Emergency Society for German Science).
NSDAP	*Nationalsozialistische Deutsche Arbeiterpartei* (National Socialist German Workers Party).
NSDB	*Nationalsozialistischer Deutscher Dozentenbund* (National Socialist University Lecturers League).
OKH	*Oberkommando des Heeres* (Army High Command).
OSRD	Office of Scientific Research and Development.
PTR	*Physikalisch-Technisches Reichsanstalt* (Reich Physical-Technical Institute).
REM	*Reichsministerium für Wissenschaft, Erziehung und Volksbildung* (Reich Ministry of Science, Education, and Culture).

xii   List of Abbreviations

RFR   *Reichsforschungsrat* (Reich Research Council).
RSA   *Reichssippenamt* (Reich Kinship Office).
SD   Sicherheitsdienst der SS (Security Service of the SS).
VDW   *Vereinigung Deutscher Wissenschaftler* (Federation of German Scientists).

Introduction

During World War II German scientists attempted to harness nuclear fission chain reactions in order to create powerful new energy sources and weapons. This is one of the most important developments in recent history, not because of what the scientists did, rather because of how their efforts were perceived. Without the German uranium project and credible reports about its existence, it is difficult to imagine the United States government investing such great amounts of manpower, resources, and money into making such a futuristic weapon as the atomic bomb. If the American Manhattan Project and the nuclear attacks on Hiroshima and Nagasaki had not happened, it is equally difficult to imagine the Soviet Union making a comparable effort. Thus without the threat of "Hitler's Bomb" there is no atomic bomb in the summer of 1945, or nuclear arms race immediately thereafter. The world would have been a very different place.

The second part of the story, the debates and arguments during the postwar period surrounding the German wartime work on uranium, is also important, for it sheds light on how people deal with and learn from the past. Confronted with the terrible legacy of National Socialism, these German scientists had to justify, both to their fellow Germans and to foreign colleagues, having worked within the National Socialist state on weapons of such destructive power. Some of these colleagues were émigrés from Germany who had suffered great personal loss. The result was one of the most enduring and controversial legends in modern science: Werner Heisenberg and Carl Friedrich von Weizsäcker's 1941 visit with their Danish Colleague Niels Bohr in occupied Copenhagen. This book examines the history of the wartime research in Germany, connects this to the postwar criticism and eventual rehabilitation of these scientists, and sheds light on this legend.

Part I

The Bomb

1 Farm Hall

I had a long talk with Professor Heisenberg, who is the most sensible of them, and he told me that their main worry was the lack of information about their families. He also said that they suspected that their potential value was being judged by the documents found at their institutions. He said that these did not give a true picture of the extent of their experiments which had advanced much further than would appear from these documents and maintained that they had advanced still further as a result of pooling of information since their detention. He begged for an opportunity of discussing the whole matter with British and American scientists in order to acquaint them with their latest theories and work out a scheme for future cooperation.

Major T. H. Rittner (June 15, 1945).[1]

Interned at Farm Hall

Two months after the end of World War II in Europe, while the conflict in the Pacific still raged, ten German scientists found themselves interned in an English country house called Farm Hall (see Figure 1.1). We know a lot about their time there because secret microphones had been installed in the walls and their conversations were overheard.[2]

After two weeks, the British officer in charge of the detained scientists described them as follows:

[Max] von Laue: A shy mild mannered man. He cannot understand the reason for his detention. He has been extremely friendly and is very well disposed to England and America.

[Otto] Hahn: A man of the world. He has been the most helpful of the professors and his sense of humor and common sense has saved the day on many occasions. He is definitely friendly disposed to England and America.

[Werner] Heisenberg: He has been very friendly and helpful and is, I believe, genuinely anxious to cooperate with British and American scientists although he has spoken of going over to the Russians.

[Walther] Gerlach: Has a very cheerful disposition and is easy to handle. He appears to be genuinely cooperative.

[Paul] Harteck: A charming personality and has never caused any trouble. His one wish is to get on with his work. As he is a bachelor, he is less worried about conditions in Germany.

[Kurt] Diebner: Outwardly very friendly, but has an unpleasant personality and is not to be trusted. He is disliked by all the others except Bagge.

[Carl Friedrich] von Weizsäcker: A diplomat. He has always been very friendly and cooperative and I believe he is genuinely prepared to work with England and America but he is a good German.

[Karl] Wirtz: An egoist. Very friendly on the surface but cannot be trusted. I doubt whether he will cooperate unless it is made worth his while.

[Erich] Bagge: A serious and very hardworking young man. He is completely German and is unlikely to cooperate. His friendship with Diebner lays him open to suspicion.

[Horst] Korsching: A complete enigma. He appears to be morose and surly. He very rarely opens his mouth. He has, however, become more human since his arrival in England.[3]

Max von Laue, a Nobel laureate for physics, was the odd man out because he had not participated in uranium research during the war, although most of the researchers at the Kaiser Wilhelm Institute for Physics that he worked in did. The Allies interned the young scientists Bagge and Korsching because they had been working on novel uranium isotope enrichment processes. The chemist Otto Hahn, like Laue an older man, had been one of the first to recognize that uranium could be split, and during the war had continued to work on the consequences of nuclear fission. Paul Harteck, a physical chemist and aside from Hahn the only nonphysicist, had been one of the most important scientists, overseeing efforts to both enrich uranium isotopes and produce heavy water. The most important administrator for the working group was Kurt Diebner, an official in Army Ordnance. The Nobel laureate Werner Heisenberg, cofounder of quantum mechanics, contributed to the theory of

Figure 1.1 The House at Farm Hall.
Source: National Archives and Records Administration (NARA).

nuclear fission and of nuclear reactors. Along with Harteck, Heisenberg was one of most important scientists researching uranium in Germany. Karl Wirtz worked under Heisenberg designing nuclear reactor experiments, while Carl Friedrich von Weizsäcker similarly assisted Heisenberg with nuclear theory. Walther Gerlach belatedly joined the nuclear physics working group near the end of 1943, taking over as the administrator in charge of research on uranium as well as physics in general.

The scientists themselves were confident that they knew why they were in Farm Hall: with one exception, they had been involved in a wartime research project to harness the energy produced by nuclear fission, in other words, nuclear power and atomic bombs. As Weizsäcker told Wirtz: "These people have 'detained' us firstly because they think we are dangerous; [second] that we have really done a lot with uranium."[4]

Who Was a Nazi?

The fall of the Third Reich and the subsequent public revelations of atrocities and war crimes begged obvious questions: had these scientists supported racist and murderous policies, or tried to provide the Third Reich with powerful new weapons? In other words, had they worked for Hitler? Bagge and Diebner admitted to having been members of the National Socialist German Workers Party (NSDAP) but denied being "Nazis." Diebner claimed that he had only stayed in the NSDAP because, if Germany had won the war, then only Party members would have been given good jobs.[5] Bagge said that his mother had applied for his Party membership on his behalf but without his knowledge, which was unlikely to have been true.[6] Gerlach maintained that no one had to join the NSDAP. Once he had left the room, Bagge added in turn that Gerlach had known Hermann Göring personally and his brother was in the SS.[7] Other scientists like Hahn also distanced themselves from the Nazis. "See what Laue did against National Socialism and I think I worked against it too. We are both innocent."[8]

Heisenberg, who enjoyed by far the most prestige and had the most influence of the scientists at Farm Hall, defended Bagge to a visiting British scientist, Patrick Blackett, claiming that Heisenberg's younger colleague had never been a "fanatical Nazi." He also told Blackett that politically Wirtz had always been "on the good side, on our side."[9] This black-and-white dichotomy was typical of how the scientists retrospectively treated the Nazi question: one had either been a Nazi, or not. But Heisenberg drew the line at Diebner. After a British officer suggested that the scientists draft a memorandum on their political convictions, Heisenberg told Hahn that if the memorandum described a general anti-Nazi attitude and Diebner signed it, then Heisenberg could not conscientiously sign it as well. In the end, their memorandum avoided such political topics.

8 The Bomb

The British wardens at Farm Hall detected the lingering effect of National Socialist ideology on the scientists. Some detainees expressed grave concern that Moroccan French colonial troops were occupying Hechingen and Tailfingen. Bagge went so far as to say:

And in the meantime my family will be dead. After all, I feel responsible for my family. I saw it for myself. The first day the French arrived in Hechingen and raped the women one after the other and a few days later they took me away. [A subsequent letter from Bagge's wife made clear that this was not true.] The day I had to leave, three Moroccans were billeted in the house--that's been going on for three months and I'm supposed to look happy here. I shall go mad. I can't stand it much longer.[10]

When the detainees were lent a copy of *Life* magazine containing articles on the atom bomb and a number of photographs of the scientists who had worked on it, Weizsäcker remarked that of course they were mostly Germans. The British commander noted that Weizsäcker's claim, which was in fact false, "merely emphasizes the conceit of these people, who still believe in the *Herrenvolk* [Master Race]." With the possible exception of von Laue, this applied to every one of the guests. As Jeremy Bernstein has pointed out, ironically many of the scientists portrayed were in fact Jewish.[11]

Even Heisenberg made a remarkable comparison between the Allied officials who had interned the Germans and were deciding their fate and some of the most infamous men in the Third Reich. While some officials were extremely friendly towards Heisenberg and his colleagues, on the other hand there were "obstinate people, these American Heydrichs and Kaltenbrunners" (the two men who served as second-in-command of the SS), who wanted to keep the Germans locked up in Farm Hall.[12] Indeed, the scientists expressed very different opinions about the worst excesses of National Socialism. Bagge argued that if the Germans had put people in concentration camps during the war – he did not do it, knew nothing about it, and always condemned it when he heard about it – and if Hitler had ordered a few atrocities in concentration camps during the last few years of the conflict, then these excesses had occurred under the stress of war.

In contrast, Karl Wirtz stated flatly that he and his countrymen had done unprecedented things. In Poland the SS had driven up to a girls' school, brought out the top class and shot them simply because the Polish intelligentsia was to be wiped out. Just imagine, he asked his colleagues, if the Allies had arrived in Hechingen, the small town where many of them had been evacuated during the last years of the war, driven to a girls' school and shot all the girls! "That's what we did."[13] Despite the apparently nationalistic and racist tone immediately after the war, the German scientists interned at Farm Hall probably would have been appalled at the scale and depth of the depravity demonstrated by some of their countrymen over the course of the "euthanasia" program, the war in the east, and the Holocaust.

Farm Hall

However, the scientists' main concern was not who among them had been a Nazi. Max von Laue summed up their situation in a letter he sent to his son Theodore in the USA:

We have always had excellent room and board here (like English military personnel, that is, better than the civilian English population), have books, newspapers, radio, a piano, and an exercise yard behind the house. Recently we have received new clothes and, as needed, shoes. Therefore we are doing very well, except for the fact that we have received no news from our families, and only today could send letters to them with some chance of being delivered.[14]

Laue wrote his letter on August 7, a day after the ten scientists' lives changed on hearing the news of Hiroshima. Indeed the discussion about Nazis now practically vanished as other questions occupied their minds.

The News of Hiroshima

When Hahn was the first to be told that the BBC had announced that an atomic bomb had been dropped, he was completely shattered by the news. He told the British officer that, since he had made the original discovery of nuclear fission, he felt personally responsible for the deaths of hundreds of thousands of people. Indeed once Hahn realized the "terrible potentialities of his discovery," he had contemplated suicide. Once Hahn was calmed down with the help of "considerable alcoholic stimulant," he joined the rest of the scientists for dinner and announced the news.[15]

Several of the scientists were hit hard by the revelation. Gerlach argued that, if Germany had had a weapon that would have won the war, then Germany would have been right and the others in the wrong, and asked rhetorically whether conditions in Germany were better now than they would have been after a Hitler victory? When he left the room later that evening, he went straight to his bedroom and began to weep. Harteck and Laue tried to comfort him. The British described Gerlach as acting like a "defeated general, the only alternative open to whom is to shoot himself." In a subsequent conversation with Hahn, Gerlach admitted that he was depressed by the fact that the Americans had outdone the Germans.[16] While Hahn could not understand why Gerlach was taking it so badly, Heisenberg explained that Gerlach was the only one of them who had really wanted a German victory. Although he recognized the crimes of the Nazis and disapproved of them, Gerlach was working for Germany. Hahn replied that he too loved his country and for this reason had hoped for its defeat. Indeed Hahn claimed that he "would have sabotaged the war" if he could have.[17]

Hahn's colleagues also feared for his safety. At 2 a.m. Laue knocked on Bagge's door, saying, "We must do something; I am very worried about

10   The Bomb

Otto Hahn. This news has shaken him horribly, and I fear the worst." They stayed awake for a long time, until finally they were able to tell that Hahn had fallen asleep. Laue also told the much younger Bagge: "When I was young, I wanted to do physics, and I have witnessed world history. I can really say that, in my old age."[18]

Their initial reaction as scientists, at a point in time when they had not heard many details about the Allied atomic bomb, was disbelief.[19] Heisenberg asked if the report had mentioned uranium, and when this was denied, he concluded that it had nothing to do with atoms and suggested that the story came from "some dilettante in America who knows very little about it." Soon thereafter Heisenberg had a puzzling discussion with Hahn. Heisenberg began by doubting that the Americans could have tons of pure uranium isotope 235, one of the materials used in atomic bombs. Hahn then objected that in the past Heisenberg had told him that one needed only very little uranium 235. A little more than a week after Hiroshima Heisenberg presented a better calculation but still failed to provide an accurate estimate.[20]

After they had all listened to the 9 p.m. news broadcast together, there was no longer any doubt. Five hundred million British pounds had been spent and 300,000 Japanese were dead. The Americans and British had atomic bombs. It was now very clear why they had been detained, why they had been hidden from the world, and why they could not send letters to their families.[21] Because of the enormous amount of effort and resources required, Heisenberg and his colleagues remained skeptical that the Americans had either managed uranium isotope separation on a large scale, or that they had been able to produce element 94 (plutonium) in a nuclear reactor, the two paths to an atomic bomb. The BBC news reports of Hiroshima were not specific and contained very little scientific information.[22] Indeed much of the confusion found in the Farm Hall transcripts arguably has more to do with the Germans' lack of information and desperate desire to believe that they had not been completely outdone, than with any lack of scientific or technical understanding on their part. However, as more details gradually trickled in, they were eventually forced to admit that the American-led Manhattan Project had far outstripped their now apparently modest efforts.

The next step these scientists took in dealing with the news was to discuss and debate whether they could have built atomic bombs. Bagge admired the courage of the Americans to risk so many millions of dollars. Harteck added that they might have succeeded if the highest authorities had been prepared "to sacrifice everything."[23] Heisenberg argued that the turning point was the spring of 1942, when they were able to convince political authorities that it could be done, with the result that for the first time large funds were made available for their research. However, he added they also would not have had the "moral courage" to recommend to the government in the spring of

Farm Hall

1942 that they should employ 120,000 men "just for building the thing up."[24] Weizsäcker added that, even if they had gotten all the support they wanted, it was still not clear that they could have gotten as far as the Americans and British: Even if the Germans had put the same energy into it as the Americans and had wanted it as much as they did, the Americans would have destroyed the German factories.

Indeed Weizsäcker tried to shift the discussion by arguing that what was important was not how far the Germans had advanced, rather the fact that they had been convinced that it could not be completed during the war. In response, Gerlach, Harteck, and Heisenberg distinguished between what they called an "uranium machine" (nuclear reactor) and atomic bombs: although they had not thought bombs could be built during the war, they had also been convinced that a uranium machine was possible. In the end the Allied air superiority also put that goal out of reach. After Heisenberg subsequently had read the British White Paper on the Manhattan Project, he told a visiting British physicist that it never would have been possible for Germany to do anything on that scale.[25]

The final stage in the collective construction of a legend came when the scientists asked themselves whether or not they had wanted to do it? Early on, Wirtz simply stated that he was "glad we didn't have it." Weizsäcker took the lead in constructing a consensus, arguing that instead of making excuses for why they had failed, they should admit that they had not wanted to succeed: "The reason we didn't do it was because all the physicists didn't want to do it, on principle. If we had all wanted Germany to win the war we would have succeeded." Hahn immediately replied that he did not believe that but was thankful that they had not succeeded. Heisenberg admitted that "at the bottom of my heart I was really glad" that they ended up working on a uranium machine and not a bomb. Heisenberg subsequently told Hahn that, if they had been in the same moral position as the Americans and had said to themselves that "nothing mattered except that Hitler should win the war," then they might have succeeded. But they did not want him to win.[26]

The emerging argument was summed up by Laue in his letter to his son:

The main question is naturally, why did Germany not get the bomb.... 1) The German physicists would never have received such resources as England and the USA made available. Neither the personnel, nor the money would have been available in nearly as large a dimension. For this reason no physicist seriously considered requesting such resources ... 2) Our entire uranium research was aimed at creating a uranium machine as an energy source, first of all because no one believed in the possibility of a bomb in the near future, second, because basically none of us wanted to place such a weapon into Hitler's hands.[27]

On the other hand, Bagge told Diebner that: "it is absurd for von Weizsäcker to say he did not want the thing to succeed. That may be so in his case, but not for all of us."[28]

12   The Bomb

Once they had learned enough from the radio and newspapers about the first atomic bombs, the older members of the group began crafting a written statement with the clear message that the Germans had worked on uranium machines, not atomic bombs. Bagge noted in his diary that this story received considerable but not complete support. Heisenberg and Gerlach composed a text, which after a few difficulties was signed by all. The key passage read:

By the end of 1941 the preliminary scientific work had led to the result that it would be possible to use nuclear energy to produce energy and thereby power machines. However, at that time the technical potential available to Germany did not appear to satisfy the preconditions for the manufacture of a bomb.[29]

Conclusion

Farm Hall was a psychological crucible for these scientists, who asked themselves several important and fundamental questions that have concerned historians, scientists and others ever since:

(1) Did the Germans know how to build atomic bombs?
(2) Could the Germans have built atomic bombs?
(3) Did the Germans try to build atomic bombs?
(4) Had they been Nazis?

Farm Hall left all these questions open. This book will try to answer them.

2   Nuclear Fission

It could still be a very strange accident, but more and more we are coming to the frightful conclusion: our Ra [radium] isotopes do not act like Ra but like Ba [barium].... I have agreed with Strassmann that for now we shall tell only *you*. Perhaps you can come up with some sort of fantastic explanation. We know for ourselves that it *cannot* actually burst apart into Ba.
Otto Hahn to Lise Meitner (December 19, 1938).

Your radium results are very startling. A process that begins with slow neutrons and ends up with barium!.... At the moment the assumption of such an extensive bursting seems very difficult to me, but we have experienced so many surprises in nuclear physics that one cannot simply say: it is impossible.
Lise Meitner to Otto Hahn (December 21, 1938).[1]

Radioactivity

On the eve of the twentieth century, scientists discovered and investigated the phenomenon of radioactivity: Radioactive substances were transmuting or decaying into other elements through the release of energy in the form of alpha, beta, or gamma rays, evoking both hopes and fears.[2] The New Zealand physicist Ernest Rutherford proposed that the nuclei of elements were composed of positively charged protons (hydrogen) and alpha-particles (helium), as well as negatively charged electrons. In 1932 the story of nuclear fission began in earnest with the discovery of the neutron – a nuclear particle without charge – by the British physicist James Chadwick.[3]

Within two years of the neutron being discovered the French physicists Irène Curie and Frédéric Joliot-Curie realized they could induce radioactivity by bombarding aluminum with alpha particles, discovering artificial radioactivity. This was taken up by Enrico Fermi and his research team in Italy. They used neutrons to induce radioactivity, proceeding to bombard one element after another, transforming each into a different, unstable element somewhere else on the periodic table.[4] When Fermi accepted his Nobel Prize in 1938, he claimed that he had transmuted the heaviest known element, uranium, into new, manmade transuranic elements.[5]

14   The Bomb

The Discovery of Nuclear Fission

Impressed by Fermi's results, the German chemist Otto Hahn and the Austrian physicist Lise Meitner, both of whom worked at the Kaiser Wilhelm Institute for Chemistry in Berlin, decided to study the apparent transuranics. They were joined by a younger German chemist Fritz Strassmann. Fermi had separated the new radioactive elements from uranium by precipitating them out with transition metal compounds. Because such new substances were present in very small quantities, radiochemists added a chemically related element as a carrier of radioactive atoms. This larger mixture was easier to handle and the radioactive atoms followed the carrier through the chemical treatments.[6] This approach structured the investigation because the Berlin researchers focused on the precipitate but ignored the filtrate, which "contained uranium, the decay products, and (as it turned out) quite a lot more." Indeed, according to Ruth Lewin Sime, this was the team's "most crucial error."[7]

After an extensive series of experiments with different periods of irradiation, the use of fast and slow neutrons, and a great variety of chemical tests, Hahn, Meitner, and Strassmann concluded that neutron bombardment had produced three different active isotopes of uranium, which subsequently decayed into different transuranic elements. Isotopes are forms of the same element with different numbers of neutrons, thereby having different atomic weights. Only one of them, an active uranium isotope with a half-life (the time it takes for half of the substance to decay into another element) of 23 minutes, was proven beyond a doubt. It was also clear that this was the result of the most common isotope, uranium 238, absorbing a neutron.[8]

The Berlin scientists were in an intense competition with French researchers – Irène Curie, Frédéric Joliot, and their collaborators – to explain the mysterious transuranics. When Curie and Paul Savitch bombarded uranium and found a substance with a 3.5-hour half-life and chemical properties similar to element 57, lanthanum, they assumed that it was a transuranic element with similar chemical properties to lanthanum.[9] By this time Lise Meitner had moved to Scandinavia, although she remained an important part of the research team. Nearly all of the subsequent experiments in Berlin were carried out in Meitner's former section of Hahn's institute using the experimental equipment she had built. She remained in close communication with Hahn, interpreting the results obtained by her Berlin colleagues and suggesting subsequent steps. As Sime has shown, the continuing collaboration proved necessary for the discovery of fission.[10]

Since Hahn and Strassmann were skeptical of the French results, and Strassmann assumed that the 3.5-hour substance might contain radium, they repeated the experiment. When they found a radioactive substance that precipitated out when combined with a barium carrier, the two German chemists

Nuclear Fission

assumed that they had found an isotope of radium, an element chemically similar to barium. However, Meitner was very skeptical of this interpretation, since it was difficult to imagine the series of nuclear reactions needed to produce radium from uranium. Meitner had remained in close contact with Hahn through the mail but more importantly, in November 1938, they met in Copenhagen, where: "Face to face, in the strongest terms, she must have told him that for all her trust in his and Strassmann's chemical expertise, their new results were a physicist's nightmare." Strassmann later remembered that in Copenhagen Meitner had urgently requested that the radium experiments be scrutinized very carefully and intensively one more time.

In response to Meitner's objections, Hahn and Strassmann began tests designed to verify the presence of radium by partially separating it from its barium carrier. These were the experiments that led directly to nuclear fission.[11] Hahn and Strassmann became convinced that they had produced barium. When Hahn reported this to Meitner, she responded that, while difficult to understand, this was probably possible.[12] Within a week Meitner, together with her physicist nephew Otto Frisch, had provided the first theoretical interpretation of the fission process, calculated the energy released, reinterpreted some of the apparent transuranic elements as fission fragments, and predicted correctly that only one of the three transuranics the Berlin team had earlier reported was real – element 93. On January 1, 1939, Meitner wrote to Hahn: "We have read and considered your work very carefully; perhaps it is energetically possible for such a heavy nucleus to burst." Two days later she added: "I am now fairly certain that you really have a disintegration to Ba and find this a truly wonderful result, for which I heartily congratulate you and Strassmann."[13]

Anxious to publish quickly, Hahn and Strassmann had submitted a manuscript to the journal *Die Naturwissenschaften* before getting Meitner's reply:

Our "radium isotopes" have the properties of barium; as chemists we should actually say that the new substances are not radium rather barium; for elements other than radium or barium are out of the question.... As chemists ... we should substitute the symbols Ba, La, Ce for Ra, Ac, Th. As "nuclear chemists" fairly close to physics we cannot yet bring ourselves to take this step that contradicts all previous experience in nuclear physics. There could still perhaps be a series of unusual coincidences that have given us deceptive results.[14]

In their subsequent article, Hahn and Strassmann were more decisive: "The formation of barium isotopes from uranium has been definitively proven."[15]

In their own publication, Meitner and Frisch used the Russian émigré George Gamow's liquid drop model of the nucleus to explain the process. The particles in a heavy nucleus would be expected to move in a collective way that resembled the movement of a liquid drop. If this movement was made sufficiently violent by adding energy, then the drop might divide into

16   The Bomb

two. Since the surface tension of a charged droplet is diminished by its charge, Meitner and Frisch estimated that the surface tension of nuclei, decreasing with increasing nuclear charge, might become zero for atomic numbers of the order of 100. This suggested that element 92, uranium, had limited stability and after neutron capture might divide itself into two nuclei of roughly equal size. Frisch chose "fission," a term from biology, to describe this new process.[16] At around the same time Frisch published his own conclusive physical evidence for the breaking up of uranium nuclei into parts of comparable size. He had bombarded uranium with neutrons, detecting high-energy particles and thereby demonstrating the liberation of enormous amounts of energy through fission.[17]

The Race to Understand Nuclear Fission

In Paris, Frédéric Joliot read Hahn and Strassmann's article and realized that each fission should release a great deal of energy and might also emit extra neutrons.[18] Using different methods from Frisch, he independently verified his result, and working in Paris with Hans von Halban and Lew Kowarski, he demonstrated in March that fission liberated "secondary" neutrons and saw their results as a step towards the production of "exo-energetic transmutation chains," which would come to be called "chain reactions." However, they noted that for such a chain, more than one neutron would have to be released per fission. A month later they published their estimate that around 3.5 secondary neutrons were produced, which made a chain reaction appear promising.[19] In the United States, Howard Zinn and Leo Szilard published an estimate that was lower, 2.3, but might still facilitate chain reactions.[20]

In June Siegfried Flügge, a physicist from Hahn's institute, published an account of nuclear fission for a general scientific audience. If every neutron that causes a fission also liberates two or three neutrons, then these neutrons should in turn lead to the fission of other uranium nuclei, increasing their number still further, so that an "endless chain reaction" would transform all of the available uranium. As an example, Flügge calculated how much energy would be liberated if all of the available uranium in a cubic meter of uranium oxide was completely transformed. This would produce enough energy to lift a cubic kilometer of water (weight 10^{12} kg) 27 kilometers high! If such a chain reaction could be controlled, Flügge emphasized, then an energy-producing "uranium machine" was possible.[21]

The news of Hahn and Strassmann's experiment, as well as Meitner and Frisch's interpretation, was brought to the USA by the Danish physicist Niels Bohr. Together with his American colleague John Wheeler, Bohr worked out the mechanism of nuclear fission. When uranium was bombarded with neutrons, sometimes this led to fission but other times the neutrons were

Nuclear Fission

absorbed – the process Hahn, Meitner, and Strassmann had discovered that presumably led to the transuranic element 93. Bohr and Wheeler found that the different uranium isotopes should behave differently in this regard: while the common isotope uranium 238 should capture neutrons, the rare isotope 235 should be fissioned by relatively slow "thermal" neutrons that move at velocities comparable to those of air molecules at room temperature.[22]

In March and April of 1940, Alfred Nier used his mass spectrometer to separate small amounts of uranium 235 that were then bombarded with slow neutrons with the Columbia University cyclotron, verifying that uranium 235 was indeed the isotope responsible for slow neutron fission. These experiments demonstrated the importance of large-scale uranium isotope separation for investigations into chain reactions in uranium. In August, Nier and colleagues followed this up with experimental proof that isotope uranium 238 was responsible for the well-known 24-minute neutron capture product.[23]

The American physicist Louis Turner noted that Bohr and Wheeler's theory also predicted that "all reasonably expectable transuranic atoms should give fission with thermal neutrons." In May of 1940, US physicists Edwin McMillan and Philip Abelson reported that they had finally found transuranic elements by bombarding uranium with neutrons to produce uranium 239 that then decayed with a 23 minute half-life to element 93. This in turn had a half-life of 2.3 days and, because it emitted negative beta particles, presumably decayed into 94. McMillian and Abelson predicted that element 94 should emit alpha-particles and therefore be stable with a very long half-life.[24]

This very public discussion of nuclear fission, uranium isotopes, and transuranic elements implied that there was a need for three technologies or processes: (1) "moderating," or slowing down neutrons to thermal velocities to control a chain reaction; (2) physically separating out the two uranium isotopes 235 and 238, or at least enriching the relative proportion of 235, to facilitate such a chain reaction; and (3) first producing element 93 and then chemically separating it or its daughter product 94 from uranium, again to facilitate such a chain reaction. Taken together, these form the heart of the technological and industrial challenges that had to be overcome to make nuclear energy possible.

But the story of nuclear fission is not merely a typical scientific race for understanding nature and professional prestige. Why was Meitner in Scandinavia when Hahn and Strassmann found barium? Hahn and Meitner had begun working on Fermi's apparent transuranics in part because of the hope that success with this research might relieve the political pressure on them. By 1938 Berlin was five years into National Socialist (NS) rule. Although classified as a "non-Aryan," Meitner's Austrian citizenship had spared her some of the effects of anti-Semitic policies, and she had been reluctant to emigrate. That came to an abrupt end with the German "absorption" (*Anschluss*) of Austria

18   The Bomb

in March. Now classified as a German Jew, the full force of NS anti-Semitism came down upon her.

Colleagues in the Kaiser Wilhelm Institute for Chemistry, close to Hitler's regime, whether enthusiastic National Socialists or opportunists, immediately attacked Meitner, claiming that the "Jewess endangers the institute."[25] When Kaiser Wilhelm Society (*Kaiser-Wilhelm Gesellschaft*, KWG) president Carl Bosch tried to arrange an exception for Meitner, the response from the Ministry of the Interior was chilling: Heinrich Himmler, the head of the SS, had personally taken notice of Meitner's case and would not allow her to leave the country:

It is undesirable that *well-known Jews* travel outside of Germany as a representative of German science or even with their name and experience, corresponding to their inner stance, in order to work against Germany there.

The Ministry instead suggested that the KWG find a way for Meitner to work for them on a private basis in Germany after she left her position.[26] Meitner now understood that she had to get out and fled Germany with the help of two Dutch colleagues, Dirk Coster and Peter Debye. Although Meitner subsequently found a position in Stockholm, she never really felt welcome or supported there.[27]

As Sime has demonstrated, after the discovery of nuclear fission, Hahn began to write Meitner out of its history.[28] Meitner's forced emigration directly affected how the work on fission was published, and thereby influenced who eventually received credit for it. In the initial letter that shared the barium result with Meitner, Hahn suggested that: "If there is anything you could propose that you could publish, then it would still in a way be work by the three of us!"[29] Meitner thought that even a joint publication retracting some of their earlier results was probably not feasible.[30] On January 2, Hahn defended the separate article by himself and Strassmann to Meitner:

I told the details only to you, so that you can form an opinion and perhaps publish something about it. But it would have been wrong for us not to publish our results as quickly as possible.... Believe me, it would have been preferable for me if we could still work together and discuss things as we did before.[31]

A joint publication between the German chemists and a "non-Aryan" physicist who had fled the country was out of the question in Germany, and probably would have been a bad idea for Hahn and Strassmann if they had published with Meitner anywhere else. But Hahn did more than just publish without Meitner. In his second publication on fission with Strassmann in *Die Naturwissenschaften*, Hahn gave no indication that the idea for several experiments had come from Meitner and "intentionally or not" characterized the work by Meitner-Frisch as "a fairly meaningless description of known results."[32] Hahn did, however, thank Meitner for their earlier collaboration:

Nuclear Fission

It was only possible to determine the countless new fission products here in a relatively short period of time and--as we believe--with considerable certainty because of the experience we gathered, together with Lise Meitner, through systematic experiments on the transuranics and thorium transformation products.[33]

After the separate sets of publications on fission, the two articles by Hahn and Strassmann, and the two published by either Meitner and Frisch or Frisch alone, Hahn and Meitner were focused on different things. While Meitner was concerned about their previous claims to have found transuranic elements that now were probably fission fragments and wondered whether the joint articles they had published before nuclear fission should now be retracted, Hahn was focused on priority.

Because I must gradually admit that [Otto] Erbacher and [Kurt] Philipp [two enthusiastic National Socialist members of his institute[34]] are right when they say that the priority for nuclear fission threatens to gradually be taken out of my and Strassmann's hands.... I am sending you [Meitner] ... for example an article from *Science*, the American *Nature*. Here you will see that "I" have observed something, but had no explanation for it!.... It is clear that such matters are well exploited during the institute coffee breaks and most agree that the work by Strassmann and me has not been handled fairly.... The fanatics among our people are already making the matter somewhat political, which I am especially sorry about.[35]

The physical separation of Meitner from Hahn and Strassmann did not affect the scientific progress leading up to the discovery and understanding of nuclear fission but it did affect the subsequent credit attributed to the three scientists. The separate publications, along with Hahn's subsequent statements, eventually led to the interpretation that it was Hahn's discovery, and no one else's.

Ironically, neither Meitner nor Hahn appeared particularly worried about the military potential of nuclear fission, even after the start of World War II. Yet the stage was now set for the wartime research and development of nuclear energy. Indeed it is striking how much was published and openly discussed before the veil of secrecy finally descended, cutting off scientists in different countries. There were no scientific secrets about nuclear fission, rather there was uncertainty whether its immense energies could be technically harnessed. This transformed the international competition to understand nuclear fission into one to exploit it for military applications.

There were some early efforts to censor work on fission.[36] On February 2, 1939, the émigré physicist Leo Szilard wrote a remarkable letter to Joliot:

When Hahn's paper reached this country about a fortnight ago a few of us got at once interested in the question whether neutrons are liberated in the disintegration of uranium. Obviously, if more than one neutron were liberated, a sort of chain reaction would be possible. In certain circumstances this might then lead to the construction of bombs which would be extremely dangerous in general and particularly in the hands of certain governments.... In the last few days there was some discussion here among

20   The Bomb

physicists whether or not we should take action to prevent anything along this line from being published in scientific periodicals in this country, and also ask colleagues in England and France to consider taking similar action.

Joliot was reluctant to take such a radical step, as was Enrico Fermi, who by now had emigrated to the United States. Publication of scientific articles related to fission finally stopped in American journals in June of 1940.[37]

Szilard did not stop with censorship. Together with another émigré scientist, Eugene Wigner, Szilard paid a visit to their more famous émigré colleague Albert Einstein and persuaded him to sign a letter to President Roosevelt. Recent scientific work by Fermi and Szilard, Einstein wrote Roosevelt, suggested that the element uranium could become a new and important source of energy in the immediate future. This could also lead to the construction of "extremely powerful bombs of a new type." Einstein also noted that Germany had stopped the sale of uranium from the Czechoslovakian mines it had taken over, perhaps because Carl Friedrich von Weizsäcker, the son of a high-ranking official in the German Foreign Ministry, was working at the Kaiser Wilhelm Institute of Physics in Berlin "where some of the American work is now being repeated."[38]

Conclusion

A collaboration of scientists investigating the puzzling behavior of uranium, driven by international competition and divided by anti-Semitism, discovered that atomic nuclei can be split, releasing energy and neutrons. Scientists around the world then elaborated and extended the research, suggesting that energy-producing nuclear fission chain reactions might be possible. All of this work took place within either a year before or after the start of the Second World War. The stage was set for a race to build the atomic bomb.

3 Lightning War

We take the liberty of calling to your attention the newest developments in nuclear physics which, in our opinion, will perhaps make it possible to produce an explosive which is many orders of magnitude more effective than the present one.... It is obvious that, if the possibility of energy production outlined above can be realized, which certainly is within the realm of possibilities, that country which first makes use of it has an unsurpassable advantage over the others.

Paul Harteck and Wilhelm Groth to Army Ordnance (April 24, 1939).[1]

Unleashing Lightning War

The German attack on Poland on the first day of September 1939, the subsequent simultaneous invasions of Denmark and Norway in early April, and of Belgium, France, and the Netherlands a month later, culminated in victory over France and revenge for the German defeat in World War I. All of this profoundly shook the scientists on both sides of the conflict. Shortly after the war began, Werner Heisenberg (see Figure 3.1), who had recently been in the United States, wrote his mentor Niels Bohr in Denmark that:

You know how sad I am about the entire development. In America we all saw it coming. I came back to where I belong. That you will certainly understand....

Since I do not know whether and when fate will bring us together again, I want to thank you again for all the friendship, for everything that I have learned from you, and for what you have done for me.[2]

Two weeks into the war came very sad news that cut close to home. Carl Friedrich von Weizsäcker's brother Heinrich had died only two days into the war. Heinrich was a "very nice person, noble and straightforward, certainly one of the best officers." Heisenberg had often played music with him and was reminded of a passage from a book by Wiechert, where he wrote that the Prussians "had always sacrificed their best blood on the battlefield."[3] Heisenberg also sounded cautious about the further course of the war. Neither France nor Great Britain had been seriously weakened and many expected the United States to enter the war in the spring. In a resigned tone, Heisenberg told

22   The Bomb

Figure 3.1 Werner Heisenberg at Farm Hall.
Source: NARA.

his wife Elisabeth that: "Since politics is being determined by higher powers, we have to be patient and attempt to arrange our lives as sensibly as the circumstances allow."[4] Three weeks into the conflict, Heisenberg was pessimistic, writing to his wife that after seeing the new reduced food rations no one believed in a short war anymore. Both a recent speech of Hitler's and an article in *Das Schwarze Korps* (*The Black Corps*), the weekly SS newspaper, appeared to be preparing Germans for a longer conflict.[5]

Together Germany and the Soviet Union, which had signed a nonaggression pact on August 23, carved up a defeated Poland on October 6. Beginning with the start of the war, the security service of the SS (*Sicherheitsdienst*, SD) began compiling and distributing secret reports on what the Germans were doing and saying, and in particular how they were reacting to the latest developments in the war. While these should not, of course, always be taken at face value, they do represent an often illuminating source for how German morale changed over time. On October 9 the SD reported that the returning victorious troops had been welcomed enthusiastically almost everywhere in Germany, with the people greeting them with flowers, cigarettes, and fruit.[6]

Organization in Germany

Just like colleagues in many different countries, several German scientists contacted military and political authorities about the possible military potential of energy-producing nuclear fission chain reactions. Georg Joos, Professor for Experimental Physics at the University of Göttingen, wrote to the Reich Ministry of Science, Education, and Culture (*Reichsministerium für Wissenschaft, Erziehung und Volksbildung*, REM) in April of 1939, well before the start of war. Within a few weeks experiments began on the purity of the uranium oxide

Lightning War

Figure 3.2 Paul Harteck at Farm Hall.
Source: NARA.

available, efforts were made to acquire significantly large amounts of uranium, and Abraham Esau, a technical physicist responsible for physics in the Reich Research Council (*Reichsforschungsrat*, RFR), organized a meeting with several leading German experimental physicists, including Joos, Wilhelm Hanle, Josef Mattauch from Otto Hahn's institute, and Walther Bothe.[7]

At least three different scientists contacted the Army directly: (1) the industrial physicist Nikolaus Riehl, a former student of Hahn and Lise Meitner and the director of research at the Auer Society (*Auer Gesellschaft*), a company with experience processing radioactive elements;[8] and (2) the physical chemists Paul Harteck and Wilhelm Groth at the University of Hamburg, who recognized that nuclear fission could possibly be used to produce energy on a large scale.[9] In April of 1939 they contacted the Army about the potential for powerful new nuclear explosives. An Army official responded that they were aware of this work, they would be interested in hearing more from Harteck (see Figure 3.2), perhaps in a meeting, and the matter must remain confidential.[10]

Immediately after the war began, news reached Germany from the United States that the American military was investing money into atomic energy research. Because it appeared possible that the Americans or the British would develop nuclear weapons, Army Ordnance (*Heereswaffenamt*, HWA), the office responsible for weapons development, forced out Esau and the RFR, setting up a "nuclear physics working group" (*Arbeitsgemeinschaft Kernphysik*, henceforth "working group") and taking over the Kaiser Wilhelm Institute for Physics in Berlin (KWIfP). Esau complained bitterly that both he and his office had been discredited in the eyes of German physicists.[11]

On September 29, HWA held its own secret conference on nuclear fission, asking the assembled scientists whether a research project on the military applications of nuclear fission should be started. According to Erich Bagge,

24   The Bomb

a young physicist who had done his Ph.D. under Heisenberg at the University of Leipzig, when someone questioned "whether one ought to do a thing like that," Walther Bothe replied, "Gentlemen, it *must* be done," while his conservative colleague Hans Geiger added that "If there is the slightest chance that it is possible – it must be done."[12] Bagge suggested that his mentor join the research group. Heisenberg was expecting to be called up for military service but was surprised to learn that he would be doing scientific research. The KWIfP became the coordination hub of the uranium working group but most scientists remained at their own institutes, with Heisenberg splitting his time between Leipzig and as an advisor at KWIfP.[13] When Heisenberg heard that he might end up "sitting in Berlin for a long time," he told Elisabeth that he was not very happy about the idea and thought he would have a guilty conscience about staying back safe behind the lines. "But perhaps one should leave war to the younger ones."[14]

Chain Reactions

Were energy-producing nuclear fission chain reactions feasible? In December of 1939, Heisenberg surveyed the available literature and asked whether it was possible to "produce mixtures of material, which when bombarded with neutrons release more neutrons than absorb them, and in what ways machines for producing energy that use such mixtures work."[15] From the very beginning, the physicist distinguished clearly between a uranium machine and a nuclear explosive, the fissile material used in an atomic bomb. "Uranium machine" was the German name for a nuclear reactor, while "uranium burner" was their name for a uranium machine that could maintain a self-sustaining energy-producing chain reaction.

Heisenberg concluded that nuclear fission in uranium could be used for the large-scale production of energy. Normal uranium could be used without uranium 235 enrichment if it was combined with a moderator, another substance that slows down the neutrons released from the uranium via fission without absorbing them. Water was not suitable for this, but according to the data available to him, heavy water (a chemical compound of the heavier isotope of hydrogen, deuterium, with oxygen) and very pure carbon in the form of graphite would satisfy this purpose. Even small amounts of impurities in the moderator would make energy production impossible. Heisenberg also mistakenly thought that such a machine would stabilize at a constant temperature, depending on the size of the apparatus.[16]

The most certain method for realizing energy production was enriching the isotope responsible for fission, uranium 235. This would allow the use of ordinary water as a moderator. The further the enrichment went, the smaller a machine could be built. The enrichment of uranium 235 was also the only method for "producing explosives that surpass the current strongest explosives by several powers of ten." However, since a considerable enrichment of large amounts of uranium 235 would probably be very expensive, Heisenberg recommended that they should look for other methods for realizing energy production from uranium.[17]

Thus in the winter of 1939–1940 Heisenberg saw two paths to nuclear energy: (1) a uranium machine built out of uranium and a moderator such as graphite or heavy water, which controls the chain reaction by slowing down the neutrons created by fission, and (2) the enrichment of the isotope uranium 235, which would allow ordinary water to be used as moderator. If pure uranium 235 could be produced, then this would constitute a nuclear explosive.

Isotope Enrichment

Could uranium 235 be enriched, or perhaps even separated? Harteck and Groth began experiments with the Clusius–Dickel separation tube, a very promising isotope separation device that had already been used successfully to enrich other heavy elements. One wall of a rectangular tube containing a gas is heated, in this case by a metal wire coiled around one side. The temperature difference between the warmer wall and the colder wall produces both a thermo-diffusion effect that causes the heavier molecules to concentrate near the colder wall, and a thermo-syphon effect that causes the gas mixture to rise along the warmer wall, to be diverted to the colder wall, and to sink along it. These two effects combine to produce a countercurrent cycle inside the tube that separates the heavier gas isotopes from the lighter ones.[18]

These were very difficult experiments because they had to be carried out with uranium hexafluoride (UF^6), a very aggressive compound that was the only known gaseous combination of uranium. Just a little more than a week after the HWA meeting in Berlin, Harteck was searching for a liter of uranium hexafluoride, which he quickly received from the chemical cartel IG Farben.[19] Officials at the HWA told Harteck that these experiments were of great interest and Harteck's group should carry them out as quickly as possible. Harteck responded by requesting that several of his coworkers be granted exemptions from frontline service so that they could remain at his institute, as well as asking for several freezers. At room temperature the uranium hexafluoride corroded the containers.[20]

At the start of December 1939, Harteck reported that they had set up a test separation tube filled with xenon and successfully enriched isotopes. These results suggested that uranium isotope 235 could be enriched to the degree and in the amounts required.[21] Unfortunately other tests showed that the uranium hexafluoride attacked glass and most metals. One promising material that uranium hexafluoride apparently did not corrode was nickel. Harteck began

26 The Bomb

contacting German companies about getting a nickel separation tube, noting that the matter was very urgent.[22] But nickel was an element in short supply in Germany and in principle the use of pure nickel was forbidden. Exceptions required exact information explaining why nickel had to be used but since the research was secret, Harteck could not provide this. He turned to HWA and asked them to intervene with the Reich Metals Office, because without nickel their work was completely shut down.[23]

In the end it took nine months to get the nickel separation tube,[24] and it quickly proved a failure. The continuous movement of gas within the tube compounded the problem of corrosion. In the previous corrosion experiments, where the gas had simply been confined within a metal container, the uranium hexafluoride had corroded the nickel walls but this green layer of nickel fluoride had also served as a barrier to further attack. As soon as the hot wall corroded in the Clusius–Dickel separation tube, the corrosion layer traveled to the cold wall, thereby leaving one wall unprotected.

Although the problem of corrosion was bad enough, it should not have hindered isotope separation but no enrichment was found in any of the trials with uranium hexafluoride. Subsequent experiments with methane succeeded in enriching carbon isotopes, so the separation tube appeared to be working correctly. Since the separation factor of the Clusius–Dickel separation tube was temperature- as well as substance-dependent, Harteck and his colleagues concluded that the separation factor for uranium hexafluoride was practically zero for any useful temperature. In theory, the gas might have had a larger separation factor at a higher temperature but then the uranium hexafluoride would be too unstable to use in a Clusius–Dickel tube.[25]

Harteck, an ambitious and energetic optimist, was not fazed by this setback. In the very same report that detailed the failure of the Clusius–Dickel separation tube, he proposed isotope separation by means of an ultracentrifuge. This process depended only on the differences in mass between the different isotopes. One potential method of uranium isotope separation, gaseous diffusion, was not taken up in Germany despite the fact that the 1925 Nobel laureate physicist Gustav Hertz had made considerable progress in this area. Hertz lost his professorship in 1934 because of his non-Aryan ancestry and moved into industry.[26]

In the spring of 1941, two months before the German invasion of the Soviet Union, Harteck assessed the relative priority of the two research areas he and his Hamburg colleagues were pursuing: uranium isotope enrichment and the production of heavy water. The latter appeared more pressing, because according to the results so far, a uranium machine would work with heavy water as a moderator, even without uranium isotope enrichment. Moreover, producing enough heavy water for a uranium machine to run would be much cheaper and easier than enriching uranium 235 to the degree needed for a machine to work with ordinary water. If a better process for isotope separation was not found, Harteck concluded, then the enriched uranium isotope would probably only be used for "special applications, for which economics are secondary considerations," in other words, weapons.[27]

Neutron Moderators

Carbon

In order for a uranium machine to produce energy through a controlled chain reaction, an effective neutron moderator, some material that could slow down the neutrons released by fission without absorbing too many of them, was needed. In his first report, Heisenberg had concluded that either ordinary water, carbon in the form of graphite, or heavy water might work. Of these, ordinary water needed to be combined with uranium isotope enrichment, and carbon appeared much easier to produce in large amounts than heavy water.[28]

By the end of February, his second report was more pessimistic. More precise published measurements now made it doubtful that the uranium machine could use carbon.[29] Georg Joos and Wilhelm Hanle, two physicists who had been involved with uranium from the very beginning of the working group, carried out experiments on producing very pure carbon. They found that most forms of carbon, including graphite, contained too many impurities, and they only succeeded in producing sufficiently pure carbon from foodstuffs: various forms of sugar or potatoes.[30]

Walther Bothe (see Figure 3.3) began experiments with colleagues at the Kaiser Wilhelm Institute for Medical Research in Heidelberg on electrographite, which appeared to be the purest carbon that could be technically produced in

Figure 3.3 Walther Bothe in 1938.
Source: AMPG.

28   The Bomb

large quantities. According to their measurements, this graphite would not work as a moderator in the uranium machine. The question remained: Was the neutron absorption caused by the graphite itself or impurities in it? Assuming that it was very improbable that the sample contained combustible contaminants, they reduced the graphite to ash in order to search for impurities but did not find significant amounts. Bothe and his colleague Peter Jensen concluded that carbon, even if it was manufactured according to the best-known technical process and was completely free of mineral impurities, probably was not suitable as a moderator unless the proportion of uranium isotope 235 could be enriched.[31]

After the war, Heisenberg suggested that Bothe had made an error when measuring the absorption of neutrons in graphite, thereby implying that he was responsible for the Germans not using graphite in their uranium machines. In the manuscript of an article Heisenberg was planning to publish about the German wartime work, he noted that as a result of Bothe and Jensen's work, "it was mistakenly concluded" that "absolutely pure carbon" would not work in a uranium burner. When Bothe politely objected, Heisenberg used vaguer language in this published article but continued to blame Bothe's "mistake" for holding the Germans back.[32] In a 1967 book review, Heisenberg wrote that Bothe's "erroneous measurement" had prevented them from realizing that pure carbon was suitable for the construction of nuclear reactors.[33]

In fact Bothe had not argued that all carbon would not work. He had both limited his analysis to the sample that he had investigated, the industrially produced electrographite from Siemens, and admitted the possibility that he had missed some impurities. This latter point was taken up by Hanle, who by now was on the periphery of the wartime fission work. He suspected that there were some impurities in this graphite, in particular boron, a very good absorber of neutrons. Most carbon contained a considerable amount of boron. With great effort, Hanle was able to manufacture small amounts of boron-free carbon from sugar that absorbed fewer neutrons than the Siemens electrographite. Hanle also pointed out that there were boron compounds commonly found in carbon that would be expected to be lost during combustion. In other words, he argued that part of the neutron absorption found by Bothe and Jensen was probably due to boron impurities, so that very pure graphite might work in a uranium machine.[34]

Heavy Water before the Invasion of Norway

In many respects, heavy water appeared to be the ideal choice for a neutron moderator. It did not require uranium 235 enrichment like ordinary water and, in contrast to carbon, could be produced in a very pure form. However, it was expensive to produce, very little was being manufactured, and Heisenberg had calculated that tons would be needed for a uranium machine. There was

Lightning War   29

very little production in Germany, in part because Norsk Hydro, a Norwegian fertilizer and aluminum producer, also used its hydroelectric power to produce heavy water inexpensively and had cornered the very small prewar international market.

Even though the German chemical conglomerate IG Farben was a part owner of Norsk Hydro, when the Norwegian company was contacted in February 1940 by HWA about selling heavy water, it refused to either send them a substantial amount or increase production. In contrast, a French government official representing a group of researchers working under the physicist Frédéric Joliot persuaded the general manager of Norsk Hydro to give them the entire available stock, 185.5 kilograms, for free.[35]

The second part of Heisenberg's report on energy production through chain reactions predicted that if uranium was used in individual pieces rather than in a homogeneous mixture with the moderator, something Harteck had suggested, then heavy water would certainly work in a uranium machine.[36] Harteck reacted to Heisenberg's report immediately by asking who in Germany was trying to produce heavy water. Unless one had access to the amount of power at Norsk Hydro, electrolysis – the chemical decomposition produced by passing an electric current through a liquid or solution containing ions, atoms or groups of atoms with electric charge – would not work in Germany. Harteck added that:

Given my experience with the army, if we left it up to them the production of the necessary large amounts of heavy water would certainly take years. However, I can imagine that, if I personally contacted the corresponding men in big business, the time would be reduced to a fraction [of that].[37]

Heisenberg responded that there had been a meeting (without Harteck) about that, with the result that the electrolysis plants in Germany would be tested to see if they contained water that was already enriched in deuterium and might be used as raw material for heavy water production. Obviously the HWA officials had not made a decision about what should be done next.[38]

Harteck then wrote HWA directly, noting that he and his colleague Hans Suess had been working on heavy water for many years and expressing surprise that, at the meeting, only uneconomical methods had been discussed. Heisenberg had shown that they would need tons of heavy water for a uranium machine but if electrolysis was used, then it would take around 100,000 tons of coal to make a ton of heavy water. The amount of enriched heavy water in German electrolytic works was irrelevant when such quantities were needed. Instead Harteck proposed two other methods: (1) elutriation, whereby lighter and heavier particles are separated by suspending them in an upward flow of liquid or gas via a catalyst, perhaps in connection with existing benzine production, and (2) desorption (the reverse of absorption) at low temperatures. In

30   The Bomb

any case it would be advisable to set up a small experimental facility as soon as possible in order to gain experience with the process. Army Ordnance encouraged Harteck to work on the process with two other physical chemists, Klaus Clusius in Munich and Karl-Friedrich Bonhoeffer in Leipzig but added both that this was to be kept secret and that in the future reports could not go directly from one institute to another but rather must always be submitted centrally to HWA, which would distribute them as necessary.[39]

Bonhoeffer was enthusiastic about the elutriation process but spent most of his letter to Harteck describing his concerns about the winter during the first year of the war. He had closed most of his institute because of a lack of coal. Only the library was still open, which during the day was full of acquaintances without fuel. The mayor of Leipzig had published a "reassurance speech" that was full of "ominous sentences and actually unusually honest." Reading between the lines, the vegetables meant for Leipzig could not be transported. The mayor claimed that the stores of potatoes in Leipzig should be sufficient but Bonhoeffer added that "in practice one only gets them from friends." There would be no additional deliveries of potatoes or coal. He noted that the official text had been "little or none." Today, he told Harteck, it had again snowed all day.[40] Harteck responded to his old friend with pleasure that they were working on the same problem once again. It was only unfortunate that "today it is so difficult to get a big thing going quickly." It was now time to set up large-scale experiments and not "only extrapolate from ridiculous measurements to larger designs." Harteck also could empathize with Bonhoeffer, having "frozen for a week in my apartment."[41]

Heavy Water after the Defeat of Norway

On April 9, Germany invaded Denmark and Norway, transforming both the war and the uranium project. Harteck wrote to Bonhoeffer that his trip to Hamburg was comfortable with the train almost empty. The invasion had obviously "shaken many to their bones." The war was going both ways, however. A month later, Harteck wrote Bonhoeffer about the latest British bombing attack on Hamburg:

There are obviously no appropriate rules for conduct during a real attack. If one stays in the apartment, then the bombs that fall on the roof are unpleasant; if one goes into a cellar that is not completely underground and the bombs fall right next to the building, then the internal walls collapse.... The small pieces that fall from the exploding grenades and in particular the bullets from the 2 cm machine guns are not harmless, so it is better that one stays at home.[42]

According to Heisenberg, Harteck might now be sent to Norway, where the powerful IG Farben had taken control of Norsk Hydro. Paul Herold, an IG chemist, questioned whether HWA would still pursue heavy water production in Germany. Harteck responded that the events in Norway had not changed much, because while Norsk Hydro was able to deliver the heavy water for one or two units, it certainly would not be able to meet the need for heavy water once uranium burners were in operation.[43]

Herold and his staff were working with Bonhoeffer to find a suitable catalyst for Harteck's proposed process. Another IG scientist and former Harteck student, Karl-Hermann Geib, had been carrying out preliminary experiments with catalysts but had not yet found significant enrichment with any of them. Only part of the small-scale pilot plant had been constructed, because until a suitable catalyst was found, other work appeared more important. Setting aside the question of the catalyst, Herold added, IG Farben needed significant support in the form of additional skilled labor.[44]

Karl Wirtz, an experimental physicist employed at the KWIfP, also had experience working with heavy water (see Figure 3.4). Together with Erica Cremer, he investigated the heavy water content of several existing German electrolysis plants but found little. Another source might be found in electrolysis plants in countries conquered by Germany. In general, it appeared that it took quite a while for heavy water to build up in such plants.[45] Moreover, as Harteck, Wirtz, and others had repeatedly emphasized, electrolysis was out of the question for the production of large amounts of heavy water in Germany because it would require so much electricity that was needed for other war production.[46]

In March of 1941 Wirtz surveyed the near- and long-term options for heavy water production. During the next year the uranium machine would still be in an experimental phase. These investigations, that were fundamental for everything else and had to be carried out as soon as possible, would require a few tons of heavy water. Only Norsk Hydro was in a position to

Figure 3.4 Karl Wirtz at Farm Hall.
Source: NARA.

32   The Bomb

produce these amounts. The company, now very accommodating to German requests, was prepared to deliver 1 ton of heavy water in 1941 and thereafter 1.3 tons a year. But Wirtz noted that they would need at least 5 tons for the first uranium machine experiments. Army Ordnance needed first to request the greatest possible expansion of the heavy water production at Norsk Hydro and second to help the Norwegians do this. If this strategy would be pursued with the necessary energy, Wirtz argued, then the Norwegian plant could certainly produce 4 or 5 tons of heavy water a year at a lower cost than current deliveries.

But in the long run, much more heavy water would be needed. Even if the nitrogen and thereby fertilizer production at the Norsk Hydro was reduced, the plant could not produce more than 10 to 20 tons of heavy water a year. For greater amounts, production within Germany would be needed. There were three different proposals, one from Klaus Clusius and two from Harteck, to do this. All of the proposals were designed to filter out deuterium from existing hydrogen production without adversely affecting the end product. However, none of these proposals had gone beyond laboratory experiments, and two of them required very pure hydrogen as feed stock. Hydrogen from electrolysis would be fine but if it came from anywhere else, for example if it was produced from coal, then it would have to be purified first. Since it was not clear which of these three processes was best, funds and resources had to be provided in order to test all of them on a larger scale.[47]

By now Harteck's institute was completely devoted to work for the working group. Along with uranium isotope separation and preliminary uranium machine experiments, they had set up several different experimental distillation columns that appeared efficient at separating light from heavy water, relatively easy to manufacture, and could use industrial waste water as a source.[48] In May of 1941 Harteck began the process of patenting a low-pressure distillation column.[49]

Both Harteck and Wirtz were impatiently waiting for HWA to agree to make substantial investments in heavy water production. Wirtz claimed to Bonhoeffer that around 3 tons a year could be obtained without difficulty from the Norsk Hydro but only if it was ordered. The problem was that HWA had not ordered it. Harteck in turn complained to Bonhoeffer that they had known for fifteen months what should happen. The necessary materials had to be acquired and transported to the right place, so that work could begin. IG Farben should also begin testing a low-pressure column. A trip to Norway, Harteck added, "would be a lot of fun for me, probably also for you."[50]

Army Ordnance made the reasonable, if consequential decision to rely upon heavy water as a neutron moderator on economic grounds. It was not clear that German industry could provide graphite pure enough to work in a uranium machine or, if this were possible, at an affordable price. Ordinary water

Lightning War

required uranium isotope enrichment but up until this point that had failed. By comparison, it was very likely that heavy water would be an effective neutron moderator and it appeared that the relatively small amounts needed for the initial uranium machine experiments could be manufactured easily and inexpensively in Norway.[51] Perhaps most important was the fact that, for HWA, heavy water, or indeed the working group as a whole, had neither urgency nor priority in the spring and summer of 1941.

Uranium and Model Uranium Machines

Harteck's CO_2 Experiment

Very little uranium was available in early January of 1940. HWA sent Harteck 500 grams of metal uranium, telling him that, if he really needed more, then they could provide this later. Harteck replied that while this amount was sufficient for manufacturing the uranium hexafluoride needed for their investigation of isotope separation, it was "a few orders of magnitude too little for experiments on practical geometric designs."[52] Along with work on the separation tube and processes for producing heavy water, Harteck took the initiative to plan an experiment to study the capture of neutrons by carbon and oxygen, and thereby their suitability as moderators in a uranium machine, by using dry ice, frozen carbon dioxide (CO_2). On his way back from a trip to Vienna, he visited both the Linde Society for Refrigeration in Munich and the IG Farben plant in Leuna, asking if they could produce pure dry ice. Where Linde had said that this was impossible, the IG Farben scientists offered to produce cubic meter blocks of dry ice that were practically pure. At this time, during the cool season, they could produce around 12 metric tons of dry ice, pack it, and ship it to Harteck. However, this had to happen before the end of May, for when the weather warmed the dry ice was needed for other purposes. Harteck would also have to arrange a closed train car and its fastest possible movement from the factory to Hamburg.[53]

Next Harteck asked HWA for a loan of 100–300 kilograms of uranium oxide and to arrange the transportation of the dry ice. This would be, Harteck insisted, the most important experiment that could be carried out at this time. Harteck was planning to visit Berlin in person to accelerate the process but less than a week later HWA responded that he would get at least 100 kilograms for a few weeks and the necessary freight car would be provided. But there was very little uranium or uranium oxide available to the researchers. Heisenberg wrote Harteck with the news that he had also ordered 500–1,000 kilograms of uranium oxide and in response Kurt Diebner, the HWA physicist administering the working group (see Figure 3.5), had asked Heisenberg and Harteck to work it out among themselves.

Figure 3.5 Kurt Diebner at Farm Hall.
Source: NARA.

At that moment there was only 150 kilograms, although more was on the way. Heisenberg wanted to get the first few 100 kilograms but if Harteck was in a hurry, then he could go first. In this case Heisenberg asked his colleague to be satisfied with 100 kilograms.[54]

Harteck responded the next day. He was going to receive one shipment of 10 metric tons of pure dry ice from IG Farben no later than the end of May. Harteck's colleagues were ready to do the measurements, and since the dry ice would not last much longer than a week, these would have to be done quickly. Harteck had asked for 100–300 kilograms from HWA because he thought that was the largest amount he could get. It was obvious that the more uranium oxide was available, the more definitive the experiment would be. For all these reasons, Harteck asked for the largest possible amount of uranium oxide during the period from May 20 to June 10. Heisenberg then agreed to send Harteck all the uranium oxide they had in Berlin.[55]

Harteck also wrote to Diebner, argued that 200 kilograms was the minimum he needed for an experiment of these dimensions, and asked Paul Herold at IG Farben to please send the dry ice as late as possible. He responded that unfortunately their request for transport trucks had been denied, and that shipping it by train would take eight to ten days. Harteck thanked Herold for his efforts, noting that "in the meantime you have also learned that the authorities in Berlin do not work exceedingly fast by themselves."[56]

On May 22 the KWIfP sent Harteck fifty kilograms, which were followed a few days later by an additional 150 kilograms brought in person by Nikolaus Riehl from the Auer Society. Harteck was admonished by HWA officials to take care that the oxide not be adulterated and be returned as soon as possible. More than 15 metric tons of dry ice arrived in two freight cars and were quickly set up for the experiment. The dry ice did succeed in slowing down

Lightning War 35

fast neutrons but because the arrangement was too small and allowed most of the fast neutrons to escape, no direct neutron increase could be measured.[57]

The dry ice experiment demonstrated Harteck's drive and creativity, as well as his excellent connections to German industry, but the small amounts of uranium available also showed how low a priority the research had. However, the availability of uranium changed dramatically after the German invasion of Belgium, France, and the Netherlands. In June of 1940, tons of uranium compounds were seized from the Belgian Union Minière Company and shipped to Germany. There was now plenty of uranium but it had to be purified and processed.

Victory over France and revenge for World War I made very many Germans jubilant and raised Hitler's popularity to new heights. When the SS reported on public opinion after the armistice, it noted that:

The surprising tempo of the military and political developments of the last days continues to completely command the mood of the population.... Everywhere the performance of the German soldiers is described as almost incomprehensible. The enthusiasm of the last days always gives the impression that it could not increase further, but with every new result the population expresses its happiness more intensely.[58]

But Werner Heisenberg had a different reaction, writing to his wife that:

This afternoon in Berlin a regiment arrived from France to return to its garrison. The city was full of flags, all [National Socialist] Party formations had to form an honor guard. There was little trace of people being truly moved, it seemed to me; if someone was happy about the return of their loved one, he did it silently for himself and told no one else about it.[59]

Layer Experiments in Berlin and Leipzig

Army Ordnance officially took over most of the KWIfP at the start of 1940, installing Diebner as the de facto head of the institute.[60] Walther Bothe had set out two questions that experiments with model uranium machines needed to answer: (1) how can an energy-producing burner be built? (2) if energy is produced, then how can this be controlled, what temperatures will be reached, etc.? Otto Hahn (see Figure 3.6) and Fritz Strassmann had continued to study the elements produced by uranium fission and their properties because, as Hahn noted at an internal working group conference in March of 1941, the fission products could accumulate and affect the operation of the uranium machine.[61]

As Heisenberg explained, the problem of building a uranium machine could be broken up into three parts. First of all, uranium fission had to produce more than one neutron per fission. This had been demonstrated by experiments in France and the United States. Second, a mixture of uranium oxide and a moderator had to be found with a negative neutron absorption coefficient, that is, if

Figure 3.6 Otto Hahn at Farm Hall.
Source: NARA.

Figure 3.7 Carl Friedrich von Weizsäcker at Farm Hall.
Source: NARA.

the entire space was filled with this mixture, the neutron density would expand exponentially. Finally, a large enough amount of this mixture had to be accumulated so that the neutron increase inside balances the neutron decrease when they leave the space.

Theoretical work began immediately, fleshing out Heisenberg's first two reports. With the help of two graduate students, Karl-Heinz Höcker and Paul Müller, Heisenberg's friend and colleague Carl Friedrich von Weizsäcker (see Figure 3.7) began calculating the efficiency of different combinations of uranium and moderator. Höcker calculated the neutron increase in an arrangement of infinite parallel plates of metal uranium (which barely existed at the time) and moderator, specifically carbon.[62]

Müller noted that, for finite machines, two models were being considered – parallel plates or spherical layers.[63] It was clear that even a slight enrichment

Lightning War 37

in the ratio of the uranium isotopes 235 to 238 would be very beneficial.[64] This work was hampered by the lack of precise experimental data for various factors, including neutron absorption in different substances.

Heisenberg began traveling to Berlin for part of the week as a consultant at the KWIfP. At first, he was not impressed. As he wrote his wife:

So far I do not like the work in Berlin very much. There is a lot of talk and little actual work. But perhaps I can change something about this state of affairs. It seems to me that the people in [Berlin-Dahlem] live on personnel politics and gossip.

In another letter three months later, he commented that:

The people in the institute are so appallingly boring, and when I arrive here on Wednesday, they are mostly exactly at the point where I had left them on Saturday. I am getting a certain respect for [Robert] Döpel [who worked at Heisenberg's institute in Leipzig], who otherwise does not look at all like an especially good physicist, but works infinitely cleaner and faster than the people here.[65]

Heisenberg's comments to his wife about the work ethic at both the KWIfP and his own institute reveal a lack of urgency in the working group. In stark contrast to Harteck and Wirtz' efforts to accelerate heavy water production, as long as the war went well for Germany, for most people uranium machines were not a pressing matter.

Berlin-Dahlem

The tempo of experiments on model uranium machines was determined by the availability of materials. Hahn's institute worked with the Auer Society to develop methods for purifying uranium compounds. Pure metal uranium would work much better in a uranium machine than uranium oxide but producing the former was a challenge. Before the spring of 1941 only very small amounts of this metal were available.[66] The situation with neutron moderators was not much better. The only substance that was clearly effective, heavy water, was also in very short supply. As a result, the first experiments used other, less effective materials.

At the KWIfP in Berlin, Wirtz led a research group that began investigating horizontal layers of uranium compounds and moderator.[67] Working with uranium oxide was dangerous for two reasons. First of all, it was a strong chemical poison when ingested into the body. Second, it was radioactive. While this radiation was not dangerous for people, it contaminated people and spaces and made scientific work impossible. Before working with the uranium oxide powder, scientists and technicians put on dust masks, dust goggles, rubber gloves, shoe covers, and protective clothing. Getting dressed and undressed took place in a separate location. All protective clothing and devices were kept as clean as possible.[68]

38   The Bomb

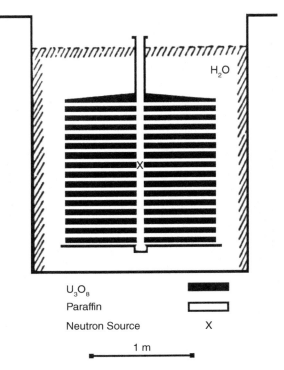

Figure 3.8 Schematic diagram of experiments B-I and B-II.
Source: Adapted from Walther Bothe and Siegfried Flügge (eds.), Kernphysik und kosmische Strahlen. Naturforschung und Medizin In Deutschland 1939–1946. Vol. 14 (Weinheim: Verlag Chemie, 1948), Part 2, 152.

The first model uranium machine was built in 1940 and 1941 in an external lab at the KWIfP out of alternating horizontal layers of paraffin, a waxy substance composed of hydrocarbons, and 6 metric tons of uranium oxide powder, all immersed under water in a watertight aluminum cylinder (see Figure 3.8). Layer designs were chosen, not because they were practical for nuclear reactors, rather because they were easy to construct and could be used to determine important nuclear properties.

As expected, this arrangement absorbed more neutrons than it produced and would not work for a uranium machine, no matter how much it was enlarged. However, because the neutron absorption was so small and the number of neutrons produced per fission was so high, it appeared that this design would work with heavy water as moderator. Indeed Heisenberg went so far as to argue that, unless unforeseen surprises occurred, the manufacture of an energy-producing, uranium burner was "purely a matter of will."[69]

Shortly after this experiment was finished, Weizsäcker and Wirtz submitted proposals for the next steps. The horizontal layer experiments with uranium oxide should continue but with varying thicknesses, to continue their measurements of various nuclear processes. Measurements in several labs suggested that pure metal uranium would be much more effective than uranium oxide in a machine but as of April 1941 only 600 kilograms were available. As soon as significant amounts of uranium metal arrived, they planned to use it with paraffin in a new experiment encased in a spherical aluminum vessel, adding more metal as it became available. Once tons of heavy water were available, they could carry out large-scale experiments that might result in an operating uranium burner.[70]

Leipzig

While the scientists at the KWIfP worked on horizontal layer designs, in Leipzig the experimental physicist Robert Döpel built spherical layers assisted by his wife Klara and at times even Heisenberg himself. First of all, they did experiments on the 9 liters of heavy water that was available, finding very little neutron absorption.[71] Next they built a model uranium machine with uranium oxide and ordinary water. The spherical arrangement, although difficult to construct, promised to provide precise measurements with small amounts of materials. Although the aluminum used to separate the layers absorbed more neutrons than expected, they concluded that a uranium machine without the aluminum and using on the order of 5 metric tons of heavy water would work.[72] After the war, Heisenberg claimed that, at this point in time, he "saw an open road to the atomic bomb."[73] However, he also understood that it would be very difficult and require great amounts of resources, labor, and time.

Transuranics

As described above,[74] by the summer of 1940 publications from American and émigré scientists had already made clear the following: uranium 238 could absorb a neutron and transmute into element 93; this transuranic element would probably transmute into a long-lived element 94; and all transuranic elements would be fissile materials similar to uranium 235. In July Weizsäcker, who had worked with both Heisenberg in Leipzig and with Lise Meitner and Otto Hahn in Berlin, and was on the staff of the KWIfP, reported to HWA on the "possibility of gaining energy from uranium 238." Since this most common isotope of uranium absorbed most neutrons rather than experiencing fission, only the rare isotope uranium 235 could contribute to energy production in a uranium machine, the purity of the materials

40   The Bomb

had to be high, and the difficult to obtain heavy water probably had to be used as a moderator. Moreover, because of resonance absorption, the preferential absorption in uranium 238 of neutrons traveling at specific velocities, the energy contained in uranium 235 could not be suddenly liberated, so that its "application as an explosive" was practically gone.

All of these difficulties could be overcome if uranium 238 could also be split by relatively slow thermal neutrons. Weizsäcker had realized that this could be done through the absorption of two successive neutrons. The first created the short-lived uranium 239, which transmuted with a half-life of 23 minutes into the transuranic element 93, which appeared to be as fissile as uranium 235. This new element could be used in three different ways: (1) to build very small uranium machines; (2) as a nuclear explosive; and (3) to transmute other elements.[75]

Scientists at Otto Hahn's institute were trying to find and investigate the properties of element 93. Indeed Hahn pointed to Weizsäcker's report in order to emphasize the importance of their work.[76] A young physical chemist working at Hahn's institute, Kurt Starke, managed first to separate out uranium 239 from the rest of the uranium, and then the transmuted element 93 from the uranium 239. Starke was not the first to discover element 93 but he did verify the results published by the American scientists Edwin McMillan and Philip Abelson in 1940. Hahn and Strassmann had also been trying to find element 93. Starke felt the climate in Hahn's institute cool after he had beaten them to the discovery and subsequently moved on to work with Klaus Clusius in Munich.[77]

Scientists at the KWIfP quickly moved to patent some of their discoveries. It is not clear when the first patent application was submitted but the Patent Office's response came on February 2, 1940, before Heisenberg had finished the second part of his report on energy production through chain reactions. This first patent had a rudimentary conception of both a nuclear reactor and an atomic bomb:

A plate of uranium 235 of a few millimeters thickness and, for example, 1 cubic meter surface area surrounded by paraffin or water, depending on its thickness, would either release a continual enormous heating ... or explosively liberate its energy with a force millions of times greater than all currently known explosives. Both cases should be protected by this patent request.[78]

Wirtz and his colleagues subsequently decided to split the original patent into one for the uranium machine, and one on transuranic elements. On June 6, 1941, a few weeks before the German invasion of the Soviet Union, Weizsäcker wrote a revised application entitled: "The Production of Nuclear Energy from the Uranium Isotope of Mass 238 and Other Heavy Elements (Manufacture and Application of Element 94)." Whereas in his 1940 report, Weizsäcker had described the end product of neutron absorption in uranium as element 93, he now assumed that this would decay into the long-lived element 94.

Lightning War 41

The best way to produce practically useful amounts of element 94 was to use a uranium machine. After absorbing a neutron, element 94 inside the machine would experience fission and produce energy and neutrons just like uranium 235. But what was especially advantageous and the main benefit of the invention was the fact that element 94 could easily be separated chemically from the uranium and produced in pure form. This artificial transuranic element could also be used in a "bomb." Indeed the "energy liberated per unit by this explosive would exceed all others by 10 million times and is only comparable to pure uranium 235."[79]

Weizsäcker did not just submit the patent application. He also met personally with Diebner to discuss the implications of their work. Both uranium 235 and element 94 were "highly concentrated potent substances" that could be used in small, energy-producing uranium burners "especially suitable to power vehicles and vessels that should have a very large operating range." The prerequisite for the production of these substances, which would be a hundred thousand times more powerful than conventional explosives, was either the construction of an energy-producing uranium burner, or an effective isotope separation plant.[80]

Three other physicists, either isolated from or on the periphery of the uranium working group, independently corroborated some of Weizsäcker's results. Hugo Watzlawek, a technical physicist in Munich who was completely cut off from the uranium working group, independently developed a surprisingly accurate understanding of how nuclear reactors and atomic bombs would work in 1944.[81] Josef Schintlmeister at the Institute for Radium Research in Vienna detected traces of what he thought was element 94, although he was never able to demonstrate this conclusively. Over the course of his work he did argue on a theoretical basis that such an element 94 could be separated chemically from uranium, thereby not requiring isotope separation, and like uranium 235 would be fissile with thermal neutrons.[82]

Fritz Houtermans was a colorful physicist who had the dubious distinction of being arrested and incarcerated by both Stalin's secret police and the Gestapo. After his release from the latter at the start of 1941, he went to work at a private scientific institute directed by the German entrepreneur Manfred von Ardenne.[83] By August he had submitted a report on "Unleashing Nuclear Chain Reactions" that corroborated much of Weizsäcker's work. Any uranium machine that relied on uranium 235 for a chain reaction would use only $1/139$ of the available uranium as "fuel." But every neutron, which instead of causing fission in uranium 235 was captured by uranium 238, thereby created a new fissile nucleus. This new element could be separated chemically from uranium, eliminating the need for uranium isotope separation.[84] Just a few months later Houtermans returned briefly to the Soviet Union and visited scientific institutes together with German officials in order to help determine which scientific equipment and scientists or technicians should be transferred to Germany.[85]

42   The Bomb

Houtermans was also the "reliable colleague" mentioned in a remarkable letter sent in April of 1941 from the émigré physicist Rudolf Ladenburg to the American engineer Asa Briggs.

It may interest you that a colleague of mine who arrived from Berlin via Lisbon a few days ago, brought the following message: a reliable colleague who is working at a technical research laboratory asked him to let us know that a large number of German physicists are working intensively on the problem of the uranium bomb under the direction of Heisenberg, that Heisenberg himself tries to delay the work as much as possible; fearing the catastrophic results of a success. But he cannot help fulfilling the orders given to him, and if the problem can be solved, it will be solved probably in the near future. So he gave the advice to us to hurry up if U.S.A. will not come too late.

At around the same time the émigré physicist Leo Szilard also reported that: "Ladenburg says he is pretty sure that a large number of German physicists are working intensively on the problem of the uranium bomb under the direction of Heisenberg."[86]

In his book *Heisenberg's War*, Thomas Powers argues that Heisenberg resisted Hitler and forestalled German nuclear weapons: "Heisenberg did not simply withhold himself, stand aside, let the project die. He killed it." Houtermans and Ladenburg's letter both play important roles in Powers' argument. Drawing mainly upon postwar sources, Powers describes discussions between Heisenberg, Houtermans, and Weizsäcker in early 1941, where they agreed: "to bottle up the significance of plutonium [element 94], saying nothing of it to the Heereswaffenamt [Army Ordnance]; Houtermans would drag out the writing of his paper for Ardenne." Powers adds that "it is true that a strange official silence on the question of the new element persisted even after Weizsäcker's study of 1940.... Weizsäcker's study disappeared as if dropped into a well, and Houtermans's work ... followed it into oblivion."[87]

In fact Houtermans' comprehensive analysis of chain reactions in uranium and transuranic elements was submitted to Ardenne eight months later and passed on to "all the significant nuclear physicists of the time."[88] This work was reprinted with a postscript in October 1944 as part of the secret series of research reports published by the uranium working group. As noted above, Weizsäcker's 1940 report was incorporated into the patent application he sent to HWA in June of 1941, which he then discussed with Diebner. As far as Ladenburg's letter is concerned, perhaps the most significant part is what Powers overlooks: Houtermans said that Heisenberg would follow orders and, if possible, solve the problem.[89]

Operation Barbarossa

Although the war was going well for Germany during the first two years, this did not mean that its negative effects were not felt by Germans. In July of 1940 Heisenberg wrote to his wife that his train from Berlin to Leipzig was diverted

Lightning War 43

to pass through Hamburg, and wondered whether in the long run he could bear the travel back and forth. Little of his own scientific work would get done. But one had to accept such hardships during the war. When he tried to go to sleep in his Hamburg hotel, there was an air raid alarm. Watching the battle from his window, he described the flak being "reflected in the clouds like a natural thunderstorm, only the noise is briefer and more mechanical." In early September he experienced a strong air raid around midnight from the safety of a cellar, from which he could clearly hear the flak and exploding bombs. Ten days later he was writing to his wife from the air raid shelter of the Kaiser Wilhelm Society's Harnack House.

I read in the newspaper that last night the Reichstag [parliament building], the Brandenburg Gate, and the American Embassy were hit. Now once again one can clearly hear the English planes. I have to ... amuse myself over the humbleness of people; who would have thought ten years ago that one would, without further consideration, travel dutifully for a few days to Berlin, in order to be bombed there every night. The next day one reads in leaflets how many houses burned and how many people died and goes reassured to work; the excited people are happy that it is even worse in London.[90]

That same month Heisenberg was visited by a young lieutenant whom Heisenberg had known as a boy. The young man told stories of France, where he had participated in the breakthrough of the Maginot Line, and was now on his way to Norway. The lieutenant's visit enlivened Heisenberg and made him feel like working again. In October Heisenberg reported on meeting the aged Max Planck at a colloquium. Planck was very unhappy about the war and how it was going. He also spoke about the intellectual and spiritual life in Germany, suddenly becoming very alive and encouraging Heisenberg "not to lose his courage," something which, as Heisenberg told his wife, "I will not do in any case."[91]

Heisenberg also told Elisabeth how Bonhoeffer and his wife had been standing at the window in Leipzig when they saw a low-flying plane drop its bombs at close range. In September Bonhoeffer wrote his friend Harteck in Hamburg, the target of many air raids:

Once again you have had an extensive visit from England. Gradually we will come closer to the stable state of the much acclaimed total war. Everything else has just been preliminaries. Will London be destroyed in this way? Or do they want to serve us a destroyed London instead of peace for the winter? Or instead of an attempted invasion?

Two months later, as what would become a very cold winter began, Bonhoeffer joked with Harteck that they were "looking forward with some confidence to winter" with their stores of potatoes, sauerkraut, and carrots, even though they had received only half of the coal they were supposed to get and "as cautious people are freezing in advance." On average they visited the air raid shelter once a week.[92]

44   The Bomb

The climactic turning point of both World War II and the Third Reich itself came in the six months between June and December of 1941. The National Socialist regime came close but ultimately fell short of realizing its ideological dream of "Living Space" (*Lebensraum*) for Germans at the expense of other peoples.[93] When the "long-awaited war against Russia" began, Heisenberg became more optimistic, "although we naturally will be fairly hungry during the winter. But perhaps this will make an agreement with the Anglo-Saxon world easier."[94] Almost immediately, "Operation Barbarossa," the codename for the attack on the Soviet Union, made itself felt on the home front. As Heisenberg wrote Elisabeth:

I find the course of the war very depressing. The Leipzig newspapers are full of death notices. A few acquaintances of acquaintances have received letters from the East, which also sound very depressing. There is still no news from Jochen Frels and from Gila's fiancé. Today an acquaintance of Gila from her dance club was listed in the newspaper as killed in action. Thus at once the war becomes serious.[95]

Government propaganda painted a sinister picture of the Soviet Union, one Heisenberg, who had fought in a militia against Communists immediately after the First World War, was predisposed to accept. A student of one of Heisenberg's colleagues got a letter from a friend claiming that: "The atrocities of the Russians were even more appalling than appeared in the newspaper." From an acquaintance Heisenberg learned of "the poverty of the population and the high living of an 'upper class' of only a few hundred people."[96] The fact that Heisenberg passed these second- or third-hand accounts on to his wife suggests that he gave them credence. In fact during the first months of Operation Barbarossa it was the Germans who were committing atrocities and making the local population suffer but as Omer Bartov has demonstrated, this "striking inversion of reality," that ascribed the unprecedented brutality of the German Armed Forces and the SS to their victims, was how German soldiers came to terms with their actions in the Soviet Union.[97]

Heisenberg's concern about the war and its toll permeated his letters to Elisabeth in the summer and autumn of 1941. "There is so much sadness in the world; we must stick together in order not to become despondent."[98] But it was news of friends, relatives, and students falling in battle that hit Heisenberg the most. When a young musician who had played with Heisenberg died in Russia, his letter to his wife described "such a nice, talented and always jolly person.... And how many other people like him will perish?" The mother of Hans Euler, one of Heisenberg's students, passed on the official letter declaring him missing in action. Again Heisenberg's biases towards the Soviet Union emerged: "Naturally the question is whether the Russians even keep lists of prisoners. But one may not give up hope that he is still alive."[99] This was another inversion of reality. Millions of Soviet soldiers were taken prisoner and then left to die from disease, lack of food, and mistreatment.[100]

Lightning War 45

At around the same time Heisenberg saw a clear path to the atomic bomb, he also became increasingly apprehensive about the war. What began to concern Heisenberg, the great loss of life, eventually became the reason why Germany began to falter. Hitler's attack, while devastating the western parts of the Soviet Union, also bled Germany white. German casualties had surpassed 200,000 by the end of July, growing to 400,000 in September, representing over 11 percent of the German forces fighting in the East. By August Hitler and the leaders of the German armed forces had concluded that the war would continue into 1942. They had reckoned with a maximum of 200 Soviet troop divisions but had already encountered 360.[101] The news from the East was troubling to Heisenberg because "the resistance of the Russians appears to be much stronger than anyone had previously assumed. What would happen if the German advance somewhere came to a stop, is hardly imaginable."[102]

Conclusion

During the first two years of World War II, when the German armed forces appeared unstoppable, a small group of German scientists researched the potential applications of nuclear fission. Two clear technological paths appeared to lead to nuclear energy and atomic bombs: uranium isotope enrichment and uranium machines (nuclear reactors). Isotope enrichment could facilitate the construction of an operating uranium burner and, if complete separation was possible, produce a nuclear explosive. Uranium burners could produce heat and thereby electricity as well as manufacture transuranic elements that also would be nuclear explosives. Progress along both of these paths was modest. Uranium isotope enrichment failed, despite great effort. Because of a shortage of heavy water and metal uranium, model uranium machine experiments had been forced to use inferior materials and remained on a small scale. It nevertheless appeared that uranium machines could in principle be built. Up until this point, the war had not significantly hampered the research and powerful new weapons did not appear necessary. That would all soon change.

Epilogue: Allied Progress by the Eve of Pearl Harbor

The progress of the German uranium project by the autumn of 1941 can be usefully measured against the standard of comparable work in the United States and Britain, often carried out by émigrés from Germany, by the eve of the Japanese attack on Pearl Harbor. The Americans and Germans both understood that pure uranium 235 constituted a nuclear explosive, and centrifuges were promising isotope enrichment and separation devices. In both Britain and the United States work also began on gaseous diffusion isotope separation. Perhaps most important, a powerful electromagnet in Berkeley was used

46   The Bomb

to produce small samples of pure uranium 235, so that its properties could be investigated. Similarly both sides realized that the transuranic element 94 would be produced in a uranium machine and could be chemically separated from the uranium, that it was fissile like uranium 235, and would facilitate small uranium machines and what the American physicist E.O. Lawrence called "super bombs." The most important difference was the availability of a cyclotron in the United States, which was used to produce small amounts of 94, which were then chemically analyzed.[103]

There was little progress manufacturing the key components of a uranium machine in either country. Metal uranium, including solid metal, proved difficult to produce. In both countries graphite (carbon) and heavy water were investigated as neutron moderators, with Americans and Germans researching catalytic exchange reactions for large-scale production of heavy water. Significant amounts of heavy water or pure enough graphite were not available in either country, but while the Germans were not sure the graphite would be a suitable moderator, the Americans had concluded that it would.[104] As a result, while the first model uranium machine experiments in the two countries measured the same things and achieved comparable results, they used different moderators: lattices of uranium in graphite in the USA, horizontal or spherical layer designs of uranium and either paraffin, water, or heavy water in Germany.[105]

Perhaps the greatest and most consequential difference between the German researchers on one hand, and émigré, British, and American scientists on the other, was that the latter were thinking more deeply about bombs. In March of 1940 the émigres Otto Frisch and Rudolf Peierls wrote a memorandum entitled "On the Construction of a 'Super-Bomb': based on a Nuclear Chain Reaction in Uranium" and submitted it to the British government. Since recent advances in isotope separation suggested that producing pure uranium 235 was possible, they calculated the critical mass of pure uranium 235, that is, how much would be needed for an atomic bomb. Their first rough estimate yielded a critical mass of less than a kilogram. A fast-neutron chain reaction in a 5 kilogram mass of uranium 235 would produce energy equivalent to several thousand tons of dynamite and release deadly radiation. "Effective protection," they noted, was "hardly possible."[106]

British scientists investigated the consequences and feasibility of the Frisch–Peierls memorandum and submitted the "MAUD" report in the summer of 1941.[107] Their estimate of critical mass was higher, 10 kilograms, with a destructive force of 1,800 tons of TNT. Because of the radiation, "the area devastated by the explosion would be dangerous to life for a considerable time." The MAUD scientists worked out how the bomb could work, bringing two subcritical masses of uranium 235 together at high velocity, and how the uranium 235 could be produced, via centrifuges or gaseous diffusion through small

Lightning War

47

holes. The estimated total cost of a gaseous diffusion plant was £5 million, each bomb £236,000. The first bombs could be ready by the end of 1943.[108]

Perhaps most important, the MAUD report had a sense of urgency. It was troubling that the Germans had tried to get heavy water, and "the lines on which we are now working are such as would be likely to suggest themselves to any capable physicist." The MAUD committee concluded that a uranium bomb was feasible and likely to lead to decisive results in the war. Even though it would be very costly, "the destructive effect, both material and moral, is so great that every effort should be made to produce bombs of this kind." The report recommended that this work be continued with the highest priority and on the increasingly large scale necessary to obtain the weapon in the shortest possible time. By November the Americans had slightly different results, estimating the critical mass as falling somewhere between 2 and 100 kilograms, and expecting that "fission bombs" would be available in significant quantities within three or four years.[109]

When Henry Smyth summarized the research on atomic bombs on the eve of Pearl Harbor, he noted that tangible progress was not great but:

Perhaps more important than the actual change was the psychological change. Possibly [the émigrés] Wigner, Szilard, and Fermi were no more thoroughly convinced that atomic bombs were possible than they had been in 1940, but many other people had become familiar with the idea and its possible consequences. Apparently, the British and the Germans, both grimly at war, thought the problem worth undertaking. Furthermore, the whole national psychology had changed. Although the attack at Pearl Harbor was yet to come, the impending threat of war was much more keenly felt than before, and expenditures of effort and money that would have seemed enormous in 1940 were considered obviously necessary precautions in December 1941.[110]

4 Selling Uranium

> The newest results of German science have been reported to me. Research in the area of atom smashing has progressed so far that, under certain conditions, the results might be used in this war. Here only the smallest deployment produces such an immense destructive effect, that one can look towards the course of this war, if it lasts longer, and a subsequent war with a certain horror. Modern technology places into the hands of people means of destruction that are unimaginable. Here German science is the best, and it is also necessary that we are the first in this area, for he who brings a revolutionary innovation into this war, has greater chances of winning it.
>
> From Propaganda Minister Josef Goebbels' diary (March 21, 1942).[1]

The End of the Lightning War

The Lightning War first faltered during the autumn of 1941 then ground to a halt in the early Russian winter without achieving its goals of capturing Moscow and Leningrad. The changing fortunes of war expanded and transformed what now truly became the second world war and forced, for the first time, careful scrutiny of the working group. In late November of 1941 Heisenberg submitted a progress report.

As Heisenberg explained, there were two paths to the uranium machine: using heavy water or separating the uranium isotopes. Although such separation was theoretically possible, so far it had not succeeded and would certainly take more time. The first path was feasible, delayed mainly by difficulties in obtaining the necessary materials, heavy water and solid metal uranium. The greatest obstacle was clearly acquiring enough heavy water, and this would also take the most time. At that moment the only heavy water available to Germany came from the Norsk Hydro, around 1.5–2 metric tons per year. With this production, Heisenberg noted, it would take at least two years to manufacture enough for only one uranium machine. An expansion of the heavy water production there, as planned by Harteck and Wirtz, might be able to increase the yearly production to 5 to 7 tons. However, the expansion had not yet begun, the necessary preliminary and pilot experiments were not completed, and someone had to coordinate all of this.

Selling Uranium 49

Storing the irreplaceable heavy water arriving regularly from Norway was an urgent problem. Currently the heavy water was kept at three different locations in small containers. If the heavy water content sunk to 99 percent, for example through exchange with the air, then the liquid would become unusable in a uranium machine. The diluted heavy water would have to be returned to Norway for regeneration, which would also hinder the production of more heavy water. For this reason, Heisenberg proposed construction of a high-concentration device at the KWIfP based on the Norwegian design. Since the heavy water had to be protected against both adulteration and other influences like bomb damage and theft, it needed to be stored in metal tanks underground. The time needed to arrange this storage depended on the allocation of restricted metals and private firms. If a trained machinist and the necessary iron and aluminum were made available, then it could probably be done in two months. The high-concentration device relied on getting more manpower. The Norsk Hydro could build such a device in half a year. Moreover, all of the heavy water arriving from Norway had to be examined. If one flask, whether through carelessness or sabotage, contained light water and was mixed with the rest, then the entire amount would become unusable. Workers at the KWIfP took half a day to check each of the twenty-five flasks that were arriving each month from Norway.

Heavy water would have to be produced on a much larger scale in Germany than was being done in Norway. Although Heisenberg could not give a definitive answer to how much heavy water would be required, he assumed that a uranium burner would need 5 to 10 tons and a yearly production of at least 50 tons, enough for five to ten uranium burners, would be needed. Since such production would be made much easier if they could begin with water that was already enriched as a byproduct of an industrial process, they were collecting and examining water samples from different German industrial works. This was also time-consuming work and would probably take three to five months. Unfortunately, the production of heavy water in Germany was still at a very early stage. Different processes had been proposed for such production but the most practical and least expensive method had not yet been determined. The experiments Harteck was running in this regard would take at least half a year. Without more help the research and development work needed for heavy water production in Germany would take at least half or three-quarters of a year. The production of heavy water on a large scale could not be expected in 1942 without a significant increase in manpower.

The heavy water was necessary for a large-scale uranium burner, one that might achieve a self-sustaining nuclear-fission energy-producing chain reaction and produce element 94. Before the scientists could attempt this, preliminary experiments needed to continue with uranium metal and paraffin (a readily available but poor substitute for heavy water) in order to improve their estimates of the amounts of materials required and provide experience for

50   The Bomb

the subsequent uranium machines. These would be followed by a large-scale experiment with the available heavy water (around 700 kilograms) and around a metric ton of uranium metal.

The form of the metal uranium was a problem. The scientists had been unable to cleanly separate the metal uranium powder without using separation walls of materials like aluminum, which strongly absorbed neutrons. It appeared clear that they would have to use metal uranium in solid form but there was little of that available. According to Nikolaus Riehl at the Auer Society, the company charged with purifying and processing uranium, there were no technical problems with casting the uranium into solid form, rather a shortage of manpower and materials at Auer and the other companies involved in uranium production had hampered progress. Once the solid uranium pieces were available, the experiment could begin two months later. Heisenberg summed up the progress so far as follows: "With regard to physics, the work on producing energy in a uranium machine has now reached a relatively clear stage. There is no longer any doubt that a self-sustaining [technical] installation can be built in principle. This main goal undoubtedly must be reached as quickly as possible."[2]

Arguably the most important part of Heisenberg's report was his estimate of how much heavy water would be needed, not just for a single uranium burner but for the industrial application of nuclear fission. The officials at Army Ordnance were probably sobered by Heisenberg's estimate that a capacity of 50 tons of heavy water each year would be needed. In the context of the German war economy such production levels must have appeared impossible, if not fantastic. Together with the fact that isotope separation had not made significant progress, Heisenberg's estimates clearly suggested that bombs using nuclear explosives could not be built in Germany before the war was over. The second strong message from Heisenberg's report, indeed one he repeatedly emphasized, was the overall need for more manpower. This was certainly objectively true but may also have reflected scientists' desires not to be called-up for frontline military service.

On December 5, a little more than a week later, the Russians launched a massive counteroffensive north and south of Moscow with large numbers of fresh troops well equipped for winter fighting. That very same day Erich Schumann, the physicist in charge of research at HWA, wrote to the leading scientists in the working group telling them that their work required an effort that, given the current military situation and shortages of raw materials, could only be justified "if it is certain that an application will be achieved in the foreseeable future." Although after the war, Schumann was often portrayed as an incompetent dilettante, in fact he was a capable physicist, expert in acoustics and explosives, and a very skillful science policy maker well versed in the political intrigues of the NS state.[3]

Selling Uranium

The institute directors were therefore summoned to Berlin for a meeting on December 16 where they would report on the progress so far and make future plans including setting deadlines for the completion of intermediary steps. Schumann would then personally report to the head of HWA for a decision as to how this matter would be handled further.[4] The conflict was transformed once again on December 11, 1941, four days after the Japanese attack on Pearl Harbor, when Hitler declared war against the United States and subsequently assumed personal control of the German army. Germany had gone from using the Lightning War to overcome countries of smaller or comparable size in a serial fashion to simultaneously confronting the United States, Soviet Union, and the British Empire in a war of attrition.

The scientists involved with uranium research were now justifiably worried about being called-up for regular military service. Two young theoretical physicists working at the KWIfP, Karl-Heinz Höcker and Paul Müller, were already serving in the army. How serious the situation had become was made clear when both Harteck and Weizsäcker were drafted in January of 1942. Bonhoeffer and Heisenberg immediately traveled to Berlin. Bonhoeffer's brother-in-law knew someone in the Army personnel office, who prepared their way. Once there Bonhoeffer found that: "The people were very reasonable. Heisenberg truly invested a great deal of time and passion into the matter," eventually succeeding in getting the call-up orders reversed. It was now very clear that the scientists in the working group had to "sell" their research to the relevant political and military authorities. Bonhoeffer told Harteck: "You can understand how happy we all are that you now do not have to go to Russia in the next few days.... How someone would then have gotten you back, only the gods would know. Right now that does not work at all."[5]

The Army Ordnance Review

In February, 1942, HWA officials composed a comprehensive report, 144 pages long and citing more than 140 secret papers, entitled "Producing Energy from Uranium." It surveyed the collective achievement of the working group up until this point, echoing Heisenberg's analysis but going beyond it, Although the report was sober and realistic, it was also optimistic about the future prospects. It argued that while the complete separation of the uranium isotopes appeared to be very far off, even an enrichment of uranium 235 to double its original percentage would allow smaller uranium machines and perhaps the use of light water as a moderator.

Whereas in Norway the Norsk Hydro could take advantage of cheap energy, in Germany a large-scale electrolytic plant with a similar design was out of the question because of the great demand for electricity. However, new processes were being developed for use in Germany that could be connected

52   The Bomb

to hydroworks, power plants, etc. but without damaging their production. "Thereby a technical and economical way will be found to produce large amounts of heavy water in Germany, a multiple of the Norwegian production."

As far as carbon in the form of graphite was concerned, the HWA officials recognized both Bothe's results, that the electrographite he tested would not work, and Hanle's argument that the true neutron absorption of carbon was probably smaller. However, the experiments that had been carried out to improve the purity of the graphite had failed, leading HWA to conclude that "in practice carbon with a higher degree of purity than what was used cannot be manufactured." This was not simply a matter of skepticism about German industry producing pure enough graphite, rather being able to do that in the context of a strained war economy. By comparison, the construction of a uranium machine using heavy water appeared promising.[6]

The most important experimental result was that a self-sustaining energy-producing uranium burner could be built with around 5 tons of both metal uranium and heavy water, although these estimates were uncertain by a factor of two. Such a burner could run 10,000 times as long as a heat engine using normal fuel of the same weight. The pace of development depended on the availability of materials. As soon as the necessary amounts of heavy water and metal uranium were available, a self-sustaining burner would be built. Once the first uranium burner had been constructed, there were three further steps:

(1) The development of the burner into a technically useful apparatus.
(2) The technical, especially military, application of the burner.
(3) The manufacture of a uranium explosive.

The second task was multifunctional. The first important application might be for ship propulsion, greatly increasing the operating range. Since the uranium machine did not require oxygen, it would be especially suitable for submarines. If uranium 235 could be enriched or element 94 produced, then the uranium machine could be made small enough to power planes and land vehicles. Finally, the machine would produce powerful radiation and radioactive substances in hitherto undreamed-of amounts, useful for science and medicine. The prospects for the third task, nuclear explosives, were uncertain because this would require very large isotope separation plants or a successful separation of large amounts of element 94 in uranium machines, neither of which had yet been built.[7]

The authors of the report made a clear distinction between a controlled and an uncontrolled chain reaction: "If this 'chain reaction' runs slowly, the uranium represents a heat-producing machine; if it runs fast, an explosive of the highest effectiveness."[8] Such an explosive, which would have "a million times the explosive power as the same amount of dynamite," could be produced by the complete separation of the uranium isotopes, something that was in principle feasible but technically very difficult. But once a uranium burner was in operation, there was a second path to manufacturing nuclear explosives. Element 94 would be formed as uranium 238 absorbed neutrons and could be separated chemically from the uranium. Unfortunately for them they did not know either how much would be produced, or what its properties would be.[9]

It is remarkable that, of all the historical sources for the German uranium work during the war, only the HWA report contains an estimate of the critical mass of a bomb using uranium 235 or element 94: "Since there are a few free neutrons in every substance, bringing together a sufficient amount of (presumably 10–100 kg) would suffice to ignite the explosive."[10] Unfortunately, in contrast to the overwhelming majority of information in the report, no source is provided for this estimate. The person who made the calculation is unknown.

The authors concluded that the technical production of nuclear energy from nuclear fission by means of a chain reaction was certainly possible with pure or enriched uranium 235 but success in the near future could also be expected with a layer arrangement of natural uranium and heavy water.[11] Just like Heisenberg had done, they also called for more support.

Once the most important scientific problems directed towards this goal have been solved, this clearly marked path requires significant investment in materials and especially trained workers, whose security [from being called-up], also in industry, is absolutely necessary. Once all these preconditions have been fulfilled, the large-scale production of heavy water has to be promoted further and the manufacture of compact uranium metal in particular has to be intensified.

Whether it is possible to produce "nuclear explosives" can only be determined after the first uranium machine [is in operation] or large-scale isotope separation is successful.

They also explained why this research was necessary, even if success appeared far off:

The tremendous significance that it offers for the energy economy in general and for the armed forces in particular justifies such preparatory work even more, since the problem is also being worked on in enemy countries – especially in America.[12]

Transfer to the Reich Research Council

Despite the enthusiasm and optimism expressed by members of his staff, General Emil Leeb, the head of Army Ordnance, told Albert Vögler, president of the Kaiser Wilhelm Society, that because the preliminary research, which had been carried out under the leadership of HWA, "had come to a certain closure," it was time that further work be managed by a different agency.[13] Now that HWA was getting out of uranium research, the KWG wanted to regain complete control over its physics institute. The director, the Dutch physicist

54   The Bomb

Peter Debye, was in the United States and not returning anytime soon. Once the Society senate had appointed Heisenberg as Debye's successor, Vögler asked Leeb to withdraw Kurt Diebner, the HWA official who had been running most of the KWIfP. Heisenberg could have kept any or all of the HWA scientists who had been working at the institute but he did not want them.[14]

An internal conference was quickly organized at the KWIfP from February 26th to the 28th, including 29 talks and representing the work of 35 different scientists.[15] This was an opportunity for the scientists to demonstrate that their research was important and deserved support. As a result of HWA withdrawing its support, the research project, although still secret, became more widely known. In agreement with Leeb, Bernhard Rust, the Reich Minister of Education, invited dignitaries to a lecture series at the Reich Research Council (*Reichsforschungsrat*, RFR), which was responsible for mobilizing basic research at universities and other institutions for the war effort.

A series of important questions in nuclear physics will be discussed, which because of their significance for national defense have up until now mainly been worked on in secret. In particular the question of utilizing atomic energy plays an important role. Given the exceptional significance the solution of this complex of questions could have for German armaments and subsequently for the entire German economy....[16]

The talks were held in the House of German Research in Berlin, with an audience including several of the most important science policy makers in Germany at this time. Collectively the talks were designed to demonstrate both the progress of the working group and the necessity of continuing the work.[17]

Nuclear Physics as a Weapon	Prof. Dr. Schumann
The Fission of the Uranium Nucleus	Prof. Dr. Hahn
The Theoretical Foundation for the	Prof. Dr. Heisenberg
Production of Energy from Uranium Fission	
Results of Investigations of Energy Production	Prof. Dr. Bothe
Basic Research	Prof. Dr. Geiger
Enrichment of the Uranium Isotopes	Prof. Dr. Clusius
The Production of Heavy Water	Prof. Dr. Harteck
On the Expansion of the "Nuclear Physics"	Prof. Dr. Abraham Esau
Working Group through the Participation of	
Other Reich Agencies and Industry	

Otto Hahn gave his listeners a basic introduction to radiation and radioactive decay, including imagery suitable for a wartime audience. The particles produced through decay can be easily detected because of the effect on their surroundings, "similar to how the effect of a musket ball leaving its path can be detected much easier than that of a bullet that has come to rest." Hahn of course described the discovery of nuclear fission in detail, noting that it had been confirmed in numerous laboratories in Europe and the United States by means of powerful radiation sources that the Germans did not possess. The

Selling Uranium 55

most important result of this discovery was the possibility of a chain reaction, "which increases the yield of nuclear disintegrations and the resulting liberated energies in an entirely exceptional way."[18]

Harteck lectured on heavy water. Just like Hahn, he provided a basic explanation of what this was but he began his talk by emphasizing why it was necessary. It had been convincingly demonstrated that a machine made of metal uranium and heavy water had to work. Since the problem of producing metal uranium had been solved (a slight exaggeration on Harteck's part), producing enough heavy water was the only problem remaining. The initial plan, which he had developed together with HWA, was to produce enough heavy water as a byproduct of other production for the first uranium machine. Fortunately the war, or as Harteck put it, a "sequence of happy circumstances," made it possible for them to use the Norsk Hydro electrolysis plant for this purpose. The next step was to develop processes for producing heavy water in Germany. These included: (1) the fractionation of water and of (2) hydrogen; (3) improved electrolysis; and (4) a catalytic exchange process using two temperatures. The investment costs of a ton of heavy water per year using processes 1, 2, and 4 would be around half a million RM a year. Perhaps understanding that this might seem expensive to his audience, Harteck used the imagery of fire to make his case.

There is an obvious question: is heavy water absolutely necessary in order for the machine to run? According to our current knowledge, we need heavy water … in order to ignite the flame of the nuclear reactions. Only experience can teach us how this flame, once ignited, will burn further. In any case we are able to produce enough heavy water so that this flame can keep burning.[19]

Heisenberg also gave a remarkable talk, which leads to perhaps the greatest mystery about the wartime German work on nuclear energy and weapons. At Farm Hall, after the scientists had learned of the attack on Hiroshima on August 6, 1945, Heisenberg appeared confused about what the critical mass of an atomic bomb would be. At first he simply did not believe a word about the bomb. The Americans might have about 10 tons of enriched uranium, he said, but not 10 tons of pure uranium 235. Hahn immediately objected that he thought that only very little uranium 235 was necessary. Could they make a bomb with 30 kilograms of uranium 235? Heisenberg replied that it would not explode. Hahn then asked why during the war Heisenberg had told him that only 50 kilograms of uranium 235 was needed? Unfortunately Heisenberg's reply, if he gave one, has not been recorded.

When Heisenberg subsequently speculated that the Americans had used an electromagnetic device to produce perhaps 30 kilograms of uranium 235, Hahn pressed him again: "Do you think they would need as much as that?" Heisenberg answered yes but added that: "Quite honestly I have never worked it out as I never believed one could get pure '235.'" Heisenberg proceeded

56 The Bomb

to try and calculate the critical mass at Farm Hall, first getting the unlikely amount of a ton, then a little more than a week later a much smaller and more accurate estimate.[20] If Heisenberg did not calculate the critical mass during the war, then someone else did. As mentioned above, it is striking that there is no source cited for the HWA estimate of 10–100 kilograms, suggesting that the calculation was made specifically for that report. Jeremy Bernstein has argued that an "apparently off-hand calculation" of the critical mass by Harteck at Farm Hall both leads "to a sensible answer" and suggests that he might have done this problem before.[21]

The confusion expressed by Heisenberg after the war in Farm Hall, as is the case for any postwar source, begs the question: What did he understand during the war? Indeed Heisenberg's February 1942 talk before the RFR reveals that he understood a great deal about how an atomic bomb would work. Heisenberg began his talk with a fantastic, indeed impossible image: If every nucleus in a ton of uranium experienced fission, then around 15 billion kilocalories of energy, an incomprehensible amount, would be liberated. Because fission released several neutrons, Heisenberg explained, it was possible to convert large amounts of uranium into energy through a chain reaction. In order to illustrate this process, Heisenberg employed the following schematic diagram (see Figure 4.1) that, after the war, he described as showing – "tailored for the level of understanding of a Reich minister of the time" – the neutron increase in pure uranium 235, compared with that in a nuclear reactor composed of ordinary uranium and heavy water.[22]

In normal uranium, after a short distance a neutron released by fission could either collide with a uranium 238 nucleus and, if it possessed enough energy, fission it and thereby release new neutrons, or what unfortunately was much more probable, only transfer energy to the atomic nucleus without splitting it, in which case the neutron travels further with less energy. After a few such collisions the energy of the neutron will become so low that there are only two possibilities for its subsequent fate: It can collide with a uranium 238 nucleus and be absorbed by it, or it can collide with one of the rare uranium 235 nuclei and fission it. In this case new neutrons are produced and the processes described above can begin again. Some of the neutrons can escape through the outer surface of the uranium and thereby be lost for any further increase. In ordinary uranium the process of neutron absorption by uranium 238, which forms a new isotope uranium 239, occurs much more frequently than fission and neutron increase. Thus the desired chain reaction cannot take place in ordinary uranium.

Heisenberg then made an analogy that, just like Hahn's use of musket balls, and Harteck's flame imagery, fit well into the National Socialist worldview. The behavior of neutrons in uranium could be compared to that of a population, whereby the fission process is analogous to marriage with children and

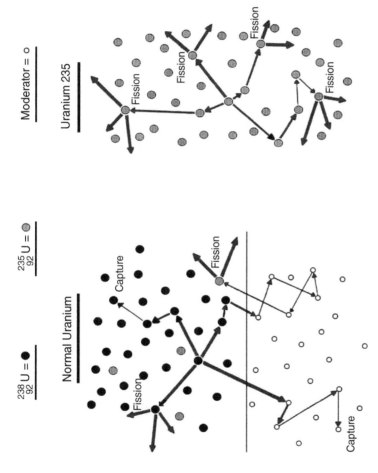

Figure 4.1 Schematic diagram of chain reactions in uranium.

Note: The smaller circles are moderator nuclei, the solid black circles uranium 238 nuclei, and the hatched circles uranium 235. The arrows represent neutrons in motion that have been released by fission. The left-hand side of the diagram represents a controlled chain reaction, in other words, a uranium machine; the right-hand side portrays an uncontrolled chain reaction, in other words, a nuclear explosive.

Source: Adapted from Werner Heisenberg, "Die Energiegewinnung aus der Atomkernspaltung" (May 6, 1943), ADM, FA 002 737.

58   The Bomb

capture an analogy to death. In ordinary uranium the mortality rate far outweighs the number of births, so that an existing population would always die out after a short period of time. The only options for improving their prospects are: (1) increasing the number of births per marriage; (2) increasing the number of marriages; or (3) reducing the probability of death. Unfortunately, Heisenberg explained, the average number of neutrons released by fission is determined by natural laws and cannot be changed.

An increase in the number of fissions could be achieved by enriching the amount of the rare isotope uranium 235, in which low energy neutrons can produce fission. If it becomes possible to produce pure uranium 235, then the processes portrayed on the right side of Figure 4.1 are produced. After one or more collisions every neutron would cause a further fission if it did not escape through the outer surface. Here the probability of death through capture is vanishingly small compared to the probability of neutron increase. Once the mass of uranium 235 is just large enough so that the neutron loss through the outer surface remains small compared to the increase inside, the number of neutrons will increase tremendously, releasing the entire fission energy in a small fraction of a second. Pure uranium 235 therefore "undoubtedly represents an explosive of utterly unimaginable effect." However, Heisenberg cautioned that this explosive was very difficult to obtain. While a significant part of the working group had been devoted to the problem of enriching or producing pure uranium 235, the Americans also appeared to be "placing special emphasis on this work."[23]

The final option for achieving a chain reaction was reducing the number of deaths, that is, the probability of neutron capture. In practice, the neutron velocity can be quickly reduced by using a suitable moderator, that is, a substance whose atomic nuclei remove some of the neutron energy when they collide with neutrons. This is illustrated on the normal uranium part of Figure 4.1. Unfortunately moderators absorb some neutrons. Therefore a moderator needed to be found that quickly removes energy from neutrons but absorbs them as little as possible. The most suitable substance was deuterium in its most practical form, heavy water but Heisenberg added that heavy water was also not easy to produce in large amounts.[24]

Such a uranium machine composed of uranium and moderator could heat a steam turbine and produce great amounts of energy over the course of time. There were practical applications of such machines in vehicles and especially in ships, which because of the great energy potential could have a vast operating distance using only relatively small amounts of uranium. Since the machine did not burn oxygen, it would be especially useful in submarines.

Heisenberg noted that, thanks to an idea from Weizsäcker, as soon as such a burner was in operation, the question of producing explosives took a new turn. Through neutron capture by uranium 238 and its subsequent transformation, a new substance (element number 94) would be created in the machine, which

Selling Uranium

"most probably just like pure uranium 235 is an explosive of the same unimaginable effect."[25] However, this substance could be produced much easier than uranium 235 from ordinary uranium, because those two elements can be separated chemically. Heisenberg ended his talk by repeating the most striking potential applications of nuclear fission chain reactions.

(1) if the enrichment of uranium 235 is successful, then it is undoubtedly possible to produce energy from uranium fission. The production of pure uranium 235 would lead to an explosive of unimaginable effect; (2) ordinary uranium can also be exploited in a layer arrangement with heavy water. A layer arrangement of these materials can transfer its great energy potential over time to a thermal engine. It is thus a means to store great amounts of technically usable energy in relatively small amounts of material. Once the machine is in operation it can also lead to the production of a tremendously powerful explosive.[26]

As Hahn noted in his diary, the talks the scientists gave at the RFR made a good impression. Remarkably newspapers even reported on the event, describing the lectures as "being concerned with problems in modern physics that are of decisive significance for national defense and the entire German economy." Wolfgang Finkelnburg, a physicist who was a high-ranking official in the National Socialist University Lecturers League, told Heisenberg that because of his talk and the press notices about it, different NSDAP offices had asked him about the military relevance of theoretical physics and especially Heisenberg's own work. Even Josef Goebbels, Minister of Propaganda, heard the news about the possibility of destructive new weapons.[27] The lecture series had an unforeseen consequence for the KWG. Although the head of HWA had suggested transferring the nuclear working group to the Society, which its President Albert Vögler wanted, when the RFR met to hear the talks, it also took control of the project, something Vögler was powerless to stop.[28]

Heavy Water

In September, 1941, HWA sent Harteck and Karl Wirtz to Norway in search of more heavy water. As Harteck wrote Bonhoeffer: "Now it suddenly starts, after I thought the matter had fallen asleep." Meetings with officials from the Norsk Hydro established that the current capacity for heavy water production was around 1,500 kilograms (1.5 metric tons) per year, which was to be increased to around 3–5 tons through a catalytic exchange process designed by Harteck and his colleague Hans Suess. Keeping the expansion work secret appeared simple, because the plant was built on a mountain and could only be reached by means of a narrow bridge guarded day and night by an armed security force.[29]

However, when Harteck and Wirtz returned to Germany, they also reported that the Norsk Hydro plant in Rjukan was unique and it was currently impossible to produce heavy water in similar amounts elsewhere in Europe. The plant

60   The Bomb

would be easy to damage or destroy. In particular, it would be easy to stop the heavy water production "through an act of sabotage." For this reason, they argued that it was absolutely necessary to begin production of heavy water in Germany. Since there were no large electrolytic plants in Germany – indeed at that time only around 20 kilograms of heavy water per month could be produced there in this way – other methods had to be found and a high concentration facility should be built that could further enrich or purify already enriched water.[30] HWA agreed that a small high concentration facility should be built, 10 percent the size of a pilot plant, and that other production methods be investigated, noting that because the different processes for enriching heavy water were still in the beginning stages, no decision could be made regarding the expansion to a large-scale facility.[31]

The expansion at the Norsk Hydro got off to a slow start. In November of 1941 Wirtz reported that their experiments on the new heavy water process would take several months more. Since German companies were so busy, Norwegian firms should be used as much as possible for the expansion.[32] The Norwegians at the Norsk Hydro found themselves in an uneasy position. The German officials in Norway wanted the expansion of the heavy water facility in Vemork according to the new guidelines to be planned and completed as quickly as possible but the Norsk Hydro had been given very little information regarding the new facility and the process it would use. As a result, they repeatedly requested more help from Wirtz and Harteck. The Norwegians were also apparently interested in doing business, because they also offered to build the small high concentration facility there instead of in Germany, indeed promising to have it running within six to eight weeks.[33]

The efforts to expand heavy water production in Norway continued to be hampered by different issues. The Norsk Hydro was shut down for several weeks in late April and early May because of a shortage of water. German officials in Norway had proposed using a second Norwegian electrolysis plant in Såheim for heavy water production but it was still under construction, so heavy water production there would be delayed. In June of 1942 Harteck was forced to borrow equipment for the Norsk Hydro expansion from Paul Herold, a scientist working at IG Farben.[34]

Harteck had reached out to IG Farben in the autumn of 1941 for help in producing a very large amount of pure heavy water. The following March, after careful consideration, Paul Herold told Harteck that, despite its unusually high demand for energy, the catalytic exchange process appeared feasible because of the expected price for the finished product. Most importantly, Herold's boss Heinrich Bütefisch wanted to work with Harteck and was prepared to build a pilot plant so long as they received sufficient support from the authorities.[35] Bütefisch was one of the most influential and powerful industrialists in the NS state, overseeing the massive IG Farben works at Leuna, directing oil

Selling Uranium

production for the Four Year Plan, serving on the IG Farben board of directors, and making financial contributions to Heinrich Himmler's "Circle of Friends," for which he was made a high-ranking honorary member of the SS.

Bütefisch wrote Harteck personally to set out his conditions. In order to lower costs, the pilot plant would be designed to achieve only a 1–2 percent enrichment as a proof of concept. IG Farben was willing to cover the costs of building the facility but only if HWA was willing to thoroughly brief Bütefisch and his closest coworkers on the main features of "this type of energy production." IG Farben also needed more manpower, not just a pipefitter and chemist but also a capable young engineer, as well as help getting the 80 tons of iron the work would require. Finally, the project had to receive a high priority rating from the authorities.[36] Within days Harteck wrote Bütefisch that HWA accepted his conditions and asked that he send a staff member to an upcoming meeting with both HWA and Abraham Esau, the RFR official now overseeing the working group.

Instead Bütefisch came himself and repeated his main demand: at least a very small group of IG Farben officials had to be well informed about the entire research program. He needed this so that, at any time, he could make his own judgment regarding the practical feasibility and prospective applications of the entire complex and correspondingly make the case for participation to IG Farben. In return, he was willing to spend up to 150,000 RM for constructing the ten-stage pilot plant and getting it running. Further developments would have to be paid for by the RFR. Esau accepted these conditions. With the agreement of all present, Harteck proposed that IG Farben be informed about any relevant patent applications and further that both the working group and IG Farben agree to inform each other about any new developments that might lead to a patent application.[37]

Isotope Separation via Centrifuges

When Heisenberg assessed the work on uranium in November of 1941, he argued that building a uranium machine using heavy water was more pressing than uranium isotope separation. This was mainly because up until that point this had failed. Indeed as far as the Germans knew, the only successful enrichment that had been achieved, by an American research group led by Alfred Nier, had produced only tiny amounts.[38] Harteck and Groth had switched from the separation tube to a multi-stage ultracentrifuge, an adaption of a technology the American Jesse Beams had already used to separate isotopes. In principle this method should work with uranium and deliver two grams of uranium hexafluoride (UF_6) per day in which the amount of uranium 235 had been enriched by 7 percent. Groth was confident that centrifuges would work if they could overcome the corrosive chemical properties of UF_6. However, in

62   The Bomb

December of 1941 even Harteck had to admit that the preconditions for planning large-scale isotope separation facilities did not exist.[39]

The Anschütz Company in the northern German city of Kiel was willing to build the centrifuges and in principle could deliver one within three months but immediately ran into supply issues. Initially they were planning to use a specially hardened steel rotor but since the Krupp Steel Company would take at least eight months to fill this order, they switched to a less robust light metal alloy. In January of 1942 the company told Harteck that they had ordered pieces needed for the centrifuge in October that were supposed to be delivered in three to four weeks but never arrived. When they asked about this, they received no reply. They then ordered the pieces from another company but again received no reply. Anschütz also made clear that it would require more technical personnel, mechanics, electrical engineers, and other workers before they would be able to produce centrifuges in large numbers.[40] Groth must have received a centrifuge by the spring, because on April 15 he noted in his work diary that a test run had caused an explosion. By May Groth was able to use the prototype ultracentrifuge to shift the ratio of xenon isotopes.[41]

This success prompted Harteck to urge that HWA reconsider its priorities regarding uranium. He reminded them that there were two paths to an operating uranium machine: machine type I, using around 5 tons of normal uranium metal and around 5 tons of heavy water; and machine type II, using smaller amounts of uranium metal enriched in isotope 235 and smaller amounts of heavy water, or even ordinary water. Whereas the Germans had taken the path of machine I, because it appeared that the development of the ultracentrifuge would take a long time, the Americans may have taken the second path. Only experience could tell which path was advantageous. The work by Anschütz and Groth had progressed more quickly than expected and they hoped to be able to shift the uranium isotopes in the next few weeks. Given this success, the second path, producing enriched uranium metal, also had to be pursued "with all energy." This path would allow significantly smaller devices, which could be used for military vehicles. Moreover, isotope separation "comes closer to the creation of explosives."[42]

Uranium Machines

Model uranium machine experiments continued in Berlin and Leipzig. Testing different models allowed the scientists to judge whether a given arrangement would increase the number of neutrons. Now that large amounts of metal uranium powder were available, scientists led by Wirtz at the KWIfP set up a spherical arrangement of alternating horizontal layers of metal uranium and paraffin. As Wirtz reported at the internal conference in February, it was clear that the paraffin would not be an effective moderator, even though it did contain a large amount of hydrogen, but it facilitated the layer design. The small

Selling Uranium 63

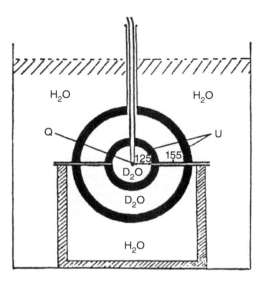

Figure 4.2 Schematic diagram of experiments L-III and L-IV.
Note: In the center was a neutron source Q.
Source: Adapted from Walther Bothe and Siegfried Flügge (eds.), *Kernphysik und kosmische Strahlen. Naturforschung und Medizin In Deutschland 1939–1946*. Vol. 14 (Weinheim: Verlag Chemie, 1948), Part 2, 150.

amount of the precious heavy water available was used in Leipzig. The results of experiments B-III and B-IV clearly showed that metal uranium was more effective than uranium oxide for producing neutrons.[43]

The real success came in Leipzig, where Robert Döpel, with the help of his wife Klara and of Heisenberg, set up an arrangement of nested alternating spherical layers of metal uranium powder and heavy water, separated by aluminum sealed with rubber, all immersed in a tank of water (see Figure 4.2). Experiment L-III, which because of the shortage of metal uranium powder used only one layer, still absorbed more neutrons than it produced but the scientists calculated that, if the aluminum had been removed, the neutrons would have increased. Finally, in April of 1942 the Leipzig group reported success.

After adding a second layer of metal uranium, L-IV yielded a neutron increase. If the aluminum support material could be removed, something planned for future experiments, then even more neutrons would be produced. Although he cautioned that these numbers were still uncertain, Heisenberg estimated that an enlargement of this apparatus to contain around 5 tons of heavy water and 10 tons of cast metal uranium would create an energy-producing uranium burner.[44]

64   The Bomb

Albert Speer

In February, 1942, engineer and Minister of Armaments Fritz Todt died in a plane crash. As Todt's successor Hitler chose Albert Speer, a young and ambitious architect and devoted follower from the Leader's (*Führers*) inner circle. Speer had made his name by designing buildings for the NSDAP, eventually rising to the post of General Building Inspector for the Reich Capital, where he oversaw plans for rebuilding Berlin. Now Speer became one of the people most responsible for armament production and the war effort.

Less than two months later, Hitler issued a decree giving Speer considerable power over the war economy. After the war Speer was credited, in part because of his own claims, with having achieved an armaments miracle. As Adam Tooze has shown, Speer did not just produce more weapons, he "made them tell a story":

The dramatic statistics of production were intended to demonstrate to the German people that the war could still be won, by the efforts of the German workers united with the heroism of the soldiers on the front line…. By elevating Germany's armaments production and by ensuring that this story was told as a miraculous story of rebirth, Speer enabled the Nazi regime to continue the war, not only in practical terms, by providing the [Armed Forces] with more equipment, but also in political terms, by expounding a propaganda story of limitless possibility.[45]

Speer's rise benefited the KWG because its president Albert Vögler was a close advisor. When Vögler complained that the Reich Ministry of Science, Education, and Culture (unofficially known as the "Reich Education Ministry," REM) was not giving enough support to nuclear physics, Speer recommended to Hitler that the RFR be transferred to Hermann Göring's authority.[46] The complaints by Vögler and Heisenberg (see below) about REM appear odd, because the working group had been supported financially by HWA. This criticism probably had more to do with the fact that the Ministry had taken over the project and thereby squeezed out the KWG.

Vögler was concerned about the support of nuclear physics because, as he told Adolf Baeumker, Minister Director of the Air Force Academy, in March: "To his surprise Professor Heisenberg and Privy Councilor Planck believed that it was definitely possible that the Americans, through their decisive and emphatic approach in this area, could in a short amount of time produce far-reaching innovations in military technology." Baeumker then advised Air Force General Field Marshal Erhard Milch to have Heisenberg report to him on nuclear physics and its military applications.[47] Parallel to this, Friedrich Fromm, commander in chief of the reserve army, told Speer in April that he was in contact with a circle of scientists who "were on the trail of a weapon that could destroy an entire city, perhaps incapacitate England."[48] Many of these top-ranking military officials had also seen the memorandum in support

Selling Uranium

of theoretical physics that German Physical Society Carl Ramsauer had submitted to Minister Rust in January.[49]

Vögler organized two days of talks by KWG scientists for Fromm, Milch, Speer, and Karl Witzell, head of the Navy's weapons development, as well as their respective staffs, to showcase the scientists' work and demonstrate the importance of the Society to the war effort (see Figure 4.3). During the previous two months, the British Royal Airforce had severely damaged several German cities.[50] Although a complete listing of all the talks on the two days has not been found, on June 3 Werner Köster from the Kaiser Wilhelm Institute for Metals Research demonstrated technology for nondestructive materials testing[51] and on the following day Bothe and Heisenberg lectured on the work of the working group.

Heisenberg's talk for Speer and the other powerful representatives of the German armaments effort and how they reacted is arguably one of the most misunderstood aspects of this history, in large part because of misleading postwar descriptions by Heisenberg and Speer. In his 1965 interview with David Irving, Heisenberg remembered that he had reported that it was possible to build energy-producing nuclear reactors but that he "did not mention that plutonium [element 94] can be made with that, because we wanted to keep these things as small as possible."[52]

In his 1969 memoirs, Speer remembered that Heisenberg had complained about how nuclear research had been neglected by REM, that they had not had enough money and materials, and that the drafting of scientifically trained staff into military service had caused German science to fall behind in an area that they had dominated a few years ago. Moreover, excerpts from American scientific journals suggested that nuclear research there received abundant technical and financial support. "America would therefore likely already have an advantage," Heisenberg concluded, "which given the revolutionary potential of nuclear fission, could be exceedingly consequential."[53]

However, the text of Heisenberg's June 1942 talk diverges from these two postwar accounts in several significant respects. Heisenberg presented the recent success from the Leipzig experiments. They had managed to build a model uranium machine that increased the number of neutrons. If this design was expanded somewhere from three to six times, it would lead to a uranium burner that could spontaneously produce great amounts of energy. In a very cautiously worded passage, Heisenberg then went on to mention element 94 even if he did not name it. Because of the positive results they had achieved and "following a path laid out by Weizsäcker," it was possible that, once the uranium burner had been built, they might have "explosive materials that surpass the effect of all existing ones by a million-fold." But even if this did not happen, Heisenberg continued, the uranium burner opened an "almost unsurveyable field" of technical applications, including watercraft and eventually

66   The Bomb

aircraft of great operating range, as well as many applications of the radioactive substances produced in the burner. Such a device could radiate around 10,000 times as powerfully as the most powerful cyclotron and correspondingly produce almost any amount of artificially radioactive materials.[54]

At the present, Heisenberg continued, the time needed to develop such a burner was determined by the supply of materials, especially heavy water. Aside from the question of materials, there still was a great deal of scientific development work to do. In conclusion, Heisenberg argued that even if one accepts how difficult such development work is, one must also recognize that here in the next few years scientists could open up "new land of the greatest significance for technology." Since they knew that many of the best laboratories in America were working on this problem, Germany also had to pursue these questions.

Even if one thinks that such developments usually take a long time, if the war with America lasts several years more, one has to consider the possibility that the technical exploitation of atomic energy could suddenly play a decisive role in the war.[55]

In both Heisenberg's February and June talks he explicitly and clearly described the powerful and destructive force of nuclear explosives like uranium 235 and element 94. He did not promise that Germany could develop such weapons in time to be deployed in the war, rather used the possible threat of American atomic bombs to justify the continuation of their research effort.

In an interview from the 1960s Heisenberg remembered that, when the scientists were asked about atomic bombs after his talk, they answered yes in principle but added that it would be enormously costly to produce a nuclear explosive, perhaps requiring billions of Reichsmark and taking many years.[56] In 1948 Heisenberg reported that some members of the audience – Heisenberg did not remember it himself – recalled that Milch had asked approximately how large a bomb powerful enough to destroy a city would be? Heisenberg supposedly responded that the bomb, that is, the effective part, would be approximately as big as a pineapple, which naturally caused a sensation among the nonphysicists.[57] By the 1960s, Heisenberg was remembering that he had said it would be as big as a (European) football.[58] Unfortunately neither of these anecdotes sheds much light on Heisenberg's understanding during wartime of the critical mass of an atomic bomb, because by 1946 at the latest he had learned a great deal about the American atomic bomb, including reading Henry Smyth's official report.[59]

Speer remembered that, when he asked Heisenberg about atomic bombs, the scientist's reaction was "in no way encouraging." While theoretically nothing stood in the way of a bomb, even if every possible support were given, it would take at least two years. According to Heisenberg, the long delay was because they did not have a powerful cyclotron at their disposal. Speer then offered to use the resources available to him to build a cyclotron as big or bigger than in

Selling Uranium 67

America but Heisenberg responded that, because of their lack of experience, they had to start with a relatively small type. Subsequently Speer visited the Krupp works, where they were constructing parts of what would be Germany's first cyclotron, and the technician there said the same thing: Germans did not have the necessary technical experience to build a bigger device.[60]

Speer asked the researchers what was necessary with regard to money, materials, and organization to support nuclear research. In response, they requested a few hundred thousand Reichsmark, modest amounts of steel, nickel, and other metals, the construction of a bunker laboratory, and that both their experiments and the cyclotron under construction be placed in the highest priority category. Speer remembered being "rather alienated by the insignificance of their demands for such a decisively important matter," increased the money to 2 million RM, and agreed to correspondingly higher amounts of materials. Apparently nothing more could be done at that time. Speer had the impression that "the atomic bomb would not matter for the foreseeable course of the war."[61] Although Speer could have massively increased investments in uranium, no one was calling for that. On June 23, Speer recorded that he "reported briefly to the Leader about the meeting on atom smashing and the support we are providing." This terse note is one of the very few primary sources for Hitler learning about atomic bombs.[62]

Heisenberg's interaction with the NS armaments elite did not end with the formal talks. Again, he described the subsequent events to David Irving. This was the first time that he "as a young man came together with these powerful men running the war." Heisenberg told Irving that he had been convinced for a while that the war was lost and thought that this was a good opportunity to hear what these men thought. That evening he was seated next to Milch at dinner, and took the opportunity of a moment when the others were not listening to ask, "What do you think about the further course of the war? It does not look good." At first Milch turned white and replied: "Well, listen, if we lose the war, then we can all take strychnine." But he quickly regained his composure and, as Heisenberg characterized it, "now came the record": Milch said, "We cannot judge that now in detail, but the Leader naturally has very well-thought-out plans." Heisenberg recalled that, from that moment on, he knew that Milch also thought war was lost. Heisenberg also had an opportunity to ask Speer that same question as they walked over to his institute.

He immediately stopped dead, and looked at me for a long time. Just so … said nothing, and after around two minutes he went further without saying a word. When you think about it, [Heisenberg told Irving,] this stare meant the following: Who are you to be so shameless to ask me this question. For you know just as well as me that the war is lost, but you also know that I may not say anything about it.[63]

However, in a letter to his wife immediately after the lectures, Heisenberg described both his talk and what happened afterward very differently.

68   The Bomb

Figure 4.3 Lectures in the Harnack House.
Note: Milch is standing at the table; Speer is seated on Milch's left; Heisenberg is in the foreground of the picture, wearing a civilian suit, with his back to the observer.
Source: Christian Kleint, Helmut Rechenberg, and Gerald Wiemers (eds.), *Werner Heisenberg 1901–1976. Beiträge, Berichte, Briefe. Festschrift zu seinem 100. Geburtstag. Abhandlungen der Sächsischen Akademie der Wissenschaften zu Leipzig. Mathematisch-naturwissenschaftliche Klasse.* Volume 62. (Stuttgart/Leipzig: Hirzel, 2005), 177.

Those were eventful days in Berlin. The powerful elite of the country were truly gathered in Harnack House – practically the entire armaments council and many other powerful people. It went better than all expectations, the talks from Bothe and me obviously made a strong impression; in any case afterwards we were treated personally and professionally fabulously. This is all very strange and eerie; suddenly I do not need to worry at all about the entire Lenard-Stark-clique [Aryan Physics movement] and can push through almost everything that is important to me. I led the minister [Speer] through the institute, strangely the planned experiments functioned completely smoothly and afterward we sat together for dinner in the Harnack House and then on the terrace for wine until midnight. At dinner I sat next to General Field Marshal Milch, with whom I had an excellent conversation. He had the same opinion as me regarding the hiring politics of the Reich Ministry of Education and expressed this openly – something I would never have dared. I found the human level of the entire group very interesting; they were loud, unusual people, many truly unusually bright, all good diplomats and used to asserting themselves in intrigues with integrity (and occasionally probably also with stronger methods). In between there were also

Selling Uranium

strange figures, who in the first moment frighten and in conversation become somewhat engaging, which can make one completely uncertain.

In general the circle was much more interesting, but also more dangerous than the circle of diplomats I know from Weizsäcker's house. Occasionally the great politics were discussed. I am happy here to be just a spectator. For better or worse I have to participate in the small physics politics. It is eerie to me that here large-scale construction, things of value, and scientific work all depend on my word. By the way, externally Speer is similar to Erwin [Heisenberg's brother], just younger and stronger; the face is mostly a mask, only occasionally does it become alive for a moment. I do not envy him that the work of many millions of people, the care of hundreds of thousands of homeless from Cologne, and all the human misery [that] depends on his word.

But enough about the festivities at court.

A few days later, Heisenberg asked Elisabeth, "Did you get my letter from last Friday, which I wrote on the train? It would be unpleasant for me if it would be lost or fall into the wrong hands."[64]

It is clear that Heisenberg and the others had indeed made a very good impression on Speer and the other dignitaries. In October, a high-ranking official in Speer's Ministry asked Heisenberg and other directors of Kaiser Wilhelm Institutes to provide quarterly one-to-two-page progress reports on the research being done in their institutes, especially the work being promoted by this Ministry. The reports should be generally understandable, that is, for Minister Speer himself.[65]

Although several historians have demonstrated how problematic Albert Speer's memoirs are, what he says about his interactions with the working group are usually supported by primary sources, or fit fairly well with them. In contrast, some of Heisenberg's statements from his 1965 interview are more problematic. Whether he misremembered, was being deceptive, or consciously untruthful in his interview with Irving, in fact Heisenberg did mention transuranic nuclear explosives produced in a uranium burner in his talk for Speer and the other high-ranking armaments officials. Both the historian Thomas Powers and the playwright Michael Frayn took this claim that he did not mention plutonium as evidence that Heisenberg had resisted Hitler and the Nazis.[66] Heisenberg's postwar accounts of how Milch and Speer reacted when asked about the war are fascinating but cannot be corroborated.

But the real problem with Heisenberg's and Speer's recollections is more subtle. What did Speer really decide or do with regard to uranium research? We know HWA began this project immediately after World War II began. When the Lightning War faltered, it reviewed the research and decided in February of 1942 to transfer it to a civilian agency, the RFR, because it appeared that this work would not be decisive for the war. When Speer came to the Harnack House four months later to hear the talks by Heisenberg and others, the question was not whether the research into the military applications of nuclear

70   The Bomb

fission chain reactions should continue, for the RFR was very interested in continuing it, but instead how much support in money, manpower, and materials Speer and others should give it. This all happened just before Germany launched their summer offensive, which was successful through to the autumn, culminating in the fateful occupation of Stalingrad.

What was the result of the June talks and discussion at the Harnack House? According to Heisenberg's postwar interview with Irving, it was decided that: "There should be no attempt made to build atomic bombs, thus we are giving that up." Speer himself had referred directly to an order from Hitler that only weapons that would be ready to use in half a year could be pursued. "This was a great relief for us, now we could do some investigations in our own institutes, how that goes with the reactors, but we did not have to worry about the atomic bomb matter."[67] Speer described it slightly differently. After asking again, how long would this take, and receiving the answer three to four years, by the autumn of 1942 they had "followed the suggestion of the nuclear physicists" and decided "not to develop the atomic bomb." The war would have been decided long before this was ready. "Instead I approved the development of an energy-producing uranium burner for the operation of machines, in which the Navy leadership was interested for their submarines."[68]

Speer did not halt work on the atomic bomb, and Heisenberg and his colleagues were not instructed or ordered to limit themselves to the civilian or peaceful applications of nuclear fission, let alone to basic research. The Armaments Minister was presented with scientific research that had great military potential but had also already been determined to be irrelevant for the war Germany was fighting. Indeed no one argued that Germany could build atomic bombs before the end of the war. Speer did not reverse this determination, and he certainly did not commit to the enormous investments in money, materials, and manpower that nuclear weapons development clearly would require but he also did not divert, slow down, or stop anything. Instead the working group scientists continued doing exactly what they had been doing before but now with much more support, all of which was predicated on the possible military applications of nuclear fission. Moreover, their work and its military potential was now widely known among the most powerful men running the German war economy.

A day after giving his talk at the Harnack House and rubbing elbows with some of the most powerful men in the NS regime, Heisenberg submitted ambitious plans for an expansion of the KWIfP. These included an underground bunker laboratory for the first uranium burner, providing protection both from radiation and against air raids. The next model uranium machine experiment was planned with 1.5 tons of heavy water and 3 tons of solid metal uranium in the form of horizontal plates. If they surrounded it with water, as in previous experiments, they expected a 60 percent neutron increase; if they surrounded it instead

Selling Uranium

with pure graphite, then it was possible that this apparatus would come "close to the critical point." On June 11th, Heisenberg signed his contract with the KWG, formally becoming the director at the Physics Institute. As he wrote to Elisabeth, "Thereby the dice have been cast, hopefully for the good of all of us."[69] A few weeks later, the German summer offensive against the Soviet Union began.

Conclusion

The period from the autumn of 1941 through to the summer of 1942 was crucial for the German research on nuclear energy and nuclear weapons because this was when the decisive question was asked: could atomic bombs win the war? The German scientists had concluded that uranium machines and nuclear explosives were possible in principle but the war itself made them impossible in practice. Everyone, including the Kaiser Wilhelm Society, the Reich Research Council, the leadership of the armed forces, Albert Speer, and of course the scientists themselves, wanted the research to continue. Despite what Otto Hahn, Werner Heisenberg, Carl Friedrich von Weizsäcker and others claimed after the war, there was no decision not to build atomic bombs or to restrict the scientific work to basic research. In the context of Germany's increasingly desperate war effort, the former would have been superfluous and the latter absurd.

The research continued with even stronger support for several reasons. First of all, it was not only a matter of atomic bombs. Better submarines and greater electricity production were also needed. An operating nuclear reactor might be valuable even if it never led to nuclear weapons. Germany was now at war with the United States. If the Americans were working on this, then the Germans should as well. While the industrial-scale effort that clearly would be needed to build atomic bombs was out of the question, the amounts of resources, manpower, and equipment needed to continue the development of isotope separation and uranium machines were relatively modest. Finally, even though the scientists were careful not to promise the delivery of atomic bombs, they had begun dangling the possibility of destructive new weapons in front of some of the most powerful men in the Third Reich.

Epilogue: Allied Progress by the Summer of 1942

Administration

Up until the autumn of 1941, the Americans had made relatively small investments into nuclear weapons research but Vannevar Bush, Director of the Office of Scientific Research and Development (OSRD), decided that "the possibility of obtaining atomic bombs for use in the present war" was great enough to

72   The Bomb

justify an "all-out" effort to develop them, a policy that was announced at a meeting on December 6, the day before Pearl Harbor. Ten days later the "Top Policy Group," consisting of Bush, Vice-President Henry A. Wallace, and Secretary of War Henry L. Stimson, decided that OSRD should press forward as fast as possible on the fundamental physics, the engineering, and particularly on the construction of pilot plants. This would cost around US$4–5 million. When James B. Conant reported this new policy to an OSRD subcommittee, he emphasized that such an effort was justified only by the military value of atomic bombs and that all efforts had to be concentrated on bomb development. The whole meeting was pervaded by "an atmosphere of enthusiasm and urgency."[70]

Bush reported general optimism to President Roosevelt but also the tentative nature of their conclusions, suggesting that the Army might be brought in during the summer of 1942 to construct pilot plants, and the project might be completed sometime in 1944. In February of 1942, when the German HWA report was written and Heisenberg lectured on chain reactions in uranium, Conant recommended that all phases of the work be pushed until at least July. There were five separation or production methods that appeared equally likely to succeed: separating out uranium 235 using centrifuges, gaseous diffusion through permeable barriers, and electromagnetic fields; producing plutonium in a nuclear reactor moderated by graphite or by heavy water. All methods were considered almost ready for pilot plant construction and perhaps even for the preliminary design of production plants. Pushing these methods to the production stage would entail a commitment of US$5 hundred million.

Although some methods would presumably prove more rapid and efficient than others, the Americans feared that the elimination of any one method might result in a serious delay and that the Germans might be far ahead of them. If atomic bombs were decisive, then there was virtually no limit to the amount of effort and money that should be invested. On June 13, 1942, Bush and Conant sent detailed plans for the expansion and continuation of the atomic bomb program to Wallace, Stimson, and Chief of Staff General George C. Marshall. All three approved the report. On June 17, 1942, six days before Speer reported to Hitler, the report was sent to President Roosevelt, who also gave his approval.[71]

Both the HWA decision that atomic bombs could not be built in time to affect the war, and the American decision to mount an all-out effort were based on accurate information and comparable, if not quite equal technical and scientific results. The German scientists did not exaggerate the cost and difficulty of building the bomb, just as their counterparts in America did not downplay it. The great difference between the two sides was context. Whereas in Germany HWA was retrenching in response to the end of the Lightning War, the American military was ramping up to enter the war in Europe and the Pacific; whereas the German leadership feared the consequences of a long, drawn-out war of attrition, this was exactly what the Americans expected.

Selling Uranium 73

Materials

The Germans had committed themselves to using heavy water as a moderator in their uranium machines because it appeared unlikely that German industry could manufacture pure enough graphite and the Norsk Hydro appeared able to produce enough heavy water for the first uranium machine experiments. The first steps had also been taken towards heavy water production in Germany with the decision to build a pilot plant together with IG Farben. In America the entire heavy water program was under review in the spring of 1942. It appeared that extremely large quantities of heavy water would be required for a plutonium production plant employing heavy water instead of graphite as a moderator. In contrast, graphite production was still unsatisfactory at the beginning of 1942 but by the middle of that year American industry had essentially solved the purity problem.[72] At this time Germany had large amounts of uranium compounds, and an increasing supply of metal uranium powder. Although at the end of 1941 the Americans had only a few grams of uranium metal, by July of 1942 around a ton a day of very pure uranium oxide was being delivered. Almost no metal uranium was available during most of 1942 but by the autumn the production problems for solid metal uranium had been solved.[73]

The Americans recognized that there were two alternative paths to an operating nuclear reactor (uranium burner): (1) build a reactor according to the best design; or (2) do experiments to determine the nuclear constants and explore intermediate designs. It was clear that (1) would lead most rapidly to plutonium but because not enough solid metal uranium and moderator were available, the Americans pursued the second path. The Germans were in exactly the same situation. The Americans carried out a series of model nuclear reactor experiments, varying the ratio of moderator to uranium oxide, surrounding the reactor with different materials, and using different three-dimensional lattice designs. The work in Germany was again very similar, with the difference that instead of a lattice, they explored horizontal and spherical layer designs. In July, when enough purified uranium oxide was available, the Americans built an intermediate nuclear reactor large enough, for the first time, to multiply neutrons. This was the equivalent of the Leipzig L-IV experiment from April of that same year.[74]

Nuclear Explosives

Whereas the Germans were concentrating their isotope separation efforts on centrifuges, scientists in America were exploring centrifuges, gaseous diffusion, and electromagnetic separation methods. The theory of isotope separation through gaseous diffusion had been well worked out by 1942, making

74   The Bomb

clear that a very large plant would be required. Good enough diffusion barriers and pumps, the most important equipment in such a plant, had not yet been developed. Nevertheless, in early 1942 a company was chosen to plan a large-scale isotope separation plant using this method.[75]

The most progress in producing uranium 235 came in Berkeley, California, where the 37-inch cyclotron, at that time the second largest ever built, was dismantled in November of 1941 and its magnet used to produce a magnetic field. Ions of a uranium salt followed a curved path in this field, dividing the two isotopes, which then could be caught in collectors. By March of 1942 the "Calutron," as it was called, had worked better than any other electromagnetic mass separator but was still very far away from producing amounts of uranium 235 that would be significant for an atomic bomb. Another magnet, which had been intended for a 184-inch "giant cyclotron," was repurposed for isotope separation and ready to use by the end of May. By the summer this larger Calutron had been used to produce milligram amounts of uranium 235.[76]

Both gaseous diffusion and centrifuges looked feasible for large-scale production of uranium 235 but both would require hundreds of stages to achieve large-scale separation and neither had actually produced any appreciable amounts of separated uranium 235. In contrast, it was clear that electromagnetic isotope separation would work: "If one unit could separate 10 mg a day, 100,000,000 units could separate a ton a day. The questions were of cost and time.... Altogether, at that time it looked very expensive, but it also looked certain and relatively quick." In September the Americans decided to build an electromagnetic separation plant in the Tennessee Valley.[77] In contrast, although German researchers were convinced that centrifuges would separate uranium isotopes, they had only been successful with other elements and were far away from being able to justify the construction of a pilot plant.

Nuclear Weapons

Of course the point of all this effort was to build nuclear weapons, or at least to determine whether or not this was possible. The German critical mass estimate from February 1942, 10–100 kilograms, was comparable to the 2–100 kilogram figure mentioned in a National Academy Committee report from November 6, 1941. According to Henry Smyth, who in 1945 wrote the official report on the atomic bomb, little attention was given in America to the theoretical understanding of how a bomb would work before the summer of 1942, when a group of around eight physicists was organized under the leadership of J. Robert Oppenheimer. While this group was small by American standards, it dwarfed the number of theoretical physicists working on uranium in Germany

Selling Uranium 75

during the war. In the American "Feasibility Report" from November 26, 1942, Oppenheimer and others wrote that the "critical size of the bomb was still unknown."[78] Ironically work on the bomb thus began in earnest in the United States just as scientists and science policy makers in Germany had given up on such weapons, which reveals the gulf between the industrial and technical resources of the two sides.[79]

The American scientists were clearly more focused on making atomic bombs than their German counterparts and saw themselves in a race to create weapons that might decide the war. As Smyth described their reasoning in June of 1942:

(1) It was clear that an amount of U-235 [uranium 235] or plutonium comprising a number of kilograms would be explosive, that such an explosion would be equivalent to several thousand tons of TNT, and that such an explosion could be caused to occur at the desired instant. (2) It was clear that there were four methods of preparing the fissionable material and that all of these methods appeared feasible; but it was not possible to state definitely that any given one of these is superior to the others. (3) It was clear that production plants of considerable size could be designed and built. (4) It seemed likely that, granted adequate funds and priorities, full-scale plant operation could be started soon enough to be of military significance....

If four separate methods all appeared to a highly competent scientific group to be capable of successful application, it appeared certain that the desired end result could be attained by the enemy, provided he had sufficient time.[80]

A Comprehensive Understanding of Bomb Physics

The physicist and historian Jeremy Bernstein was not impressed with Heisenberg's efforts at Farm Hall to calculate the critical mass of an atomic bomb: "All of these simplifications and confusions make it very clear to me that Heisenberg had never done this problem before.... The Germans had no comprehensive understanding of bomb physics."[81] More recently, Manfred Popp has argued that the discussion at Farm Hall "reveals to any physicist how little the German scientists knew about the bomb."[82] What we mainly have for evidence of Heisenberg's understanding of how an atomic bomb would work are his popular lectures from February and June of 1942.[83] Of course these were nontechnical, qualitative accounts but are also corroborated by some of his technical reports.[84] Taking these two lectures together, Heisenberg demonstrated a clear understanding that, in a pure, sufficiently large mass of a nuclear explosive like uranium 235 or element 94, a fast-neutron, energy-producing chain reaction will increase exponentially and constitute an explosive of tremendous power. This is the heart of an atomic bomb. It is not surprising that Heisenberg's talks do not reveal how much nuclear explosive would be needed, since at Farm Hall he admitted that he had never made that calculation.

76 The Bomb

However, when assessing Heisenberg's understanding in 1942 of how an atomic bomb would work, the standard should not be the final achievement of the Manhattan Project, rather what émigrés, British, and Americans working in the United States had accomplished by the summer of 1942. Heisenberg hardly demonstrated a comprehensive understanding of bomb physics but during this stage in the war, no one in Britain or the USA had such an understanding either. The important difference between the two sides is that, whereas no further theoretical work was done on the physics of an atomic bomb in Germany, American and émigré scientists subsequently pursued this goal with dedication and determination.

5 Total War

> It is quite striking how everyone is becoming thinner, including different people in the KWG who I last saw in May, before the summer break. I was shocked at how they now look.... People who look completely healthy and well-fed can scarcely be found anymore. And the state of the war does not make people more optimistic.

> Perhaps it is all connected to the illness: I still occasionally have a light fever and am tired, but nevertheless strangely inwardly stimulated. I have worked all day, yes actually almost an entire week intensively on my physics and am making wonderful progress.
>
> Werner Heisenberg to Elisabeth Heisenberg (September 13 and 22, 1942).[1]

Stalingrad and Total War

The German offensive in the summer 1942 was at first a success, expanding even farther than the previous year into the Soviet Union, but began to falter as the autumn turned to winter. The battle for the southern city of Stalingrad began on August 19, with extraordinarily fierce fighting and every street and block contested. When the German offensive in the Caucasus bogged down, Hitler's generals advised him to withdraw to less exposed positions but he refused. In November the Soviet forces counterattacked and encircled around 240,000 troops. The German commander asked that his forces be permitted to break out, but Hitler again rejected the request, choosing to believe overly optimistic claims that the air force could supply the encircled troops. When defeat appeared certain, Hitler yet another time refused the beleaguered commander's appeal, insisting that they must fight on to the last man in order to gain time. When the German forces finally surrendered on February 2, 1943, Germany and its allies had taken more than 150,000 casualties with an additional 90,000 taken prisoner. During the winter of 1942–1943 the Germans lost virtually all the territory they had gained in the summer offensive of 1942, as well as large amounts of men and equipment.[2]

As the military situation became steadily more grave on the eastern front, Propaganda Minister Josef Goebbels, one of the most powerful and ruthless members of the NS elite, began calling for the introduction of "total war" at home. At a ministerial conference he held on January 4, Goebbels argued that:

78   The Bomb

A more radical conduct of the war is alone capable of producing military victories. Every day brings further proof of the fact that in the East we are facing a brutal opponent whom one can overcome with the most brutal means and for this purpose there must be a total commitment of the whole of our forces and reserves. This will then put German propaganda on the rails again and the contradiction between theory and practice will disappear. If the nation felt that total war is not simply a matter of propaganda but that the necessary conclusions were being drawn then propaganda would prove really substantial and effective.

The propaganda message itself had to be reduced to a few key sentences: "(1) The war had been forced on the German people. (2) In this war it was a matter of life or death. (3) There must be total war." At a different conference ten days after the fall of Stalingrad, Goebbels added: "The fight against Bolshevism and the threat of the Bolshevization of Europe is now preoccupying friend and foe in the same way. Our struggle against Bolshevism must dominate all the propaganda instruments as the great and all-pervading propaganda theme."[3]

On February 18, Goebbels gave a major speech, broadcast over the radio, at the Berlin Sportpalast. He began with three propositions:

(1) if the German armed forces are unable to break the danger from the East, Germany, and soon afterwards the whole of Europe, will fall victim to Bolshevism;
(2) the German Armed Forces and the German nation, together with their Allies, represent the sole force capable of delivering Europe completely from this menace;
(3) delay involves danger. Swift and thorough action is required, otherwise it will be too late.

Goebbels then turned to dire warnings of what might come, cynically flipping the roles of victims and perpetrators. "Behind the onrushing Soviet divisions we can see the Jewish liquidation squads – behind which looms terror, the specter of mass starvation and unbridled anarchy in Europe."[4]

Goebbels was aided by a large, handpicked audience of National Socialist activists when he turned to what he expected from the home front. Goebbels claimed that, although most people were bearing the whole burden of the war, a small passive group was attempting to evade its burdens and responsibilities. When he argued that burdens must be justly distributed, he received shouts of bravo and applause and the crowd called for the shirkers to be hanged. In this "serious phase of our fateful struggle," Goebbels insisted, every man must fulfill his duty to the nation; if necessary, he would be compelled to do so. The Minister of Propaganda ended his speech with ten rhetorical questions as the obsequious audience roared its approval, including: "I ask you: Do you want total war? Do you want it, if necessary, more total and more radical than we can even imagine it today?"[5]

Most Germans did not share the enthusiasm of Goebbels' Sportpalast audience. Even before the Germans entered Stalingrad, local officials reported that the German population was becoming exhausted by the war.

Total War

The longing for the war to come to an end at last manifested itself recently in particular in the eagerness with which people seized on the rumors of armistice negotiations with the Russians. The fact that for a long time the eastern front has been at a standstill, that Stalingrad has still not been taken, that news of deaths at the front never stops coming in, that the cancellations of the reserved status positions of young farmers are increasing at an alarming rate, and that the youngest cohorts are already being called up are interpreted as signs of exhaustion. Speeches by the Leader, the Reich Marshall, the Foreign Minister, the Reich Propaganda Minister and the other propaganda measures and local propaganda campaigns no longer have a lasting effect. Tiredness with the war is already so strong that all appeals to do more have no effect.[6]

Moreover, the propaganda authorities hid the true nature of the battle for Stalingrad from Germans. On January 11, Paul Harteck told Karl-Friedrich Bonhoeffer that he thought the war would not last much longer.[7] Although the German Sixth Army was surrounded on November 22, 1942, only on January 16, 1943 did Germans hear that their troops were involved in a defensive battle against an enemy attacking from all sides.[8] On January 28 the Security Service of the SS (*Sicherheitsdienst*, SD) reported that the whole nation was deeply shaken by the impression that the fate of the Sixth Army was already sealed and concerned about the further development of the war. People were asking above all why Stalingrad was not evacuated or relieved, and how it had been possible, only a few months ago, to describe the military situation as secure. Fearing that the war might end badly, many Germans were thinking seriously about the consequences of defeat, with most people convinced that losing the war would "amount to extinction."[9]

A few days earlier, regional NSDAP leaders had made a similar report. With a certain bitterness people had noticed the striking contrast between the previous reporting and the latest news. The media had portrayed things in much too rosy a light. Not only were the Soviets underestimated, a completely false picture had been given of their powers of resistance and armament potential. As a result, there was a considerable crisis of trust in the media. The German people wanted to hear the truth. They knew that their existence was at stake and that everyone was fighting for their lives. But while they did not want to be given a rosy picture, they did want to know that their struggles would lead to success.[10]

Goebbels' Sportpalast speech, which a large portion of the population heard, had a mixed reception. In general, reports from the Security Service were favorable. Goebbels' frank description of the seriousness of the situation had eased tensions and strengthened confidence in the leadership, that was now "speaking frankly at last and telling the plain unvarnished truth." But people were asking "where the front would be stabilized, why there had to be a Stalingrad, and what the withdrawals would cost in terms of losses of men, weapons, materiel, and territories."[11]

Centrifuges

Wilhelm Groth finally had proof of uranium isotope enrichment in August of 1942. The content of uranium 235 in three small samples had been enriched in the centrifuge by 2.7, 2.4, and 3.9 percent respectively.[12] But the step towards industrial application appeared difficult. Konrad Beyerle from the Anschütz Company told Harteck and Groth that more technically trained workers were needed to develop and manufacture the ultracentrifuges. Harteck and Beyerle also began discussing patent applications.[13] As Abraham Esau reported to Rudolf Mentzel in November, the next step was to build a series of ultracentrifuges in order to produce the enriched uranium needed.[14]

The Hamburg researchers reported on their progress with the ultracentrifuges In February of 1943, they had improved, simplified, and automated the design (see Figure 5.1), which now allowed the apparatus to run continuously for hundreds of hours without service. A rocking process would be used to multiply the separation effect. The drum of the centrifuge, which rotates around a central axis, would be divided up into chambers such that the portion of one chamber near the axis communicates with the part of the next chamber near the outer wall.

As the gas is centrifuged, the heavier portion tends to concentrate itself on the outer wall of each chamber. Next, the gas is periodically pushed (or pulled) from one chamber to the next by means of an oscillating gas stream. This oscillation is achieved by connecting two centrifuges. Most of the time, the centrifuges run at the same number of revolutions per minute. But the rate of

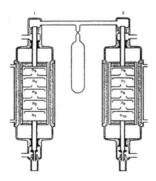

Figure 5.1 Schematic diagram of a double ultracentrifuge.
Source: Adapted from Konrad Beyerle, Wilhelm Groth, Paul Harteck, and Johannes Jensen, *Über Gaszentrifugen. Anreicherung der Xenon, Krypton, und der Selen-Isotope nach dem Zentrifugenverfahren* (Weinheim: Verlag Chemie, 1950), 9.

Total War 81

revolution of one centrifuge is periodically altered, creating a sudden drop in pressure. This regular change in pressure causes the gas stream to oscillate in turn, thereby pushing (or pulling) the gas near the outer wall of one chamber into the central region of its neighbor. Thus a sort of separation column is produced, that multiplies the separation effect of a single centrifuge.[15]

In his budget submitted in April, Esau allocated almost a third of the money to the development of double ultracentrifuges. A month later, in a lecture to the Academy for Aeronautic Research, he explained why: the enrichment of uranium 235 would probably liberate them from the necessity of using heavy water and reduce the dimensions of the uranium machine. Klaus Clusius, who followed Esau with his own lecture on isotope separation, praised both Harteck's "energetic advocacy" and the unique expertise of Anschütz. Thanks to them Germany now possessed an excellent electrically powered ultracentrifuge.[16]

The Hamburg researchers' success with the ultracentrifuge brought increased expectations as well as support. In July, after Esau had received a favorable report on the progress of the centrifuge work, he wrote Harteck that "It would be very important to me personally" if Harteck could manufacture a sufficiently large sample of enriched uranium as soon as possible for an experiment Walther Bothe was planning. Harteck was instructed to tell Esau what the centrifuge currently under construction could produce, and when he would be able to provide the sample. Harteck responded that, at first their main goal had not been to produce samples, rather to ensure an absolutely dependable operation of the centrifuge. Moreover, this had required more work than it perhaps appeared after the first positive results. The provisional model at Anschütz in Kiel could be used beginning next week for separation experiments, and the double model that was being set up in Freiburg in southwest Germany should be finished in a few weeks. "From your letter," Harteck continued, "I see that samples for Bothe's measurements are considered urgent." Harteck had therefore come to an agreement with Groth and Beyerle that samples would be produced in the next weeks under any circumstances.[17]

The war made it impossible for Harteck to keep this promise. Allied air raids caused a firestorm in Hamburg during the night of July 27–28 that killed some 35,000–40,000 people. The official report by the Police President of Hamburg contains horrifying details:

The impression created by viewing a burnt-out city pales beside the fire itself: the howling of the firestorm, the cries and moans of the dying and the crashes of the falling bombs.... The horrific scenes which occurred in the area of the firestorm are indescribable. Children were torn from the hands of their parents by the tornado and whirled into the flames. People who thought they had saved themselves collapsed in a few minutes in the overwhelmingly destructive force of the heat. People who were fleeing had to make their way through the dead and the dying. The sick and frail had to be left behind by the rescuers since they themselves were in danger of burning.... The streets were covered with hundreds of corpses.

82   The Bomb

Mothers with their children, men, old people, burnt, charred, unscathed and clothed, naked and piled like wax dummies in a shop window, they lay in every position, quiet and peaceful, or tense with their death throes written in the expressions on their faces The situation in the air raid shelters was the same and made an even more gruesome impression because, in some cases, it showed the last desperate struggle which had taken place against a merciless fate. Whereas in one place the occupants were sitting quietly on their chairs, peaceful and unscathed as if they were sleeping and had unsuspectingly been killed by carbon monoxide gas, elsewhere the existence of the fragments of bones and skulls showed how the occupants had sought to flee and find refuge from their prison tomb.

In seven subsequent air raids on the city between July 25 and August 3, which involved around 3,000 British and US aircraft, at least 42,000 people were killed and over 100,000 injured; more than 40,000 apartment blocks with around 225,000 apartments, 24 hospitals, 277 schools, 580 industrial plants, and some 3,000 other businesses were destroyed.[18] The physicist Max von Laue, who was vacationing away from Berlin on the northern coast of Germany, watched as refugees from Hamburg arrived. Potable water was so short there after the attacks that people had begun drinking out of the canals, resulting in a typhus epidemic. Two weeks later he witnessed another attack, hearing the drone of the American and British planes. "An eerie sound! Eerie especially because nothing happened to oppose it.... One has the impression as if we were only passively participating in the air war."[19]

At the end of August Karl-Friedrich Bonhoeffer was relieved to get a telegram from Harteck: "Institute exists. We are all alive." Bonhoeffer immediately telegraphed the news to Harteck's mother, but then the questions came: "What does it mean that you are 'living'? Are you all unhurt? Obviously not!" Harteck should get out of Hamburg. "What you are living through is certainly the most horrendous thing that has happened in the war so far." Up until now such concentrated attacks had not occurred one after another in the same place. "And you are exactly in the middle of the witches' cauldron! Does your apartment with its beautiful piano still exist? Do you have things to eat and drink?" It would be "madness" to try and continue Harteck's experiments in Hamburg. If Bonhoeffer was Harteck, then he would sleep every night out in the open outside of the city. Bonhoeffer himself thought continually that he should get his children out of Leipzig but it was probably too late for that, about Harteck and what he was living through, and about the general misery that would inevitably follow.[20]

As early as June Esau and Harteck were planning to set up the double ultracentrifuge in the relatively safe city of Freiburg in southwest Germany instead of Hamburg. Esau wanted to move it as soon as possible, while Harteck wanted to find and fix all the bugs in the centrifuge first, because the relocation would interrupt their work. The attacks on Hamburg made Harteck's concerns moot. On August 3 Anschütz was ready to send the prototype centrifuge and other centrifuge pieces south. Harteck's two collaborators Groth and Albert Suhr

Total War 83

were missing. A truck was provided by HWA to ship the important institute equipment, but Harteck would have to organize the transport, loading, and unloading, including finding the necessary labor. Hermann Beuthe, an HWA official, ended his letter to Harteck on a cheerful note: "I am glad that you and hopefully your colleagues have personally survived the difficult days in Hamburg and hope you will continue to work successfully soon."[21]

By the middle of September Harteck could report good news back to the HWA in Berlin. His institute and most of the staff had had "improbably good luck" during the attack. In order to get the work back on track as soon as possible, shortly after the firestorm Groth traveled to Freiburg, with Suhr following him with the truck loaded with the apparatus necessary for the centrifuge project. Now the experiments in Freiburg had also demonstrated uranium isotope enrichment. Harteck closed his letter with his pleasure at hearing that the recent attacks on Berlin had been ineffective. "Let us hope for the best in the future!"[22]

The deteriorating state of the war had made the German home front truly dangerous by the autumn of 1943. But there was another reason why Germans now had to take great care. Growing public discontent with the state of the war had been met with increasing intense repression by the German secret police. As opposed to the first years of the Third Reich when, within certain limits. German citizens enjoyed some personal freedom of movement and expression, careless remarks now became a potentially fatal matter. One of the most disturbing aspects of life in Germany at this time was the fear of betrayal. Along with distrusting the officials of the police, secret police, government, or military, Germans had to suspect anyone of being a potential informer.

In the late summer of 1943, a confidential report on Paul Harteck was submitted to the secret police, accusing the Hamburg scientist of "morally-undermining" remarks. Harteck, who it was claimed had openly revealed himself as an enemy of the state, should be both removed from his position at the university and immediately prosecuted by the police. The secret police contacted the local Party official in charge of the university faculty, but he replied that he knew nothing about any such behavior by Harteck. The report had to be an exaggeration. Harteck was from Vienna, was a Catholic, was perhaps a little politically unstable because of his world view and of his temperament, but in any case this Party official found Harteck tolerable as an instructor. The secret police nevertheless paid a visit to Harteck in his apartment.[23]

The informer was the Hamburg experimental physicist Peter Paul Koch, a dedicated National Socialist. Although he had been well respected by his peers while in his prime, by 1943 it had been a long time since Koch had made an original contribution to physics. Koch may have been motivated by personal and professional differences. Harteck had supported an attempt by several Hamburg physicists to force Koch into early retirement and to call a young nuclear physicist to Hamburg in his place.[24]

84   The Bomb

Unknown to Harteck, one of the mechanics in his institute was also an informer for the secret police. Harteck's outgoing, joking demeanor brought him good fortune. The informer/mechanic was so fond of his boss that he revealed himself and assured Harteck that he would not betray him. When Koch betrayed Harteck, the latter was forewarned by his mechanic. When the dreaded Gestapo agents arrived and interrogated Harteck, he replied that if there had been a complaint, then it must have come from Koch, who detested Harteck. The secret police acknowledged at once that Koch had been the informer. Afterward, much to Koch's discomfort, Harteck openly told his colleagues that Koch had betrayed him.[25] Fortunately for Harteck, apparently the police investigation went no further. However, Harteck was not simply cleared of all suspicion. He probably considered himself to be under surveillance and in constant danger of some reprisal until the end of the war. Like many other German scientists, the members of the working group were now daily faced with death from above and with betrayal from within. Their reaction was often to lower their heads, bury themselves in their work, and try to hang on to the end.

Heavy Water

Norsk Hydro

In July of 1942 Friedrich Berkei from HWA, Hans Süss, and Karl Wirtz traveled to the Norsk Hydro to meet with plant engineers and German officials in charge of the Norwegian economy.[26] The additional process Harteck and Süss had designed for increasing the heavy water output at the Norsk Hydro required a chemical catalyst. Unfortunately the best candidate catalyst, just like the separation tube, used the difficult to obtain nickel and would have to be ordered from IG Farben. The German officials agreed to provide 230 kilograms of nickel for this purpose. IG Farben sent 1,000 kg of the catalyst to Norway in late August.[27] But this was only the first installment. In order to produce the tons of catalyst the Norsk Hydro would eventually require, IG Farben would need more nickel. When they ordered it from the appropriate German office, they were told that it would have to come from Norway. The German officials there responded that these amounts were significantly larger than had been mentioned before but could provide half a ton right away. The rest would have to be negotiated.[28] By the beginning of March IG Farben had still not received the nickel.[29]

Since the heavy water output had not met the Germans' expectations, and it would take some time to get the additional process working, the Germans pressed the Norwegians to get heavy water production going at an additional plant in Såheim, and insisted that electricity produced at the Norsk Hydro first go towards making heavy water.[30] The German Army had ordered 1,500 kg

Total War   85

(1.5 metric tons) to be delivered over the course of a year. The average delivery would therefore have been 125 kilograms a month, but the amounts actually received were significantly smaller.

From 9.10.1941 – 31.12.1941	361 kg
January 1942	100 kg
February 1942	91 kg
March 1942	100 kg
April 1942	0 kg
May 1942	51 kg
June 1942	94 kg
July 1942	128 kg
August 1942	121 kg
September	96 kg
Total	1,142 kg

The German officials in Norway understood why production had fallen in April and May, when a water shortage shut down the plant, but not why output dropped in September. Süss noticed a suspicious periodicity in the levels of heavy water, with the percentages in the various stages rising at the start of the week, but then falling again at the end. The Germans wanted to know what was causing this periodic reduction and what was being done about it.[31]

The Norsk Hydro replied that the reduction in September was caused by the expansion of electrolysis apparatus in order to incorporate the Harteck-Süss expansion. As a result, they had to reduce the amount of heavy water they drew off. Moreover they now realized that they had overestimated the capacity of the plant in the summer and drew too much in July and August. A build-up of foam was also lowering output, but they were working on reducing this by adding activated charcoal. They told the Germans that they were not sure what was causing the periodic rising and falling of the concentration levels but promised to continue to look into it.[32] In fact some Norwegians at the Norsk Hydro were causing the foaming by adding castor and cod liver oil, and sabotage may also have caused the periodic dips in output.[33]

Sabotage

The highest levels of the American military were both aware that the Norsk Hydro was making heavy water for the Germans and were concerned about it. Major General George V. Strong wrote to General Eisenhower in September of 1942, warning him that the Norwegian heavy water was being sent to Berlin for use in experiments to develop "fission bombs based upon uranium." Noting that both American and British scientists were making progress along this line, it was obvious to Strong that whichever nation could deploy such bombs would have "a destructive agent which may determine the final outcome of this war."

86   The Bomb

Since Strong had been told that such bombs could not be developed or built without heavy water, the Norsk Hydro should either be sabotaged or bombed.[34]

As David Irving has argued, the first attempt to sabotage heavy water production at the Norsk Hydro, Operation Freshman, was "ill-conceived and underplanned." Two gliders full of volunteers were towed by bombers from Britain to Norway. One of the towing aircraft along with its glider crashed, as did the second glider. The former crash killed nine people outright; the survivors were captured by the Germans and executed. The Germans found the second glider the next day, this time questioning the survivors before shooting them. It was now clear to the Germans that the Allies knew about heavy water and what it was good for.[35] The German officials overseeing the Norsk Hydro also began to question the importance of heavy water production.[36]

Freshman was followed four months later by Operation Gunnerside. From the very beginning, this action has been mythologized. Leif Tronstad, a Norwegian physicist who had helped design the heavy water plant at the Norsk Hydro, but was now in London working for the Norwegian High Command on intelligence, espionage, and sabotage, told the volunteers before they embarked on their mission that they "might not fully realize the importance of their mission, but it would live in Norwegian history for hundreds of years." This time the saboteurs made it safely into Norway and then into the Norsk Hydro. On February 16, 1943, in a perfect piece of sabotage, every cell was damaged, with the partially enriched heavy water disappearing down the drains. A little more than a third of a ton of pure heavy water was thereby lost. This surgical action had not cost any lives on either side, inflicting the maximum damage on the heavy water plant without harming the hydroelectric power station that was so vital to the civilian Norwegian economy.[37]

Consul Schoepke, head of the German military economic liaison office in Oslo, now suggested that pieces of the heavy water high concentration plant and the remaining concentrate be moved to Germany.[38] Swedish radio reported the sabotage, including the news that heavy water was being used in Germany to manufacture high-quality explosives. According to Schoepke, because the military had shown so much interest in this plant, for many Norwegians it had become "almost a national sport to help with the destruction of this facility." The Germans were planning to accelerate the resumption of heavy water production at the Norsk Hydro by seeding it with heavy water they already possessed. But Schoepke cautioned that the return to production of heavy water would be a signal for new attacks. If the Germans made sabotage impossible by introducing security measures and eliminating traitors within the plant, then they should expect the entire facility to be bombed.[39]

The heavy water equipment at the Norsk Hydro was quickly repaired, using some heavy water brought back from Germany as feedstock. By late June they had produced 120 kilograms of heavy water ready for shipment to Berlin.[40]

Total War   87

In the meantime Süss had found a better catalyst that used less nickel. Although Harteck admitted that the sabotage in Norway had raised the question whether more investments should be made in the Norsk Hydro, he argued that they should take advantage of the significant investments already made.[41] Esau, who was now in charge of the working group, was more pessimistic. They had to assume that despite all security measures another sabotage attempt would be made, perhaps destroying the entire facility.[42]

Indeed the Allies were planning another attack. In August US intelligence reported that a reliable source claimed that the "Germans have progressed so far that there is a possibility of using uranium in present war" and "that heavy water is absolutely necessary for splitting [the] atom and also in [the] making of explosives." The Americans decided that the heavy water plant at the Norsk Hydro, which had been restored to operation, should be "sufficiently damaged by bombing to put them out of commission for a considerable period of time." Moreover, the "killing of scientific personnel employed therein would be particularly advantageous."[43]

Leuna

Esau now wanted to shift heavy water production from Norway to Germany.[44] At the beginning of August, 1942, IG Farben was ready to begin building a heavy water pilot plant using the Harteck–Süss process at their facility in Leuna. IG Farben had received the necessary materials and two powerful and influential men, IG director Heinrich Bütefisch and Carl Krauch, Plenipotentiary for Special Issues in Chemical Production both backed the project.[45] Harteck was eager to get started because, assuming the process worked well, it would take two and a half years to begin large-scale production.[46] A little more than a month later, the Leuna scientist Paul Herold told Harteck that, whereas the project had been approved for the last quarter of 1942, because of its low priority rating it was unfortunately shifted to the first quarter of the next year.[47] Harteck now suggested that a novel electrolytic facility under construction in Leuna be connected to the new pilot plant, so that pure heavy water could be produced.[48] Again Herold was pessimistic. What Harteck was calling a facility would in fact at first be just a small laboratory device able only to produce 400 grams of water enriched to 3–4 percent heavy water per day. However, Herold agreed to begin building the electrolytic device immediately as well.[49]

In early May, at a meeting with Harteck and other leading scientists in the working group, Esau announced that there would be no further expansion of heavy water production at the Norsk Hydro because an attack or air raid on the entire plant would endanger nitrogen production in the areas under German control. For this reason heavy water facilities would have to be built in Germany as quickly as possible. If the Harteck–Süss process worked well in

88   The Bomb

Leuna, then a large facility using the same process would be built and manufacture sufficient heavy water to make them independent of Norway and other countries. Along with this process, they would reassess a fractional distillation process proposed by Klaus Clusius.

Italy

Both the Harteck–Süss and Clusius–Linde processes would be more effective and efficient if they had a feedstock that was already enriched in heavy water. Electrolysis plants enriched deuterium in water as a byproduct, which was why the Norsk Hydro had originally got into the heavy water business. Unfortunately there were no such facilities in Germany, but electrolysis plants in areas controlled by or friendly to Germany could in principle also provide enriched feedstock. Karl Wirtz surveyed the options in Europe and found a plant owned by the Montecatini company in Sinigo near Merano in northern Italy. Esau was interested in achieving a minimal amount of security in heavy water production for the next few years without large investments.[50]

In May Esau and Harteck visited the Montecatini plant. The Italians were very interested in doing business. The facility had around one-third the capacity of the Norsk Hydro to produce heavy water. The Germans planned to produce 1 percent heavy water there and ship it to Germany for further enrichment. However, the electrolysis works were open, so that around 40 percent of the water fed into the plant escaped as steam into the air, taking some of the heavy water with it. The plant would have to be modified. If the Montecatini plant could produce and ship 1 percent heavy water to Germany, and the pilot plant in Leuna worked, then the combination could produce around half a ton of pure heavy water each year.[51] In September and October important meetings were held on the topic of heavy water production. Hartek was told by HWA in Berlin that most of the heavy water production at the Norsk Hydro would have to stop, but the concentrate there would be shipped to Germany for further processing. This constituted around a ton of pure heavy water. The electrolysis troughs at the Montecatini would be covered to increase output.

A month later the Berlin scientists traveled to Leuna to meet with IG Farben officials, telling them about the new situation in Norway. The IG Farben representatives then reported on the progress of their work. The model high-concentration device using a new electrolytic-elutriation process worked very well and was suitable for enriching concentrate with 1 percent heavy water to around 99 percent. All agreed that a larger plant should be built with the new process capable of producing two tons of heavy water per year, both to process the Italian concentrate and purify any heavy water that had been diluted.

Another process for heavy water production was developed by an IG Farben scientist with the help of Johannes Jensen, a physicist at the Technical

Total War

University of Hannover who collaborated with Harteck's institute. This process was also promising but was still at a preliminary stage. More experimental work needed to be done in order to find the best catalyst. When Harteck asked the IG Farben officials about the Clusius–Linde process for heavy water, they were pessimistic, arguing that the Linde Company would take a long time to build the plant, and once built a large facility would consume a huge amount of electricity that could hardly be made available.

The model plant using the Harteck–Süss elutriation process had just gone into operation, so that they did not have results yet, but upon inspection made a very good impression. However, the IG Farben officials told Harteck that an independent plant using the Harteck–Süss process would have, in Harteck's words, an "improbably high price." This stood in stark contrast to the first estimates made by IG Farben.[52]

The Return of Abraham Esau

In the summer of 1942 atomic bombs must have appeared far off to the scientists in the working group, even if they continued carefully hinting to potential patrons that they might come sooner. The motivation for these scientists to continue their work was clear: working on uranium would hopefully keep them out of the war, and they might be the first in the world to build a self-sustaining nuclear reactor. In 1942 Carl Friedrich von Weizsäcker accepted a professorship at the recently refounded Reich University of Strasbourg and moved to the newly annexed German province of Alsace, taking Karl-Heinz Höcker with him as his assistant. Although Weizsäcker and especially Höcker continued to contribute to the working group, their willingness to trade working full-time on war-work for an academic appointment speaks volumes about how pressing the uranium work appeared.

In June of 1942 around seventy people worked in Germany on the uranium project. The two younger theoretical physicists at the institute, Höcker and Paul-Otto Müller suffered different fates. Both were called up in 1941 for military service. Höcker was fortunate to be wounded and sent back; Müller died on the eastern front in March of 1942.[53] Diebner and the other HWA officials had left the KWIfP. By July Diebner was complaining that the HWA was still doing the considerable administrative work, but Abraham Esau was making the decisions, leading the KWG General Secretary, Ernst Telschow, to call for the working group to be returned to the Army.[54]

Explosions

The Leipzig experiments came to a sudden explosive end. Under certain conditions the metal uranium powder they were using could oxidize, liberating

90   The Bomb

flammable hydrogen gas as a byproduct. In December of 1941, as the mechanic Paschen was loading the uranium a spoonful at a time, a sudden explosive flame burned his hand and ignited the nearby uranium container. This was quickly carried outside of the lab and covered with sand. The next day the uranium was a red, glowing mass. From then on, they streamed CO_2 into the container while inserting the uranium.

After the experimental spherical layer system of metal uranium and heavy water used to verify the increased production of neutrons had been immersed in water for twenty days, bubbles of hydrogen gas were regularly observed coming from the seal between the two half spheres. After some time, the release of gas stopped, and they carried out their measurements. When the experiment was over, they decided to open the device to see how much moisture had entered the sphere. With Döpel looking on, Paschen removed the cap from the filling tube. About three to five seconds later they heard a sound like air streaming into a vacuum and saw a gap open in the device. After three more seconds, they saw glowing uranium and the now familiar explosive bursts of flame. The glowing mass quickly became a flame 20 cm high that melted the aluminum and exposed the uranium. Using water they stopped the flame, leaving the uranium almost completely submerged in water. After a while, they noticed increasing heat and smoke from the uranium, so they added more water, stopping the smoke.

The scientists hurriedly removed all the precious heavy water they could. The temperature continued to rise, making an explosion appear imminent. By this time Heisenberg had arrived. Flames then erupted from the water, producing a rain of burning metal uranium. At this point Döpel called the fire department. They managed to douse the flames by smothering them with wet blankets covered by fire-retardant foam. It took two days for the gurgling mass to stop. Döpel now considered the manufacture of solid cast pieces of metal uranium to be the highest priority. While it was "self-evident that the development of the uranium machine will cost human lives" and this danger would not stop them from being built, a machine made of tons of metal uranium powder would be so dangerous that it was out of the question.[55]

After the Leipzig accident, it was clear that solid metal uranium would have to be used instead of the "scary" powder, which essentially ended work with the spherical layer design. The Auer Society, which purified and processed the uranium, had to build the necessary custom-sized casting ovens, but there were other, more difficult problems: not much metal uranium powder was available and Auer lacked the necessary machine tools to process the cast plates. In October of 1942 Auer scientist Karl Zimmer told Heisenberg that unless the priority rating was increased, the plate production would drag out until March, if not longer.[56]

The highest priority rating, DE, had to come from the Ministry of Armaments, with Minister Speer personally deciding whether or not to grant this level of

Total War   91

priority on a case-by-case basis. Fortunately, Speer had taken a personal interest in the research and even asked the KWG how he could support the work at the KWIfP. Metal uranium production was classified DE in November, but even with this priority Auer director Nikolaus Riehl could only hope that the plates would be finished by the end of May.[57]

The scientists needed a safe place to carry out the next experiment, but since Berlin was already the target of Allied air raids, the Kaiser Wilhelm Society began building a bunker laboratory near the KWIfP. The necessary work crews had to be ordered from Speer's ministry through the HWA. Both the Army and Speer approved the request, with the latter again granting the highest DE priority. The concrete was poured in November, and in December Heisenberg hoped that the bunker would be ready for experiments in April. However, despite the high priority, the Siemens Company estimated that the electrical wiring of the underground lab would not be done before the end of 1943. In January Heisenberg again asked for help from Speer, this time to stop the call-up of a key worker at Auer.[58] Even the highest priority from Speer's ministry did not mean that metal uranium production and the construction of the bunker laboratory subsequently proceeded quickly or without problems. The uranium research had been given priority, but it was still not considered urgent.

Hermann Göring's Plenipotentiary for Nuclear Physics

Abraham Esau was a respected technical physicist with industrial experience who had overseen physics in the Reich Research Council since 1937 and two years later was appointed president of the Reich Physical-Technical Institute as well. At the start of the war he had moved quickly to set up a nuclear fission research project, only to be abruptly halted by Army Ordnance. After the working group was moved to the RFR in 1942, Esau was technically in charge, but the various institutes continued to enjoy considerable autonomy.

In late November Esau submitted a progress report on the working group to his superior at the RFR, Rudolf Mentzel. Esau defined his responsibilities much more broadly than just uranium isotope enrichment and uranium machines, although these were the most important. The technical solution of the problem, what Esau described as "the exploitation of this energy in the form of heat engines," had not yet been achieved, but continual progress had been made and parts of this main problem had already been solved. The full list of tasks included:

(1) The manufacture of luminous paint without using radium;
(2) Utilizing the nuclear energy of uranium (uranium machine);
(3) The manufacture of powerful sources of fast neutrons, including in particular particle accelerators, for the testing of materials and biological purposes;
(4) Investigations of protective measures for working with neutrons.

92   The Bomb

There was no mention of nuclear explosives or atomic bombs. Uranium 235 enrichment was only discussed in the context of allowing smaller uranium machines that used less heavy water, while transuranic elements were not mentioned at all. On December 4 the physicist Erich Bagge noted in his diary that at a meeting that day: "Esau is preparing to begin cutting back in January and February…. Evidently someone thinks that the solution of a certain problem could not be decisive for the war."[59]

At this stage, when hopes of creating a weapon to win the war were fading and the home front was involved in total war, conflicts between individuals began to influence the course of the project. Up until now, there had generally been a common effort towards shared goals but this now changed. Esau felt disrespected and was clearly jealous of the close working relationship the KWG enjoyed with Speer and his Ministry of Armaments. Thus in his November report to Mentzel, Esau reported that Vögler had received the highest DE priority level for construction at the KWG, adding "something that is not possible for other mere mortals."[60]

Werner Heisenberg's appointment as director at the KWIfP alienated his colleague Walther Bothe. Shortly before Christmas 1941, as HWA research director Erich Schumann was chairing a meeting of the leading scientists in the working group, he suddenly and unexpectedly brought up the need to find a successor to Peter Debye, the KWIfP director who had left for the USA in 1940, and suggested that Bothe was the right man. After only about twenty seconds of silence, Schumann said that everyone clearly agreed with him and asked Otto Hahn to send a nomination letter for Bothe to him at HWA. Indeed there was no objection at the time.

A month later, Harteck visited KWG general secretary Ernst Telschow, described what had happened, and argued that Heisenberg, who had only not nominated himself "out of modesty," was the suitable director. When Hahn contacted Bothe about the appointment, he replied that everyone had had a chance to vote and in a sense had already promised the director position to him. Harteck also told Telschow that while Bothe was the best experimental physicist in Germany, adding that "unfortunately no one is better," he was not in the same class as Heisenberg. Hahn and Laue subsequently agreed with Harteck, telling Telschow that Bothe was "difficult to work with."[61]

Bothe's potential for difficulty became clear in the summer of 1942 when he and Heisenberg began planning a joint uranium machine experiment in order to maximize the use of limited materials and combine their efforts. The design would use horizontal plates of cast metal uranium with heavy water as moderator, all surrounded by a mantle of carbon. Since this experiment might come close to achieving a sustained nuclear-fission chain reaction, it would also allow them to study the stability of the uranium machine design. Whereas there was a consensus regarding the form and goals of the experiment, the two scientists

Total War 93

did not agree on where it would be held. Heisenberg clearly expected it to run at the KWIfP, but Bothe suggested that the site be "discussed with HWA and Esau." With a touch of frustration in his prose, Heisenberg responded: "I hardly need to say that I welcome every type of collaborative work; I have often expressed the wish that you come regularly to Berlin." As Telschow told KWG president Vögler, Esau, with Bothe's backing, wanted the experiment at his institute or a "neutral site."[62] Finally, the relationship between Kurt Diebner on one hand and Heisenberg and Weizsäcker had also deteriorated. This shows through a note Heisenberg sent to his younger colleague:

I am very much in agreement with your plan to be in Berlin.... If you want to work in the institute, I would like to ask if you are willing to use the colloquium room. Diebner is so exceptionally rarely in the institute, that a collision is not to be feared.[63]

Lattices versus Layers

In the summer of 1941, when Heisenberg wanted to switch from uranium oxide to metal uranium, Diebner assembled a group of young physicists at the Army Ordnance weapons testing facility in Gottow in order to begin a parallel series of uranium machine experiments. Using uranium oxide and paraffin, leftover materials no one else wanted, they decided to study three-dimensional lattices of uranium cubes in moderator (see Figure 5.2). The wax-like paraffin was set with wooden cubes as molds for the uranium oxide. Since they were unable to press the uranium oxide powder into solid forms, they inserted it a spoonful at

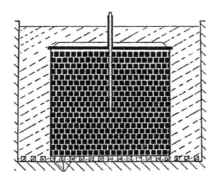

Figure 5.2 Schematic diagram of experiment G-I.
Note: A cylinder consisting of alternating horizontal layers of paraffin and uranium oxide cubes arranged in a lattice, all surrounded by water.
Source: Adapted from F. Berkei, W. Borrmann, W. Czulius, K. Diebner, G. Hartwig, W. Herrmann K. Höcker, H. Pose, and W. Rexer, Bericht über einen Würfelversuch mit Uranoxyd und Paraffin in der Versuchsstelle Gottow des Heereswaffenamtes (November 26, 1942), ADM, FA 002 629.

94   The Bomb

a time, wearing protective boots, clothing, gloves, and face masks as protection against ingesting the poisonous uranium oxide.

When their experiment was finished more than a year later, it had produced more neutrons than any previous arrangement using uranium oxide.

Höcker argued that this experiment had "urgently thrown open the question of the best arrangement of uranium and moderator." Setting aside the problem of resonance absorption, he noted that a design that surrounded the pieces of uranium completely with moderator would be best, that is, uranium spheres or cubes would be better than cylinders, that in turn would be more effective than plates. For the rest of the war, Höcker found himself in the awkward position of being simultaneously Weizsäcker's assistant in Strasbourg, the critic who had to extend and sometimes correct Heisenberg's work on uranium machines, and the theoretical physicist who consulted with Diebner's reactor group.[64] By the time the report on the lattice design was finished, it was not clear whether these experiments would be continued, but that all changed along with Esau's fortunes.

Although in December of 1942 Esau was planning to cut back on work related to uranium, this suddenly changed when Göring appointed Esau as his plenipotentiary for nuclear physics, giving him far-ranging powers and authority. When Rudolf Mentzel nominated Esau, he closely followed the latter's report from the previous month and characterized the goal of the working group as "coming closer to utilizing the tremendous energies bound up in atomic nuclei, possibly for the construction of a new type of thermal engine that could be operated with atomic energy." Again there was no mention of atomic bombs, or even the potential use of uranium 235 or element 94 as nuclear explosives. Indeed Mentzel was quite explicit about the status of the work: "Here we find ourselves absolutely in the area of basic research." However, this did not mean that the work was not important.

Setting aside the fact that the tempo of a scientific development can never be exactly calculated beforehand, and that in the area of nuclear physics surprises are possible, the entire complex of questions appears so important to me that it may not be neglected for a moment, even during the war. Moreover, boundary problems in nuclear physics have an immediate relevance for the war.[65]

Because of Esau's new status a meeting was held with Esau, Mentzel, and two representatives of the KWG, Telschow and Vögler in the offices of the KWG president's steel company. According to the minutes of the meeting, Esau agreed to grant the Kaiser Wilhelm Institutes participating in the working group considerable autonomy.[66] However, when Esau subsequently began asserting his authority as if that meeting had not taken place, Telschow and Vögler separately wrote to Mentzel, calling for another meeting, this time including both the leading scientists in the project and a representative of Reich Minister Speer. Mentzel replied that he would be happy to attend such a meeting, so long as

Total War 95

Esau and Vögler jointly invited him. "Otherwise I am afraid that misunderstandings and annoyance will be unavoidable."[67] Erich Schumann similarly wrote to Heisenberg, Harteck, and the other institute directors, telling them that the working group was "exclusively in Esau's hands" and henceforth if they wanted to contact the HWA, then they would have to go through him.[68]

In March Esau did meet with the leading scientists in the working group, but without Vögler, Telschow, or a representative of Reich Minister Speer. Esau began by emphasizing that: "the leadership and supervision of the entire U-enterprise has been definitively transferred to me." The HWA department that had been handling the administration of the work, including Kurt Diebner, had now been moved to Esau's office. Esau directed the scientists to submit plans for how the work should be continued, including the resources that would be needed. He also hinted at a change that would affect Heisenberg's plans for the uranium machine: as far as the continuing experiments were concerned, the main goal was improving the experimental design.[69]

A week later, Esau called Heisenberg and ordered the 600 liters of heavy water stored in the air raid shelter at the KWIfP to be moved to a bunker at the Reich Chemical-Technical Institute because, until the KWIfP bunker laboratory was finished, it would be safer there. Heisenberg was powerless to stop this and urged Telschow to arrange a meeting, with Vögler present, in order to establish a fixed protocol for which experiments would be performed at which institutes, which apparatus would be available, which construction would be carried out, etc.[70] It was hardly a coincidence that Diebner and his collaborators were setting up an experiment using uranium oxide and frozen heavy water in the low temperature room of the Chemical-Technical Institute (see Figure 5.3).[71]

In July Diebner's group submitted their final report on the heavy ice experiment. They embedded the uranium directly in the frozen heavy water in order to avoid using any supporting materials. Once again they used what was available, 200 liters of heavy water and small uranium plates that were cut up and assembled into cubes. Ideally they wanted to use cubes 6.5 cm a side, but cutting up the plates only allowed 108 cubes measuring 5 cm.

During the freezing of the heavy water and construction of the experiment, they could not avoid allowing pieces of heavy ice to interact with the air, potentially diluting the heavy water. The experiments yielded the highest neutron increase so far, although they recognized that comparisons with the very different L-IV design were difficult.[72]

In May of 1943 Heisenberg wrote Esau with his plans for future work. First of all, the long-planned large-scale uranium machine experiment with metal uranium plates and around 1.5 tons of heavy water, all surrounded by a mantle of water and carbon as moderator, should be carried out in collaboration with Bothe's institute. A great deal of preliminary work had already been done, including investigating important properties of the materials to be used, the two

96 The Bomb

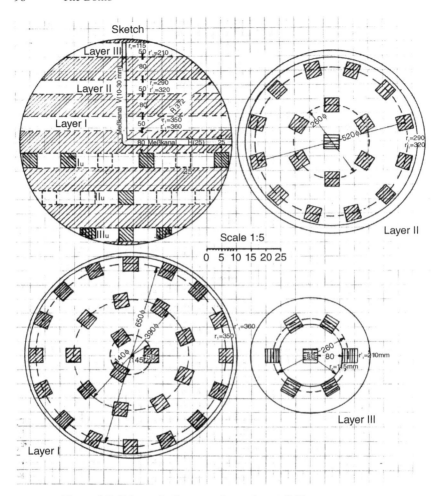

Figure 5.3 Schematic diagram of experiment G-II.
Note: A sphere consisting of alternating horizontal layers of frozen heavy water and metal uranium cubes arranged in a lattice, all surrounded by a mantle of ice.
Source: Adapted from K. Diebner, G. Hartwig, W. Herrmann, H. Westmeyer, W. Czulius, F. Berkei, and K.-H. Höcker, Bericht über einen Versuch mit Würfeln aus Uran-Metall und Schwerem Eis. (July 1943), ADM, FA 002 651.

containers for the heavy water and the moderating substances were finished, and the bunker laboratory would be finished in around four to six weeks. Heisenberg also recognized Höcker's theoretical work and agreed that it might be desirable to vary the arrangement of the uranium metal in the planned experiment.[73]

Total War 97

In January of 1943, the chancellor of the German Academy for Aviation Research (*Deutsche Akademie für Luftfahrtforschung*, DAL), invited Heisenberg, along with Bothe, Clusius and Hahn, to give lectures on the production of energy from uranium fission. Heisenberg noted that such matters were secret, but the chancellor responded that they often heard talks on top secret matters. Recognizing that things had changed with Esau's appointment as plenipotentiary, Heisenberg asked him to lead the talks. Esau introduced the session with a talk that was a slightly updated version of his November report to Mentzel.[74]

He began with what had become almost a ritual by invoking the threat of nuclear physics in the United States, where with "the greatest support" American scientists were "exceptionally successful." Although Germans had made fundamental discoveries in this area, as the rest of the speakers would describe, the further development of the "main thing" (energy from nuclear fission) had only progressed slowly because of insufficient support, with the unavoidable result that foreign physicists had outperformed their German counterparts. Esau now reassured his listeners that, under his guidance, German research would catch up as quickly as possible and "regain the position in this area that is its due and necessary for its reputation abroad."[75]

When he turned to nuclear energy production from uranium, he must have surprised Heisenberg by telling his audience that it was now clear that the "application of metal uranium in the form of plates is not optimal and that the yield of neutrons, which is what matters in practice, improves with cubes or columns." The manufacture of the necessary uranium metal in the greatest possible purity and the desired form could be regarded as assured. Although there had been "temporary difficulties" in acquiring sufficient amounts of heavy water, they had enough to carry out the next round of experiments. Esau mentioned uranium isotope enrichment, but only in the context of allowing uranium machines to use ordinary water as a moderator.[76]

Heisenberg's talk at the Academy was his third and final nontechnical lecture on energy production from uranium, following his talks in February 1942 before the RFR and the following June for Speer, Milch, and their respective staffs. This lecture covered much of the same territory as in 1942 but was different in significant ways. Using the same schematic diagram of a uranium machine on the left and a pure mass of uranium 235 on the right, Heisenberg told his audience that, if a nuclear fission chain reaction began in the latter, then "the number of neutrons will increase in a fraction of a second enormously, explosively liberating a corresponding great amount of energy." This was the closest he came to mentioning explicitly nuclear explosives or atomic bombs.

There were two paths to the production of energy from uranium fission: (1) the pure production or enrichment of uranium 235, and in the past year Harteck had achieved a small enrichment of what were still very small amounts of material; and (2) using ordinary uranium with a suitable moderator. Along with emphasizing the success of the L-IV experiment by Robert Döpel, Heisenberg

98   The Bomb

also mentioned that: "In the meantime a working group from Army Ordnance has investigated a slightly improved apparatus of a similar type in the Chemical-Technical Institute, which led to the same result, and in which the neutron increase was even a little bit higher." The next step would be to carry out an experiment including around 1.5 tons of heavy water and 3 tons of metal uranium in the form of layers in the bunker laboratory being built at the KWIfP.[77]

Heisenberg hoped to begin this experiment in the summer. Once they had successfully achieved a self-sustaining chain reaction in a uranium burner, the first important technical application would be the manufacture of artificial radioactive substances. If they could build many such burners, then they could be used to power thermal engines in ships and other vehicles for which it was important to store as much energy as possible in a small space. As Heisenberg ended his talk, he told the Academy that they had taken the first step towards a very important technical development. There could no longer be any doubt about the possibility of liberating atomic energy for technical purposes. However, the practical continuation of this development in the strained economic situation caused by the war "naturally ran into great external difficulties."[78]

A day after the Academy lectures, Esau met with Bothe, Harteck, Heisenberg, Weizsäcker, Höcker, and three scientists including Diebner from the HWA group. The purpose of the meeting was to clarify the current state of uranium metal and heavy water procurement as well as the continuation of experiments on the basis of the most recent results. Heisenberg responded that, for the time being, nothing had changed regarding the plans for the large-scale experiment. On cue, Diebner then reported on the successes of his group, including the ongoing heavy ice experiment. Both Höcker and Bothe followed by suggesting that the Leipzig IV experiment, that had appeared to verify that energy-producing uranium machines could be built, had been interpreted too favorably. Heisenberg coolly responded that it had been interpreted correctly. Esau now suggested that any further experiments should use the best design, which obviously was the lattice of cubes.

Heisenberg gave several reasons for continuing with the planned layer experiment. The dimensions of the previous experiments had been too small to produce absolutely secure data. The Auer Society was now set up to cast plates, so that these would have to be finished before they could switch to cubes, otherwise the company would be delayed. They had just enough heavy water to carry out the layer experiment, which would allow them to estimate precisely how large the uranium machine would have to be. After the experiment, the plates might be able to be cut up for cubes. Although Bothe had just criticized Heisenberg, he also did not want Diebner to direct the next large-scale experiment. Bothe agreed that the lattice design was superior, but supported Heisenberg's arguments that the layer experiment should be carried out.

Esau ended the meeting by emphasizing that he would decide whether the layer or lattice experiment would be done. His decision would depend on how

Total War 99

long it would take to produce the plates.[79] Three weeks later he announced that, although a cube lattice system was probably superior to a layer design, he nevertheless agreed to Bothe and Heisenberg's suggestion that the layer experiment be performed as planned. Diebner's group would also begin work on another lattice machine.[80]

When Heisenberg subsequently read the minutes of the meeting, he found that it "still contained a few passages that could be misunderstood" and wrote Esau with corrections. He and his colleagues had considered other geometric designs than layers from the very beginning. Heisenberg made a back-of-the-envelope calculation using the values of the nuclear constants known at the time and concluded that layer designs would be better. When Diebner and the physicist Heinz Pose suggested investigating a cube lattice in Gottow, Heisenberg encouraged them because the theory was not complete and the experiment promised to produce interesting results. Experiment G-I gave Höcker reason to reexamine the different designs theoretically, with the result that a cube lattice design with the appropriate dimensions could produce a "slightly larger" neutron increase than a layer design. This result was then confirmed by the heavy ice experiment.[81]

However, Heisenberg argued, the experiments so far had been too small to yield conclusive results. For this reason, the planned large-scale layer experiment, which would vary the thickness and gap between the layers, would provide valuable data and experience for the future uranium machine. Perhaps most important, Heisenberg pointed out that the cube lattice was not technically practical and, as Höcker had argued, they would probably have to consider other designs, for example, using cylinders. On the other hand, since they could not afford unlimited experiments, Heisenberg suggested continuing with the layer design. Indeed the cube arrangement was as impractical as the layer design was inefficient. Heisenberg's argument of using layers to fine-tune constants and values made some sense. In any case, he did not want the layer experiments to be delayed by other work.

Two scientists from Diebner's group, Heinz Pose and Ernst Rexer, now carried out a systematic series of experiments with pressed uranium oxide and paraffin in different geometric arrangements. Their results mirrored Höcker's predictions. As far as neutron increase was concerned, cubes were better than columns, which in turn were better than plates. However, since with regard to construction and heat transfer a cube lattice was "extremely unfavorable," a design using columns appeared best.[82]

Diebner's group now constructed a larger cube lattice experiment. Because heavy ice had been so hard to work with, G-III used a spherical lattice of metal uranium cubes suspended by a minimum of aluminum-magnesium alloy cables and immersed in heavy water (see Figure 5.4). They avoided a metal container, which would absorb neutrons, by using a reflective mantle of paraffin instead of water.

Figure 5.4 Photograph of experiment G-III.
Source: K. Diebner, W. Czulius, W. Heremann, G. Hartwig, E. Kamin, and F. Berkei, Bericht über die Neutronenvermehrung einer Anordnung von Uranwürfeln und Schwerem Wasser (G III). (December 1943), ADM, FA 002 634.

The experiment was run with 180, then 240 metal uranium cubes weighing 564 kilograms and the just under 600 liters of heavy water that was available at the time, producing a neutron increase of 106 percent. This was clear evidence that an energy-producing uranium burner could be built. In November Karl Wirtz wrote an anxious letter to Heisenberg. Höcker had told Wirtz that the neutron production of a layer machine would always be lower than a cube lattice or a shell design like the Leipzig experiments. Although Wirtz did not believe that Höcker's calculations were always correct, he was worried that their long-delayed layer experiment might turn out badly.[83]

Although Heisenberg, Wirtz, and the KWG scientists had fallen out of Esau's favor, they did have other, more powerful supporters. Speer's ministry

Total War 101

shifted priority away from some less important Kaiser Wilhelm institutes to the KWIfP and asked Heisenberg again for a list of his needs.[84] However, as the war steadily deteriorated, it nevertheless became harder and harder to get the materials and expertise they needed. In March of 1943 construction at the KWIfP had halted because of a lack of tool machines. Fortunately KWG President Vögler had excellent informal connections within German industry and got the machines three weeks later. In April the bunker was finished except for the ceiling, but Heisenberg was waiting for the cast metal uranium plates, which now would not be finished until the end of June.[85]

The production of uranium plates was threatened by Esau's support of Diebner's group and their cube lattice experiments. Although on May 29 Esau wrote to the institute directors that Auer could manufacture the necessary uranium forms for both the plate and cube experiments, suggesting that both would go forward, he quietly ordered the company to cast the cubes and stop working on the plates. When Heisenberg learned of Esau's intervention, he asked Johannes Goerner, an official from Speer's ministry for help. Goerner in turn told Auer that only the plate production had DE priority, and it had to be done before anything else.[86]

In fact Auer did continue with both orders, since cube production was much easier. The rough casting of the large metal uranium plates was straightforward, but the processing of them to the specifications from Heisenberg and Wirtz required hardened metal milling tools Auer did not possess. In June the delivery of such tools, even with DE priority, would take nine months or more. Heisenberg again asked Vögler to help them acquire them sooner.[87] By the middle of August a large number of cast uranium plates had been delivered to Auer, but they could not process them. The company that had promised to deliver the hardened tools had backed out, and the other possible supplier would need at least two months to provide them. Again, Heisenberg asked Vögler for help.[88] Another firm was found in September, but Heisenberg was told that they would have to keep pressure on them to deliver the tools. An official from Speer's ministry similarly told Wirtz that they should pressure Dr. Zimmer at Auer to deliver the plates.[89]

By the end of July the bunker was finished except for the interior work. Heisenberg now invited Esau to come by for a tour, adding that, since the heavy water would now be significantly more secure against air raids than its previous storage areas, he hoped that it would be returned.[90] Heisenberg also wrote to Bothe and invited his institute to join them for the collaborative experiment. Bothe offered to send a young physicist, Erwin Fünfer, but said he could not come to Berlin because that would delay his vacation. Since so many people had fled from Berlin, there would be no problem finding a place for Fünfer to stay.[91] Bothe, who of course had wanted to run the experiment at his own institute, now had even less reason to travel to war-torn Berlin.

In July of 1943 Esau submitted his first progress report as Plenipotentiary for Nuclear Physics. When Mentzel passed this onto Fritz Görnnert, a high-ranking

102   The Bomb

official in Göring's office, he argued that the work was important and had been supported very strongly during the past few months: "Even if this work will not lead to the creation of practically useful machines or explosives in a short time" on the other hand it demonstrated that "the enemy powers will not be able to surprise us in this field."[92] When Vogler received a copy of the report, he forwarded it confidentially to Heisenberg with the dismissive comment that Esau had "made his job a little easy."[93] Heisenberg tactfully responded by surveying the progress of the working group, noting that: "Unfortunately the difficulties caused by the war appear to increase with every month." Hopefully they would be able to carry out the planned experiment in the KWIfP bunker without too much disruption from air raids.[94]

Evacuation and Holding On

Heisenberg's letters to his wife Elisabeth document the deteriorating state of the war and the effect it had on him. His large, young family had been moved to safety in the remote and rural town of Urfeld in the Bavarian mountains, while Heisenberg continued to commute between Leipzig and Berlin. Heisenberg only rarely saw his wife and children. In May of 1943 he wrote to Elisabeth explaining how much he regretted missing his young son Jochen's birthday. He felt very lonely in Berlin and slept badly because of the many air raid alarms. Even before the alarms it was difficult to fall asleep because he knew that "it will start soon."[95]

The stress also had a physical effect. Heisenberg's neuritis and the nerve pain that accompanied it had reappeared. By July it had become significantly worse. He realized that he was "not up to the unpleasant side of my tasks here." He should not have taken over the institute. "For this one would have to be more robustly built than me." Heisenberg consoled himself with the realization that: "This is a piece of the front, and not home. Moreover an especially quiet and comfortable piece of the front, where enough houses are still standing that one can sleep in beds, and is only seldomly shot at."[96]

Heisenberg resolved to put his enforced aloneness to good use and make progress on his own physics and a philosophy project. But his thoughts kept returning to the war. He found it "difficult inwardly to let go of all the horrible things that were happening" and did not have the strength to concentrate on scientific work. During this period, when so little progress was being made, he became darkly pessimistic about the working group. "The days pass here, while I do some senseless work. Inside or outside of the institute, it is all the same."[97]

In late May he wrote to Elisabeth that, after thinking about the difficulties for a long time, he concluded that they had to see things as they were. It would probably go badly for both of them until the war ended. Elisabeth was struggling with unmanageable tasks in trying to keep the household together.

Heisenberg was alone and "mostly had to do work that made no sense." Even the possibility of helping each other through letters would naturally become harder because they would be too weary to write and the letters would not be delivered. All that remained, Heisenberg wrote, was his willingness in an emergency to travel to Urfeld. In this case, he would have no qualms about leaving his work in Berlin, which was "basically completely irrelevant."[98] In December he visited Leipzig. His former institute and the apartments of colleagues had all burned down. A new book on cosmic rays Heisenberg had edited had apparently been destroyed when the publisher was bombed. "Here the war is so near that it is difficult to stop thinking about it."[99]

The deadly nexus between the catastrophic state of the war, the increasingly desperate effort to both increase armaments production and introduce qualitatively new weapons into the conflict, and genocide became crystal clear in October 1943 at the annual meeting of the NSDAP regional leaders (*Gauleiter*) in Posen, a city German troops had reclaimed from Poland for the German Reich. Reich SS Leader (*Reichsführer-SS*) Heinrich Himmler's speech bound his listeners even more tightly to the NS regime and war effort by making them accomplices to genocide.[100]

Let me point out one question that you, my party comrades, have all taken for granted, but which for me has become the most difficult question of my life, the Jewish question. You all happily take for granted that there are no more Jews in your district…. The sentence, "The Jews must be exterminated," with its few words is easy to say. For those who have to carry it out, what it demands is the hardest and most difficult thing there is….

I ask you to really only listen to what I am telling you in this circle and never to speak about it…. The difficult decision had to be made to make this people disappear from the face of the earth. For the organization that has to carry out the job, it is the hardest we have ever had.

It has been carried out without, as I believe I can say, our men and our leaders suffering damage in spirit and soul. This danger was very real. The line between the two possibilities here, either to become too raw, to become heartless and no longer respect human life, or to become soft and go crazy to the point of nervous breakdowns, the line between this Scylla and Charybdis is terribly narrow….

With that I would like to conclude the Jewish question. You know now, and you will keep it to yourself. Perhaps in the distant future one will be able to consider telling the German people something more about it. I think it is better that we, all of us, have done this for our people, taken responsibility (responsibility for an act, not just an idea) and then take the secret with us to our graves.[101]

Albert Speer, now promoted to the Minister of War Production, also spoke in Posen and gave the NSDAP elite an important message: the state of the war was dire and could only be reversed by squeezing a greater production of higher-quality armaments out of the German economy. This would mean politically unpopular policies so the regional leaders had to be on board. "There is no point in concealing the fact that our armament economy only has a chance of

104   The Bomb

supplying the armed forces with the necessary weapons if the whole people stands behind this armament and if the regional leaders in particular understand the seriousness of the situation ... [Speer's lecture was] intended to take away any excuse in the future of not having known exactly what is going on here."[102]

The Posen speeches reveal the close cooperation between Speer's ministry and Himmler's SS: Speer ruthlessly used the terror of the SD to coerce a greater and more focused effort out of German companies and the workers they employed, which often included forced labor from other countries.[103]

As far as the so-called slackers are concerned, who contaminate the spirit of the well-intentioned work force ... I am grateful that ... right now a few thousand slackers are being arrested and transferred to a concentration camp. I believe that these slackers, who are well known in the factories, are getting a just punishment and that the worker who is earnestly going about his job will see this as a just, not unjust matter.

Hitler had ordered Speer to find around 20 divisions worth of soldiers in the armament economy for the armed forces. Since the only young men still working in the economy were highly skilled labor, this would inevitably affect armaments production. Speer's solution was to close down the production of consumer goods and transfer these workers to armaments factories.

Speer demanded that the regional leaders assist him in mobilizing the last reserves of the civilian economy by eliminating all unnecessary production. "I have asked Reich SS Leader Himmler to place the SD at my disposal in order to find fabrication [that should be halted]. I have come to an agreement with the SD that it will have access to all businesses producing armaments in order to make the necessary determinations."[104] In his speech, Himmler had made clear how this would be carried out. After describing how the SS had cleared Jewish ghettos, including those in which Jewish labor had been exploited, he added: "This was part of alleged armaments factories that Party Comrade Speer and I want to clean up together over the next few weeks and months. We will do this just as unsentimentally as in the fifth year of the war everything has to be done, unsentimentally, but with a big heart for Germany."[105]

The only hope Speer offered the NSDAP leaders was that the German war effort would soon reap the benefit of technological miracles and new weapons systems. "If we carry out these measures with the necessary brutality and if you help me do this, then I am firmly convinced that we will be able to maintain quantitatively the lead in quality that we have undoubtedly achieved in the field of armaments in order to withstand the enemy and then finally defeat him."

Speer's speech had an additional remarkable, if not surprising component: his generous praise of scientists and engineers and plea to the regional leaders to take care of them.

Here I would like to mention in particular the work of engineers and scientists and ask you of all people to give special care to the engineers and scientists in your district, just

Total War 105

as it seems natural for every regional leader to take care of the artists there. In exactly the same way, there should also be additional support for the scientists, who are just as clumsy and unworldly as an artist.

I would be very grateful if you would give these scientists the necessary support. They find it difficult to cope with life during the war and much of their manpower is crippled by having to take care of things that the Party could reasonably do for them. It is precisely the engineer and the scientist who must give us the opportunity to ensure through superiority in the quality of material the unconditional superiority in quantity....

It is necessary for us to give technology and science all the support they need, beginning with young researchers. And I can assure you that if you give this support, our engineers and scientists will continue to maintain the lead that we already have in the field of army armaments and probably also naval armaments.[106]

Speer's Posen speech, juxtaposed with his reaction to Heisenberg's talk in June of 1942, shows that the minister's patronage of uranium research was not unique, rather was a manifestation of his general belief that promising scientific research had to be supported in the hope that it might become decisive for the war.

Hans Frank, the regional NSDAP leader of the General Government, a portion of occupied Poland, had also been in Posen. Around six weeks after the conference, Heisenberg, who was an acquaintance of Frank, traveled to Cracow to give a talk at the Institute for German Work in the East.[107] After the talk, Frank pulled Heisenberg off to the side and mentioned that he often heard talk of a wonder weapon, perhaps an atomic bomb or something similar? Heisenberg responded that the Germans did not have anything like that.[108]

In November the evacuation of the Kaiser Wilhelm Institutes was the main topic at one of the last meetings of KWG institute directors. These evacuations were only possible because of a personal request made by Vögler to Reich Minister Speer, who then offered his full support.[109] Vögler ordered the evacuation of the KWIfP to an area less dangerous with regard to air raids. Erich Bagge organized the evacuation, and by September around a third of the institute was already in Hechingen in southwest Germany. Like much of the German war economy, the evacuation of the KWIfP relied upon forced labor, including Polish prisoners guarded by Hitler Youth. Otto Hahn's KWIfC also moved from Berlin to nearby Tailfingen, assisted by Soviet prisoners of war.[110]

Vögler noted that the war had "thrown open the question of the performance and impact of German science" because in some areas the enemy powers had a significant advantage over Germany. Recently scientists had often been called up for military service. Such call-ups for Kaiser Wilhelm Institute staff should be approved if the scientist's work at the institute was finished. However, Vögler was prepared to fight to keep scientists all the way up to Speer. Finally, the Society president appealed to the institute directors to "act sharply against defeatist views" in their institutes and in "especially crass cases" not to "shy away from" reporting the offender to the authorities. "Now is not the time for debates and asking questions--the only thing necessary is working for a German victory."[111]

106   The Bomb

Conclusion

During 1943 the war came home to Germany with a vengeance, making the research on heavy water, centrifuges, and uranium machines increasingly more difficult. Very small samples of uranium 235 were slightly enriched using an ultracentrifuge. When the Allied attack on the Norsk Hydro threatened their source of heavy water, the Germans struggled to find alternative solutions in Italy and inside of Germany. The strained war economy hampered the production and processing of uranium and construction of the KWIfP bunker laboratory, thereby delaying the experiment with layers of cast metal uranium. In contrast, a group of HWA scientists made progress with uranium machines using three-dimensional lattice designs. Bombing raids eventually made work in Hamburg and Berlin almost impossible, forcing the institutes to evacuate to the German countryside. But the worst was yet to come.

Epilogue: Allied Progress by the Summer of 1943

Whereas in Germany control of the uranium research moved from the Army to civilian authorities, in America it moved in the opposite direction. In the autumn of 1942 the United States Army set up the Manhattan District for an atomic bomb project.[112] It became clear to the Americans that it would take up to two years to produce enough heavy water for a plutonium plant. Since they had a viable alternative in graphite (carbon), in November of 1943 they decided to move forward with the more modest goal of building a laboratory-scale heavy water nuclear reactor. Heavy water production using a catalytic exchange process began at a Canadian mining company in order to take advantage of a hydrogen source produced by electrolysis. By the end of 1943, around 300 liters of heavy water had been produced.[113] Graphite production had also been unsatisfactory at the beginning of 1942, but the purity problem had been solved by the middle of that year and large-scale manufacture began. Although almost no uranium had been available for most of 1942, by November the production problems had been solved and around 6 tons of uranium oxide were available.[114]

By the autumn of 1942 the Americans had enough graphite, uranium oxide, and uranium metal to build a self-sustaining chain-reaction nuclear "pile" in Chicago, Illinois. Ironically this was around the same time Heisenberg had hoped his large-scale uranium machine would achieve this result. Similar to the uranium machine design used by Diebner's group, the Chicago pile used a three-dimensional lattice of lumps of uranium or uranium oxide embedded in graphite, but also included control strips of neutron-absorbing material designed to slow down a chain reaction. This turned out to be fortunate, because the chain reaction began earlier than had been expected.[115]

Total War 107

The Chicago pile, led by the émigré Enrico Fermi, began operation as a self-sustaining system on December 2, 1942. A comparison of this experiment with the German working group reveals differences in scale. Fermi described having a "relatively small amount" of uranium available, but it contained about as much refined uranium as the Germans had in total during the war. Again Fermi noted that the graphite used as moderator was "of various brands of different purity," but the sheer amounts available dwarfed the mass of heavy water in Germany. Finally, Fermi noted that "an experiment of this kind requires a collaboration of a large number of physicists." Indeed there may well have been as many scientists, engineers, and technicians working on this single experiment as the total that worked in the working group in Germany during the war.[116]

The Chicago pile was as far removed from a practical nuclear reactor as the designs being investigated in Germany, but it was quickly followed up with plans for a pilot plutonium-producing plant. Construction began in January at Clinton, Tennessee. This design, created by engineers and scientists working together, consisted of a graphite cube containing horizontal channels filled with metal uranium cylinders protected by gastight aluminum casings. The cylinders could be slid in or out of the channels. There were also channels for control rods and instruments. The Clinton pilot plant, which was considerably larger than the Chicago pile and included a cooling system, thicker radiation shields, and a system for changing the uranium, went into operation in November of 1943.[117]

Fermi's success was crucial for the future course of the Manhattan Project. By this time, the American authorities had also become confident that the uranium isotopes could be separated on an industrial scale. Now they had to decide whether or not to attempt the industrial-scale production of atomic bombs. Vannevar Bush sent Roosevelt a report in December of 1942, explaining that the atomic bomb would cost more and take longer than previously thought, and recommending that several facilities be constructed simultaneously: full-scale plutonium and gaseous diffusion isotope separation plants; an intermediate electromagnetic isotope separation facility that could be expanded; and heavy water plants capable of producing 2.5 tons a month. Roosevelt approved the report, with its estimated costs of around $400 million. The contrast with Speer's report to Hitler is stark.[118]

The Army responded within months by starting several very expensive construction projects. Using the powerful cyclotron in Berkeley, California, the Americans had been able to produce enough plutonium by the end of 1942 to yield considerable information about its chemistry. By January 1943 the Army had decided to build a large-capacity production plant on the Columbia River in Hanford, Washington and enlisted the DuPont corporation to design, construct, and operate it.[119] Similar decisions were made early in 1943 to build large-scale gaseous diffusion and electromagnetic uranium

108   The Bomb

isotope separation plants in Clinton. The latter plant was ready for operation in November.[120] This step, from the laboratory to the industrial scale, never happened in Germany.

The success of the Chicago pile also made a better understanding of the physics of the fast neutron chain reactions in atomic bombs a priority. Serious attention to these theoretical problems began in the summer of 1942, when J. Robert Oppenheimer organized a group of physicists for this purpose. By the spring of 1943 several estimates of critical mass had been made using various methods of calculation and using the best available nuclear constants, but "the limits of error remained large."[121] When Smyth summarized the status of work on the atomic bomb in America in April of 1943, he noted that the available information needed to design atomic bombs was "preliminary and inaccurate" and the problems connected to the instantaneous assembly of the bomb were "staggering in their complexity."[122]

The introductory lectures physicist Robert Serber gave for new arrivals at Los Alamos early in April of 1943 were still preliminary regarding several crucial aspects of how an atomic bomb would work. Serber began by clearly defining the objective of the project: "To produce a *practical military weapon* in the form of a bomb in which energy is released by a fast neutron chain reaction in one or more of the materials known to show nuclear fission." Serber argued that the critical mass would be around 60 kilograms for an untamped weapon (a tamper would reflect neutrons back into the mass) but added that the critical masses would have to be determined by actual tests when materials became available. Similarly, in a meeting on April 15, Oppenheimer estimated the critical mass of a uranium 235 bomb with a tamper as 25 kilograms but noted that his result was only as accurate as the values of the still uncertain nuclear constants. These would have to be determined by experiment.[123]

The sometimes harsh criticism of Heisenberg's understanding of how atomic bombs would work[124] appears misplaced. Implicit in this criticism is a comparison with the Manhattan Project. Teams of physicists worked on this problem in America, comparable to the total number of physicists who worked in the working group in Germany. Most important, even in the United States the effort necessary to develop a sufficient theoretical understanding of the physics of nuclear weapons did not begin in earnest until after it was clear that nuclear fission chain reactions could be controlled and the uranium isotopes could be separated, in other words, that plutonium and uranium 235 could be manufactured. These technical milestones were never reached in Germany, so it should also be no surprise that Heisenberg and his colleagues never attempted to master this level of "bomb physics."

6 The War is Lost

Deep distrust in a totalitarian state can exist between people, sometimes must exist, even between those who work closely together. Trust in the false place could be fatal, as some of our friends had to experience during the Third Reich. It often became clear to us only after the end of the Third Reich that because of this mistrust we sometimes also were bitterly unjust.

> Werner Heisenberg in a 1967 review of David Irving's
> book *The German Atomic Bomb*.[1]

A New Plenipotentiary for Nuclear Physics

In October of 1943, Abraham Esau held an internal conference, the first since he had taken over the working group. There were twenty-four talks over two days, demonstrating the impressive breadth of the research he had been supporting. Along with producing energy from uranium, the talks included the manufacture of energetic ion and neutron sources, radiation safety, research at the Paris cyclotron, new types of particle accelerators, and applications of artificial radioactivity in biology and medicine. This was Esau's last hurrah. Two weeks later Rudolf Mentzel, Esau's superior at the Reich Research Council, asked for his resignation.[2]

Esau, who had never represented the interests of the Kaiser Wilhelm Society, ran afoul of both KWG president Albert Vögler and his powerful ally Reich Armaments Minister Albert Speer. Mentzel mollified Esau by appointing him as the plenipotentiary for high frequency technology, the latter's own field of research. Before agreeing to swap plenipotentiaries, however, Esau insisted that Speer approve the new appointment because he did not want "to be shot at from there again."[3]

Mentzel proposed the experimental physicist Walther Gerlach (see Figure 6.1), professor of physics in Munich, as Esau's successor. Speer personally approved the appointment and on December 2, 1943, Gerlach became the new plenipotentiary for nuclear physics. Klaus Clusius, Gerlach's colleague in Munich, commented to Heisenberg that: "Now that Gerlach has taken over physics in the Reich Research Council, let us hope that everything will be handled reasonably." However, this was not simply a matter of a respected

Figure 6.1 Walther Gerlach at Farm Hall.
Source: NARA.

physicist finally taking charge of the working group. Gerlach had also been very active in military research for the Navy, including ship degaussing and torpedo physics, and had been working closely with NS science policy makers like Mentzel. The new plenipotentiary for nuclear physics set up shop in the KWIfP and, as he wrote Paul Harteck and other institute directors in the working group, hoped that their cooperation would lead to "the greatest success."[4]

The Heavy Water Dries Up

The Bombing of Norsk Hydro and Sinking of the DF Hydro Ferry

As had been predicted, once the heavy water facility at the Norsk Hydro was back up and running the Allies attacked it again, this time bombing the facility on November 16, 1943. Although the part of the plant producing heavy water was not touched, the raid had its desired effect and effectively ended heavy water production in Norway.[5] Less than a month later, in a tense meeting at the Norsk Hydro, the head of the plant, Dr. Aubert, reminded the Germans that they had urgently requested the halt of heavy water production. What was decisive now was not what the German side claimed, that the heavy water had no military use, only scientific and economic value, rather that the Allies clearly saw the heavy water production as a threat. If the Norwegians resumed making heavy water, then there would be another attack on Rjukan, where the Norsk Hydro was located, with the result that they would lose both heavy water and nitrogen. Aubert, who was not willing to take responsibility for exposing the staff of the Norsk Hydro to more "catastrophic bombing" and investing more millions of Norwegian crowns that would be lost in the next attack, urgently requested that the Germans stop demanding heavy water.

The War is Lost   111

Esau's representatives accepted this, and both sides agreed that the partially enriched heavy water in the plant would be shipped to Germany.[6]

Harteck traveled to Norway again to see what could be saved from the heavy water production there. A German official offered to ship all partially enriched heavy water to Germany in a way that would be "inconspicuous and safe." They also discussed other facilities inside and outside of Germany that might be able to provide partially enriched feedstock but agreed that these possibilities would be discussed in the smallest circles and only by word of mouth, in order not to "endanger valuable facilities." But Harteck did not stop there. In a subsequent meeting he and German officials in Norway agreed upon a strategy of encouraging the Norsk Hydro to manufacture and store low-level heavy water concentrate for commercial reasons without appearing to connect it to Harteck's visit. Otherwise, the Norsk Hydro would "correctly fear that one day their concentrate will be confiscated."[7]

The Allied attacks in Norway had serious consequences for the work on uranium machines. As Heisenberg reported to Vögler, heavy water now became a very difficult bottleneck for the working group. Production in Norway had halted, and it would be a long time before it could begin in Germany. This came as a disturbing surprise to Vögler, who thought that production in Germany had already begun and, since the Norwegian heavy water had been coming for months, plentiful stocks were on hand.[8]

By the end of January 1944, thirty-nine drums containing varying concentrations of heavy water from the Norsk Hydro were ready for transport. The actual total heavy water in this shipment was around 600 liters. Although the British authorities instructed Norwegian resistance to do everything possible to destroy the shipment, the Norwegians hesitated because of the inevitable loss of civilian lives. After the British reiterated that this was very urgent, the DF *Hydro* ferry carrying the heavy water across a lake was sabotaged on February 20, killing fourteen Norwegian passengers and crew, as well as four German soldiers. Four of the thirty-nine containers bobbed up to the surface and were sent on to Germany.[9] The attacks on Norwegian heavy water production, sabotaging the plant, bombing the Norsk Hydro, and sinking the ferry, were all carried out in good faith. But despite the heroization and mythologization of this resistance since the end of the war, they did not stop a German atomic bomb. That was already inconceivable when the sabotage began in 1943, if it had ever been possible.

Independence from the IG

In December, 1943, Heinrich Bütefisch reminded Esau that at the beginning of their cooperation on heavy water they had agreed to work closely together on patent matters. In particular, any relevant patent applications by scientists should

112   The Bomb

be shared with IG Farben. This had not happened. Harteck had argued that he could not share his papers because of secrecy restrictions. Since IG Farben scientists at the Leuna plant wanted to submit a patent application that did not infringe on what Harteck's group had already submitted, Bütefisch requested access to these materials. Six months later, IG Farben went ahead and sent Harteck a copy of their patent application without receiving anything from his institute.[10]

A few weeks later Harteck's colleague Hans Süss complained to Gerlach about the IG Farben patent. The Hamburg scientists had worked out a countercurrent exchange process for producing heavy water or deuterium (heavy hydrogen) and had expected Leuna to patent the details of the equipment and how to construct it. Instead IG Farben was attempting to patent in a very general form facilities that use exchange processes in a countercurrent. The Hamburg scientists had made such a suggestion in a secret report as well as in their own 1941 patent application. Although the Hamburg scientists thought that they could easily dispute and hinder the IG Farben application, they suspected that it was not really a matter of getting patent rights. Part of the patent application from the Leuna scientists contained practically all the proposals that the Hamburg scientists had made concerning heavy water, including several that were not in their 1941 application. By including these proposals, which represented the results of several years of work by the Hamburg scientists, the IG Farben patent application would make them appear to be common knowledge – even if the patent was not granted. As a result, it would be very difficult for the scientists to patent any of them after the war or in other countries. Harteck and Süss now quickly submitted a revised patent application that covered their work mentioned in the Leuna submission.[11]

The termination of heavy water deliveries from Norway endangered the entire uranium project. Harteck composed a comprehensive report on the efforts to produce heavy water from the beginning of the war to the spring of 1944, including reflections on how they had gotten into this position. In 1941, when it appeared that they might need as much as 5 tons of heavy water for the first uranium machine, it had been reasonable to try and increase the Norwegian production as much as possible and begin planning heavy water production in Germany. At that time a lot of armaments production was being moved to occupied territories and Norway appeared secure from air attack and sabotage. The Norsk Hydro promised to produce enough heavy water for the first large scale experiment with much less effort and in a much shorter time than would have been possible in Germany. Once Harteck and Süss had developed their exchange process, which could be added to the Norsk Hydro plant, it appeared that 4 tons could be produced in Norway per year, which would have been enough for the entire development work and the first uranium machines. Moreover, during the crucial years 1941 and 1942 an investment of millions of Reichsmark for heavy water production could not have been justified.[12]

The War is Lost   113

In April of 1944 there were four different heavy water production methods under consideration:

(1) (Harteck) Distillation from water in low-pressure columns;
(2) (Clusius–Linde) Distillation from hydrogen at low temperatures;
(3) (Harteck–Süss) Exchange at two different temperatures using the equilibrium $H_2 + HDO = HD + H_2O$;
(4) (Geib–IG Farben) Exchange at two different temperatures using the equilibrium $H_2S + HDO = HDS + H_2O$.

Each option had advantages and disadvantages. Harteck's distillation would use little energy and cheap materials and could be built relatively quickly but needed the waste heat from a larger plant, so that air raids against the heavy water production might endanger the entire facility. The Clusius–Linde process for distilling hydrogen would cost little to construct and could produce 100 percent heavy hydrogen but used large amounts of electricity and the facility for liquifying hydrogen would be very vulnerable to air raids. It also might, as Harteck put it, "have a price-reducing effect on IG Farben." As Harteck wrote his colleague Klaus Clusius: "Right now it appears necessary to demonstrate to IG Farben that we are not necessarily dependent upon them."[13]

The Harteck–Süss exchange process could be placed anywhere, its various elements had already been tested, and a facility could be expanded simply by adding more units. However, it would use large amounts of energy, IG Farben had quoted an "astonishingly high" price for construction, and around 100 tons of nickel, a material in short supply, would be needed. The other exchange process, proposed by the IG Farben scientist Hans Geib, could also be built anywhere and expanded but used less energy. The hydrogen sulfide it used is very poisonous and it would be difficult to defend against releases of the gas caused by enemy attack. Originally they had planned to connect these processes to a larger facility that produced waste products enriched in heavy water, as was done at the Norsk Hydro but the danger posed by air raids made this strategy less appealing.[14]

A little more than a month later, Harteck set out a very optimistic timetable for heavy water production in Germany. Two high-concentration devices using electrolysis were needed, one in the KWIfP to purify adulterated stocks of heavy water being used in experiments, and a second at IG Farben that would use feedstock of 1 percent heavy water to manufacture pure product. The former should be finished in two months, while the latter might take half a year.[15] However, Harteck was "shocked" to learn that IG Farben wanted to build this facility in Upper Silesia, in the East near the ever-advancing Soviet armies.[16] The facility using the Clusius–Linde process, which would produce a few tons of heavy water a year, could be completed in a year and a half. A pilot low-pressure column that would produce 40 liters of heavy water a year was

114   The Bomb

under construction by IG Farben and should be finished by October. A larger column would take a year if it received the highest priority. IG Farben was also working on the Harteck–Süss exchange process. Finally, the Italian plant that was supposed to provide the partially enriched heavy water as feedstock could begin production in half a year.[17]

When Walther Gerlach also surveyed heavy water efforts in May, he was far more pessimistic. The Norwegian facility and its partially enriched heavy water was destroyed. The high-concentration facility using 1–10 percent feedstock only made sense if enough feedstock was available. The Montecatini Works in Meran could only produce the equivalent of 100 liters of pure heavy water per year but "these amounts are far from sufficient." Therefore, along with the small high concentration device at the KWIfP, two processes that promised to produce pure heavy water without feedstock, Clusius–Linde and the low-pressure columns, had to be pursued, even though it probably would be two years before they were running at full capacity.[18]

Gerlach was subsequently distracted by a long illness and the bombing of Munich. At the end of July, he sent Herold a detailed letter setting out his new heavy water policy, which included three new projects. The IG Farben high concentration plant had been designed in two stages. The first would enrich 1 percent concentrate to 10 percent, the second 10 percent to 100 percent, with the first stage using four times as much electricity. Since sufficient amounts of 1 percent feedstock would not be available, that stage was canceled, and the I.G Farben should build only the second, smaller section. The second new project was a low-pressure column designed to produce 10 percent heavy water. Both of these projects could be set up anywhere, and Gerlach expected that they would not be constructed in the East. Since IG Farben did not have enough technicians, Gerlach had persuaded the Armaments Ministry to provide four pipe-fitters.

Finally, Gerlach "took the liberty" of mentioning a third project with an industrial competitor of IG Farben, a plant using the Clusius–Linde process designed to produce 1.5 tons of heavy water a year. On the very same day Allied bombers destroyed the IG Farben Leuna complex, including the heavy water pilot plant they had been building using the Harteck–Süss process. Several weeks later Herold told Gerlach that the two IG Farben projects would be located at their facility in Bitterfeld, in central Germany.[19]

The ever-worsening state of the war continued to hamper their efforts. The necessary materials could not be shipped to the Italian plant, with the result that no Italian concentrate ever made it to Germany. Harteck continued to look for ways to circumvent IG Farben but when he discussed the construction of large low-pressure columns with the Bamag company, he was told that any such construction would invite Allied air raids. In January of 1945, IG Farben told Harteck that experiments with the low-pressure column were about to begin and invited Süss to come and observe. However, it clearly was delayed

The War is Lost   115

again, because in March Harteck told Herold that while both he and Süss were very interested in the device, it would not be easy to get to Bitterfield from Hamburg by train. Instead Herold should telegraph Süss when the experiments were running. Süss never made it to Bitterfeld, and no significant amount of heavy water was ever produced in Germany.[20]

Uranium Isotope Separation

Harteck, who had always gotten along well with Esau, was quick to congratulate Gerlach on his appointment, although not without expressing some frustration: "As you know, the small Hamburg group has with great enthusiasm completely dedicated itself to the cause and never shied away from working on apparent side issues, if the entire enterprise was thereby served." At the end of 1943, Harteck had reported to Esau on the progress his colleague Wilhelm Groth, working with Konrad Beyerle from the Anschütz Company, had made with the ultracentrifuge. Experiments with a small centrifuge with a new rotor arm and internal structure had produced 7.5 grams per day enriched by around 5 percent. Extrapolating to the larger double ultracentrifuge, Harteck hoped to be able to produce more than 20 grams a day with 10 percent enrichment. Because of this success, they decided to stop work with the small centrifuge and put all their energy into the larger UZ III, the definitive model. The armaments command in the southwestern city of Freiburg had found a factory in nearby Kandern that Harteck could use but the current tenants fought against their eviction. By April the factory had been officially allocated to Harteck's group.[21]

The German working group had always relied upon plunder. The uranium came from Belgium and the Sudetenland in Czechoslovakia, two countries invaded and occupied by German forces. The heavy water was produced under duress in Norway without compensation. As the war and German economy deteriorated, and scientific equipment became harder to find, scientists relied upon the exploitation of occupied and dependent countries. Setting up and running the centrifuges required several machines the Hamburg researchers did not have. Harteck spoke with the Freiburg official in charge of armaments, who recommended they visit the nearby "plunder camp" (*Beutelager*) in Strasbourg. There was a series of plunder camps in Germany, with new machines constantly arriving and being distributed on a monthly basis to interested parties. In September Harteck complained to Gerlach that the four tool machines they needed had been set aside for them in Strasbourg but Harteck had not received them, adding his hope that the verse from *Faust*, "Who is right and patient, their time will come," would also hold in this case.[22]

All the scientists working for the working group were anxious about being called up for frontline service, as had already happened to Harteck. In July of 1944 Harteck asked for help from the engineer and SS member Werner Osenberg, who

116   The Bomb

in June of 1943 had been given responsibility for a planning office in the RFR. Osenberg worked tirelessly to mobilize scientific and technical manpower for the war effort, including recalling 5,000 engineers, technicians, and scientists from the front and classifying a further 10,000 as "indispensable" (*unabkömmlich*) for the war effort. Although working at the University of Hamburg, Harteck and Groth's indispensable status was registered in Berlin. As a result, they had no documents on hand, which had "already repeatedly led to unpleasantness" that could only be rectified by a call to Berlin. Since they were expecting "special call-ups" in the near future, Harteck asked Osenberg to send them paperwork that they could show to the district military command and other offices.[23]

On July 28 the factory of the Anschütz Company was hit hard by Allied bombs, completely destroying the development laboratory that had been working on centrifuges. Konrad Beyerle now moved south and joined Harteck's group in Kandern. When the western front drew closer to Kandern and Freiburg, secure locations were found in northern Germany closer to Hamburg. At the end of September Groth began building an ultracentrifuge in the city of Celle, a half an hour south of Hamburg by train. Shortages of materials and manpower hindered the work but in January of 1945 Harteck hoped to start experiments before the end of the month. The five double centrifuges that had been set up in Kandern now had to be moved, because the armed forces had confiscated the factory building.[24]

When members of the American Alsos Mission, charged with finding and neutralizing any German atomic bomb project, inspected the Celle centrifuge laboratory on April 17, they found a "small-scale set-up." They estimated that, when working smoothly, something that was never achieved, the equipment would have been capable of producing 50 grams a day of enriched material, with a maximum enrichment of around 15 percent.[25] Centrifuge development was decisively influenced by the war, including the bombing of Hamburg, repeated evacuations, and the destruction of the Anschütz Company factory. It is remarkable that, both for heavy water and uranium isotope separation, Harteck drove the work and his colleagues forward with so much energy and enthusiasm. By the end of the war, they had essentially demonstrated in a proof of concept that the proportion of isotope 235 could be enriched in uranium. Given their hardships, this was a great success. However, there is no evidence that they, or anyone else in Germany, produced appreciable amounts of significantly enriched uranium.

Uranium Machines

Gottow and Stadtilm

In early 1944 the Gottow group was planning two experiments at the HWA site: (1) an expanded version of G-III with more heavy water and larger uranium cubes; and (2) an arrangement of uranium cubes and dry ice, suggested by Harteck.

The War is Lost   117

Since Gerlach gave Heisenberg and Bothe most of the heavy water for the large-scale layer experiments, the termination of heavy water deliveries from Norway halted the expanded experiment in Gottow. It appears that the dry ice experiment never got started. Instead Diebner and his colleagues set up an experiment with uranium cubes and ordinary water as moderator. By November they had taken measurements but the experiment may never have been finished, since apparently no report was ever written, and there was no mention of it after the war.[26] In the autumn of 1944 Diebner's group began evacuating Gottow for Stadtilm, a small town located roughly halfway between Berlin and Munich. They brought with them some uranium cubes and 500 liters of adulterated heavy water (see below) as well as an electrolysis device. They made no progress on the expanded lattice or dry ice experiments, and never got the electrolysis device running.

In the Bunker

Although Gerlach was much more supportive of Heisenberg's group at the KWIfP than Esau had been, the long-delayed layer experiments still had to wait for the casting of the large metal uranium plates at Degussa and their processing at the Auer Society. There was a great deal of pressure on Auer scientists Nikolaus Riehl and Karl Zimmer to deliver the plates. In December of 1943 they responded with an example of what they had to deal with. Allied attacks disrupted trainlines, making it difficult to ship the cast uranium from Frankfurt to Berlin. As soon as it was clear that all nonessential transport of freight had been halted, Riehl and Zimmer contacted the Armaments Ministry for a special permit for the uranium. After a delay of five weeks, the permit was received and immediately sent on to Degussa. However, the national train office in Frankfurt "attached no value to this certificate" and waited until the freight stoppage had been halted to accept the uranium for transport. Riehl and Zimmer wanted to make clear that they were doing everything conceivable to complete the order and "under the current circumstances even orders from the highest offices do not always have the desired effect." On the other hand, Auer had managed to develop an effective anticorrosive coating for the metal.[27]

   In January Vögler asked for an update because Armaments Minister Speer had again inquired about the uranium machine. Heisenberg responded that the bunker was finished and the plates had finally begun arriving. The only apparent problem was the shortage of heavy water. On February 15, Heisenberg took stock of the uranium production in a letter to Gerlach. Although all the plates Heisenberg had ordered had not been produced, they had enough to carry out their large-scale horizontal layer experiment. Since there were enough plates and cubes, Heisenberg made a new proposal: Auer should be directed to cast 300 cylinders of 7 cm diameter and 7 cm height. Höcker had already suggested cylinders as an effective compromise between the ideal but impractical shape

118   The Bomb

of spheres or cubes on one hand and the less effective layers on the other. According to Degussa, the 300 cylinders could be cast in a month, if their operation was not disturbed. By late June Heisenberg had formally canceled plate and cube production and requested the highest priority for cylinder production.[28]

When Heisenberg first planned the experiments with large metal uranium plates and heavy water in the summer 1942, it was a natural continuation of their previous experiments with layer designs. Throughout the autumn of 1942, all of 1943, and the first months of 1944, Heisenberg and Karl Wirtz waited for the uranium metal plates and heavy water to be delivered and the bunker laboratory to be finished. By the time Gerlach had made the heavy water available and the bunker was ready for the experiment, the plates were finished, so that it made sense to carry this out. Heisenberg was perhaps a little reluctant to give Diebner's group the credit they deserved, but while he recognized that a lattice of uranium cubes would probably produce a higher rate of neutron increase than horizontal plates, it was also clear that the Gottow design was impractical and would not be the final design for an operating uranium burner.[29]

The young group of scientists that Diebner had gathered to work on three-dimensional uranium machine designs had upstaged the work of Werner Heisenberg, Karl Wirtz, and the other scientists at the KWIfP but they were inexperienced. They themselves recognized that their experiments ran the risk of adulterating the heavy water with ordinary water but thought that the precautions they had taken had been enough. In March 1944, as Wirtz had finally set up the large-scale uranium machine with metal uranium plates and heavy water, he recognized to his dismay that the heavy water that had come from the Gottow experiments had only been 97 percent heavy water. Because some of this had been used, the 1,500 liters contained in the experiment were now only 98.85 percent pure. As Heisenberg had calculated, even only a small percentage of ordinary water would significantly reduce the heavy water's effectiveness as a neutron moderator. Since they now could not get additional heavy water from Norway, or send adulterated water there to be purified, this was a serious problem.[30]

The working group desperately needed to be able to purify adulterated heavy water. An electrolysis device was ordered from the Lüde Company, which was only willing to build and set up the device, not install it. Eventually Diebner found an electrical engineer to finish the electrical work. They still needed someone to configure, manage, and operate the device. Wirtz insisted that he could not do this on top of all his other responsibilities. Harteck asked Karl-Friedrich Bonhoeffer if he could spare a young scientist but the latter was not very enthusiastic about the idea, since he needed his remaining staff to try and get his institute working again. Bonhoeffer pointed out that there were two young scientists at the evacuated KWIfP who could do the work but they were probably also not enthusiastic about leaving the relative security of Hechingen and returning to war-torn Berlin.[31]

The War is Lost

In late September it was decided that Wirtz and another KWIfP scientist still in Berlin, Gerhard Borrmann, would have to finish installing and operating the electrolysis device. Wirtz, who himself was temporarily in Hechingen, wrote Borrmann with instructions, including a list of parts that he would have to get from companies in Berlin. Gerlach emphasized that, although the electrolysis device was very important, existing "institute resources" would have to suffice. When this became difficult they attempted to get parts from a similar device at the Norsk Hydro. By January of 1945 Wirtz was in Berlin but because Borrmann was not, no work on the device had been done since Christmas. In the end, it never went into operation.[32]

Gerlach in June of 1944 asked Heisenberg for an update on the KWIfP experiments for a collection of secret nuclear physics research reports the former was editing to be printed and distributed to high officials in the RFR and armed forces, the Minister of Education, and Armaments Minister Speer. Heisenberg reported that the first large-scale layer experiments (see Figure 6.2), along with

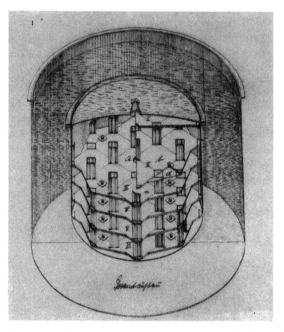

Figure 6.2 Schematic diagram of experiments B-VI and B-VII.
Note: Cylinders consisting of alternating layers of cast uranium metal plates and heavy water, all surrounded by a mantle of water.
Source: Adapted from Werner Heisenberg, "Die Energiegewinnung aus der Atomkernspaltung" (May 6, 1943), ADM, FA 002 737.

120   The Bomb

the investigations in Gottow, demonstrated that it must be possible to build an energy-producing uranium burner with 2.5 tons of heavy water, approximately half the amount they had assumed earlier. Whether this amount could be reduced even further would be known when the layer experiments were finished. Heisenberg and his colleagues were also beginning to study the question of stabilizing such a uranium burner.[33]

The layer experiments were finally finished in October of 1944. Along with the Gottow experiments, these had for the first time provided reliable experimental values for the coefficient of neutron production and neutron increase factor. The arrangement of horizontal uranium plates, immersed in 1.5 tons heavy water and surrounded by a mantle of graphite, yielded a significant neutron increase and demonstrated that only a small enlargement of the design would produce energy. Indeed the 2 tons of heavy water available in Germany now appeared to be enough to achieve a self-sustaining chain reaction. However, 500 of these 2,000 liters, which had been used by Diebner's group, had been adulterated and would have to be purified before being used. Heisenberg began planning the next experiment using metal uranium cylinders, 2 tons of heavy water, and a mantle of uranium oxide to increase the neutron increase still further.[34]

The Last Experiment

The scientists in the working group were preoccupied with three things in the late autumn of 1944: (1) their scientific work; (2) their personal safety; (3) the possibility that they would suddenly be called up. As Heisenberg wrote his wife: "I believe that the danger that individuals will be sent to the front – this has happened to a few men from Hechingen – has been averted for the time being. But we have to participate energetically [in civil defense] here in town." By late October the Degussa plant had been bombed out and, despite great efforts by Gerlach's staff, Degussa, and Auer until the very end, it proved impossible to cast any more uranium. On October 30, Gerlach made an unexpected suggestion to Heisenberg.

I am very excited to learn what you think of the proposal to use all the cubes to do a large experiment as soon as possible. I consider it urgently necessary that the interim period, until the [uranium] cylinders are finished, be fully utilized. We are constantly being pushed by the departments that oversee research and development, and I cannot deny them a certain right to this pressure, since in the end many people have been classified as indispensable in order to carry out such experiments. I have now begun, not only in the entire area of physics in general but also in nuclear physics, to put on hold work that is less important than the main problem [producing energy from uranium]. In this way physicists and technicians have been freed up from individual positions and can be used for the most important work.[35]

The War is Lost 121

Karl Wirtz began setting up an experiment with a uranium cube lattice surrounded by heavy water as moderator in the Berlin bunker. The cubes arrived on January 26, 1945. The high-strength nylon they had hoped to use to hang the cubes did not work, so they switched to aluminum cables. If the front came too close, then they were planning to evacuate the uranium machine. After speaking on the telephone first with Heisenberg, then Gerlach, Wirtz decided not to evacuate, rather instead keep working on the experiment right through the weekend. Wirtz brought in five scientists from the Gottow group to help and regretted not bringing a skilled mechanic back from Hechingen. As he wrote Heisenberg on January 29: "Unfortunately I did not completely comprehend how much work this experiment entails.... We have far too few workers for an experiment this large."[36]

The next day Gerlach ordered the dismantling and evacuation of the uranium machine. On January 31 Gerlach, Wirtz, and Diebner, dressed in his Army uniform, left by car, followed soon afterward by trucks carrying the uranium, heavy water, and other equipment. The caravan stopped first at the HWA testing site in Kummersdorf to pick up more materials, then continued on more than 300 kilometers to the small town of Stadtilm, where to Wirtz' surprise Gerlach ordered that the trucks be unloaded. It appeared as if Gerlach had decided to let Diebner's group continue the experiment. Wirtz telephoned Heisenberg in Hechingen, who called Gerlach in turn. Heisenberg and Carl Friedrich von Weizsäcker, who in the meantime had fled Strasbourg and joined the KWIfP in Hechingen, set off first on bicycles, then endured a hazardous train and automobile journey. They reached Stadtilm on February 5 and began lobbying Gerlach to move the experiment to Hechingen.[37]

Diebner may well have tried to convince Gerlach to let him run the experiment, which after all used his group's design. Gerlach may also have been daunted by the prospect of transferring the uranium and heavy water the further war-torn 200 kilometers from Stadtilm to Hechingen. But there was another, more existential reason why the two groups were fighting over the experiment. As Heisenberg wrote to his wife on February 1: "In our nuclear physics club the internal struggle (Diebner against the KWI) has been reignited, which is undoubtedly connected to the new wave of call-ups and the looming danger from the East."[38] The group that did the experiment had relative security; the other feared becoming Soviet cannon fodder. In the end, Heisenberg's prestige prevailed. Gerlach agreed to let his institute run what became the last uranium machine experiment but not before personally traveling to Hechingen to inspect the preparations that had already been made there.[39]

One of the youngest scientists in Hechingen, Erich Bagge, now traveled to Stuttgart to collect some trucks, then with a driver proceeded to Stadtilm. There he picked up Wirtz, most of the uranium, and the 1.5 tons of usable heavy water, leaving behind some uranium and the adulterated heavy water.

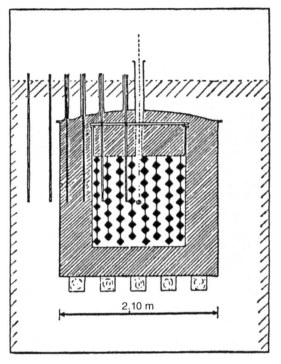

Figure 6.3 Schematic diagram of experiment B-VIII.
Note: A cylinder filled with heavy water, into which a lattice of metal uranium cubes is suspended, all surrounded by a mantle of carbon.
Source: Adapted from Walther Bothe and Siegfried Flügge (eds.), *Kernphysik und kosmische Strahlen. Naturforschung und Medizin In Deutschland 1939–1946.* Vol. 14 (Weinheim:. Chemie, 1948). Part 2, 159.

They made their way in an "adventurous ride" back to Hechingen. They traveled mostly at night without lights, once going off the road into the ditch but were still attacked by bombers. By the end of February the work was proceeding "quite energetically," despite being disturbed by low-flying aircraft.[40]

Using the same magnesium container, graphite mantle, and 1.5 tons of heavy water employed in the large-scale layer experiments in the bunker laboratory, Wirtz set up experiment B-VIII in a cave in Haigerloch using the lattice of uranium cubes design developed by the Gottow group (see Figure 6.3). Altogether there was around 1.5 tons of uranium distributed among 680 metal uranium cubes.[41] In the middle of the experiment they suddenly realized that they had ignored most safety precautions and had only a block of neutron-absorbing

The War is Lost   123

cadmium on hand to throw into the tank if the chain reaction got out of control. Heisenberg appears to have believed that the machine would stabilize itself at a given temperature but even if this had been true, he did not know what this temperature would have been. No one suggested stopping the experiment: they were determined to reach their goal.[42]

On March 1, Heisenberg sent a telegram to Stadtilm with the news that a tenfold increase in neutron density had been achieved. They needed to expand the volume of the machine by 50 percent in order to reach the critical point and achieve a self-sustaining nuclear-fission chain reaction but the remaining heavy water at Stadtilm was too adulterated to use and by this stage of the war it would have been impossible to transport uranium or heavy water from Stadtilm to Haigerloch. Instead the KWIfP scientists were considering adding pieces of uranium oxide they had on hand to the carbon mantle in the hope of increasing the neutron production.[43]

The scientists did not expect the experiment to achieve criticality, because they knew they did not have enough heavy water but they nevertheless hoped to achieve this goal. In fact the last uranium machine experiment was not the well-thought-out culmination of their wartime work but instead a desperate attempt, using what was available rather than what was needed, to achieve something great for themselves and Germany and ensure that they survived until the end of the war. On April 17, Heisenberg, Wirtz, and the other KWIfP scientists saw villages burning in the distance and for the first time artillery shells on the horizon. They waited until night and buried the uranium.[44]

Hitler's Bomb?

According to Rainer Karlsch, once it became clear in the summer of 1942 that Germany could not build an atomic bomb, some scientists turned towards nuclear fusion in order to create a weapon that might influence the war.[45] In his 2005 book *Hitlers Bombe*, Karlsch argued that German scientists were able to "trigger nuclear reactions" by means of their "perfected hollow-point technology," thereby developing a "tactical nuclear weapon."[46] In a subsequent collection of essays Karlsch went further by suggesting that small amounts of enriched uranium were also included in the design in order to increase the temperature, what he called a "hybrid system" composed of chemical explosives, fissile material, and substances that could be fused. Instead of a tactical nuclear weapon, in 2007 Karlsch speculated that the Germans might have tested the "ignition mechanism" for a hydrogen bomb, which itself had a "considerable destructive potential." Moreover, he asserted that this test was successful in the sense that it released kinetic energy and radioactivity.[47]

124   The Bomb

Soviet Documents

There are three wartime Soviet documents used by Karlsch, a Soviet intelligence report from November 1944, a second report from March 23, 1945, and a response to the latter report by the Soviet physicist I.V. Kurchatov a week later. The first document reports that the Germans were planning to "test a new secret weapon with a powerful destructive force." The bomb had a diameter of 1.5 meters and consisted of several hollow spheres nested inside of each other.[48]

The second document, apparently a second-hand account, describes two explosions that produced strong detonation waves and high temperatures. Trees were felled 500 to 600 meters away and buildings and other structures built for the test were destroyed. Prisoners of war were placed at the site of the explosions. Some were killed, often without a trace, while others suffered burns, the degree of which depended on the distance from the center of the test site.[49] Karlsch used witness statements from the 1960s to corroborate the fact that there were powerful tests producing bright light, causing great destruction, and killing and maiming concentration camp inmates but in a 2007 article was ambivalent about the strength of these sources. In any case, the oral history does not provide any insight into the design of the weapon.[50] The March 23 report first notes that the two-ton bomb "probably contained uranium 235," then goes on to state without qualification that it included "a sphere of metal uranium 235." The report concludes with a warning: "Undoubtedly the Germans are carrying out tests of a powerfully destructive bomb. If the tests are successful and such bombs are manufactured in sufficient numbers, then they will have a weapon *that can slow down our offensive.*"[51]

Kurchatov read the March 23 report through the lens of his own understanding of how an atomic bomb would work. While he considered the details of the construction very plausible, other parts of the description were unclear. Based upon these materials, Kurchatov was not completely convinced that the Germans "had actually tested an atomic bomb." Because the destruction caused by such a weapon would stretch for several kilometers, not a few hundred meters, Kurchatov speculated that the mechanism of the bomb had been tested without the uranium 235.[52]

In 2006, a year after the publication of Karlsch's book, a German television channel employed the Federal German Physical-Technical Institute to investigate the site where the nuclear test was supposed to have taken place. After taking measurements, they concluded that the radiation they had found was caused by fallout from above-ground nuclear tests during the 1950s and 1960s and the Chernobyl nuclear power plant accident in 1986. As far as a test of a nuclear device at the end of the war was concerned, they reported "no result."[53]

Hollow-Point Fusion Experiments

After the war, HWA physicist Erich Schumann described experiments he had planned with fellow physicist Walter Trinks that were designed to provoke nuclear fusion by detonating high explosives around a metal sphere containing a gas. This is called a "hollow-point" (*Hohlladung*) design (see Figure 6.4), whereby the energy and heat from the explosives are focused onto one point inside the shell. If these explosives were detonated correctly, they would produce a spherical shock wave that very quickly concentrated and heated the gas to high temperatures.[54]

Trinks had calculated that, if the sphere was made of iron and enclosed hydrogen, then nuclear reactions in the compressed and heated hydrogen could produce 10,000 to 100,000 times the energy of the most powerful chemical explosives. However, the scientists recognized that, in practice, the temperatures and pressures that would be needed to produce fusion could only be "approximately reached." Schumann and Trinks began planning such experiments late in 1943 but the Ministry of Armaments forbade them.[55]

Sometime in 1944, a group of HWA scientists led by Trinks, working under the direction of Kurt Diebner and with the support of Walther Gerlach, carried out more modest experiments designed to test whether nuclear fusion could be achieved in this way. Their report noted that it had often been suggested that chemical explosives could be used to initiate nuclear reactions, that would in turn then enhance the effectiveness of the explosives. Although "simple considerations" suggested that "this path was impassable," they wanted to test it experimentally. A sphere of paraffin enriched in deuterium was placed in a

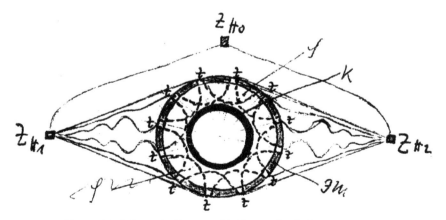

Figure 6.4 Schematic diagram of hollow-point design.
Source: Schumann-Trinks-design from 1944, Federal German Military Archives (*Bundesarchiv Militärarchiv*) Freiburg, Erich Schumann Papers.

126   The Bomb

hollow cylindrical device composed of chemical high explosives. The pressure waves created by detonating the explosives were supposed to fuse deuterium atoms and produce neutrons. As expected, no measurable activity was found. After the war, Diebner described similar experiments using heavy water instead of paraffin with similar results.[56]

Occam's Razor

Was there a powerful test of a weapon in the spring of 1945? Neither the Soviet reports nor the witness accounts from the 1960s are persuasive sources. There is no evidence at the supposed test site of radioactivity caused by a nuclear test in 1945. The fact that traces of radioactive fallout from a little more than a decade later can be found suggests either that there was no such test, or that the test did not successfully provoke nuclear reactions.

If the Soviet documents are correct and there was a successful test, then there is no solid evidence that it used a hollow-point hybrid bomb design. The first Soviet document does mention a hollow sphere but it also describes a series of nested spheres. Given that it is so difficult to make one hollow sphere implode symmetrically, a series of nested hollow spheres appears implausible. There is no other evidence that connects the reports of the tests to the hollow-point design. Moreover, because the hollow-point experiments during the war did not ignite nuclear fusion, indeed probably could not have done so, a test using this design would probably not have been successful.

Throughout Karlsch's book and articles, the author often argues that things happened for which there is no evidence because scientists were secretive and unwilling to discuss what they did, even after the war. There is, of course, no documentation for Karlsch's suggestion that there were undocumented experiments and tests during the war. For example, Karlsch's hybrid device would have required highly enriched uranium or perhaps element 94 but neither Groth, Beyerle, and Harteck's work on centrifuges nor the uranium machine experiments in Leipzig, Gottow, or Berlin ever achieved this. In his book Karlsch argues that other researchers could have enriched the uranium with other isotope separation methods and devices, and experiments with other reactor types could have produced element 94 but there is no compelling evidence that this happened.

This also raises the question, why would scientists be unwilling to speak up and take credit after the war for such scientific breakthroughs? Karlsch might argue that the difference was that the test caused great loss of life, killing and maiming concentration camp prisoners but here he is assuming that the test happened, used the hollow-point fusion design, and was successful, all of which appear unlikely. Moreover, scientists were willing to admit having worked on uranium isotope separation and uranium machines, even though Hiroshima and Nagasaki had made very clear where this research could lead.

The War is Lost   127

Karlsch's thesis, that Germans tested a tactical nuclear weapon or the ignition mechanism of a hydrogen bomb, can be illuminated by applying Occam's razor, a philosophical rule that requires that the simplest of competing theories be preferred to the more complex.[57] In the absence of proof to the contrary, the evidence should speak for itself. If scientists did not mention wartime work after the war, and there is no evidence that they did such work, then we should assume that they did not. Indeed Karlsch's argument should be inverted. Instead of assuming that the Soviet reports of a powerful weapon test causing great destruction and loss of life were true, so that the Germans must have been able to build such a device, and it must have been the hollow-point design, we should recognize that the Germans were unable to make such devices work and that a test using this design would not have been successful. The simplest, and most compelling explanation is that Germans did not successfully test a tactical nuclear weapon or ignition mechanism for a hydrogen bomb during the war. Instead the efforts to build an atomic bomb led by Kurt Diebner, Paul Harteck, Werner Heisenberg, and others is all there is.

Downfall of the Gods

The Devastation of War

"*Götterdämmerung*" literally means the downfall of the gods but is also used to describe the collapse and destruction of a regime, society, or culture. National Socialism came to power thanks in part to violence; ruled through oppression, discrimination, and scapegoating; unleashed world war; committed unprecedented genocide; and ended violently. Moreover this process accelerated and intensified towards the end. In the first five months of 1945, 1.4 million German soldiers died, including 450,000 in January alone. These numbers do not include the tens of thousands of civilians who perished under Allied bombs.[58]

By 1944 the scientists in the working group were as much preoccupied with their physical survival as their research. Hamburg was the closest major German city to airbases in the United Kingdom and suffered repeated air raids. Harteck was personally affected. In the winter of 1943–1944, for the first time in many years, he did not visit family in Vienna. The difficulty of the journey, which would have taken more than seventy hours and required Harteck to "storm" the trains in order to get on, put him off. By May Hamburg had forbidden all vacation trips by state employees. As Harteck wrote Bonhoeffer: "What will happen by August, that can only be known by people who are significantly wiser than us." In June Harteck noted that, in the meantime, he had "come to respect the air raids," especially after getting to know them up close.[59]

A month later he wrote to his colleague Klaus Clusius in Munich, having not seen any "sign of life" from him since a powerful attack on the southern

128   The Bomb

German city. Although he apologized for bothering Clusius during the Munich catastrophe, Harteck added "life has to go on." As a Bavarian, Heisenberg had strong personal connections to Munich, including having gone to university there. In August Heisenberg was in the city for an hour changing trains and saw the surroundings of the train station. As he wrote his mentor Arnold Sommerfeld, "even in Berlin, such a degree of destruction is rare. And how long will it take until the traces of this madness are wiped away?"[50]

Heisenberg had been a professor for many years in Leipzig and his family had lived there before moving to Urfeld. Because Berlin could be so frustrating and discouraging for him, he took several short trips back to Leipzig for relief. In May of 1943, after his house had been rendered uninhabitable, Heisenberg stayed with his neighbors. As he told his wife Elisabeth:

Sunday morning we had breakfast in the garden. It was not so easy for me to look over into our garden, where I had planted almost every flower; often I thought that I must have heard Woi's [his son] voice from behind the sandbox. I really had to pull myself together in order not to let anyone notice anything…. Greet all the children for me. Do not worry about me, I will get through this.

The following January Heisenberg was in Leipzig again. Their street "appeared bleak." It took him quite a while to recognize the sidewalk and which building was their house. It appeared impossible to rebuild. As long as he only saw the destruction, also inside the house, the "picture remained foreign and hardly touched" him. But here and there were some intact corners, for example the window in his office with the green shutters, or the oven in the living room, which "rips me apart."[61]

The bunker laboratory built for the KWIfP in Berlin was a convenient air raid shelter but complications soon arose. Because the lab had been built with support from the Ministry of Armaments for secret research, civilians were not allowed entry, even during an air raid. This was enforced by the Gestapo, that learned during an inspection in July of 1944 that family members of KWIfP personnel had been granted access to the bunker. This had to stop. Henceforth only KWIfP personnel and members of the armed forces in uniform could seek shelter in the bunker. Two weeks later a neighbor, Emil Karl, followed soldiers into the KWIfP during an air raid. The man had no identification on him, and when informed of the rules refused to leave, even when threatened with the Gestapo. Instead he responded that "they knew who he was" and "he would see who makes the rules." Noting that the KWIfP in fact did not know who he was but in the meantime had determined his name and address, Heisenberg passed on this information to the Gestapo, noting that "It would be a great help to the institute" if they "could explain the inadmissibility of his behavior to Mr. Karl."[62]

On February 2, 1944, Otto Hahn's Kaiser Wilhelm Institute for Chemistry (KWIfC) suffered a direct hit, with a bomb destroying the left wing of the building and firebombs setting the institute on fire. The nearby institute director's villa was also considerably damaged. Institute staff, who were with their families in the air raid shelter, emerged before the attack was over to begin putting out the fires. Other KWIfC staff members quickly arrived, along with scientists and staff from the nearby Kaiser Wilhelm Institute for Physical Chemistry, Heisenberg and Max von Laue from the KWIfP, and Rudolf Mentzel, a high-ranking official in the Ministry of Education. All helped to douse the flames and search through the rubble for whatever could be saved. Shortly thereafter the SS provided a fifty man "cleanup squad" composed of forced laborers and prisoners to help with the work. Because the KWIfC was destroyed, the institute moved to its evacuation site in Tailfigen, near the KWIfP in Hechingen.[63]

Heisenberg had never really enjoyed being and working in Berlin on uranium but by 1944 the ever-encroaching war made life difficult at best. His letters to his wife Elisabeth chronicle the stresses of day-to-day life. In early January the air raid alarms sounded but it was so dark, caused in part by shutting off lights, that for quite a while he could not find his way to the institute. Then "wild shooting" began, which caused him to run into a tree. When he got to the KWIfP, the shooting stopped. After Heisenberg drank a strong tea, his "mental balance" returned. In July, while he was heading for Berlin, the train stopped and everyone ran into the woods, but then no attack came. By now Heisenberg found his time in Berlin "quite horrible" and was "counting the days" to when he could leave Berlin for Hechingen. Laue was about to move there as well. As he wrote Otto Hahn: "When I was young, I wished to experience world history. A very foolish wish! Experiencing world history is never a pleasure but sometimes it can be as boring as hell."[64]

The Holocaust, certainly one of the most important consequences of National Socialism, only intersected with the working group in a few places. One such example is the case of Nikolaus Riehl, the industrial physicist and director at the Auer Society who was responsible for uranium production and processing. Because Riehl had a connection with the Technical University in Berlin, its administration required certification of Riehl's Aryan – in practice, non-Jewish – descent. The Reich Kinship Office (*Reichssippenamt*, RSA) was the sole administrative body for determining descent. While RSA officials did not participate in the actual killings at the death camps, their decisions sometimes made the difference between life and death.[65]

In June of 1943, when the deportations to Auschwitz and mass murder of Jews there were in full operation, a Technical University official contacted the RSA about Riehl, only to be told that "despite repeated prompts" the scientist had not submitted some of the documents needed for the RSA report. Riehl, who was born in Russia to a Russian Jewish mother, could not submit the paperwork that would classify him as Aryan, and if he fell into the category of a half-Jewish Mischling (half-breed), then he would be in danger of deportation. By

130   The Bomb

December of that year Riehl had been reminded a few more times without submitting the documents but was given a reprieve when all the paperwork for his case at the Technical University was destroyed in a fire. When the official took up the case again in July of 1944, Riehl told him that the documents must have been lost in the mail but in the meantime more photocopies of the necessary certificates had been made and sent to the RSA. Although mass murder continued at Auschwitz until November, the chaos caused by the war apparently let Riehl slip through the cracks of the machinery designed to find and eliminate Jews in areas under German control. He probably continued to fear that his non-Aryan status might be discovered until the very end of the war.[66]

Another very important event during the Third Reich, the attempt to assassinate Hitler and its aftermath, also intersected with the lives of scientists in the working group. In November of 1942, after his dual appointment as Professor of Physics at the University of Berlin and Director of the Kaiser Wilhelm Institute for Physics, Heisenberg became a member of the Wednesday Society, or Free Society for Scientific Discussion, an influential group of sixteen or seventeen men who were either recognized experts in their field or held important positions in public life who met every second Wednesday for a lecture and discussion.[67] In his memoirs, Heisenberg remembered these gatherings as some of the happiest aspects of his life in Berlin. On July 12, 1944 Heisenberg was the host of what would be the last meeting of the Society during the Third Reich. The KWG's Harnack House contributed some milk and wine, while Heisenberg had some cookies baked with rations he had saved and picked raspberries from the KWIfP garden in order to offer his guests at least a frugal meal. Heisenberg then lectured on atomic energy in stars and, as far as the demands of secrecy allowed, its technical application on earth.[68]

A week later, on July 19, Heisenberg dropped off the protocol of the meeting and took a night train south to first Munich and then the town of Kochel, from which he had a two hour walk to his house in Urfeld. Along the way he met a soldier pulling his backpack on a hand cart. Heisenberg added his bag and helped pull. The soldier then told Heisenberg that he had just heard on the radio about an attempt on Hitler's life and a revolt among the leaders of the Armed Forces. A few hours later Heisenberg was sitting in Urfeld listening to the radio himself. Several members of the Wednesday Society were either dead, arrested, or named as confidants of the conspiracy and Heisenberg "knew what that meant." Heisenberg probably wondered whether he would be arrested as well. A few weeks later Heisenberg wrote his wife from Hechingen:

The Army reports from the West worry me; I also found the report today about the trial of the assassins very depressing. I find it almost impossible to consciously bear the general fate, so one retreats back into his small world and to the duties that are simple and always clearly fulfilled; perhaps it is also enough, if everyone does that.[69]

The theologian Dietrich Bonhoeffer, brother of the physical chemist Karl-Friedrich, became involved with groups plotting resistance to Hitler. In April 1943, Dietrich and his brother-in-law Hans von Dohnanyi were arrested and accused of "subverting military strength" (*Wehrkraftzersetzung*), a crime that carried the death penalty. After the attempt to assassinate Hitler, the prisoners' situation became even more precarious. In February of 1945, Karl-Friedrich Bonhoeffer sent his friend and colleague Harteck a "sign of life" and shared some of his pain. The recent air raids had cut Bonhoeffer off. The train station in Leipzig was out of commission, mail was no longer being delivered, and the telephones in his apartment and institute were not working.[70]

Karl-Friedrich learned on a trip to Berlin that the judgment in his brother's recent trial in the People's Court, a special tribunal that tried political crimes, had been "unusually harsh." The family had both appealed and asked for a pardon, even though Bonhoeffer considered success very unlikely. He ended his letter to Harteck with resignation: "No one can foresee how things will develop.... But one will probably only have the freedom of decision as long as he cannot make up his mind for other reasons." Harteck was "shocked" by Bonhoeffer's letter, writing that "what has happened to you all is something that cannot be expressed in words and in a letter.... Keep your head high, hopefully we will see each other soon." Bonhoeffer wrote Harteck again in late March, a month before his brother was finally executed in a concentration camp, in a despairing tone:

Gradually one becomes numb to everything and lives like livestock. One no longer knows whether the people you love are still alive; separated from everything that one likes, one cannot even fulfill one's true calling.[71]

Perhaps the most striking and thought-provoking evidence of a "Downfall of the Gods" mentality among the scientists working on uranium comes from a letter Heisenberg wrote to his wife Elisabeth in October of 1943 about Weizsäcker.

I basically do not get along with him at all. The way he takes everything as a matter of principle and everywhere forces the "last decision" is so completely alien to me. Weizsäcker can say such sentences as: he would be completely content in a totally destroyed city, for then one would be certain that it would not come again and that people, because of the experience of guilt and punishment, would mature to a different way of thinking--whereby the new belief [National Socialism] is meant, which he himself avows.

Then he says further that this belief is naturally irreconcilably hostile to that of the old world, that is the Anglo-Saxon, and that even Christ said that he had not come to bring peace, rather the sword--whereupon one is back to where he was at the beginning, that is, whoever does not believe the same things as I do, must be exterminated.

I find this eternal circle of belief in the most sacred goods, which must be defended with fire and sword, quite unbearable; apparently I am completely un-German about it.

132   The Bomb

At around the same time, National Socialist officials charged with assessing Weizsäcker reported that the physicist was neither politically active, nor willing to become so. Weizsäcker's infatuation with National Socialism appears to have been purely intellectual.[72]

Riding the Tiger

The last year and a half of the war in Europe was characterized by frenzied efforts in Germany to build wonder weapons like rockets and jet aircraft in a desperate attempt to forestall defeat. By the time Walther Gerlach had taken charge of the working group, if not long before, it was clear to the scientists and administrators involved with research that Germany could not possibly create atom bombs in time to influence the outcome of the war. They had two equally dangerous options. If they admitted that their research would not lead to decisive weapons, then they might all be sent as cannon fodder to the front; if they said that they could deliver powerful atomic bombs, then they would be put under tremendous pressure to do so.

The two individuals who most often served as intermediaries between the researchers and the powerful National Socialist elite, Gerlach and Heisenberg, trod a very thin line, never promising to deliver atomic bombs but at the same often dangling the possibility of a sudden breakthrough. KWG President Albert Vögler asked Heisenberg in April of 1944 for an update on whether "the experiments have brought us closer to the manufacture of the so-called energy bombs?" In January of 1945 Gerlach reported that, with regard to the uranium work, "we are everywhere in uncharted territory, in which every carefully investigated research question could open up new possibilities." After the war at Farm Hall, Gerlach said that he had told NS leaders that "the man who could threaten the use of a bomb would be able to achieve anything."[73]

Of course, the NS leadership did not just oppress and threaten scientists. It also rewarded and honored researchers who were helping them advance their policies. In late November of 1943, at around the same time as the administrative transition from Abraham Esau to Walther Gerlach, Reich Marshal Hermann Göring, in his capacity overseeing the RFR, called for nominations of scientists who had made a special contribution to research important for the war. Harteck, Hahn, and Heisenberg were subsequently all awarded the war service cross first class by Hitler. Armaments Minister Speer, who had nominated Hahn and Heisenberg, planned to award the crosses to them personally. That apparently did not happen, since Speer's adjutant Johannes Goerner wrote Heisenberg in December that Hitler's congratulations, as well as the cross, were destroyed in the last air raid. A second cross would be sent on as soon as possible. Heisenberg thanked Goerner in January when the replacement cross and certificate arrived, asking him to pass on Heisenberg's thanks to Speer.[74]

The War is Lost

It is striking how many of the most powerful men in the NS regime became interested in nuclear energy, especially during the dying months of the regime. Although the NS leadership was intent on extracting the last reserves of manpower for fighting the war, they were also aware that this would not suffice; some other sort of breakthrough would be needed. In an article published in the main NS newspaper in the summer of 1944, Propaganda Minister Josef Goebbels raised the hopes for such weapons when he reported that: "I would be ashamed to speak such language, if the facts did not justify it. I recently saw modern German weapons, which not only made the heart beat faster, rather stopped it for a moment.... The German inventive genius has passed its crucial test."[75]

Gerlach and the uranium scientists also received strong support from Rudolf Mentzel, the de facto head of the RFR. In June of 1944, Hitler issued a decree on behalf of Speer for the Concentration of Armaments and War Production. From now on only "revolutionary" research that promised to give Germany an advantage over its enemies would be supported. Mentzel ordered that all research supported by the RFR be scrutinized but interpreted the decree in a way that kept scientists away from the front, noting:

The goal of this action is less to free up workers, rather much more to create possibilities with the scientific and technical staff still left in the research sector for pursuing the most important research projects with the greatest possible intensity and bring them to completion as quickly as possible.

In other words, some research programs should be closed down and the researchers shifted to other, more pressing projects. Gerlach, who oversaw all physics, now began doing this, keeping the research on heavy water, ultracentrifuges, and uranium machines going.[76]

In June of 1944, a high-ranking SS officer quoted SS Leader Heinrich Himmler discussing the possibility of new weapons that sounded like atomic bombs. First of all, it was "not clear how long this war will last and this will not be the last war." Moreover, advances in technology could "very suddenly produce new explosive devices whose effects and speed dwarf the latest explosives in our revenge weapons." Shortly thereafter, as a consequence of the attempt on his life, Hitler transferred to Himmler control of the reserve army, and therefore of the recruitment and training of replacement soldiers. When Himmler subsequently learned of plans to call up 14,000 scientists and engineers, he immediately halted the action, "because I consider the dismantling of our research madness." A few months earlier Himmler had ordered that scientists imprisoned in concentration camps be put to work on basic research, a policy Gerlach also supported.[77]

Martin Bormann, head of the NSDAP Chancellery and as someone who controlled access to Hitler, one of the most powerful people in the regime,

134   The Bomb

added his support. The uranium researchers were already exempt from being called up for the Army. Bormann now ordered the powerful regional NSDAP leaders (*Gauleiter*) to spare these scientists, engineers, and technicians from being sent out of their region on "special missions." Werner Osenberg circulated this order widely, commenting that Göring, Himmler, and Bormann had all made clear that "war research, which serves as the starting point for military technology, must be fully maintained with all means."[78]

By far the most important and enthusiastic supporter of the working group among the National Socialist elite was Armaments Minister Albert Speer, without whose support the KWIfP bunker would never have been built, most of the uranium would never have been cast, and some of the scientists probably would have been sent to the front. In October of 1944, KWG President Vögler reminded Heisenberg that he would be happy to ask for more support from Speer, "who as you know, is extremely interested in these questions and asks me about it at every opportunity." Just before Christmas, Speer also made this clear to Gerlach:

I attach great importance to research in the area of nuclear physics and follow your work with great expectations.... I am certain that you are pushing the experiments forward with all possible intensity. You can always count on my support for overcoming difficulties that would hinder the work. Despite the exceptional demands on all forces for armaments, the relatively small resources for your work can still always be provided.[79]

The People's Storm

Once Heisenberg had moved to Hechingen from war-torn Berlin, he focused on the well-being of his family in distant and isolated Urfeld. Elisabeth had a maid to help with their six young children but the family faced increasing challenges. Heisenberg wrote frequently, often urging his wife to take steps to ensure that they would have enough to eat. In August 1944 he reminded her to ask about deliveries of coal, potatoes, and carrots. Elisabeth should buy anything that she could get with their ration cards, bread, flour butter, and especially salt, "which will perhaps soon become very scarce!" In March Heisenberg wrote that "now the struggle for existence really starts, and it is horrible that right now I cannot help you."[80]

Heisenberg was also worried about the safety of his family. In October he told Elisabeth that a radio announcement had claimed that 70 percent of all sixteen-year-olds had volunteered for the Army. "How good it is, that our children are still so small." Perhaps most threatening were the Allied attacks, which Heisenberg was experiencing on a daily basis in Hechingen. At the beginning of March 1945, he sent Elisabeth detailed instructions for keeping the children safe.

The air offensive that erupted over Germany eight days ago will be the most horrific thing a people in Europe will have to endure since the Thirty Years War. Because of

The War is Lost 135

my experience over the last few days, I want to give you a few security measures that I consider necessary for Urfeld, especially if the front comes closer to your region. The greatest danger for so small a location is low flying attacks.... On clear days the children should never go down to the street. It would be best if someone continuously sat in front of the house and observed the sky.... On such days the children should play only on the patio. If ... an airplane suddenly appears, then it would be best if you all simply threw yourselves behind the patio wall, nestled close to the ground and I would simply practice that with the children. I think that they could get used to having to hide from every airplane, without becoming very nervous about it ... When having lunch in front of the house you must be very careful about the planes![81]

In late August, Heisenberg's plans to visit Urfeld suffered a serious setback when Goebbels, now in charge of mobilizing the home front for the war, canceled all vacations by decree and increased the work period during the week to sixty hours. Heisenberg thought that the new decree would "cause a lot of bad blood." In practice Heisenberg doubted that it would increase performances but it would cause "significant anxiety among people who have already become insecure." But he added that "the leadership must have considered that." By January of 1945 it appeared that the war in the East could "turn in sudden and unexpected ways." If the Russians approached the Bavarian border, then Heisenberg would try to get to Urfeld.[82]

He was doing well physically and mentally but after a bicycle trip to Haigerloch noticed that his reserves of physical strength were even smaller than he had thought. He was not sure whether they would suffice for a bicycle trip to Urfeld. By March the trip appeared even more doubtful because travel with the trains was too risky, it was too far for a bicycle, and the roads were dangerous. "In any case, do not worry if I do not come soon, and you do not hear from me for a fairly long time. I will do everything so that it is best for us, and that can only be decided at that moment." Eleven days later Elisabeth wrote Werner: "You will not be able to come, my beloved heart! What will we face? Here in Urfeld the atmosphere is excellent. Everyone is convinced that the war will turn. So much steadfastness is actually really shocking."[83]

By September of 1944 the war had moved noticeably closer to Hechingen. "Columns of army wagons travel through the village; not cleanly scrubbed trucks, rather filthy ones, close to carts drawn by horses covered by straw or foliage, alongside the soldiers, tired and apathetic. One senses that the front is no longer far away." Air raid alarms were so common, sometimes with hundreds of planes at a time flying overhead, that they no longer noticed when they began or ended. In late October Heisenberg saw a "tremendous number of airplanes" over Hechingen on their way to the city of Stuttgart. Even from a distance, the attack was so "horrific" that he "dreaded the thought of going through this mill again." But the next morning he could "see the golden light of the trees again and life went on, as always."[84]

136   The Bomb

In October of 1944 all available manpower in Germany between the ages of sixteen and sixty was conscripted into a national militia. These men were to be the last line of defense against the advancing Allied armies. The young physicist Erich Bagge noted in his diary: "The time of the German People's Storm [*Volkssturm*] has begun…. The front moves ever closer…. The heavens become darker and darker for Germany." On November 6 all of the scientists had to register with the People's Storm. Laue reported to Heisenberg that "naturally they did it with great enthusiasm." As Heisenberg told his wife, for the time being the danger of the KWIfP scientists being sent to the front had been averted, "but we have to participate energetically here locally." Copying Heisenberg, Gerlach sent a letter to Martin Bormann and the local NSDAP officials, reminding Hitler's deputy of his order that the scientists should not be sent outside of their area. In this letter Gerlach also took care to mention that their scientific work "could unexpectedly become decisive for the war."[85]

The People's Storm was trying, and at times apparently pointless. On one day in January they spent two hours learning the songs "The Watch on the Rhine" and "O Esteemed Germany." As Heisenberg noted to Elisabeth: "How this will be applied during action was not clear to me." A few days later Heisenberg had to get up early and spend several hours freezing outside. He had a weapon in his hands for around three minutes and took one shot. Otherwise he stood in the cold. But then he was suddenly and unexpectedly picked up by a few high-ranking officers in a plush automobile for a meeting, which included a few glasses of vermouth. Naturally this "powerfully impresses the good people of Hechingen, which doesn't hurt either."[86]

Early in the morning of January 11 it was "barbarously cold," -20° Celsius. Heisenberg heated his apartment a little but "when I no longer get any coal, I will not be able to afford this luxury very often." By the end of January the coal had run out and Heisenberg was wearing two layers of underwear and undershirts. The electricity for all factories and shops had also been cut off. Heisenberg was trying to keep the institute running, even if at a low level. If it closed completely, then he feared that his staff would be "taken away" for military service. Since Heisenberg now had nowhere to keep warm during the day, he expected his cough and rheumatoid arthritis to get worse, "but there are much more pressing concerns."[87]

The news from the East was very alarming. Heisenberg did not see how the war could continue if Berlin was occupied but "one has to hope for the best." Their People's Storm service continued but without having any weapons. In mid-February they had another strange experience. This was not training, rather an "action." They were supposed to comb through the woods for refugees. Since they had no weapons, "it was difficult to see how we would arrest armed people." They marched in a column through pouring rain to another village. Because they were very wet, a farmer's wife came with a large tray full of

The War is Lost   137

schnaps glasses and kept filling them as long as they wanted. For this reason they stayed there almost two hours, with "the mood becoming quite cheerful." They then realized that they had missed their train connection, so they "wandered home jolly in small groups without having seen any enemies."[88]

Food became progressively harder to find. On March 9, 1945 Heisenberg told his wife that "I will not starve here, there are many friends who can help me if necessary." A week later things looked much worse. Now getting enough to eat was "really a matter of life and death." Even in Hechingen, Heisenberg no longer came close to being full. He was continually becoming leaner and physically weaker. Although he occasionally was given food, he still did not have enough. "Who would have thought ten years ago," he wrote Elisabeth, "that one day one would be grateful for every piece of bread?"[89]

The bombers now made scientific work almost impossible. They appeared so quickly that Heisenberg just had enough time to run from his living room to the more sheltered kitchen. The planes usually attacked automobiles or trains, dropped a few bombs, then were gone. Heisenberg felt like "wild animals in the forest, which listen for every sound and with a fast leap bring themselves to safety." Indeed when Heisenberg had time, he often took his scientific work into the woods and "enjoyed the peace of safety." Sometimes he remembered the old soldiers' saying: "Dear God, let it become evening, tomorrow will then take care of itself."[90]

Heisenberg's Odyssey

Despite all its hardships, at the end of the war Hechingen proved more tranquil than the other outpost of the working group at Stadtilm. Once most of the uranium and heavy water had been transported to Hechingen, Diebner and the other scientists had little if anything to do. Their boredom abruptly vanished in early April when the SS suddenly appeared, told them that the Leader had ordered that the bearers of secrets be evacuated, and threatened to shoot those who refused. Most of the uranium, heavy water, and equipment was loaded onto trucks, along with Diebner and some of the scientists. The column of trucks then headed south. Eventually the scientists were able to lose their SS guards, hide the materials in various places in Bavaria, and wait for the end.[91]

Very early in the morning of April 19, shortly before Allied forces entered Hechingen, Heisenberg set off on bicycle, including a few train rides, for Urfeld. As soon as the sun rose, he exited the train at the first opportunity in order to avoid attack from low flying planes. As he rode his bicycle, he passed many destroyed autos. He boarded the second train again very early in the morning but it soon came to a halt. Another train was provided but it did not do much better, so Heisenberg decided to travel on with his bicycle. By 8 p.m. he had reached Kaufbeuren and had to fight for a glass of tea in the overcrowded

138   The Bomb

waiting room in the train station. The train took him to Schongau, where he had to wait from 1 a.m. to 5 a.m. in a room filled with "a bunch of teenage boys in SS uniform, presumably from the Balkans." Heisenberg did not dare sleep, because he feared losing his baggage and bicycle. The train took him to Weilheim, where he got back on his bicycle.

On April 21, as Heisenberg approached a wooden bridge, he saw SS autos parked in front and weapons hidden under nearby haystacks. The SS men looked at Heisenberg with suspicion but did not stop him. After the war Heisenberg told the story of how he bribed a SS man with American cigarettes in order to let him pass. Now Heisenberg had a long and exhausting climb up the Kesselberg mountain. A little before noon he saw the Walchensee lake before him and knew that "this part of the struggle is won." Soon he was home, greeted by his wife and children. There were changes at home that he would have to get used to. The chickens on the first floor of the house bothered him a little but he certainly recognized their usefulness.[92]

On April 23 the radio reported that Berlin and Hitler were encircled. The frequent trips to buy food in local towns, which included waiting for hours in long lines, also reminded Heisenberg of the encroaching war. On April 27 the road was full of soldiers including generals "who take walks in the sun and obviously have given up on the war." The next day Munich radio first proclaimed the "Bavarian Freedom Movement," but by noon the channel was cut off. When it returned in the evening it announced that this movement had been put down and local NS officials urged people to hold on for victory.[93]

While out to get milk, Heisenberg ran into local friends Colin Ross and his wife. Heisenberg jumped up and greeted them happily. Ross responded that he was happy that Heisenberg had made it back to Urfeld but the couple was otherwise a little curt and quickly left. The next day Elisabeth learned that Ross and his wife had shot themselves. Heisenberg noted in his diary that Ross was popular and considered respectable before adding: "The decent Nazis draw the consequences, leaving just the rascals." When Elisabeth and Werner got back to Urfeld around six in the evening, they were asked to come to the burial. When Heisenberg saw the two dead bodies laid out, Ross's distinctive and calm face made a deep impression. But the general situation was so tense that "even death did not move me very much." Elisabeth felt the same way. The dead were carried by soldiers to the graves that had been dug a few meters away from their house. A Lieutenant read the last words of Ross: "He did not want to survive the ruin of Germany and the new idea. His wife, companion on so many hikes, also wanted to accompany him on this trek." As Heisenberg noted in his diary: "For the last time we gave the Hitler salute [*Heil Hitler*]."[94]

The ring around Berlin had become tighter, so that Hitler would one day disappear. Heisenberg had also heard that Himmler had offered to capitulate to the Western Allies. But it was not clear how the war would end in Urfeld.

The War is Lost

Heisenberg went shopping on April 29 in the nearby town of Kochel, which was like "an anthill" with soldiers, SS, and foreign workers milling about. Some of the SS were foreigners, young men who "clearly earned their bread through plunder." At the train station he saw a freight train full of prisoners from the Dachau concentration camp, who "looked terribly starved and pale." By the next day, the train was gone.[95]

Most of the other inhabitants of Urfeld had already fled to the other side of the lake but SS were there. Above them on the mountain was an intact infantry company. When the skies cleared he could see two nearby villages on fire, and suddenly realized the seriousness of their position. Moreover, Heisenberg would have to travel with small children. They decided to stock the cellar and stay there. By this time the Heisenberg's had been joined by an Army officer named Schuster, who had decided to try and ride out the rest of the war with them. As Heisenberg and Schuster approached the house, they were confronted by the leader of the infantry company, who asked what they wanted to do up on the mountain, and whether they were trying to defect. Fortunately Schuster with his identification papers was able to talk their way out of it. Urfeld, which had been "a real NS nest," had a NS leadership school. On May 1 the children from the school took their songbooks, Hitler pictures, etc. to a large field and set them on fire. Around eleven at night a neighbor called from her open front door: "Hitler is dead!" Perhaps, Heisenberg hoped, they might avoid a military conflict in Urfeld.[96]

The next day, May 2, Heisenberg's bicycle broke down so he had to push it to a bike repair shop. There he met the owner of a local tavern who had hoisted the white flag but told Heisenberg "with all the signs of horror" that the night before when sixteen soldiers had left their camp, they were intercepted by the SS, who hanged them. The woods around Sachenbach were supposed to be full of SS, which was where Heisenberg was headed. The news of Hitler's death had not yet reached the soldiers there but when Heisenberg told them, they reacted with "complete indifference." A peasant woman said that the SS were sitting in the woods, plundering and burning houses with white flags. Heisenberg noticed that "no one dared express an opinion whether that was right or wrong. Basically everyone was hoping that the Americans would come soon."[97]

Later that afternoon, as Heisenberg was visiting his nearby mother, three armed men suddenly appeared on the patio, pushed open the door, and confronted Elisabeth and Shuster with drawn submachine guns. Both thought at first that it was SS but instead they were Americans asking for Werner Heisenberg. Elisabeth telephoned Werner to come back and speak alone with Colonel Boris Pash, the leader of the group. As Pash and Heisenberg were sitting in armchairs, wild shooting started outside. Pash leapt up and ran with the submachine gun onto the patio. Heisenberg himself was so moved that what

140   The Bomb

he had expected, feared, and hoped for so many years had finally happened, he "watched the small firefight with complete calm and in the best of moods." Everyone else in the house, especially the children, quickly hid in the cellar. After around ten minutes it became quiet. An American major reported that one SS man was dead, two wounded, and the rest had fled.[98]

Now the conversation continued. Pash had orders to arrest Heisenberg but he would take care of him and the family in every way. They would leave the next day, up until then Heisenberg could make preparations. The military situation in Urfeld was very precarious. There were ten Americans, an entire company of German infantry that probably wanted to surrender, and SS scattered through the forest. In the evening the Heisenbergs had a "small peace celebration" with the last amounts of alcohol. Everyone was in the best mood, although Elisabeth was very tired and Wolfgang kept asking why Heisenberg was going away again. His father had promised that, when peace came, he would stay with him.[99]

The next morning Heisenberg went shopping in an American military vehicle and was able to collect large amounts of food staples. The entire region was full of tanks, trucks, and troops. The material superiority of the Americans was clear to everyone. Heisenberg said goodbye to his mother and family, then set out around 4 p.m. for the city of Heidelberg. Their departure caused quite a stir. First came a jeep, followed by a huge tank, then Heisenberg in an armored car with a mounted machine gun, a second tank, and finally a second jeep, all of which drove through Urfeld while the whole village lined the street. As Heisenberg described to David Irving in an interview many years later, afterward some locals told him that "even Stalin could not have been so well escorted." Heisenberg had dinner in Augsburg and for the first time in many months became so full that he could not eat any more. They arrived in Heidelberg, completely frozen, around two-thirty in the morning. Heisenberg climbed into a warm bed, and quickly fell asleep. After the excitement of the past few days, he would have been forgiven if he thought that the Allies considered him very important.[100]

Conclusion

During the last year-and-a-half of the war the heavy water production dried up, the production of metal uranium stopped, and Allied planes and the ever-encroaching fronts drove the scientists into the countryside, where their main focus was on survival. The research on heavy water, uranium isotope separation, and uranium machines was severely hampered but nevertheless continued until the very end, with the scientists coming close to but falling short of building machines capable of sustaining a nuclear fission chain reaction or producing nuclear explosives.

The War is Lost   141

Epilogue: Allied Progress by the End of War in Europe

Although the Americans used graphite-uranium nuclear reactors to produce plutonium and a combination of gaseous diffusion, thermal diffusion, and electromagnetic isotope separation for enriching uranium 235 for atomic bombs, they also surpassed the German efforts with heavy water and centrifuges. Using essentially the same two basic approaches to manufacture heavy water, the fractional distillation of water and catalytic exchange reactions using hydrogen and water, the Americans started building heavy water plants in early 1943 and put them into operation by January of the following year. The catalytic exchange plant was situated at a mining company in British Columbia, Canada, in order to take advantage of electrolytic hydrogen produced as a byproduct. The DuPont company built three fractional distillation plants in the United States. By the end of March 1945, when the German uranium effort halted, the Manhattan Project had produced almost 20 metric tons of heavy water, dwarfing the German effort. The Americans had plenty of electricity and did not have to worry about their plants being attacked.[101]

In the spring of 1943, even though it appeared that it would take two years to produce enough heavy water to construct a nuclear reactor large enough for plutonium production, there were so many uncertainties related to the duration of the war and the production of materials that scientists in the Manhattan Project decided to build a small laboratory-scale heavy water reactor at the Argonne lab in Illinois. By November of that year the program was limited to a small reactor capable of producing 250 kilowatts of power. By May 15, 1944, the Argonne uranium and heavy water reactor went online. Similar to the scientists' experience with Fermi's first graphite and heavy water reactor, the Argonne reactor achieved a self-sustaining chain reaction before all the uranium had been added. The Germans never got to the point of designing a nuclear reactor from an engineering perspective. Even if the Haigerloch uranium machine had succeeded, it would probably have been the second, as well as the second best, of its type.[102]

In 1946 Jesse Beams, whose research Wilhelm Groth had used as a foundation when developing centrifuges, reviewed the wartime German work. Beams noted with approval that the Germans had concluded that centrifuges, despite being expensive, probably had the best chance of successfully separating out uranium 235. The air war had prevented this research from getting beyond the experimental stage but Groth and colleagues had made some headway both with theory and experiment. By the end of the war the Germans were still far behind the American centrifuge effort, which was effectively ended at the end of 1943 when production plants using gaseous diffusion and electromagnetism started to come online.[103]

The first samples of enriched uranium were sent to Los Alamos in February 1944. When the first large shipment of uranium 235 arrived the following

142   The Bomb

August, it appeared unlikely that enough uranium 235 would be produced in time to use in a wartime weapon but by January 1945 production was increasing steadily.[104] The uranium 235 "gadget," nicknamed "Little Boy," used a gun design, whereby one piece of fissile material would be shot at the other in order to detonate the critical mass. The design was finished in early May, the first uranium 235 insert was completed and tested by July 25, and the first atomic bomb was dropped on Hiroshima twelve days later. Despite great efforts, the Americans only managed to build one uranium 235 bomb by the end of the war.[105]

Once plutonium production began, it would produce fissile material significantly faster than isotope separation. Following Fermi's successful demonstration of a sustained chain reaction, Manhattan Project scientists began building a second graphite and uranium nuclear reactor in Clinton, Tennessee as a pilot plant for plutonium production. The much larger Clinton reactor consisted of a graphite cube perforated by horizontal channels, with cylindrical uranium slugs covered by gas-tight aluminum casings that could be slid in and out of the reactor. Operations began in November 1943. By the following March grams of plutonium had been sent to Los Alamos. The first plutonium production reactor in Hanford, Washington began in September 1944 and by early 1945 had delivered kilograms of plutonium.[106]

During the summer of 1944 the Manhattan Project was suddenly faced with an existential crisis. A group of scientists tested the plutonium from Clinton and were shocked to observe that, in contrast to the plutonium that had been produced by cyclotrons, the reactor-plutonium had a very high rate of spontaneous fissions and would probably cause a premature detonation in a gun design. The only alternative was a design that would require a perfectly symmetrical implosion, something that appeared very difficult, if not impossible. Oppenheimer quickly refocused the efforts of the Los Alamos laboratory on the primary technical objective of developing a plutonium implosion assembly.

The relatively small existing implosion research group was expanded into a well-coordinated, multidisciplinary big science research effort involving hundreds of workers distributed across more than fourteen different groups. By February 1945 the scientists had selected an implosion design, the plutonium hemispheres for the Trinity test were delivered on July 2, and the "Fat Man" gadget successfully detonated in the desert of New Mexico two weeks later. The plutonium hemispheres for the next implosion bomb were completed on July 23 and incorporated into the atomic bomb dropped seventeen days later on Nagasaki. The war in Europe, of course, had ended months ago.[107]

A comparison of the German working group with the Manhattan Project reveals both the great differences in scale as well as the destructive effect of the war on research and development in Germany. The sudden challenge presented by the discovery of spontaneous fission and the herculean American

The War is Lost

efforts needed to overcome it make very clear that the small number of scientists working with relatively modest resources in Germany under the National Socialist regime could not have built atomic bombs.

The German understanding of how to build an atomic bomb was commensurate with the progress they had made and the task they had undertaken. Of course they did not know exactly how to build an atomic bomb but the Americans also did not understand this until early 1945. But let us give the peers of Heisenberg and his colleagues the last word. Alvin Weinberg and Lothar Nordheim, who had worked on nuclear reactors during the war, were given a few of the German uranium machine reports.

Generally we would say that their approach was in no wise inferior to ours; in some respects it was superior ... from the few reports we have seen, we would say their understanding of the principles is comparable to ours.... The Germans knew how to design a lattice which will work. From the practical standpoint this is all that matters....

The general impression from the German reports is that they were on the right track and that their thinking and developments paralleled ours to a surprising extent. The fact that they did not achieve the chain reaction is primarily due to their lack of sufficient amounts of heavy water....

It is also fairly clear that the total German effort was on a very considerably smaller scale than the American effort. This may be due to the strained German economy or to the less favorable attitude of their government. The fact remains that an independent group of scientists, of much smaller size than ours, operating under much more adverse conditions achieved so much.[108]

Part II

Living with the Bomb

7 Oversimplifications

[Heisenberg was] … surrounded by a group of scientists who hardly ever doubted his judgment…. None of his associates ever seemed to have understood that the real solution lay far beyond academic laboratory effort and involved huge industrial capacities…. In any case, their notion of a uranium bomb was so far off the right track that it could never have succeeded….

I feel certain that Heisenberg would have been one of the leading figures on the atomic energy project, if he had been working on our side. In Germany, Heisenberg worked in a vacuum, the only atmosphere present being the one created by his own ability. Even in the case of a great scientist like Heisenberg, this ability was not enough.

Samuel Goudsmit in "Secrecy or Science" (1946).[1]

The Alsos Mission

In 1944 the American Manhattan Project sent an intelligence-gathering unit to Europe to search for, and if necessary, neutralize any threat of a German atomic bomb. This Alsos Mission was jointly led by Colonel Boris Pash and the physicist Samuel Goudsmit (see Figure 7.1). A well-respected Dutch physicist who had become a naturalized American citizen, Goudsmit personally knew some of the scientists likely to be involved in the German effort and had up until then been involved in RADAR research during the war, so that he could not betray much about the Manhattan Project if captured. He was also Jewish.

The Alsos Mission followed behind the advancing Allied armies. In Strasbourg, just west of the Rhine river in the province Alsace that Germany had seized from France in 1940, Goudsmit and his colleagues found the first real evidence of German uranium work. Karl-Heinz Höcker and Carl Friedrich von Weizsäcker had already fled from Strasbourg to Werner Heisenberg's group in Hechingen. The uncooperative physicist Rudolf Fleischmann was captured, along with papers and correspondence from the institutes he and Weizsäcker directed. Almost immediately Goudsmit recognized that the German uranium work was in a very preliminary stage and very far from an atomic bomb.[2] However, he also found misleading reports from Fleischmann,

148 Living with the Bomb

Figure 7.1 Samuel Goudsmit during the Alsos Mission.
Source: American Institute of Physics, Emilio Segrè Visual Archives, Goudsmit, Samuel B37.

who had worked on isotope separation in Walther Bothe's institute and was a peripheral figure in the working group.

In a 1942 report arguing for support to build a cyclotron, Fleischmann mentioned uranium machines, both for energy production and as a weapon: "It may also be possible by means of rapid ignition to give the uranium machine the character of a buzz bomb [a crude early cruise missile]." A chemist interrogated at Strasbourg also told the Alsos Mission that he had heard from an inventor (neither one had anything to do with the nuclear physics working group) that the minimum weight of an atomic bomb was 8 tons. This improbable estimate was reinforced when Goudsmit found a draft report Walter Gerlach had written in January describing progress made on the uranium machine but without mentioning bombs, which Goudsmit took as evidence that the Germans had not understood how an atomic bomb would work. This is the origin of Goudsmit's mistaken belief that the Germans had conceived an atomic bomb as a uranium machine gone out of control.[3]

The Alsos Mission rounded up the majority of the most important working group scientists as quickly as possible. They reached Stadtilm just four days

Oversimplifications 149

after Kurt Diebner had been forced to leave under SS guard, finding revealing documents, parts of uranium machines, and a lot of equipment. Three days after Heisenberg had left, American and French troops entered Hechingen. The Germans had hidden the heavy water in gasoline drums, buried the uranium, and sunk the documents in a cesspool. Shortly thereafter Alsos personnel arrived and began interrogating Karl Wirtz and Weizsäcker. The two physicists quickly realized that there was no longer any point in keeping secrets and led the Americans to the hidden materials.[4] Subsequently Diebner, Gerlach, and Heisenberg were picked up in Bavaria.[5]

After navigating the dangerous political and ideological shoals of the Third Reich for years, Heisenberg was both relieved and ready to start a new chapter in his life. As he wrote to Elisabeth the day after he left:

In my feelings the misfortune of the past time and the sight of the endless destruction are mixed with the intense happiness at being able to begin anew and once again rebuild.... I personally feel that, for the first time in twelve years, I can truly do something for Germany and am as fresh and lively as I have not been in years. Hopefully fate will show that I am up to my task.

Two days later Heisenberg wrote his brother-in-law in England with similar sentiments:

If during the negotiations that will come I can do something to help Germany be rebuilt, first and foremost in the scientific sector, then that is a goal worth a great deal of sacrifice.... Germany looks, as you know, grim. All of the large cities, with the exception of Heidelberg, are up to 80 percent destroyed. Moreover the mentality of the people has been hopelessly twisted by twelve years of propaganda. But it does not help to complain about it, one has to rebuild again from the beginning.[6]

Goudsmit and Heisenberg had known each other for many years. Heisenberg had visited Goudsmit several times, including a trip to the United States just before the start of World War II. The two physicists came together again in Heidelberg. As Heisenberg described it to Elisabeth, his meeting with Goudsmit was "friendly as if the last seven years had not happened. I feel inwardly and outwardly better than I have in years. I am full of hope and adventurousness for the future. Naturally there will be setbacks but that should not make one crazy."[7] In an interview in the 1960s, Heisenberg recalled that he had asked Goudsmit whether the Americans had a program like the German uranium project and received the clear answer that they had done nothing along those lines.[8] In her memoir from the 1980s, Elisabeth Heisenberg recalled that Heisenberg had told her that "with a smile, Goudsmit [had] answered that there had been more important things to do during the war, and that there had been no efforts in that direction."[9]

In 1947 Goudsmit published his account of the meeting while promoting a forthcoming book in *Life* magazine:

150   Living with the Bomb

I greeted my old friend and former colleague cordially. Purely on the impulse of the moment I said, "Wouldn't you want to come to America now and work with us?" But he was still too impressed by his own importance and that of his work, to which he ascribed his internment.

"No, I don't want to leave," he said. "Germany needs me. If American scientists wish to learn about the uranium problem, I shall be glad to show them the results of our researches if they come to my laboratory."

It was sad and ironic to hear him say this, when I was aware how much more we knew about the problem than he did. But I did not enlighten him. I merely thanked him for his offer and left him secure in the belief that his work was ahead of ours.[10]

After World War II nuclear fission did appear to have great future promise for Germany, or for that matter any other country. For a short period of time from May to August of 1945, the combination of Germany's catastrophic defeat, the apparent willingness of Allied authorities to help rebuild the devastated nation, and the false impression that they were ahead of the Americans led Heisenberg and others to believe that they could leverage their wartime work to benefit their country.

Perhaps most surprisingly, Goudsmit did not question Heisenberg and his colleagues thoroughly about their work. Weizsäcker recalled that he had been willing to tell the Americans everything but Goudsmit spoke with him for only one hour and appeared uninterested, leaving Weizsäcker feeling unhappy and slighted.[11] Goudsmit probably did not interrogate them because he had already discovered what he wanted to find, apparent evidence that the Nazis had ruined German science and the German uranium work was unsound.

The German hope that the Americans and British would be very interested in their work lasted until the news of the atomic bomb. The profoundly surprised and sometimes incoherent reaction of the Germans at Farm Hall to Hiroshima was in part due to Goudsmit's deception. Indeed Heisenberg complained bitterly that Goudsmit had "lied to him very cleverly."[12] Goudsmit had been an intelligence officer in the service of an enemy power and had to act as he did, including deceiving his colleagues, while Heisenberg, who had carefully survived the most dangerous last years of the Third Reich, had now lowered his guard. However, afterward, when Goudsmit was no longer in the employ of the Army or US government, the physicist did not recognize that he had in fact helped create this response and instead used it as evidence of German arrogance and incompetence.

Keeping Control

Back in Germany

After the atomic bomb the Farm Hall detainees now understood why they had been interned but not why they were still being held. The desire to return home

Oversimplifications

151

and reunite with their families dominated their lives. On the day of the attack on Hiroshima, Heisenberg wrote his wife that:

> If I was not separated from you [his family], then I would be doing wonderfully here.... The only thing that depresses me very much is my concern for you. I have a very bad conscience, that now in this worst time I am not with you, but I cannot do anything about that. Please write to me in great detail about how you are doing, whether you have food, whether you have anyone helping you, where mother lives and whether you all are healthy.[13]

Two weeks later Elisabeth wrote back, asking Werner to "brace his heart" for very sad news. HIs mother fell, then lost her mind, and died. The children were all healthy, even if they had few vegetables to eat. Elisabeth had become very thin but was now calmer and once again was more confident about their future.[14]

The mood of the detainees brightened considerably once it was clear that their release was imminent. The Americans forbade any return to the French zone of occupation, and of course the Soviet zone was out of the question, but as part of their policy to use Germans to rebuild the country the British occupation authorities subsequently made great efforts to make Heisenberg and his colleagues as comfortable as possible in postwar Germany. On December 7, 1945 the official order was given for the detainees' return to Germany. The British wardens had quite often been both amused and exasperated by the conduct of their charges, so that it was with considerable humor that they described how Wirtz hauled down his colors. Even though they had all cursed their warden, Wirtz admitted, it would be wise to stay on his good side. They did not know when they might have another use for him.[15]

The Farm Hall scientists were returned first of all to the British zone of occupation, with Erich Bagge, Horst Korsching, Otto Hahn, Heisenberg, Max von Laue, and Wirtz settling down in the relatively untouched city of Göttingen, where the Kaiser Wilhelm Society and the Kaiser Wilhelm Institute for Physics were reestablished as the Max Planck Society (*Max-Planck-Gesellschaft*, MPG) and Max Planck Institute for Physics (*Max Planck Institut für Physik*, MPIfP) respectively. As soon as Heisenberg was back in Germany, he wrote Elisabeth that, because she had probably been asked what he had to do with the atomic bomb, he was sending her an excerpt from a letter from Weizsäcker to his wife that portrayed this problem exactly and correctly.

> We were spared the difficult moral decision, whether we should build an atomic bomb. The technical and organizational possibilities that we had in Germany would not have allowed the effort that the Americans invested in this problem. We restricted ourselves to preliminary work for the more modest task of building a heat-producing machine, moving along paths that clearly were similar to the ones followed in America, and by the end of the war were close to final success. We thereby did what was within our power to ensure that our country could participate in an inevitable technical development.[16]

152   Living with the Bomb

The legacies of National Socialism overshadowed life in Germany. Heisenberg critiqued the beginning of denazification:

We had to fill out questionnaires that, except for the sign [swastika], are almost identical to those of the Third Reich. I was reminded of the stupid joke from many years ago, which assumed that the questionnaires of the Fourth Reich would contain the questions: were you in a concentration camp? If not, why not? The first question is in fact in another form included; only the second is missing.

Elisabeth was shocked by what was happening in the East. It was "monstrous" that "once again revenge is being taken on innocent people." In part as retribution for murderous German occupation policies during the war, as Soviet troops pushed to the west, some of them killed, raped, and robbed civilians, driving them back to Germany. After the war, new regimes in Poland, Czechoslovakia, and other countries forcibly expelled Germans, again sometimes violently. Elisabeth had believed that Germans were "the only ones incapable of thinking really reasonably, honorably, and humanely." But it was clearly no different in the rest of the world and had probably never been any different.[17]

Elisabeth asked Werner whether they had the choice of staying in Germany or going to America. It was obviously Heisenberg's decision to make, and he had thought about it carefully. Although it was clear that America was the center of scientific life and working conditions for Heisenberg would be much worse in Germany, he was not needed in America where there were many other capable physicists, and intellectual life had to resume in Germany.[18] Heisenberg thought that he would get used to Göttingen. The fertile landscape was in some respects more lively than Bavaria, and the people were hardly as "self-serving and pig-headed" as the Bavarian peasants. But sometimes he was homesick.

I think about the immaculate beauty of the view from our terrace and I would have loved once to have experienced the entire course of the year, spring, summer, and autumn up there. You know, such an October, where the fog begins after the pass, and the lake is illuminated in a blaze of color like Italian lakes. But one cannot have everything. In the end I have to do my work and we will have it better in Göttingen than most other people.

Elisabeth replied that she was getting used to the idea that they would end up in Munich but pointed out that he would not be happy there now. Their house was confiscated and "Munich is dead and dismal, especially for someone who once loved it as much as you." But one day they would move there and "you will have your mountains again."[19]

Goudsmit's Crusade

In an August 1945 letter to the influential American science policymaker Vannevar Bush, Goudsmit gave his suggestions for US policy towards German

Oversimplifications 153

science. While it was "nonsense" to attempt to prohibit scientific research or to destroy laboratories, Goudsmit thought it best to let the Germans solve their own problems regarding the revival of science and scientific industry. "Let them reopen their universities and research institutions when they can do so without outside material help. Let them publish their results again if they can find the paper and presses." Americans should adopt the attitude that German scientific developments were insignificant as far as they were concerned. "The rather common worship of German science, even after its rapid decline, is detrimental to our own progress and development."[20]

Shortly after he returned to the USA, Goudsmit began publishing short popular articles on the German uranium work.[21] Goudsmit rejected out of hand one of the major findings of this author's book, that the conditions of the steadily deteriorating war decisively influenced the progress of the German uranium work. Moreover he criticized the Germans for realistically concluding that it would not be possible for them to build an atomic bomb in Germany during the war, blaming this on their "lack of insight."[22] Even the German hopes that the progress they made on the uranium machine might be beneficial for Germany after the war was portrayed by Goudsmit as sinister: "The main motive ... was the firm belief that Germany could win the peace if she again dominated the world of science, irrespective of the outcome of the military struggle."[23]

Perhaps one of the most damning claims by Goudsmit, for it made the Germans appear arrogant, was his assertion that the Germans believed that they were ahead of the Americans when it came to uranium, even though he admitted that they "knew practically nothing about Allied developments, aside from what they picked up in the summer of 1939."[24] There is no evidence from the war period to corroborate such a belief, rather there are several documented cases where German scientists warned that the Americans, with their far greater resources, were working on the same problem.

Goudsmit had two sources for his claim. During the last desperate months of the war, when the scientists had to fear sudden conscription and sacrifice as cannon fodder, Gerlach's reports dangled the possibility that they might still be ahead of the Americans in front of powerful Nazi patrons in order to secure support. Goudsmit took these statements at face value.[25] Goudsmit's other source was Heisenberg's statement that Allied scientists would be interested in the work done in his laboratory but Heisenberg said this after Goudsmit had told him that the Americans had not worked on uranium during the war. Goudsmit not only took both sources out of context, he embellished them: "The remarkable thing about the Germans is that throughout the war they believed that they were ahead of our effort along those lines. Not until the news broke that the atomic bomb had been dropped did they realize that they were not ahead but that they were behind.... They were convinced that they were far ahead of the Allies."[26]

154   Living with the Bomb

Although Goudsmit had spent a year following the trail of the German atomic bomb and was now devoting a considerable amount of time spreading the gospel of how the Nazis had ruined German science in general, and the uranium research in particular, this was only a vehicle to achieve his main goal: stopping and reversing restrictions on scientific freedom and communication in America. The effective mobilization of science for war, coupled with the approaching Cold War, had ignited a vigorous debate in the United States over civilian or military control of scientific research. Goudsmit sought to contribute to this debate by using the German uranium project as a cautionary tale of what can happen when politics and ideology interfere with science.

According to Goudsmit, the principal factor in scientific progress is the free exchange of information among the world's scientists and engineers. Isolation, on the other hand, can lead to stagnation, error, and decay. The wartime restrictions in the United States placed on the exchange of scientific information as well as on scientists' ability to travel and attend international meetings should be ended. The benefits of science and technology, Goudsmit added, have been so great that only a "Nazi-like regime, run by lunatics, would want to do anything that would put an end to them."[27]

Telling Their Side of the Story

In the waning months of the Third Reich, with the help of Albert Speer some physicists founded a new physics journal, the *Physikalische Blätter*, which served as a news organ for the physics community. As an industrial physicist, its editor Ernst Brüche was relatively independent of powerful academic physicists like Heisenberg. Brüche had read Goudsmit's article "Secrecy or Science" and decided to include an excerpt in German translation in the *Blätter*.[28] Heisenberg and Weizsäcker had wanted to publish an account of their uranium work but the British authorities initially did not allow it.[29]

Weizsäcker advised Heisenberg that they had no way of stopping Brüche from publishing and "further I have the feeling that in the long run we will not be able to avoid a discussion of the questions broached by Goudsmit." For this reason it was important that they be allowed to "say for ourselves what we think of these things."[30] Since the British authorities now granted permission, Heisenberg drafted a manuscript of his article on the wartime uranium project and circulated it among a few scientists who had played a prominent role, noting that he no longer had the wartime reports and asking his colleagues to make sure that the work of their institutes was cited correctly.[31]

Bothe thought that the article was excellent, with two exceptions. He did not think that Heisenberg had given enough credit to Diebner and his coworkers, and was "not so convinced that our absorption cross section [measurement] for pure carbon was so false."[32] Heisenberg softened his language but

Oversimplifications

in the published version still suggested that Bothe had made a mistake that held back the German project:

The absorption cross section for neutrons in the technically purest electrographite was measured in the Kaiser Wilhelm Institute in Heidelberg ... and from this the behavior of pure carbon was inferred; it appeared that, according to the state of knowledge at the time, even the purest carbon was unsuitable for manufacturing a uranium burner, while as is known carbon was applied with great success in the United States.[33]

Bothe's measurement was the only error in the working group to which Heisenberg was willing to admit. In contrast, it is striking and perhaps telling that a very consequential mistake for which Heisenberg's collaborator Wirtz was partially responsible, allowing some of the limited heavy water to become adulterated and then failing to purify it, was never mentioned after the war.

Overall Heisenberg's article was a clear, succinct, fair, and very accurate account of the wartime work. A German atomic bomb was impossible because of the strained war economy as of 1942, the damaging effects of Allied bombing, and what he called the "psychological assumptions of the leadership" (it is striking how reluctant Heisenberg appeared to be after the war to mention the National Socialists by name) who as late as 1942 still expected a swift end to the war. In order to get the necessary support for an industrial-scale project, the German scientists would have had to make promises they could not have kept. Since an atomic bomb appeared out of the question, they concentrated their efforts on the energy-producing uranium machine.[34]

However, at the end of his article, Heisenberg moved beyond his factual account to a subjective analysis of their motives by introducing the concept of "keeping control," thereby implying that he and his colleagues had deliberately refrained from building atomic bombs for the National Socialist regime.

From the very beginning, German physicists had consciously striven to keep control of the project, and had used their influence as experts to direct the work into the channels which have been mapped in the foregoing report. In the upshot they were spared the decision as to whether or not they should aim at producing atomic bombs.[35]

Although the published version is suggestive enough, the corresponding passage in the draft version went still further:

For the researchers who worked on the uranium enterprise, this decision [not to attempt the construction of atomic bombs] also had a different, human side. These physicists understood the great responsibility carried by a person who can unleash such natural forces and from the very beginning had worked consciously and with much effort towards keeping the control of the enterprise in their hands. They also had to consider from the very beginning the difficult question, whether the thing is good for which the greatest natural forces should be deployed. External circumstances took the difficult moral decision, whether they should manufacture atomic bombs, out of their hands.[36]

156   Living with the Bomb

Although there is no clear and compelling evidence, one way or the other, from before the end of the war that Heisenberg and his colleagues were thinking about such moral questions, they certainly were now.

Alsos

In his article, Heisenberg had suggestively juxtaposed the American and German projects:

In the United States, the final decision was taken to go for the production of atomic bombs, with an outlay that must have amounted to a considerable fraction of the total American war expenditure; in Germany an attempt was made to solve the problem of the prime mover driven by nuclear energy, with an outlay of perhaps a thousandth part of the American.[37]

Goudsmit was infuriated because Heisenberg had implied that "it was a deliberate decision of the German scientists to refrain from making atom bombs."[38] In response Goudsmit wrote a book, *Alsos*, expanding upon his recent articles and designed to bring his arguments to a much wider audience.[39]

Failures

When Goudsmit described the Germans' skeptical reaction to the news of Hiroshima (this was clearly from Farm Hall, although Goudsmit did not state this explicitly) he revealed that "some of the younger men hit upon a brilliant rationalization of their failure," turning it to their advantage by denying that they had ever wanted to make nuclear weapons, telling the world that "German science never, never would have consented to work on such a horrid thing as the atom bomb." This would become the "new theme song" of German science: "Germany worked on the uranium problem for peaceful uses only; the Allies, for purposes of destruction." While it was true that the Germans had worked on a uranium machine and not an atomic bomb, this was *true only because they failed to understand the difference between the machine and the bomb*. The bomb is what they were after. And what the whole world knows now about plutonium, *the German scientists did not know – until they were told about it after Hiroshima*."[40]

While Goudsmit accepted that while the Germans knew that an atomic bomb could be made with pure uranium 235, in *Alsos*, as well as several articles and letters to colleagues, he claimed that they, and in particular Heisenberg, had "never thought of using plutonium in the bomb" and that the German idea of the bomb was "quite different from ours and more primitive": a uranium machine "in which the chain reaction went so fast that it would produce an explosion." The German bomb was "merely an explosive pile and would have

Oversimplifications 157

proved a fizz compared to the real bomb." Goudsmit went so far as to explain the initial Germans confusion in Farm Hall because they "still believed that what we had dropped on Hiroshima was a complete uranium pile."[41]

Although the Germans lagged very far behind the Americans and were very far removed from being able to construct an atomic bomb, what Goudsmit claimed in *Alsos* about the Germans' technical understanding of how an atomic bomb would work was simply wrong. Weizsäcker's 1940 report and 1941 patent application demonstrated an understanding that plutonium (element 94) could be manufactured in a nuclear reactor (uranium machine) and used as fissionable material in a bomb. The text of Heisenberg's February 1942 talk before the Reich Research Council, which Goudsmit had in his files, clearly conceived of atomic bombs as fast-neutron chain reactions in pure masses of either uranium 235 or plutonium.[42] Aside from a few preliminary analyses by Paul Müller that were superseded by Weizsäcker's work on transuranic elements[43] and despite Fleischmann's 1942 report, they never conceived of a bomb as a runaway reactor.

The Armorers of the Nazis

After the war in the United States a new scientific journal appeared, the *Bulletin of the Atomic Scientists*, founded by a group of former Manhattan Project scientists concerned, like Goudsmit, about issues of science policy. Philip Morrison, a Manhattan Project scientist who had personally participated in the bombings of Hiroshima and Nagasaki, reviewed *Alsos* for the *Bulletin*. Goudsmit had described how German science had "atrophied because of its arrogance and complacency, its narrow political domination, with the barring of many of its greatest men from work or even from the land itself, and its increasing emphasis on technology," which were errors Goudsmit and Morrison worried the United States might repeat. Turning to Heisenberg's claim that the German scientists' motivations had been peaceful since "they wanted not bombs but merely a pile," Morrison agreed with Goudsmit that this was a rationalization:

No different from their Allied counterparts, the German scientists worked for the military as best their circumstances allowed. But the difference, which it will never be possible to forgive, is that they worked for the cause of Himmler and Auschwitz, for the burners of books and the takers of hostages. The community of science will be long delayed in welcoming the armorers of the Nazis, even if their work was not successful.[44]

Following Goudsmit, Morrison also made an exception for the "brave and good men" like Laue, who remained aloof from the German war effort and resisted the Nazis in the sphere of science.[45] Both in letters to colleagues and publications, Goudsmit highlighted the political and moral failings of most German scientists by exaggerating how well Hahn and especially Laue had behaved during the

158 Living with the Bomb

Third Reich. This came close to a deification of Laue as the exception that proves the rule. In fact both Hahn and Laue had also made concessions to the National Socialist authorities, despite also opposing some NS colleagues and policies.[46]

Ironically both Hahn and Laue also worked very hard in the postwar period to exonerate and rehabilitate almost all of their colleagues, including some with problematic Nazi pasts. This included squelching the voices of scientists who had been the victims of the Third Reich like Ursula Martius Franklin, a young physicist who survived a forced labor camp during the war.[47] In a postwar letter to his son Theodore, Laue claimed that during the war German scientists and engineers did not act differently from their English, French, and American colleagues. Although in response these colleagues might say, "we fought against Hitler, you for him," Laue was "not certain that those who make this accusation would have done differently, if they had by chance been born in Germany." Laue believed that, while the "great criminals" needed to be taken care of one way or the other, there should be a "GREAT AMNESTY" (Laue's emphasis) for the others. Indeed he went so far as to argue that, whether through law or social understanding, accusations against specific people for what they did during the Third Reich should be forbidden.[48]

It was therefore perhaps no surprise that Laue was the German scientist who responded to Morrison's review. Noting that he had not read Goudsmit's book, Laue attacked Morrison for his "monstrous suggestion that German scientists as a body worked for Himmler and Auschwitz." Laue then argued that it was not always possible for a scientist to avoid war service. Indeed by putting their institutes at the service of the war effort, the directors could shield many younger scientists from a much more direct mobilization for the war and protect "political suspects from concentration camps or worse," including some "non-Aryan Germans." Would severe critics like Morrison describe such cases as being the "armorers of Himmler and Auschwitz?" Laue rhetorically asked. Finally Laue denounced publications like Morrison's review because they "keep alive hate."[49]

Morrison responded that Laue had misrepresented what he had written. "I said in the review of which he writes that these men worked, not for Himmler but for Himmler's cause, the victory of a National Socialist Germany." Turning to the directors of large institutes that Laue had defended, Morrison noted that

many of the most able and distinguished men of German science, moved doubtless by sentiments of national loyalty, by traditional response to the authority over them, and by simple fear, worked for the advantage of the Nazi state. These men were in fact the armorers of the Nazis.... It is not for the reviewer to judge how great was their peril; it is certainly not for him to imply that he could have been braver or wiser than they. But it was sentiments like theirs, weakness like theirs, and fear like theirs which helped bring Germans for a decade to be the slaves of an inhuman tyranny, which has wrecked Europe, and in its day attacked the very name of culture. Are we to forget the tragic failure of those German men of learning?[50]

Oversimplifications 159

It is interesting to note that in the *Blätter* Brüche published only Laue's spirited defense of German scientists, containing his misrepresentation of Morrison's review, so that German readers got a very different impression of the debate than their American counterparts reading the *Bulletin*. In the same issue containing Morrison's response to Laue, the editor of the *Bulletin* Eugene Rabinowitch appended a comment. Noting that Laue had a right to a "respectful hearing" from American scientists, Rabinowitch extended Morrison's criticism to "some men of great prominence in science, whose apparently unreserved collaboration with the criminals in power undoubtedly helped to subdue the qualms of many a rank-and-file German scientist."[51] Although no one was mentioning his name, they all were thinking of Heisenberg.

Perhaps an Oversimplification

Waldemar Kaempffert, an American with a very German-sounding name, reviewed both Goudsmit's book and Heisenberg's article as the science editor of the *New York Times*. While Kaempffert found Heisenberg's account convincing and objective, he described Goudsmit's book as a "popular, somewhat emotional and therefore biased account" that portrayed the Germans as conceited and arrogant and Heisenberg in particular as a "sly villain." Kaempffert extended Heisenberg's argument by including examples from the American Manhattan Project. Along with the destruction of the Norwegian heavy water plant, the lack of anything like the massive Tennessee Valley Authority or Columbia River hydroelectric plants in Germany and the other demands on the German war economy forced the German uranium work to proceed on a small scale.[52] As Kaempffert put it in a subsequent letter to Goudsmit, if the German authorities had put the necessary industrial resources at the disposal of the German scientists working on uranium, then this "would have been the equivalent of losing the war."[53]

Goudsmit responded in the *New York Times* by repeating his claim that the Germans had not understood how an atomic bomb would work and criticizing Heisenberg for not blaming "the Nazis for their fatal interference in matters of science."[54] In a private letter to the science editor Goudsmit expressed surprise that Kaempffert had been "taken in" by Heisenberg's report but did reveal that his description in *Alsos* of Heisenberg's offer to share the German work on uranium problem with Allied scientists was "not clearly written." Whereas the passage in *Alsos* portrays this as evidence of Heisenberg's conviction that the Germans were ahead of the Americans, in fact Goudsmit now admitted that Heisenberg had meant that American colleagues were welcome to work again at his institute on sabbatical leave or on fellowships, as had been the case before the war.[55]

160   Living with the Bomb

The Goudsmit–Heisenberg Dialogue

In late September of 1947 Heisenberg wrote Goudsmit directly, noting that he had read several of his articles about the German uranium work during the war. As far as the technical work was concerned, Heisenberg believed that his December 1946 *Naturwissenschaften* article contained the essentials, perhaps more precisely than Goudsmit had known at the time. Heisenberg had the impression that Goudsmit perhaps did not understand "the details of our work and especially the psychological situation in Germany." One point in particular, Heisenberg argued, must be the result of a misunderstanding: Goudsmit's assumption that the Germans had conceived of the uranium work to some extent as a "race with America" and "if not the war, at least wanted to win the peace."

Heisenberg reminded Goudsmit that in Heidelberg he had told him that the Germans believed that the Americans, with their incomparably better infrastructure, would be able to solve the uranium problem quicker and better if they decided to do so. The Germans never thought about a real race but did consider the possibility that the Americans would not even take up this problem because it appeared to the Germans that the chances of it affecting the war were very small. "Therefore when you told me in Heidelberg that the physicists in America had essentially only worked for the war effort and did not take up atomic questions (naturally at that time you had to give me this answer), this appeared plausible to me, and we were then pleased that we had apparently performed useful work for the peace."

Heisenberg recognized that it must be very difficult for Goudsmit to empathize with their psychological situation during the war. On one hand, it was very clear that a victory of National Socialism in Europe would have terrible consequences but on the other hand precisely because of the hate that National Socialism had planted, the German scientists could not have great hopes about the consequences of a total defeat. "Such a position leads automatically to a more passive and modest conduct, whereby one is content to help on a small scale or to save what is possible, and furthermore to do work that might perhaps be useful later."[56]

Goudsmit responded, noting that he had in the meantime written a "small rather popular book which contains a few sections you may not like." In America and probably everywhere, people were reformulating the relationship between government and science and Goudsmit was determined that the United States not make the same mistakes that Germany had. Goudsmit was shocked and surprised by some omissions and understatements in Heisenberg's article, that appeared mainly intended as a defense of German physicists under Hitler. It sounded as if Heisenberg was afraid to blame the Nazis for their "deliberate and stupid frustration of pure science.... Does one still have to

Oversimplifications 161

make a compromise in Germany? Are the Nazis still so powerful that you dare not openly accuse their doctrine for being responsible for the rapid decline of once superior German science?"[57]

Of the many other things Goudsmit wanted to talk about with Heisenberg, he chose only one, "the most difficult one to write about," the "middle position" taken by many of the Germans, including Heisenberg. When he found out about the attempts to compromise with the Nazis, Goudsmit was "deeply disappointed" and most surprised that Heisenberg had not seen that such a compromise was impossible. Goudsmit now must have shocked Heisenberg in turn by including copies of letters he had found from the SS leader Heinrich Himmler to Reinhard Heydrich, his second-in-command, and to Heisenberg himself. Also reproduced in *Alsos*, these letters made clear that Heisenberg had asked Himmler to intervene in order to stop political attacks on him by the physicist Johannes Stark, and that Himmler had agreed. Why, Goudsmit asked, did Heisenberg believe that he could work with someone like Himmler?[58]

In *Alsos*, Goudsmit painted an unflattering picture of Heisenberg. First of all Goudsmit noted that his German colleague had defended Einstein's theory of relativity in the leading Nazi newspaper and was severely criticized for doing so. But in Goudsmit's telling, even this had a dark side:

Although he fought courageously against Nazi excesses and especially Nazi stupidities, his motives were not as noble as one might have hoped from such a great man. He fought the Nazis not because they were bad but because they were bad for Germany, or at least for German science. His principal concern was that Germany might lose its lead in science, especially physics. That is why he strenuously objected to the exile of German Jewish physicists.

Goudsmit similarly interpreted Heisenberg's decision to stay in Germany in a negative way:

Heisenberg had many offers of positions in the United States. He was so convinced of his own important role in Germany, however, that he consistently refused to emigrate. He was always convinced that Germany needed great leadership and that he could be one of the great leaders.... His extreme nationalism led him astray, however, during the war. He was so convinced of the greatness of Germany, that he considered the Nazis' efforts to make Germany powerful of more importance than their excesses. He still was stupidly optimistic in his belief that these excesses would eventually stop after Germany had won world domination.[59]

It is striking how diametrically opposed Goudsmit and Heisenberg's perceptions of the latter's actions and motives were. Where Heisenberg saw himself sacrificing, at considerable personal risk, personal security, and professional opportunities for the good of Germany, Goudsmit saw an arrogant nationalist, rejecting out of hand the possibility that working for the benefit of German science could be a positive goal.

162   Living with the Bomb

What Goudsmit really wanted from Heisenberg was the last thing his German colleague would have been willing to do. Now, not during the war, Goudsmit argued, was the time for the more modest conduct Heisenberg had mentioned in his letter. Heisenberg and "some of the greater men among you" should "show their real greatness, swallow their pride, and courageously tell the world of the German mistakes as a warning for the future." Based on his experiences and admitting his own errors of judgment, Heisenberg was supposed to describe: "the hopeless fight with the opposition among colleagues and in the government, the decline of interest in pure science, the clash of science with Nazi dogma, the ultimate death of German science."[60]

Heisenberg wrote Goudsmit a second letter in early January. In contrast to his American colleague, Heisenberg found most important: "the question, whether the German physicists had known that an atomic bomb functioned with fast neutrons and that atomic bombs can be manufactured from uranium 235 or plutonium 239." The first point was basically taken for granted after the publication from Niels Bohr and John Archibald Wheeler, "whereby it is completely clear to me that the actual construction of the atomic bomb required the solution of some difficult physical questions that you [the Americans] solved and, for the reasons already given, we did not take up." As far as plutonium was concerned, although Weizsäcker did not know when he wrote his 1940 report whether the stable element caused by neutron capture was 93 or 94, it was again clear from the Bohr–Wheeler article that the transuranic would be fissionable like uranium 235.

Next Heisenberg referred to his February 1942 talk before the Reich Research Council and the diagram comparing the neutron increase in pure uranium 235 with that in a uranium machine composed of ordinary uranium and heavy water, including providing Goudsmit with a sketch drawn from memory (see Figure 7.2).

"What these represent," Heisenberg added, "I do not need to explain to you further." Suggesting that perhaps Goudsmit had not seen these reports, Heisenberg added that he did not think that their understanding was especially significant, rather that after the discovery by Hahn and Strassmann and the work by Bohr and Wheeler, the entire development was practically inevitable. Heisenberg saw the great achievement of the Manhattan Project physicists above all in "the tremendous effectiveness of the technical implementation, in the systematic use of the greatest resources that could only have been provided by the giant industrial potential of America."

Only after they agreed on the facts, Heisenberg argued, should they begin discussing political motives, and perhaps the discussion would be better postponed until they could speak in person. "I do not believe that much can be gained from handling this matter in public." However, Heisenberg nevertheless immediately responded to several of Goudsmit's points. Heisenberg had

Oversimplifications 163

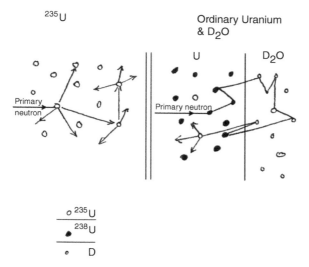

Figure 7.2 Hand-drawn diagram of chain reactions in uranium.
Source: Adapted from Werner Heisenberg to Samuel Goudsmit (January 5, 1948), SGP B11 F98.

always believed that science in Germany had suffered badly under National Socialism, first through the expulsion of many capable scholars from Germany, and second through the support of nonsensical scientific theories. Moreover, Heisenberg did not just occasionally mention this within a circle of friendly colleagues, rather at a time when this could certainly have been dangerous, he repeatedly made this case in a series of petitions to offices of the German government in order to try and bring about change.

It would never have crossed Heisenberg's mind to believe that the German scientists were different people than their colleagues in the Allied countries. But Goudsmit had to recognize that the German physicists were in a "different psychological situation" than their colleagues in England and America and had to "take up a different position towards the worldview of their government than the Allied physicists towards the worldview of their people." As far as the "complacency" of the German physicists was concerned, in every meeting with high-ranking government agencies about the uranium project Heisenberg had warned that the Americans were much better equipped with people and laboratories and would solve the atomic energy problem much faster than the Germans if they took this up during the war.

Finally, Heisenberg wanted to comment on the "political conduct, which you consider correctly described as compromises with the Nazis." Heisenberg never doubted for a minute that a considerable part of the German government

164   Living with the Bomb

of the time consisted of "fools and rogues." But he also knew that if the Germans did not succeed in undermining this system from within and finally eliminating it, then "a great catastrophe would erupt that would cost millions of innocent lives in Germany and other countries." Heisenberg was not so naive as to believe that they had a good chance of success before the catastrophe erupted but he still believed that

I would have criminally neglected my duty if I had not at least in my small circle tried everything in order to break through the blindness of the political rulers in the hope that others in other positions were doing the same.... I have never had the slightest understanding for the people who withdrew from all responsibility and then during a safe conversation at a table told you that "You see, Germany will perish, I have always said it."

Heisenberg believed that the world would have benefited if National Socialism had been replaced from within with something better instead of being eliminated from the outside through force of arms. There was now indescribable hardship in Germany that made it difficult to influence people in the direction that every serious person considered necessary. "What we need in Germany now is not a hateful reckoning with the past, rather a quiet reconstruction and the gradual beginning of a life worthy of living." The German physicists would certainly be happy to help with any effort that led to a better world understanding, as Goudsmit had written. Unfortunately their discussions in the United States and Heidelberg had demonstrated "how infinitely difficult it is, to really understand another person. But we may not give up, rather have to redouble our efforts."[61]

Heisenberg's Lawyer

At this point a mediator temporarily emerged between Goudsmit and Heisenberg, the uniquely qualified Bartel van der Waerden, a Dutch mathematician now in the United States who had been Heisenberg's colleague at the University of Leipzig and had spent the Third Reich in Germany.[62] After reading *Alsos*, van der Waerden asked Goudsmit what he had meant when he wrote "the bomb is what they were after"? Did he mean that the German scientists, knowing who Hitler was, planned the "horrible crime" of giving him an atomic bomb? Goudsmit did not agree that it would have been a crime to work on the atomic bomb, rather this was something "you cannot stop. It is a kind of scientific triumph, of which you realize the consequences only when it is too late."[63]

Since van der Waerden had come to the United States, he had been cautiously defending his former Leipzig colleague. After meeting with Goudsmit, van der Waerden wrote Heisenberg again. Goudsmit was not one of those people who considered "you and your friends accomplices to the horrific events of

Oversimplifications 165

the Nazi era" and sincerely wanted to reestablish both the international cooperation and friendly relations with German physicists. Van der Waerden did tell Heisenberg that his claims regarding what they had known were correct. Goudsmit had the reports. Goudsmit and van der Waerden discussed the question of guilt for a long time. They disagreed on what Heisenberg's group would have done if they had known more about plutonium but after thinking about it, Goudsmit admitted that one may not judge someone according to what he might have done if his situation had been different.[64]

Although van der Waerden was defending Heisenberg to Goudsmit and others, he also asked him direct and uncomfortable questions. When Heisenberg discussed possible nuclear explosives with higher officials in the Nazi regime, was this just a tactic to get money for physics? Was he determined that it would never come to delivering a weapon? "Then everything would be fine," van der Waerden wrote, "because with these people any deception was allowed." As Heisenberg's self-styled lawyer, van der Waerden had enough data to defend him; but as his friend, he wanted so very much to believe that "your decency in any circumstances would have been stronger than your nationalism plus ambition."[65]

Heisenberg responded immediately, noting that because every letter from Germany was read by a censor and, especially if it deals with atomic bombs, might be made public, Heisenberg had to write more "officially" than he would like. When by the end of 1941 Heisenberg knew that the uranium machine would work and that atomic bombs were probably possible, he was "deeply shocked over the possibility that some political leader (not just Hitler) could get such weapons." By early 1942 Heisenberg was pleased that the decision had been taken out of their hands because it was clear that Germany would never be able to build atomic bombs during the war.

In any case I would have considered it a crime to make atomic bombs for Hitler; but I also do not think that it is good that they have been given to other political leaders who have used them. On the other hand, I have learned something during the past years that my friends in the West do not quite want to see: that in such times it is almost impossible for anyone to avoid committing atrocities or by doing nothing to support them, whether by Germans, Russians, or Anglo-Saxons.

When Heisenberg read through his letter, he saw that his last sentence could be misunderstood in two ways. In a P.S. he continued: "First someone might think that I wanted to describe [J. Robert] Oppenheimer or [Enrico] Fermi as criminals, or further assume that under certain circumstances I myself would have been willing to commit any crime 'for Hitler.'" Van der Waerden knew Heisenberg well enough to understand that he meant neither of the two. Instead Heisenberg believed that the disintegration of the rule of law in large nations also forced nations that were fighting for self-preservation to be as brutal as

166   Living with the Bomb

their opponents, that "then accelerates the process of disintegration in a scary way." But Heisenberg did not want to write a lot about such things.[66]

When Goudsmit responded to Heisenberg, he admitted that: "It is clear that I had to simplify the scientific facts in my book to bring this important idea to the readers. One cannot impress the non-physicists by discussing highly technical papers." His principal aim in *Alsos* was to warn against "incompetent control of and interference with science." While nuclear research was too expensive for universities to conduct on their own, all around the world governmental agencies and the military were getting more and more interested in it. This situation threatened to "damage scientific progress seriously, like it happened under the Nazis and for many branches of learning under the Communists. Over here, as you know, some scientists are having serious difficulties already." When Goudsmit read over his letter, he saw that its contents differed little from the last letter sent to Heisenberg. Like Heisenberg, Goudsmit thought that it would be much easier to discuss these things in person.[67]

But Heisenberg, who had written in length about his personal experiences, perceptions, and motives, now wanted a retraction. It was clear that Goudsmit had the reports that verified what the Germans had known. After quoting at length Goudsmit's most inflammatory claims about their scientific understanding in *Alsos*, Heisenberg proposed that Goudsmit publish this text in the *Bulletin of the Atomic Scientists*:

The German physicists understood the difference between a uranium machine and an atomic bomb. They also knew since 1940 about the possibility of obtaining atomic explosives from the uranium burner and since 1942 knew that this was element 94 (plutonium). They knew at least enough about the manufacture and construction of atomic bombs for it to be clear to them that the manufacture of bombs in Germany during the war could not succeed. For these reasons they were spared the moral decision, whether they should make atomic bombs, and they only worked on the uranium machine.

Heisenberg added that he would rather not respond to the rest of the content in Goudsmit's letter because he considered "many formulations to be incorrect," but did not want a critical discussion between them to increase the differences between them. He had hoped that by coming to an agreement on the facts they would also come to an understanding about motives and "did not want to give up this hope for now." Of course Heisenberg agreed that a totalitarian system greatly damaged science. Indeed he had often said and written that, "but in your book this view is justified with incorrect arguments, and I find that very unfortunate."[68]

At this point Goudsmit wrote his colleague and fellow émigré Victor Weisskopf, who had just come back from visiting Germany, asking, "When will the German colleagues work for the future instead of trying to justify the past?" Weisskopf responded that, on the whole, their colleagues were less prone to justify that past that one might think, although there were "a few

Oversimplifications 167

notable exceptions such as Mr. Heisenberg, and they will learn too." Goudsmit then shared Heisenberg's last letter with Weisskopf. Although he could see how exasperating the situation was, Weisskopf counseled Goudsmit not to publish anything in the *Bulletin*. "Let's stop this useless prying into the past." Yes, Heisenberg's attitude was "tragicomic," but Weisskopf added that this was what Goudsmit got for his "unavoidable simplifications." By writing a popular book on a complex situation, Goudsmit inevitably made statements that he now had to qualify before defending them. "A *simplified* expression of my criticism of your book: The style is not appropriate to the subject. This is not to defend Heisenberg but to explain it."[69]

After waiting two months for a retraction, with the help of Kaempffert, Heisenberg took his case directly to the American public via an interview in the *New York Times*. Responding to Goudsmit's repeated criticisms of him for not explicitly blaming the Nazis for the decline of German science, Heisenberg began by placing "the blame squarely on the Hitler regime and its 'racial' theories." In contrast to the American physicists, during the war the German physicists never had the wholehearted support of the "totalitarian government." Heisenberg also explicitly criticized the expulsion for political or "racial" reasons of some of the ablest physicists in Germany and the cultivation of nonsensical scientific theories. Fortunately the German physicists "never had to make a moral decision" because "they and the Army agreed on the utter impossibility of producing a bomb during the war."

Without mentioning Goudsmit's name or book, Heisenberg next took aim at criticism of their scientific competence:

According to the tales which have been circulated we reached the absurd conclusion that a whole atomic pile or furnace had been dropped on Hiroshima and allotted to explode. Such was our alleged ignorance that we did not know the difference between a bomb and a [nuclear] furnace. The truth is that the general principles which must of necessity underlie the design and construction of an atomic bomb were well known to German physicists. So was the possibility of transmuting uranium into plutonium in a furnace.

Noting that around 300 German wartime uranium reports were now in Washington, Heisenberg called for the publication of the titles, if not the reports themselves. The reports would demonstrate that

top nuclear physicists of Germany were not far behind American physicists in their theoretical knowledge of chain reactions, of the essentials of pile or furnace design and of the general principles that would have to be applied in making an atomic bomb.[70]

When Goudsmit responded in the *New York Times*, he rejected Heisenberg's statement that the Germans had not been far behind their American counterparts but did grudgingly qualify some of his claims: "In my book 'Alsos' I have stated that the German scientists did not know the difference between

168   Living with the Bomb

a pile and a bomb. This is perhaps an oversimplification, as far as a few key men were concerned but I used it to avoid technical explanations." Having now read the text of Heisenberg's February 1942 talk, Goudsmit accepted that Heisenberg understood that plutonium was a fissile material that could be produced in a nuclear reactor but insisted that most of his colleagues had not. Inexplicably, however, Goudsmit continued to insist that "the German physicists also missed the crucial point that a bomb is a reaction produced by fast neutrons in plutonium or in U-235 [uranium 235]." According to Goudsmit, instead of the "hindsight conclusion of Dr. Heisenberg," the main lesson to be learned from the German wartime uranium work was that "German science, once inferior to none, had been so weakened by years of Hitlerism that it could not produce the decisive weapon for which German science itself had paved the way."[71]

Heisenberg sent one more letter to the *New York Times*, noting that Goudsmit had retracted some of the statements he made in Alsos, and again argued that, since "even so good a physicist as Dr. Goudsmit can be misled by distrust and incomplete information," the German reports should be published. Betraying some frustration, Heisenberg also asked why Goudsmit had ended his letter by saying "that German physicists ought to tell the world the detrimental effects of the Nazi regime on science rather than convince the public of the excellence of their war-time research," when Heisenberg had begun the interview by criticizing the "Hitler regime and its' racial theories'" and subsequently described the "progress made after Dr. Hahn's and Dr. Strassmann's discovery not as a great and unexpected scientific achievement but as a natural practical evolution." Heisenberg ended his letter by expressing the "greatest admiration for the efficiency of American physicists who in such a short time went the whole way from theoretical knowledge to the most important practical results."[72]

When Goudsmit asked Heisenberg whether he thought it would be better to stop their "exchange of ideas" altogether, Heisenberg responded with his sharpest tone yet:

You know that I would have preferred that the German atomic energy work had not been wrenched through a public discussion. But since you have over and over again spread false information about the German physicists in very many American journals and through your book, it appeared justified to me that for once a correct description of the facts appeared in a newspaper. I thought that you, even if you do not agree with me about the facts, would recognize this as right and just, and I am disappointed that this is not the case.

Goudsmit sent one last letter on "our controversial subject." Because he was afraid that they might lose their tempers, he laid out his point of view one last time, and expressed the hope that they would continue to correspond on scientific matters. Goudsmit had heard that Heisenberg would come to America to attend a scientific meeting in the fall, and cordially invited him to visit Goudsmit at the

Brookhaven Laboratory. Heisenberg immediately responded that he would be very interested in seeing the scientific work at Brookhaven. That visit did not work out but a year later in the autumn of 1950 Heisenberg came to Brookhaven as Goudsmit's guest, including a tour of the facility, discussions with the staff, and a talk by Heisenberg. The two men reconciled through physics.[73]

Although Goudsmit forgave Heisenberg, he did not exonerate him. In the summer of 1951, Goudsmit was contacted by his colleague at Yale, Gregory Breit. Someone had offered to donate money so that Heisenberg could join the Yale Faculty on a permanent basis. Recognizing that Heisenberg was controversial, before accepting the offer the Yale administration asked Breit to collect a few representative opinions from American physicists. Goudsmit began by praising Heisenberg, who was undoubtedly one of the greatest physicists, "almost as great as Einstein and Bohr." Heisenberg was an excellent teacher and lecturer and would certainly contribute to the success of any research project to which he was connected. However, Heisenberg had resisted calls to come to the United States because he believed that Germany needed him. Only if western Germany became dominated by the Russians would he probably be willing to emigrate.[74]

Goudsmit doubted that Heisenberg would fit well into American society. Although Heisenberg was never a member of the Nazi party and did not sympathize with the Nazi excesses, he was a "loyal German whose loyalty went too far." Even now, Heisenberg maintained that "the Nazi excesses were merely a normal by-product of a revolution and that the criminals at the top would soften or be replaced as soon as the revolutionary forces came to an equilibrium." Ever since the end of the war Heisenberg had been trying to "place the German research in a more favorable light than it deserves and to rationalize some of its shortcomings to the point of being dishonest." Finally, Goudsmit's recommendations to Breit were strikingly similar to those he had made immediately after the end of the war to Vannevar Bush.

Heisenberg's employment in the U.S.A. should be based entirely upon his possible future contributions to physics. It would be wrong to put him in a high position where he may have an influence on policy matters, such as the relation between physics research and defense, policies of the American Physical Society or even general problems of education. I fear that his opinions in such matters will often be in disagreement with ours.

Breit nevertheless continued trying to bring Heisenberg to Yale but warned his German colleague that: "I should explain that some people do not realize that World War II is over. Some unpredictable person might object and delay the approvals which are required by our regulations." Heisenberg, who after all had not emigrated during the Third Reich, made clear to Breit that he would only consider leaving Germany if another war came and the Soviet Union occupied Göttingen.[75]

170   Living with the Bomb

In fact Heisenberg sometimes appeared reluctant to criticize his countrymen for what they did during the Third Reich. Several of his émigré colleagues were surprised when he made comments after the war that appeared to downplay the horrors of National Socialism. According to Rudolf Peierls, during a trip to England in 1947 Heisenberg told a colleague who had been forced to emigrate from Germany that "the Nazis should have been left in power for another fifty years, then they would have become quite decent." A year later, Lise Meitner described an awkward conversation with Heisenberg and others. After German colleagues had said that Germans had done terrible things, Heisenberg responded: "Unfortunately, every spiritual upheaval has always been accompanied by great cruelty." When Meitner asked whether one could really compare the French Revolution, which had a spiritual and ethical basis, with Nazism, or the Napoleonic wars of conquest with the World War II, Heisenberg had no answer. In contrast, when Heisenberg responded to Breit, he wrote that it was "completely understandable to me that some colleagues are still hostile towards us Germans, for some of my countrymen in fact did horrible things, and we are ashamed that we could not stop them."[76]

Sins of the Father

The Shadow of Auschwitz

In *Alsos* Goudsmit also revealed the devastating blow he received while searching for a German atomic bomb: learning the fate of his parents. When he visited his family home in the Netherlands, he was

gripped by that shattering emotion all of us have felt who have lost family and relatives and friends at the hands of the murderous Nazis—a terrible feeling of guilt. Maybe I could have saved them....

It was too late. If I had hurried a little more, if I had not put off one visit to the Immigration Office for one week, if I had written those necessary letters a little faster, surely I could have rescued them from the Nazis in time. Now I wept for the heavy feeling of guilt in me. I have learned since that mine was an emotion shared by many who lost their nearest and dearest to the Nazis. Alas! My parents were only two among the four million victims taken in filthy, jampacked cattle trains to the concentration camps from which it was never intended they were to return.

The world has always admired the Germans so much for their orderliness. They are so systematic; they have such a sense of correctness. That is why they kept such precise records of their evil deeds, which we later found in their proper files in Germany. And that is why I know the precise date my father and my blind mother were put to death in the gas chamber. It was my father's seventieth birthday.[77]

In a real sense, Goudsmit was punished twice by his parents' death: once when he learned of it, and again when critics used this to question his objectivity. Kaempffert made this very clear:

Oversimplifications

I hope you will not be offended when I say that you should never have headed the Alsos Mission, and this because of the tragic end of your relatives at the hands of the Nazis. The whole tone of your book indicates that you set out on a witch-hunting expedition, determined to put the worst possible construction on any documents that you might find or on any testimony that you might hear. By contrast Heisenberg's *Naturwissenschaften* article is sober and plausible.[78]

It is perhaps not surprising that their correspondence broke off two months later. However, Laue's criticism must have been the most painful.

After Goudsmit had gone out of his way to praise his German colleague's conduct during the Third Reich, Laue used the fate of his parents to try and discredit both him and his reviewer Philip Morrison:

How far Morrison has suffered personally through [Himmler and Auschwitz] ... is unknown to us. We do know that Goudsmit lost not only father and mother but many near relatives as well, in Auschwitz and other concentration camps. We realize fully what unutterable pain the mere word Auschwitz must always evoke in him. But for that very reason we can recognize neither him, nor his reviewer Morrison, as capable of an unbiased judgment of the particular circumstances of the present case.[79]

Morrison rejected Laue's ad hominem criticism. No, he had not suffered personally but did not "see that it is fair or relevant to ask." It was not Goudsmit, the person who "most surely should feel an unutterable pain when the word Auschwitz is mentioned," who was biased, rather instead

many a famous German physicist in Göttingen today, many a man of insight and of responsibility, who could live for a decade in the Third Reich, and never once risk his position of comfort and authority in real opposition to the men who could build that infamous place of death.[80]

In fact Heisenberg, who was of course the "famous German physicist in Göttingen," was personally involved in the fate of Goudsmit's parents. During the war the Dutch physicist Dirk Coster had written to both Heisenberg and Laue, asking them to write letters on the parents' behalf. Unfortunately, both letters arrived too late and "the inevitable had already happened." Heisenberg answered Coster as follows:

Responding to your inquiry, I am pleased to say that I consider Dr. Goudsmit to be one of the best researchers in the field of theoretical physics. He has become well known throughout the entire scientific world because of the development of the magnetic properties of the electron. At scientific conferences he attended, I was always impressed by his scientific personality.

Since Goudsmit has always been very hospitable to us Germans in America, also at a time, when hostility to Germans could already be clearly sensed (I was his guest in the summer of 1939), I would be very sorry if, for reasons unknown to me, his parents experienced difficulties in Holland.[81]

Of course, there was nothing either Heisenberg or Laue could have done to forestall the deportation and murder of Goudsmit's parents. This must also

172   Living with the Bomb

have been clear to Heisenberg, who assumed that his letters were intercepted and read. At this stage of the Third Reich, even such an apparently bland letter could have caused significant problems for the physicist. It would have been much easier, and safer, simply to not respond. Goudsmit knew of Heisenberg's intervention, indeed he brought Heisenberg's letter back with him from Europe. In his 1976 obituary of Heisenberg, Goudsmit wrote: "Heisenberg was asked in 1943 to intercede in the case of acquaintances who were being sent to a concentration camp. He responded merely with a vague letter. I doubt that he could have done anything else. I doubt that I or most physicists I know would have done better under the circumstances."[82]

Active and Passive Opposition

Carl Friedrich von Weizsäcker came from a very well-connected aristocratic family. His father Ernst, a high-ranking official in the Foreign Ministry, was a prominent example of a member of the traditional German elites who stayed on and worked for Hitler's government. Although the elder Weizsäcker was initially very skeptical about the new regime, he decided that he had to provide it "with all help and experience in order to make sure that the second stage of the new revolution that was just starting will be constructive." In 1938 he rose to the position of State Secretary, essentially the level below the Foreign Minister himself, and as a consequence also joined the NSDAP and the SS.[83] By all accounts the elder Weizsäcker tried but failed to stop the outbreak of World War II.

German diplomats proved to be "willing helpers" of the SS in the Holocaust. Ernst von Weizsäcker told a Swiss diplomat in 1938 that the Jews had to leave Germany or "sooner or later they will be completely destroyed." The Foreign Ministry was well-informed about the *Einsatzgruppen* killing squads and their murders of Jews in 1941, with Weizsäcker and other high-ranking officials initialing the summaries of the reports that included vital statistics on Jewish executions. In the spring of 1942, SS official Adolf Eichmann asked the Foreign Office to approve the deportation of thousands of French and stateless Jews to Auschwitz. When presented with a draft response Weizsäcker changed the comment that the Office had "no concerns" to "no objection" before initializing it.[84] In 1943, at the height of the Holocaust, Weizsäcker moved on to become German ambassador to the Vatican.

After the war, Ernst von Weizsäcker's conduct during the Third Reich came under close scrutiny. Heisenberg, who was very close to the Weizsäcker family, remarked to Elisabeth in this regard that: "It is really sad to see how many decent men are now being thrown into the same pot with the most evil Nazi criminals." In November of 1947, less than two weeks after Ernst von Weizsäcker's indictment was announced, Heisenberg composed a remarkable manuscript, never published, with the title "Active and Passive Opposition in the Third Reich."[85]

Oversimplifications 173

If most Germans had refused to work with the National Socialists in 1933, Heisenberg began, then a great deal of harm would have been avoided. Instead the "generally undiscriminating masses" were won over, so that the "relatively thin layer of people" who instinctively recognized that the new system was fundamentally bad only had two possibilities: passive or active opposition. If someone recognized that the "Hitlerian system" would lead to a catastrophe for Germany and Europe but saw no way to change that from inside of Germany, then they could "go as a martyr into the concentration camp [this option was removed in the second draft of the manuscript], emigrate, or in any case pull back from any responsibility in Germany," waiting until the system was eliminated through war from the outside, including "unprecedented sacrifices in property and blood." Heisenberg described these stances as passive opposition. Some of the "most consequent of this group" subsequently decided to fight on the side of the Allies but (again a phrase removed from the second draft) many had "contented themselves with being safe from persecution in a foreign land."

Another group of people reasoned that a war would be so terrible that they had to do whatever was in their power to stop, shorten, or diminish this catastrophe. Many such people, who did not understand the stability of a modern dictatorship, attempted open, direct resistance during the first few years and ended up in a concentration camp. For others, who recognized the hopelessness of a direct attack on the dictatorship, the only remaining path was to acquire a certain amount of influence, thus a stance that from the outside must have appeared as participation. Heisenberg argued that it was "important to understand that this was in fact the only way to truly change something," describing this stance, the only way to "replace National Socialism with something better without enormous sacrifice," as active opposition.

Moreover, Heisenberg explained, these people were in a more difficult position. Over and over again a member of the active opposition had to make compromises with the system at unimportant places in order to be able to influence important things for the better. In a sense they had to "play a double game." In order to illustrate the unavoidable, morally difficult problems faced by a member of the active opposition, Heisenberg anticipated the trolley problem in ethics. Let us assume, he wrote, that someone who wishes to save a human life finds himself in a position where he can really decide whether someone lives or dies and, "as is conceivable in a truly evil system like National Socialism," he can only hinder the execution of ten innocent people by signing the death warrant for another person. The fate of the individual innocent, Heisenberg argued, was so-to-speak already sealed. Signing his death warrant makes no difference. What should be done? In such a case, Heisenberg argued, he should sign the death warrant, as long as he was ready to accept the consequences for himself personally. Heisenberg argued that such a stance was morally superior to someone simply refusing to have anything to do with it.[86]

174   Living with the Bomb

Ernst Weizsäcker became the lead defendant in a trial of German diplomats for war crimes. As Norbert Frei has shown in his study of the "Politics of the Past" (*Vergangenheitspolitik*) in postwar West Germany, the former State Secretary became the figurehead for former Foreign Ministry officials seeking a collective moral rehabilitation. Although the judges allowed that Weizsäcker may not have known how the killing machinery at Auschwitz operated in detail, he must have known that these people were being deported to their deaths. Even his son Carl Friedrich testified that "of course [they] knew" that the Jews were being killed. When the court found the elder Weizsäcker guilty and sentenced him to seven years imprisonment, these former officials redoubled their efforts to win his early release. His sentence was first shortened to five years for technical reasons. Prominent figures like Theodor Heuss, the first president of the Federal Republic, petitioned for Weizsäcker's release. John J. McCloy, the American High Commissioner, released Weizsäcker in October 1950 after three years and three months in prison. Weizsäcker then passed away in August 1951.[87]

Although he did not have access to Heisenberg's manuscript, on the basis of other published sources that subsequently echoed it the political scientist Joseph Haberer perceptively characterized Heisenberg's argument as "resistance through collaboration" and concluded that it provided a "rationalization for joining any winning side."[88] Heisenberg's analysis of active and passive opposition was clearly connected to Weizsäcker's trial but it also reads like a perhaps unconscious autobiographical account of Heisenberg's own sometimes harrowing journey through the Third Reich.

A Real Diplomat

The lives of Samuel Goudsmit and Carl Friedrich von Weizsäcker had become inextricably intertwined through the fates of their parents. In 1943, Goudsmit's mother and father were transported to Auschwitz where they were murdered; in 1947 Carl Friedrich's father Ernst was first charged and then sentenced to prison as a war criminal because he had approved the transport of French and stateless Jews to the same camp. The discussion of Ernst von Weizsäcker's role in the Holocaust and subsequent efforts by his son Carl Friedrich and others to clear his name must have been especially painful for Goudsmit. This may explain why, although Goudsmit had made peace with Heisenberg, he never forgave Weizsäcker.

Today one often asks, why did Heisenberg, Weizsäcker, and their colleagues work on nuclear weapons for the Nazi regime? However, this was not the most important question debated by physicists after the war. Instead émigrés and foreign scientists, many of whom had themselves worked on atomic bombs, asked why their German colleagues had stayed in Germany, worked within the Nazi system, and compromised with the Nazis? Although as we have seen,

Oversimplifications 175

Goudsmit also questioned Heisenberg's decisions in this regard, he saved his real criticism for Weizsäcker.

Goudsmit's most damning example of Weizsäcker's making concessions to the Nazis involved Laue, again using him as an example of a German scientist who did the right thing in order to discredit Weizsäcker by comparison. In 1942 a physics meeting dubbed the "theological dialogue" was held in Seefeld to find a compromise between the representatives of two physics factions: on one side a small group of scientists who followed the Aryan Physics of Philipp Lenard and Johannes Stark, two scientists who were early supporters of Hitler; on the other mainstream physicists who taught and researched in modern physics. As one of the most prominent intellectual scapegoats of the Third Reich, Einstein's theory of relativity was the main bone of contention. For mainstream physicists like Heisenberg and Weizsäcker, the goal of this meeting was to rehabilitate Einstein's physics, although not Einstein himself, and end the ideological attacks on modern physics.[89]

Goudsmit highlighted the difference between how Laue and Weizsäcker reacted to a reprimand the former received from the Reich Ministry of Science, Education, and Culture (REM) for mentioning Einstein's relativity during a lecture a year later in Stockholm. Weizsäcker suggested a compromise formulation worked out at Seefeld: "The theory of relativity would have been developed without Einstein but it did not develop without him." Laue instead published a paper on relativity and told Weizsäcker: "That is to be my answer."[90] The prominent émigré James Franck was so agitated by Goudsmit's reporting of Weizsäcker's attempt to convince Laue to compromise with the Nazis that an attempt by his fellow émigré physicists George Gamow and Edward Teller to invite Weizsäcker to lecture in the United States had to be abandoned.[91]

Teller was undeterred and a year later used personal connections in the Navy to arrange a trip for Weizsäcker and his wife to America, including talks at the University of Chicago, where both Teller and Franck taught.[92] Goudsmit wrote directly to Robert Hutchins, the President and Chancellor of the University, protesting Weizsäcker's invitation and arguing that it might "hamper the spread of democratic ideas and ideals among the younger German intelligentsia, ideals so essential to the freedom of thought." Since German academics could gain "tremendous influence" by being invited by an American university, only Germans who would "strengthen the spread of democratic concepts in the German educational system, a very difficult task after so long a period of authoritarianism," should be brought over. Weizsäcker, Goudsmit argued, would not.

Goudsmit's opposition to Weizsäcker was not based on what he would do. "Even if he were an extremist of the left or right, which he is not, I would never object against his right to explain his views. A true democracy is strong enough to allow absolute free speech." Weizsäcker was an excellent physicist and

176   Living with the Bomb

Probably no Nazi. Even his father, who recently has been found guilty at Nuremberg, of participating in war crimes, cannot be accused of having been a fanatic follower of Hitler, though he was his Secretary of State for a while.... The objectionable characteristic of both father and son lies in their philosophy of compromise. This is a very common and usually forgivable weakness but it should not occur in a man whom we single out to teach our way of life to German youth.

Using the Seefeld example, Goudsmit argued that Weizsäcker's "illogical position of compromise" showed through most clearly when he tried to "twist some of the basic ideas of physics into the Nazi philosophy." Moral support should be given to the German colleagues who, unlike Weizsäcker, could spread democratic ideas of freedom and saw the defeat of Germany as a "liberation from totalitarian rule." As Goudsmit's letter to Hutchins showed, the physicist struggled to reconcile his implacable opposition to "honor" Weizsäcker by invitations to lecture in the United States with his convictions about free speech and intellectual freedom. Hutchins replied that they were thoroughly familiar with Weizsäcker's career and did not believe that his visit would "hamper the democratization of Germany."[93]

Teller had done his Ph.D. with Heisenberg in Leipzig and had studied with Weizsäcker. Although Teller had also lost family members in the Holocaust, he quickly reestablished ties with the two German physicists. Sometime during the fall of 1949 Goudsmit met together with Teller and Weizsäcker. When Teller tried to defend his German colleague, Goudsmit had none of it:

I have not quite recovered from the meeting with Von Weizsäcker: I was especially disturbed by the manner in which you presented yourself as his "lawyer".... The general theme you followed, namely that the position of his father forced him to act as he did, is utterly ridiculous. If his father had jumped out of the window of the chancellery, would he have followed him too? This wouldn't have been a bad solution.[94]

When Goudsmit learned that Franck had met with Weizsäcker when he visited Chicago, he protested.

As you probably already heard, I am not at all happy about von Weizsäcker's visit and I imagine you can well understand why. The other day I was told that you, too, have talked to him and "forgiven" all the things he did during the war.

It was tragic that Weizsäcker could come to the United States without any trouble, while Goudsmit had failed to obtain permission for other, more deserving Germans.[95]

Franck responded with a long, detailed explanation. Like Goudsmit, he thought that it was a bad idea to "have asked Weizsäcker to come to this country instead of other men who had made no compromises whatsoever in respect to the Nazis and who had behaved excellently." At first Franck refused to have any contact with Weizsäcker but when the German physicist approached him through an intermediary, Franck agreed because, now that he was in the country,

Oversimplifications 177

Franck wanted Weizsäcker to know "why we felt the way we did about him." Moreover, Franck did not "sugar-coat in any way the things I had to say to him." Weizsäcker was "exceedingly sincere" and did not "gloss over the things he had done." He had decided to take a "realistic attitude toward the situation," which Franck understood to mean: "The Nazis are in power; I have to find a way to live under their regime and do some useful work instead of vegetating." In the beginning Weizsäcker believed that "the fury and criminality of the Nazis would eventually calm down," but eventually recognized that this hope was in vain. Of course, Franck did not agree with him but hopefully impressed him by explaining that he was talking with him in order "make him see that he had been wrong, and that if a man of his intelligence is unable, now that the pressure has ceased, to recognize where he has been wrong, the moral atmosphere in Germany can never become pure."

Franck neither forgave Weizsäcker, nor forgot what he did but did clear the air between them and decided that it would be wrong to avoid further contact with him. Now that Weizsäcker was in the United States, Franck considered it his duty to "see that he does not go away without having learned something." Two years later, Weizsäcker thanked Franck for the discussions, "which were also not easy for me either … to be addressed at this level and to be asked to examine oneself is an act of human seriousness that does not happen often."[96]

Goudsmit then heard from Bart Bok, a Dutch-American astronomer at Harvard, that Victor Weisskopf had been involved in inviting Weizsäcker to the Harvard Astronomy Department and MIT. Weisskopf had supposedly gone so far as to say that what Goudsmit said about Weizsäcker was "either not true or not relevant." Enraged, Goudsmit asked how could Weisskopf and Teller be "so utterly stupid to promote such a character as your friend von Weizsäcker," who once he was back in Germany, would describe the two physicists as "gullible imbeciles who, because of a sentimental attachment to old Germany, can easily be used to promote German influence here." Goudsmit had heard that Weizsäcker had started a campaign to "help his poor innocent father get out of jail. This poor man just couldn't help being Under Secretary of State for Hitler – it wasn't his fault at all. And, of course, signing the death warrant for only 8,000 Jews is just a minor offense." It was clear that Weisskopf was helping Weizsäcker because of an "inner kindness." Goudsmit knew that Weisskopf's heart was still in Germany but he needed to "snap-out of that attitude because that Germany of the Weimar Republic existed only in our imagination and in a small corner among a few of the intellectuals. It certainly doesn't exist anymore now."[97]

Weisskopf was deeply shocked by Goudsmit's "nonsensical" conclusions. Weizsäcker had asked Weisskopf last year to be invited to MIT but Weisskopf responded that he had no funds and refused to have him come "with some polite phrases." At the same time, Weisskopf told Bok that Weizsäcker was available

178   Living with the Bomb

but Weisskopf would never invite him for political reasons. Subsequently Weisskopf ran into Weizsäcker in Washington and in a frank personal conversation attacked him "as strongly as one could." When Weizsäcker admitted that he had been "blinded" when he had supported the Nazis, Weisskopf answered that a man who could be blinded by the Nazis would be "dangerous under all circumstances." Weisskopf took it "almost as a personal offense to be put in the same category as Teller in these matters." Goudsmit apologized for the misunderstanding and for causing him "any undue anxiety but this von Weizsäcker case just irritates me no end."[98]

Yet despite his personal loss, his ambivalence about Heisenberg, and his hostility towards Weizsäcker, Goudsmit eventually reversed course. Whereas he had advocated leaving the Germans to their own devices in 1945, writing in the *Bulletin* three years later, he now called for "renewing our relations with German scientists." Although it was understandable that many scientists in America would be "reluctant to converse with our German colleagues again as if nothing had happened," and fundamental science in Germany had declined rapidly in quality and quantity, it was important to promote democratic ideals among their German colleagues. In order to do this, American scientists had to

morally support those German colleagues in whose integrity we have confidence. There are many of them. We do not have to agree with all their opinions and should make allowances for the disturbing circumstances under which they have lived and are still living. We must again communicate with them as in the days before Hitler. The exchange of scientific literature, now practically at a standstill due to our indifference, should be actively promoted. German scientific research should again be helped by grants and supplies. By thus supporting the right persons, institutions or programs we might finally create an atmosphere of mutual understanding, beneficial to the spread of democratic ideals and practices.[99]

Conclusion

World War II brought Samuel Goudsmit to Europe in the search for a German atomic bomb. There he suffered tremendous personal loss and found what he considered evidence that Werner Heisenberg and colleagues had failed to understand how to make atomic bombs, something which fit into Goudsmit's preconceived conviction that the Nazis had ruined German science. For several years this became a public crusade as he used the German uranium work and the specter of politics or ideology influencing science to argue for the freedom of scientific research in America. Unfortunately some of Goudsmit's claims were false, leading to a wrenching dialogue with Heisenberg in which the two men often talked past each other but eventually agreed to set the controversy aside. The other main target of Goudsmit's criticisms was Carl Friedrich von Weizsäcker. Here the bad blood between the two men ran much deeper and was never resolved.

8   Compromising with Hitler

I must admit that I was deeply disappointed when I found out about these attempts at a compromise. What surprised me most was that you, yourself, did not see that a compromise with the Nazis was impossible. Your attempts to convince them of the soundness of relativity and quantum theory seem so out of place. How could you ever hope to be successful, how could you ever think that these were important issues? Didn't you know what you were up against? Men like von Laue should have opened your eyes. Many did not understand it but from you everyone expected a clearer insight. Why didn't you sense the hopelessness of ever convincing a Himmler?

Samuel Goudsmit to Werner Heisenberg (December 1, 1947).[1]

Weimar

It All Begins with Einstein

Samuel Goudsmit criticized both Carl Friedrich von Weizsäcker and Werner Heisenberg for attempting to compromise with the Nazis.[2] This suggests several questions: (1) did the German scientists think that they were compromising?; (2) did they compromise from Goudsmit's perspective?; (3) did they compromise from the historian's perspective?; and (4) what does compromise mean in this context?

The answers to all these questions begin with Albert Einstein, the Jewish, German-born physicist who became both well known and well respected within the international physics community through a series of fundamental publications in 1905. These included what soon was called special relativity, a branch of physics that, by denying any preferred frame of reference, accepting the finite speed of light, and only considering constant velocity, produced a series of apparent paradoxes such as twins aging at different rates or trains contracting – at least in thought experiments. In 1914, on the eve of World War I, the prominent German physicist Max Planck coaxed Einstein to Berlin with a package of scientific appointments that would allow him to concentrate on his physics without teaching, including membership in the Prussian Academy of Sciences and becoming the director of a Kaiser Wilhelm Institute for Physics. The latter was a paper institute, essentially giving Einstein research funds he could allocate.

179

180   Living with the Bomb

Einstein had been working on a generalization of special relativity since 1907. General relativity included accelerated frames of reference and constituted a theory of gravity. In a herculean effort, despite illness, malnutrition caused by the war, the difficulty of the mathematics, and the stress caused by the prominent mathematician David Hilbert's attempts to find the correct equations first, Einstein solved the problem and presented his final equations of general relativity to the Prussian Academy of Sciences in 1915. This did not make Einstein famous, that would come later. Indeed Einstein caused more of a stir during the war with his public support of pacifism and internationalism, the diametrical opposite of the political stances taken by the majority of German scientists.[3]

For most Germans, defeat in World War I was sudden and shocking, turning their world upside down in a wave of anger and despair. Just two weeks after the armistice, Einstein published what he undoubtedly thought was a playful response to scientific critics of relativity modeled on Galileo's famous dialogue between the advocates of the Aristotelian and Copernican world views. Whereas Einstein himself was the Relativist, the conservative experimental physicist Philipp Lenard, professor at the University of Heidelberg, played the role of the conservative Anti-Relativist. Just as the Catholic Church did not appreciate Galileo's portrayal of Aristotelianism, Lenard was probably not amused by Einstein's joke.[4]

A year later, Einstein's name was on the front page of newspapers around the world. A British expedition led by the astronomer Arthur Eddington used an eclipse of the sun to show that gravity can bend light, a prediction of general relativity. Eddington, a pacifist Quaker, had sought to confirm Einstein's theory for both scientific and political reasons: by verifying the theory of a German scientist, he would make a strong statement about the internationality of science despite the bitter war.[5] Politically Einstein was an especially attractive scientist in the West. As an article in the *New York Times* entitled "Lights All Askew in the Heavens" noted, Einstein, a Swiss citizen, had both opposed German nationalism and welcomed the postwar revolution. Einstein became a popular icon, while relativity became much more than just a scientific theory, and the opposition to it grew into something that reached far beyond science.

Anti-Relativity

Despite the fact that Einstein's physics appeared to have supplanted that of Isaac Newton, Eddington's results and Einstein were greeted warmly in Britain. In an article published in the *Times* of London, Einstein made another joke:

The description of me and my circumstances in *The Times* shows an amusing feat of imagination on the part of the writer. By an application of the theory of relativity to the taste of readers, to-day in Germany I am called a German man of science, and

Compromising with Hitler

in England I am represented as a Swiss Jew. If I come to be regarded as a *bête noire* [literally a "black beast," someone who is strongly destested], the description will be reversed, and I shall become a Swiss Jew for the Germans and a German man of science for the English!

Less than a year later, Einstein's prediction appeared to be coming true. A public anti-relativity event was held in Berlin. Einstein himself was in the audience, expecting to be amused but instead was confronted by pseudoscientific and anti-Semitic attacks. In a step the physicist subsequently regretted, he published "My Answer: Regarding the Anti-Relativity Company." His critics were hardly worthy of a response, he noted, and were not motivated by a quest for truth. Einstein rhetorically asked: "If I was a German nationalist, with or without a swastika instead of a Jew with a liberal international disposition." Although Lenard had not participated in the event, Einstein nevertheless attacked him:

As far as definite opponents of the theory of relativity among physicists of international significance are concerned, I could only name Lenard. I admire Lenard as a master of experimental physics; but in theoretical physics he has achieved nothing and his objections against the general theory of relativity are so superficial, that up until now I have not considered it necessary to respond to them extensively. I am now considering making up for that.

There would be a scientific discussion of relativity at the upcoming meeting of the Society for German Natural Scientists and Physicians in Bad Nauheim where anyone could voice their objections.[6]

Arnold Sommerfeld, Professor of Theoretical Physics at the University of Munich and current chairman of the German Physical Society, tried to intervene between Einstein and Lenard. He wrote Einstein both suggesting that Lenard had no connection to the Berlin anti-relativity event and exclaiming:

You must not leave Germany! Your entire work is rooted in German (and Dutch) science; you will never find as much understanding as in Germany. I cannot believe that you would abandon Germany now, as it is being anonymously mishandled by all sides.

Einstein had in fact considered "desertion" and worried that his continued silence towards the objections and allegations would be interpreted as agreement. "It is unfortunate that every comment by me is exploited by journalists for business. I have to close myself off very tightly." Sommerfeld urged Einstein to send a conciliatory message to Lenard before the meeting but this did not happen.[7]

Sommerfeld also wrote to Lenard but the Heidelberg physicist responded by "rejecting with indignation" the suggestion that an apology from Einstein would suffice. Einstein's "degrading" comments were a sign of his "personal contempt" for Lenard. If Einstein regretted his remarks, then he should publicly disavow them. The session on relativity at Bad Nauheim was run

182   Living with the Bomb

by physicists who backed Einstein. The speakers supported relativity and the debate, although civil and professional, was tightly controlled. Lenard insisted that physics should make "common sense," but Einstein responded that "clarity" in physics was itself relative and changed over time, indeed: "physics is conceptual, not clear."[8]

Foreign Policy

While colleagues like Planck and Sommerfeld defended Einstein's science, they did not share his pacifist and internationalist political views. When a French publication quoted Einstein arguing that the Germans had played a disastrous role in the war and deserved defeat, Sommerfeld assumed that it was all a lie. After Einstein told him that the statements in the interview were substantially accurate, he was devastated.[9] In 1922 the French physicist Paul Langevin invited Einstein to give lectures in Paris. At first Einstein begged off, noting that his German colleagues were still excluded from international meetings and that some individuals "whose touchiness has risen to almost pathological levels due to the events and experiences of the last years, would regard my trip to Paris at this moment as an act of faithlessness and be so hurt that very nasty consequences might develop." However, a subsequent conversation with Einstein's friend Walther Rathenau, an influential industrialist, Jew, and German Foreign Minister, convinced Einstein to go.[10]

While Einstein was still in France, he was criticized in a letter to a newspaper by the conservative experimental physicist Johannes Stark. Einstein traveled to Paris at a time when Stark claimed that the German people were being "repressed by the French in the most brutal way. They are ripping one piece after another from Germany's body, they are subjecting the Germans to extortion after extortion, they have stationed colored people in the Rheinland to control them, in their last message to the reparations commission they have made unbearable demands." Stark noted that since Einstein was a "pacifist and international-minded Jew" who lacked the "feeling of a German towards the French oppressors," this was no surprise but as a director of a Kaiser Wilhelm Institute with several other official positions, Einstein should not "pander to the French."[11]

Along with his scientific talks, Einstein asked to see the regions devastated by the war. In an article subsequently published in a French magazine, Einstein was quoted as saying: "We ought to bring all the students of Germany to this place – all the students of the world – so they can see how ugly war is." He also allowed himself to be photographed amidst the destruction. A few months later Rathenau was assassinated by right-wing extremists. When Einstein memorialized his friend, he noted that he had regretted that Rathenau had become Foreign Minister.

Given the attitude held by a great many of the educated class of Germany toward the Jews, it is my conviction that it would be most natural for Jews to keep a proud distance

Compromising with Hitler

from public affairs. Yet I could not have imagined that hatred, blindness, and ingratitude could go so far. I would like to draw the attention of those, however, who have directed the moral education of the German people for the last fifty years, to the following; by their fruits shall ye know them.[12]

Philipp Lenard had a very different reaction to Rathenau's death. The day of the funeral was declared a day of national mourning but the physicist demonstrably refused to fly the physics institute flag at half-mast or stop work. When union members gathered and shouted for Lenard to come out, they were drenched with cold water from a fire hose. The crowd then broke into the institute and forced Lenard to accompany them to the union hall, where he was taken into protective custody by the police to appease the crowd. When the union members were subsequently tried for breaking into the institute, the Jewish defense attorney managed to shift blame onto Lenard. The student who had started the conflict was cleared of any blame at a disciplinary hearing chaired by a Jewish professor. Lenard was supported by right-wing students and the case attracted a lot of attention for the young National Socialist movement.[13]

Along with being politically and scientifically conservative, despite winning the Nobel Prize in 1905, Lenard was convinced that his science had not received the attention and honor it deserved. Lenard believed that he, and not Wilhelm Röntgen, was the real discoverer of x-rays, and that the English and J. J. Thomson in particular had not given him credit for his work. Einstein's growing fame and the attention given to the theory of relativity were also direct threats to Lenard's conception of the ether, an intangible medium hypothesized to allow the transmission of electromagnetism and other things but which relativity had made redundant.

In 1922 the Society for German Natural Scientists and Physicians celebrated their centenary. Planck organized a special session on relativity with Einstein as the main speaker. Einstein reluctantly agreed, only to back out because of threats against his life. Instead Einstein took advantage of his fame and began touring other countries. Planck bitterly responded that "thus we have truly come so far that a band of murderers ... can dictate the program of a purely scientific society."[14]

In the second edition of a book published just before the meeting, Lenard made a clear distinction between Jewish and German science.

It is a known Jewish peculiarity to easily and quickly shift professional questions to the area of personal conflict ... if the German spirit – which certainly needs care and protection – will be revitalized, then it will have to free itself from the alien spirit that appears everywhere as a dark power and also so clearly forms everything that belongs to the "theory of relativity." We are living in a time no less dark than the Inquisition was.[15]

Instead of a triumph, the Leipzig meeting brought more disappointment for Lenard. Probably because of his political extremism, he received much less scientific support from colleagues than at Bad Nauheim.[16] The announcement

184   Living with the Bomb

that Einstein had been awarded the Nobel Prize, not for relativity, rather for the theoretical explanation of the photoelectric effect, something which had derived from Lenard's own experimental work, must have been the final blow.[17]

Stark also began a public campaign against Jewish influence in German science. Like Lenard, Stark was a Nobel laureate and respected experimental physicist who became alienated by developments in modern physics and from the German colleagues who practiced it. In 1922 Stark resigned from his professorship at the University of Würzburg over the criticism he received for using his Nobel award to buy part of a porcelain factory, something that went against the spirit of the Nobel Prize. He also resented faculty opposition to a student who tried to earn his *Habilitation* (essentially a second German doctorate, a prerequisite for an academic career) with a work on the optical properties of porcelain, which some of Stark's colleagues considered mere technology, not science. Stark probably hoped that he would be appointed president of the Reich Physical-Technical Institute (*Physikalisch-Technisches Reichsanstalt*, PTR). When this did not happen, and Stark was passed over when he tried to return to the university, he became alienated and bitter.[18]

In the same year he left Würzburg, Stark published a polemic against modern physics, dedicated to Lenard for his sixtieth birthday, entitled: "The Current Crisis in German Physics." Stark, who was positioning himself as the spokesman and defender of experimental physics against modern physics, considered it outrageous that "Einstein was being portrayed to the broad public by some people as the greatest physicist in several centuries." General relativity, that claimed to eliminate the ether, was being spread through propaganda. Quantum theory, led in particular by Sommerfeld, was as dogmatic as the Catholic Church. Perhaps most demeaning, Stark noted, the critics of relativity and quantum theory were dismissed as second-class scientists unable to follow the mathematics. Einstein and his supporters had forgotten that "theory in physics was not an end in itself, not just for the theoreticians and mathematicians, rather it should help experimental physicists by stimulating or formally concluding their work."[19]

Embracing Hitler

The long-standing cordial personal and professional relationship which Lenard and Stark had enjoyed now became a political collaboration. Like a significant number of Germans but unlike most academics and scientists, because of professional disappointments both Lenard and Stark turned to Hitler and National Socialism, where they found fulfillment.[20] Although they both opposed all or part of quantum mechanics and the theory of relativity, for Lenard the distinction between "Aryan" and "Jewish" science was a matter of ideology; for Stark it was a weapon to use against those who he felt had kept him a pariah for so long.

Compromising with Hitler

Philipp Lenard

Philipp Lenard was driven by personal resentment over priority, hated the English as much as anybody, became truly and viciously anti-Semitic, and during Weimar embraced Hitler's movement like no other scientist, even including the racial eugenicists. Through National Socialism Lenard hoped to realize his aspirations for an Aryan research and education policy.[21]

It is striking how deeply the leadership of the new NS movement was engaged with Einstein and relativity. Alfred Rosenberg, a Baltic German, anti-Semite, editor of the NSDAP newspaper *Der Völkischer Beobachter*, and the self-proclaimed philosopher of National Socialism, contacted Lenard in early 1923 about participating in a "polemical fight against Einstein." Rosenberg had been gathering material about Einstein and wanted an article that would "illuminate Einstein's political agitation." When Lenard declined but offered to recommend one of his students, Rosenberg replied that the student's article need not appear under his full name for the National Socialists had "no interest in having them added to the black lists of the Jews."[22]

In 1924 the experimental physicist Ernst Gehrcke, one of the speakers at the 1920 anti-relativity event in Berlin, published a book entitled *Die Massensuggestion der Relativitätstheorie* (*The Mass Suggestion of the Theory of Relativity*). Drawing upon Gustav Le Bon's theories of mass psychology, Gehrcke used thousands of press clippings to investigate how the theory of relativity was popularized, including Einstein's lecture tours, his advocacy of Zionism and pacifism, the construction of an observatory outside of Berlin nicknamed the Einstein Tower, and an animated film about relativity. Gehrcke's book inspired Rosenberg to ask Lenard and Stark to write an article on mass suggestion for his newspaper. Josef Goebbels, the future Minister of Propaganda in the Third Reich, discussed the book in his autobiographical novel *Michael*, arguing that the theory of relativity had a "hypnotic effect on the masses, even though most people did not understand it."[23]

During the first five years after the end of World War I, several *völkisch* groups coalesced into the National Socialist movement. *Völkisch* can be defined as a romantic, ethnic German nationalism, usually racist and anti-Semitic. By the autumn of 1923 Lenard was a member of the Association of *völkisch* German Teachers. On November 8–9 the National Socialists staged what came to be known as the Beer Hall Putsch, a failed attempt to take control of Munich by force. After a spectacular public trial, in which Hitler portrayed himself as a martyr for the German people, the NS leader was sent to Landsberg Prison. As Hitler sat in jail, Lenard and Stark took an unprecedented step for scientists by publishing an outrageous letter of support in a newspaper. Although most German academics were conservative and nationalistic during Weimar, they rarely participated in party politics, and very few university professors came out in public support of Hitler and National Socialism.

186   Living with the Bomb

Lenard wrote the text, and as Stark said in 1936, it was "so written from the heart" that he did not change a single word.

> We are speaking here as scientists ... we recognize in Hitler and his comrades ... the same spirit that we have always sought, strived for, and pulled out of ourselves: the spirit of complete clarity, the honesty with regard to the external world, as well as the inner unity, the spirit, that hates every work of compromise, because it is untrue. It is also the spirit that we have recognized and honored early on as exemplary in the great researchers of the past, in Galilei, Kepler, Newton, Faraday....
> Experience tells us that these spirits are only embodied in Aryan-Germanic blood, just as the great scientists named were of this blood.... It is the same activity, always with the same Asiatic people [the Jews] in the background, who put Christ on the cross, burned Giordano Bruno at the stake, shot at Hitler and Ludendorff with machine guns and locked them up behind prison walls: the struggle of the dark spirits against the bringers of light ... we only want clear, whole people, just as Hitler is one. He and his comrades in struggle appear to us as gifts from God from a long ago sunken past, because races were purer, people greater, and spirits less deceived.[24]

Rosenberg, who was tirelessly working to expand the influence of National Socialism into the intellectual sphere "alongside the daily politics and struggle," was often in contact with Lenard, asking him to lend his name to Rosenberg's NS cultural organization and to suggest other intellectuals who "would be prepared to help us." When the physicist agreed, Rosenberg thanked him and added that Hitler would be "delighted with the keen interest you have shown in his work." When Lenard offered to make a financial donation to Rosenberg's organization, the latter responded that he "had really not considered that, since your moral support of us is more valuable than anything else."[25]

In fact Lenard was a very strong and generous financial supporter of Hitler's movement. He was a regular supporting member of the SS and contributed to other National Socialist organizations and election campaigns. He also responded to special calls to help pay for the transportation of SS men to Party rallies, the support of SS and Party members who were involved in legal proceedings, or if they had been injured or killed, in support of their families. The physicist received personal letters of thanks for his generous gifts from SS leader Heinrich Himmler and Hitler himself.[26]

In 1926 Lenard attended a rally for Hitler and found the experience invigorating. That same year Hitler and Lenard were planning on meeting at a rally in Karlsruhe but the visit was canceled when the regional government banned Hitler from speaking. Hitler and his adjutant Rudolf Hess visited Lenard in his home in 1928. Hess subsequently wrote Lenard that "Hitler often and happily thinks of his visit with you and your just as harsh and unfortunately correct judgment of your [academic] colleagues." The NS leadership recognized Lenard's value to their movement and appears to have treated him with genuine respect, something Lenard felt his professional colleagues did not give him. Hitler clearly found Lenard to be a kindred spirit.[27]

Compromising with Hitler

Johannes Stark

While Johannes Stark was definitely anti-Semitic, this was focused on his conflicts with Arnold Sommerfeld – who ironically was not Jewish – over academic positions and quantum theory. Even before the end of World War I, in 1915 when Stark's hopes of being called to a professorship in Gottingen were dashed by the appointment of Sommerfeld's student Peter Debye, Stark blamed the "Jewish and pro-Semitic circle" of mathematicians and theoretical physicists there and its "enterprising business manager" Sommerfeld. When Stark sent Lenard a scientific paper in 1927, the elder Heidelberg professor gently chided him. The publication should help him in his efforts to get another position, "not because it contains valuable new things," but instead because "you praise so many Jews. Hopefully this will have the effect of making you personally acceptable again."[28]

When Stark sent Lenard another publication a year later, he justified his work in anti-Semitic terms: "In order to wrest the monopoly on atomic research away from the physics-Jews around Einstein, Bohr, and Sommerfeld, it appears necessary to me to create new ideas from the spirit of experimental research, not just to criticize their sophistry.... Although I fear that the credit for creating this will be taken away by Jews." In the margins of Stark's letter, here Lenard commented "of course!" Stark went on to describe the tactics he predicted that the "Jewish enterprise" would pursue. First, no one would comment on or review Stark's two publications; next a new clamor would start about the new advances in atomic research, naming Planck, Erwin Schrödinger, and Louis de Broglie; this would give Sommerfeld and his consorts the opportunity to revise their theory and incorporate the parts from Stark's publications, presenting them as their own work. "But I am by no means willing to let the Jews take advantage of and bury me. On the contrary, I will do everything that I can do in order to break the domination of the Jews over my science."[29]

By 1928 Stark had become obsessed with his quest to be appointed professor of experimental physics in Munich. In a letter thanking Lenard for recommending him to the Bavarian Ministry of Culture, Stark responded that, "The entire group Sommerfeld-Einstein-Planck-Debye is namely very disturbed by the prospect of me being appointed. They fear that I will have a strong influence over German physics." Stark had informants about the selection process, and usually interpreted what they told him in terms of Jewish influence. Everyone who opposed him, or supported someone else, was either Jewish, Catholic, or a friend of the Jews. Stark even confronted Sommerfeld directly, accusing him of controlling the selection process and passing him over, which constituted a "public downgrading of my person and scientific achievements." Sommerfeld responded that he was offended by the accusation that he had acted in an unprofessional manner, that he had always emphasized the significance of Stark's discoveries in his books, and had not responded to his criticism of a supposed "quantum orthodoxy" because it

188   Living with the Bomb

was not real. By the spring of 1929 it was clear to Stark that he would not get the Munich professorship because "the Minister gave in to the concentrated pressure of the Jews and decided to comply with their wishes."[30]

Like Lenard, Stark was involved in *völkisch* organizations early on. A few days before the Beer Hall Putsch, Stark had merged the local *völkisch* group he led into the NS movement. In 1924 he published his own weekly newsletter supporting Hitler. When Hitler was in prison, Stark's wife, also an enthusiastic supporter, brought him food. After Hitler's release from prison in December of 1924, Stark invited him to recuperate at his house, an offer for which the NS leader was very grateful.[31] Stark often discussed Hitler with Lenard. Of all the contemporary political figures, Stark thought the highest of Hitler, even if the physicist was pessimistic about his prospects. "I wish that chaos would arise, which would allow him to come to power." In July of 1929, at a time when the National Socialists' prospects appeared bleak, Stark told his colleague that: "You are right, dear Lenard. Hitler is our last hope. The Jewish domination in Germany can only be broken with force."[32]

A few months later the chaos Stark had called for began with the collapse of the New York stock market, heralding the beginning of the Great Depression. On April 1, 1930, Stark officially joined the NSDAP. He closed the doors of his private laboratory in order to help Hitler in his final struggle for power through speeches and publications. When manipulative politicians called for unnecessary national elections in September, the National Socialists gained a shocking 18.3 percent of the vote and 230 seats in the German Reichstag (parliament). By this time, Stark had been completely won over to the NS cause, as he wrote Lenard.

I consider it a great fortune that I hear Hitler speak so often and along with the study of his brilliant book [*My Struggle (Mein Kampf)*] can experience the immediate effect of his personality. In my eyes he is the greatest German man for centuries, researcher, statesman, organizer, and hero. He will certainly lead German youth to victory over the enemies of everything German. Even for an old man like me he has such a strong effect that I feel tempted to intervene in the political struggle, even if only in a literary way.

Stark' wife added a handwritten note to a letter Stark wrote to Lenard, telling the latter that she was involved in the stormtrooper's women's auxiliary, providing food and raising money for unemployed party members. "I have a lot of work to do there. But I do it so gladly, because we of course do anything for the Leader [*Führer*]."[33]

Nazification

The Einstein Affair and the Prussian Academy of Sciences

Beginning in 1930, the politicians and power brokers who ran Germany worked systematically to end democracy. The last, fateful step came when

Compromising with Hitler 189

President Paul von Hindenburg appointed Adolf Hitler chancellor on January 30, 1933. Einstein was in the United States and never returned to Germany. When he began criticizing the repressive policies of the new nationalist–National Socialist coalition government, his elder colleague Max Planck predicted that, because of the criticism, "the already difficult position of your tribal and religious colleagues will be in no way relieved, rather put under more pressure." While on board a ship bound for Europe, Einstein informed the Prussian Academy of Sciences that he was resigning because of the "currently prevailing conditions" in Germany but went out of his way to thank the Academy and its members.[34]

On the same day, in a statement that appeared in French and German newspapers, Einstein publicly attacked the new German government.

The actions of brutal force and oppression taken against all free intellects and against the Jews ... have fortunately shaken the conscience of all countries that remain faithful to humane thought and to political freedoms. The International League for Combating Anti-Semitism has done a great service in defending justice by establishing the unity of peoples who have not been infected by the poison.

We can only hope that the reaction will be strong enough to prevent Europe's relapse into a barbarism of times long past. May all friends of our so imperiled civilization concentrate their efforts to abolish this mental disease from the world. I am with you.

A commentary in the *Kölnische Zeitung* was equally sharp. Einstein had been able to research unhindered in Germany but that did not stop him now from describing the Germans as barbarians and to hope that "Europe unites against us." Let him move to a place where he thinks that he is free from the "poison" of patriotism.[35]

On March 30, the Academy noted Einstein's resignation and decided that any further action was moot. However, the National Socialist Prussian Minister of Culture Bernhard Rust personally asked the Academy to make a public statement about Einstein on April 1, coinciding with the national one-day boycott of Jewish businesses and professions. Ernst Heymann, one of the four permanent secretaries of the academy, then issued a press release expressing "outrage over the participation of Albert Einstein in atrocity agitation in America and France" and adding that they had "no reason to regret Einstein's resignation."[36]

Einstein responded to the Academy that he had never participated in atrocity-mongering, indeed had never seen it. Instead people merely reproduced and commented on "the official statements and orders of responsible members of the German government, together with the program for the annihilation of the German Jews by economic methods." However, Einstein did add that he had described the current conditions in Germany as "a state of mental illness of the masses" and discussed the causes. Einstein wrote a more thoughtful letter to Max Planck, asking him to imagine that he was a professor in Prague when a Czech government came to power that "robbed the Czech Germans of their

190   Living with the Bomb

source of existence and simultaneously hindered them by force from leaving the country." Would Planck then think that it would be right to accept this silently and not try to help them?[37]

Planck, also a permanent secretary of the Academy, found a compromise that the majority of his colleagues could accept and read this via a speech into the permanent record.

I believe that I am speaking in the spirit of my physicist colleagues in the Academy as well as the overwhelming majority of all German physicists when I say: Einstein is not only one of many outstanding physicists, rather Einstein is the physicist, through whose work, published in our Academy, physical knowledge has experienced a deepening, the significance of which can only be measured by the achievements of Johannes Kepler and Isaac Newton. It is especially important to me to say this, so that posterity does not believe that Einstein's physicist colleagues in the Academy were not able to comprehend his significance for science.

However, Planck went on, through his political conduct Einstein had himself made it impossible for him to remain in the Academy.[38]

Another colleague, academy member, and close friend of Einstein, Max von Laue, used "an opportunity" to send him a letter, that is, evading the National Socialist censors, telling Einstein that of course he was very sad about what had happened. "The worst thing is the complete powerlessness to do anything about it. What attracts attention, only makes matters worse." Aside from Planck, Schrödinger (who would soon leave) and a few others, Berlin was now deserted for Laue. "But why do you have to take prominent political stands? It is far from my intention to criticize you for your statements. I just believe that scholars should stay away from that. The political struggle requires other methods and interests than scientific research. As a rule the scholar ends up being run over." Einstein disagreed. Such restrictions left "leadership to the blind and irresponsible." While he did not regret a single word, the physicist added that his "feelings of warm friendship for you and a few others there remain. Hopefully we will see each other again in better times." A week later Einstein asked Laue to arrange his resignation from other organizations like the German Physical Society "in order to avoid new theatrical effects."[39]

The Haber Affair

The frustrated National Socialist leadership was forced to limit the national boycott of Jewish businesses to one day because of the weakness of the German economy, negative reactions from abroad, and the ambivalence shown by many Germans. In response, new anti-Semitic policies were implemented, including the euphemistically named law for the Restoration of the Professional Civil Service decree on April 7. Civil servants who had one Jewish grandparent could now be dismissed or forced into early retirement.

Compromising with Hitler

President Hindenburg had required that exceptions be made for non-Aryan civil servants who had their positions before August 1914 or had served at the front in World War I. Although the Nobel laureate and staunch German nationalist Fritz Haber had certainly served at the front – indeed he was mainly responsible for the introduction of chemical weapons into World War I – as director of the Kaiser Wilhelm Institute for Physical Chemistry he would now have to dismiss his Jewish staff members. As he wrote in his resignation letter to Prussian Minister of Culture Rust, the traditions of scientific research required that he consider only professional abilities and character when selecting staff, not their race. Haber went into exile, where he died the next year. In his obituary in a scientific journal, Laue highlighted Haber's discovery of how to extract nitrogen from the atmosphere but also compared him to the Athenian general Themistocles, who led the Greeks to victory over the Persians but was subsequently ostracized and sent into exile.[40]

Two weeks later Stark wrote to the German Physical Society, outraged that Laue had suggested that the NS government banned Haber, and demanded that he immediately step down from the executive committee running the society. An official in the Prussian Ministry of Culture subsequently told Laue that his comparison with Themistocles had been read "with a certain astonishment," but added the Minister had not ordered that any further steps be taken. Laue sent Einstein a copy of the obituary and Stark's letter, suggesting that the latter was just "blowing off steam." Einstein was delighted: "If I have a fervent desire to see someone again, it's you."[41]

In January of 1935 the Kaiser Wilhelm Society (*Kaiser-Wilhelm-Gesellschaft*, KWG), German Physical Society, and initially the German Chemical Society announced that they would hold a memorial celebration in honor of Haber. The REM, which in the meantime had subsumed the Prussian Ministry of Culture, quickly condemned the event. Haber's resignation letter had clearly expressed "his inner opposition to the current state." The plan to honor Haber, whose staff of forty scientists had included twenty-three Jews, was a "challenge to the National Socialist state." Everyone under the authority of the Ministry was forbidden to participate in the memorial.

KWG President Max Planck responded by writing directly to Minister Rust, protesting that there had been a "grave misunderstanding." This was not a challenge to the NS state, rather merely a memorial to a former member who made "undying contributions to German science, economy, and military technology." Planck pointed out that canceling the event would have negative repercussions outside of Germany and argued that: "The Kaiser Wilhelm Society has proven often enough through word and deed its positive attitude towards the current state and its profession of faith to the Leader and his government."[42]

Rust responded by recognizing Planck's positive attitude but added that Haber left his position because he had "placed himself in opposition to the

192   Living with the Bomb

National Socialist state." Rust refused to lift the ban in general, but because the foreign and domestic press had been informed of the event and foreign guests were expected, was willing to allow the event as a private celebration of the KWG and offered to grant permission to certain members of the societies who wanted to participate. In fact, when Karl-Friedrich Bonhoeffer, a former student of Haber, requested such permission it was not granted. Instead Otto Hahn read his speech. No university professors, not even Laue, attended. The Haber Memorial in 1935 was the closest scientists came to organized public protest during the Third Reich. Nothing even remotely like it ever happened again.[43]

The Dictator of Physics

As long-standing supporters of Hitler, Lenard and Stark benefited immensely when the National Socialists came to power. "The time has finally come when we can bring to bear our conception of science and research," Stark wrote Lenard. Stark was acquainted with NS Minister of Interior Wilhelm Frick and asked him to ensure that the two physicists be consulted regarding jobs at scientific institutes. Lenard wrote directly to Hitler, asking that the Education Ministers in the different German states ask Lenard for his advice before making any appointments. Both Hitler and Frick agreed.

In May of 1933 Frick appointed Stark president of the PTR, something the physicist had wanted for years. Lenard proclaimed the news in the *Völkischer Beobachter* as a sign of a new age for science.

It had gone too far in physics, namely from the top down. By powerfully inserting Jews into important positions, also at universities and academies, the basis of all natural knowledge, the observation of nature itself had been forgotten and invalidated.... The theoreticians who stood in distinguished positions should have guided this development better. Now Hitler is guiding it. The spook has crumbled; the alien spirit is actually already voluntarily leaving the universities, even the country.

But Stark was nevertheless worried. As he told Lenard:

I do not fear the Jews and our other opponents, rather the arrogance, envy, and intrigue in the leading National Socialist circles. We also have to see things here as they really are. People like me and you are not appreciated in the circle of National Socialist leaders. First we are old and for that reason alone inferior; second we have achieved something and many around Hitler consider this a reproach in itself; third we are men of science ... and Hitler is fundamentally unsympathetic to science.[44]

Stark now followed a strategy typical of leading National Socialists by trying to consolidate personal control over everything in a particular sector, which he portrayed as reorganizing and expanding the physical sciences.[45] His next target was control of the German Physical Society but Laue stood in his way. In a famous opening lecture at the yearly meeting of the Society in Würzburg,

Laue noted the 300-year anniversary of the ending of Galileo's trial before the inquisition and made a direct and clear connection between the Church's opposition to a solar system centered around the sun and the contemporary controversies surrounding the theory of relativity. Repeating the perhaps apocryphal story of Galileo saying "but it nevertheless moves" as he signed a document renouncing Copernicus' theory, Laue suggested that the Italian scientist must have asked himself: "What does this matter? Whether I, whether anyone claims it or not, whether political or religious power is for or against it, that changes nothing about the facts! Political power can hold back knowledge for a while but at some point it breaks through."[46]

An undoubtedly enraged Stark subsequently announced that he would become the "Dictator of Physics" and control physics publications, threatening that if the publishers were not compliant, "then I will use force." Unfortunately for Stark, he had not sufficiently corrupted the democratic process or intimidated the assembled physicists. When the vote for society chairman was held by secret ballot, the industrial physicist Karl Mey was selected. Stark subsequently publicly denounced Laue for supporting Einstein, the theory of relativity, and suggesting that "the National Socialist government was violating the freedom of scientific research."[47]

A few months later, Stark was nominated for membership in the Prussian Academy of Sciences. The nominators included Friedrich Paschen, the previous president of the PTR, and Max Planck. Although this was an honor a PTR president normally could expect, Paschen and Planck may have done this under pressure. Laue addressed the Academy and again opposed Stark. Repeating Stark's claim for his dictatorship over physics, Laue added that after becoming PTR president Stark had abruptly ended a series of important investigations that he "hated." Most disturbing were Stark's plans for physics journals. If Stark got his way, Laue argued, theoretical work might no longer be able to be published in Germany. He also addressed Stark's public criticism of recent developments in modern physics in a "not very tactful way, not separating the personal from the professional or the scientific from the political." It was understandable that a man like Stark, who had "never allowed strict scientific training to rein in his extravagant imagination" did not accept the "inexorable logic of the theory of relativity and the unfamiliar mathematical methods of quantum theory," but this could not justify the way Stark spoke about these things in public. Following Laue's intervention, the nomination was withdrawn.[48]

Laue's success in opposing Stark suggests several questions. Why was Laue not punished? If Stark had Hitler's support, why did the physicist not get whatever he wanted? Laue was, after all, part of an older generation that could be ignored. When National Socialist officials investigated the mathematicians and physicists at the University of Berlin at the end of December 1934, shortly after the academy had rejected Stark, Laue was assessed as an excellent scientist,

194   Living with the Bomb

pedagogically less talented, with nothing known about his political conduct. All of Laue's interventions were in scientific contexts – scientific meetings and publications. In his own mind, the physicist no doubt thought that he was following his own advice to Einstein and staying out of politics.[49]

Stark's failures suggest he was not that powerful, or ruthless, or perhaps both. He repeatedly denounced Laue in private and public, with apparently little effect. The fate of the writer Ernst Wiechert provides a telling contrast. When Wiechert published implicit criticism of the National Socialist claim to total power and protested against the arrest of the pastor Martin Niemöller in 1938, Goebbels had him locked up in the Buchenwald concentration camp. After his release three months later, Goebbels summoned him, not disguising his glee at being able to show off the power he had over life and death. In his diary, Goebbels noted that: "I am in great shape and mentally stab him. One final warning!.... At the end, the delinquent is very small and explains that his imprisonment has given him food for thought and insight. That is very good. Committing a new offense will lead to physical destruction. We both know that now."[50]

However, Laue's success probably had more to do with Stark's enemies. On May 1, 1934, REM was created with authority over all education. When a month later Frick's Reich Interior Ministry transferred responsibility for scientific institutions to the newly formed REM, Stark and Lenard lost a powerful patron. While REM officials did not see Laue as a threat to their authority, Stark was clearly a competitor for power and influence. Max von Laue was very useful to REM as Stark's colleague and tormentor.

Although REM considered Stark a threat, the physicist had Hitler's ear. A few days before he decided to create REM and install Rust as minister, Hitler received Stark, listened to his plans for organizing research, and subsequently told Rust that he should take Stark's concepts into account. In June of 1934 Rust appointed Stark president of what would soon be called the German Research Foundation (*Deutsche Forschungsgemeinschaft*, DFG), the institution that allocated research funding, realizing one of Stark's greatest aspirations, the ability to influence what was researched and how.[51]

Stark's main adversary in REM was the chemist Rudolf Mentzel, a specialist in chemical weapons. Like Erich Schumann, after the war Mentzel was portrayed as incompetent,[52] but he also resembled Schumann in being an effective science policy maker in the NS state. Although Mentzel was hardly a first-class scientist, politically he had impeccable credentials, fighting in the paramilitary *Freikorps* immediately after the First World War, joining the SA and NSDAP early on, and becoming a member of the SS in 1932, on the eve of the Third Reich. In 1934 Mentzel was appointed the head of a science unit in REM, rising to the top-ranking official for science in 1939. Two years earlier he became a senator in the KWG, again rising to vice president of the Society in 1940, two years before he effectively took control of the Reich Research Council.

Compromising with Hitler

In early 1935 REM circulated a draft law creating a Reich Academy for the coordination of research that would have replaced the DFG and been directly under the control of the Ministry. Stark protested to Hitler, and although he managed to kill the proposed Reich Academy, his request for a personal audience with Hitler was denied. From this point onward, Mentzel worked towards ousting Stark from the DFG and sidelining him as a political rival.[53]

Stark's fall began with his attempts to influence the KWG. He was elected senator of the society shortly after becoming president of the PTR in May of 1933. When REM official Theodor Vahlen asked Lenard whether he would consider becoming the society's president if Planck stepped down. Lenard immediately refused. This "purely Jewish business" first of all needed to be "smashed in order to make something reasonable." The KWG was planning to reestablish a Kaiser Wilhelm Institute for Metals Research in Stuttgart but Stark instead wanted to incorporate it into the PTR in Berlin. Stark complained about his lack of influence over decisions in the KWG, whose patrons were "Jews, democrats, and freemasons." When Stark did not get his way with the metals institute, he resigned as senator in December 1933.[54]

When Max Planck announced at the beginning of 1936 that he did not want another term as KWG president, Rust wrote Hitler that Stark, who was "overloaded" as president of the PTR and DFG, had now offered to become KWG president as well. Rust added, "However, I must point out that, to my great regret, Professor Stark is rejected by so many prominent leading men and the highest governmental agencies that cooperation with him would encounter great difficulties." On the very same day, Stark wrote Lenard that talk of Planck stepping down was being used to "intrigue against me again with the lie" that Stark had asked Rust to be Planck's successor. In fact Stark would not agree to head the society, even if the Minister urgently requested it. Hitler left it up to Rust to decide, and the industrialist Carl Bosch became KWG president. Whether Stark had asked to succeed Planck or not, Hitler's decision suggested that Stark was not the Leader's favorite and therefore vulnerable.[55]

Although Rust had strengthened Stark by making him DFG president, REM controlled the foundation's budget. When Stark submitted his first budget request early in 1935, he asked for the very generous sum of 19.2 million RM but received the same 4.4 million RM given to his predecessor. Moreover REM reserved the right to determine how 2 million of the marks would be dispensed. Stark's plans for massively expanding the PTR and using it to coordinate research were thereby throttled. The physicist blamed the "young, narrow-minded, unscrupulous, [and] power-hungry" Mentzel.[56] REM and Stark were now in an uneasy standoff: each could thwart the other's plans but not realize their own ambitions.

Now that Stark appeared vulnerable, he was attacked on all sides and continued to make new enemies. Stark refused to fund research at the SS Ancestral Heritage Foundation because he did not consider the science good enough,

196   Living with the Bomb

incurring the enmity of Himmler's organization.[57] Eduard Wildhagen, Stark's most important staff member at the DFG, was denounced by the historian Walter Frank for having supported Jews and Jewish interests during Weimar. Incriminating materials were supplied by scholars that Wildhagen had dismissed from the DFG, Mentzel passed on Wildhagen's personnel file, and the SS Security Service (SD) also provided documents. Within two months Stark was forced to let Wildhagen go. Stark was finally forced out by his own financial mismanagement. A dentist named Fritz Oberländer claimed that he could obtain gold from wetlands in Upper Bavaria. Stark paid 50,000 RM from DFG funds for the rights to Oberländer's process, which proved to be worthless. Both REM and the Reich Accounting Office threatened to hold Stark personally responsible.[58]

Once Stark offered his resignation, the charges were dropped. The physicist also received guarantees for future support of the PTR. As Mentzel took over as DFG president, he found that the physicist had given out far more money that had been in the budget. Stark told Lenard that for two and a half years he had been working for German research and "fighting hard against its bureaucratization." Now that he had laid down the heavy burden of the DFG presidency, he felt emotionally and physically relieved and looked forward to getting back to his science.[59]

However, just as Stark was ending one conflict with fellow National Socialists, another was beginning. In Traunstein in rural Bavaria, where Stark had his estate, a local National Socialist official named Karl Sollinger shocked local people by participating in a brutal beating and stabbing of a police commissioner who had tried to enforce the curfew in a local tavern. Sollinger was tried and sentenced to eight months in prison. His friend, the powerful regional NSDAP leader in Upper Bavaria Adolf Wagner, persuaded the Minister of Justice, Franz Gürtner – no National Socialist, rather a holdover from the initial Nationalist-National Socialist political collaboration– not to carry out the sentence "for reasons of state and party politics."

Sollinger was subsequently sentenced again by a Traunstein court to six months prison and a fine for embezzling from one of the main National Socialist charities, the Winter Relief Fund. This sentence was eliminated in the general pardon decreed by Hitler on August 7, 1934. When Sollinger refused to obey the curfew again, bragging about his power and declaring he would never obey the police, Stark was convinced that, for reasons of both state and party, Sollinger needed to be punished. After twice complaining to Wagner without result, Stark took the consequential step of informing Gürtner of Sollinger's continuing transgressions.[60]

When Gürtner ordered Sollinger's arrest, Wagner reacted angrily. In March of 1936 he formally requested that Stark be expelled from the NSDAP. By circumventing all Party offices and going directly to the Ministry of Justice, Stark had caused considerable public damage to the image of both Wagner and

Compromising with Hitler

the party. Moreover, in 1934 Rudolf Hess, Hitler's personal representative in charge of the NSDAP, had decreed: "From now on I will ruthlessly expel every Party member who complains to external state or other agencies, or turns to their leaders." As an old National Socialist Stark should have known, Wagner subsequently told the Highest Party Court, that "a National Socialist may not sell out another one to the judiciary."[61]

Stark in turn angrily denied that he had been undisciplined or damaged the reputation of the Party. Indeed that was what Sollinger and Wagner had done. If the physicist had known that such complaints had to go through Hess, then he would have done so. He also petitioned in turn for Wagner's expulsion from the NSDAP, an extremely unlikely outcome that either demonstrated Stark's fearlessness, his rage, or his naivete. In the meantime Wagner, who was pleased that Stark had lost the DFG presidency, thought that the physicist had been punished enough and was prepared to halt the expulsion process, if Stark would recognize his error and apologize to Wagner and Sollinger in writing. Stark refused and instead had to defend himself in court.[62]

Stark described his trial as the tragic end of his fourteen-year struggle for Hitler and his movement and flatly rejected the charges against him. The physicist was shaken by the fact that the Highest NSDAP Court began a trial against him for conduct that he had felt obligated to do precisely in the interest of National Socialism. Stark had been fighting longer for Hitler than had Wagner, and could judge for himself what benefited or damaged the Party. Moreover, the physicist told the court that he had no intention of taking his expulsion quietly: he would inform Hitler personally of the tragic end of his struggle for the NS movement and its Leader. Hitler, Stark was convinced, would not judge his conduct as an offense against the efforts of his political movement.[63]

After careful consideration of all the testimony and evidence, the Party court saw no point in proceeding with Stark's trial. There was no doubt that Stark truly believed that Sollinger should have been disciplined. Stark could only be punished for not going through official party channels to Hess with his complaints. Although the physicist should have taken his complaint to Hess, the court had to agree with Stark that the Sollinger affair had hurt the image of the party. Stark may also not have known the proper procedure. Thus he had very little guilt. Since Sollinger had not been punished in any way and Stark had already lost the presidency of the DFG, the court and the NSDAP leadership quashed the proceedings in January of 1938 because of Stark's valuable past services to the NS movement.[64]

The Sommerfeld Succession

By 1934 Arnold Sommerfeld, Johannes Stark's greatest nemesis, was planning to retire in Munich and wanted one of his most successful pupils, Werner

198   Living with the Bomb

Heisenberg, to replace him. Most German physicists and members of the Munich faculty probably would have agreed that Heisenberg was an ideal choice. But Stark was adamant that Heisenberg would not succeed Sommerfeld and fought resolutely and tenaciously against this. What came to be called the "Sommerfeld Succession" was Stark's last political campaign and decisively changed the relationship between the NS government and the German physics community.

Heisenberg, along with the Danish physicist Niels Bohr, Erwin Schrödinger, and others, was one of the founders of quantum mechanics and in 1928 had become full professor of physics at the University of Leipzig at the young age of 27. Although Heisenberg himself was not affected by the Civil Service Law, many young scientists who were working with him had to leave his institute. Heisenberg subsequently received several very generous offers of positions in the United States once the National Socialists came to power, including from Columbia and Harvard Universities but did not want to leave Germany.[65]

In order to influence the search for Sommerfeld's successor, which "was close to my heart," Stark enlisted allies in Munich and tried to get information from former colleagues inside of REM but the latter effort was initially unsuccessful. The physicist increasingly denounced other scientists in public. In his 1934 book *Nationalsozialismus und Wissenschaft* (*National Socialism and Science*) Stark claimed that during the previous decades the "theoretical physics enterprise" centered around Einstein and Sommerfeld of "Jewish-spirited scientists" had dominated their areas of science, sometimes through "intellectual terror." In the published version of the speech he gave in December 1935, when the Heidelberg physics institute was named after Lenard, Stark began to turn his attention to Heisenberg:

After the sensation and the advertising for Einstein's theory of relativity came the matrix theory of Heisenberg and the so-called wave mechanics of Schrödinger, each as opaque and formalistic as the other.... Today Einstein has vanished from Germany ... but unfortunately his German friends and supporters are still able to continue working in his spirit ... the theoretical formalist Heisenberg, spirit of Einstein's spirit, is even supposed to be honored by a call to a professorship.[66]

The denunciation campaign escalated with an exchange in the *Völkischer Beobachter*. First came an article by an unknown physics student who quoted liberally from Stark's Heidelberg speech, which in turn had quoted liberally from Lenard, again denouncing Heisenberg. After discussions with a NS official in Leipzig and the Dean of the Philosophical Faculty at the University of Munich, Heisenberg decided that he had to respond. In an article also published in the leading NS newspaper, the physicist defended modern physics, including quantum and relativity theory and concluded that theoretical physics was "one of the most noble tasks for young German scientists." Heisenberg's essay

Compromising with Hitler

was immediately followed by a response from Stark, who again argued that the scientists practicing Heisenberg's style of physics should not be appointed to professorships and, in bold type, attacked his younger colleague: "In his article Heisenberg still represents the fundamentals of Jewish physics, indeed he even expects young Germans to adopt this and take Einstein and his comrades as scientific role models."[67]

Despite Stark's rejoinder, the very fact that Heisenberg had been allowed to publish an article in the *Völkischer Beobachter* suggested that leading National Socialists were ambivalent about Stark. Mentzel, who at this time was still working to oust Stark from the DFG, asked Heisenberg and two experimental physicists to draft a memorandum for REM on the position of theoretical physics.[68] The resulting document, that gathered seventy-five signatures from Germany's most important physicists, described German physics as in a "crisis": the great demand for physicists in industry and the armed forces could not be met; it was often difficult to fill open professorships and the number of physics students during the most recent semester was much too small. These problems were exacerbated by attacks that the signatories found "unfounded and harmful" because they frightened students away from physics, and theoretical physics in particular, when a good theoretical education was necessary for both scientists and engineers. In closing, the signatories desired a halt to "the public discussions in the daily newspapers that try to reduce the value of one direction of research in favor of the other."[69]

Heisenberg sent Lenard the memorandum before it was submitted to the Ministry. Along with a few younger colleagues sympathetic to "Aryan Physics,"[70] Lenard contacted the Ministry directly with objections. For Lenard and his younger colleagues, it was all about race: "What the researcher who cares about true knowledge, and especially the German researcher who has inwardly experienced the spiritual revolution of the past three years, must reject in the strongest terms are those methods of theoretical physics that came to dominate in the most harmful way before the National Socialist revolution and that we can simply describe as the methods of non-Aryans." Rudolf Tomaschek, an experimental physicist, told the Ministry that it was not a struggle between experimental and theoretical physics, as the memorandum implied, rather between "German natural research and the Jewish spirit."[71]

By the spring of 1937 it appeared that Stark had been sidelined. Wilhelm Dames, Mentzel's assistant at REM, offered Heisenberg the opportunity to take over in Munich in April as Sommerfeld's temporary replacement, with a permanent appointment to follow. Heisenberg miscalculated, perhaps assuming that the regular procedures would now be followed, and turned down the offer, preferring to wait for the professorship.[72] This gave Stark an opening, which he pursued with increasing ferocity. In May he denounced Heisenberg to the Reich Governor in Bavaria:

200   Living with the Bomb

Although Heisenberg provided formal proof of Aryan ancestry, in his spirit he is worse than a racially-pure Jew.... If the Jewish spirit will maintain its domination of German physics, then it would be less damaging to bring back Einstein than to give a proxy for Einstein, stamped as an Aryan, the opportunity to continue work in his spirit to influence German youth.

Stark again tried to convince Minister Rust to oppose Heisenberg, first by claiming that Sommerfeld was undoubtedly Jewish, even if he had provided evidence of Aryan ancestry, then arguing that, because of Heisenberg's past Jewish connections, his mentality was "un-German and Jewish-related."[73]

Along with tying Heisenberg as tightly to Einstein and Jews as possible, Stark had a trump card yet to play. In August 1934, when President von Hindenburg died, the National Socialists moved quickly to further consolidate their power by merging the political offices of president and chancellor into "Leader." The Ministry of Propaganda asked Stark to organize a public declaration of support from the twelve Aryan German Nobel laureates for Hitler. The physicist then sent telegrams to his colleagues, including Werner Heisenberg and Max von Laue, asking them to add their names to this text: "We German scientists see and admire Adolf Hitler as the savior and leader of the German people. Under his protection and with his support, our scientific work will serve the German people and raise Germany's standing in the world." The response was so negative that Stark abandoned the project but not before sending Propaganda Minister Goebbels the responses to his call and Stark's rejoinders. Laue refused to participate, arguing that scholars should not participate in a political demonstration. Stark countered that it was not a demonstration, rather "a part of the great national commitment of the German people to Adolf Hitler before the whole world." Heisenberg told Stark that: "Although I personally vote 'yes,' political demonstrations by scientists appear incorrect to me, and for this reason earlier never common. Therefore I do not sign."[74]

By June Stark was convinced that Dames was going to give Heisenberg the Munich professorship. Stark now took the consequential step of placing an article in the weekly SS newspaper, *Das Schwarze Korps* (*The Black Corps*). As he wrote to Lenard, it was "regrettable" that they had to deal with this "worst sort of comrade of the Jews," but it was a matter of not letting the Jewish spirit "triumph with the call of Heisenberg to Munich." Stark hoped that the article would be a "devastating blow against Heisenberg and his comrades."[75] It was in fact a masterful example of character assassination in the Third Reich.

The article, "White Jews in Science," referring to racially Aryan scientists who were Jewish in spirit, had two parts. The first anonymous section contained the political, ideological, and racist attacks; the second, appearing under Stark's name, was more sober and professional but still thoroughly anti-Semitic. The entire essay probably came from Stark, since the arguments in the first section mirrored things he had written in letters or articles in the

Compromising with Hitler

recent past. Immediately after the title came another heading: "Einstein as Cornerstone." Indeed it is striking how dominant a presence Einstein, or his specter, remained in German physics. Stark was thorough, using almost every argument he had and turning Heisenberg's strengths against him.

The fact that Heisenberg had been appointed a professor at a very young age was supposedly proof that he had not deserved it and only got it through Sommerfeld's machinations. Once in Leipzig, Heisenberg had fired the German assistant and instead mostly given jobs to Jews and foreigners. The article Heisenberg had published in *Völkischer Beobachter* had been "smuggled into an official party institution" and sought to encourage young German scientists to follow Einstein. The memorandum Heisenberg and others had composed in support of modern physics was described as an attempt to silence his critics.

Although these attacks can be described as conventional for Stark, the attacks on Heisenberg entered much more dangerous territory with the second heading, "The Ossietzky of Physics." Carl von Ossietzky was a journalist and pacifist who had revealed German rearmament during Weimar that violated the Treaty of Versailles and continued to criticize militarism after the National Socialists came to power. In 1933 he was imprisoned in a concentration camp. When during his confinement he was awarded the 1935 Nobel Peace Prize, Hitler was so angry that he forbade German scientists from henceforth accepting Nobel Prizes. The article in *Das Schwarze Korps* stated that: "In 1933 Heisenberg, along with the Einstein-disciples Schrödinger and Dirac, received the Nobel Prize – a demonstration of the Jewish influenced Nobel committee against National Socialist Germany that should be equated with the 'honor' for Ossietzky."

Immediately after the connection was made to Ossietzky, which implied that Heisenberg belonged in a concentration camp, the article continued with Stark's strongest accusation against his younger colleague. "Heisenberg repaid his thanks in August of 1934 by refusing to sign an appeal of German Nobel laureates for the Leader and Reich Chancellor" demonstrating his "Jewish spirit" and rejecting "solidarity with the German people" and the "national responsibility" of scientists. Ominously the first part of the article ended with a clear threat: Heisenberg was just one example of scientists who were "all proxies for Judaism in German intellectual life and must disappear, just like the Jews themselves."[76]

Heisenberg and Himmler

Appeal to the SS

Although Planck, Sommerfeld, and Laue had also been repeatedly denounced by Stark, Heisenberg was different because he fought back. When Heisenberg complained to the university rector in Leipzig about the "shameless" attacks by

202   Living with the Bomb

Stark, he made clear that he wanted: "a fundamental decision by the ministry. Either the ministry agrees with the standpoint in '*Das Schwarze Korps*,' then I will resign. Or the ministry condemns such attacks; then I believe that I am entitled to the same protection that, for example, the armed forces would give their youngest lieutenant."[77]

Here the story takes an unexpected turn. Heisenberg's mother was an acquaintance of the mother of Heinrich Himmler, the Leader of the SS. Heisenberg asked his mother to intervene with Mrs. Himmler, who in turn advised Heisenberg to request a meeting with her son. Heisenberg's mother delivered his letter to Himmler's mother, who passed it on when her son visited her. Heisenberg did not get a meeting but his message did get through.

Heisenberg was of course writing because of Stark's attack in *Das Schwarze Korps*. He began by attacking Stark and Lenard at their weakest point, their age, thereby subtly emphasizing his relative youth. The older members of the physics community had not fully participated in the development of modern physics. In particular the two "old researchers" Lenard and Stark rejected and opposed this development. Since the National Socialist revolution, the two physicists had led this struggle with the argument that: "the science, in which the Jew Einstein achieved something, is just as unpleasant as Einstein's political views and in any case is to be rejected as 'Jewish.'" Heisenberg assured Himmler that he was always willing to participate in an objective discussion of scientific questions. However, he was not willing to be described as a white Jew or the Ossietzky of physics.

The form of the attack was especially unacceptable because Heisenberg was a civil servant of the National Socialist state. What should students who listen to his lectures or are examined by him think, Heisenberg asked, when they read Stark's article? Again Heisenberg asked for a fundamental decision. If Stark's views aligned with those of the government, then he would ask to be dismissed; but if this was not the case, as REM had explicitly assured Heisenberg, then he asked Himmler as SS Leader for "effective protection" against such attacks in the newspaper under his control.

Heisenberg ended with information about his political position. He did not belong to any party and "had remained aloof from the National Socialist revolution." For this reason he had not considered it right to join the NSDAP in order to gain advantages he did not deserve. However, he had intended to work as a German civil servant in the position he was placed and was thankful for every opportunity given him. As political references he offered the commander in his post-World War I *Freikorps* (paramilitary unit), other military officers, and the National Socialist student leadership at the University of Leipzig. Of course, the letter ended with "*Heil Hitler!*"[78]

Heisenberg's letter was passed on to the editor of *Das Schwarze Korps*, who in turn asked Stark for a response. Heisenberg could not deny, Stark replied,

Compromising with Hitler

that he had fired a German assistant and replaced him with two foreign Jews, that he had refused to sign the appeal for Hitler, and that through his memorandum he had tried to enlist the support of REM. In order to distract from his "Jewish past," Heisenberg had twisted in a "truly Jewish way" the facts regarding Lenard and Stark's attacks on the Jewish spirit in physics. With his "typical modesty," Heisenberg had presented himself as a young representative of progress in physics while Lenard and Stark were "old and backward." Stark went on to argue that even Einstein and Schrödinger should be valued higher than Heisenberg. Einstein's hostility to National Socialist had been in accordance with his Jewish character, while Schrödinger, whose theories had been "infected by Jewish spirit," gave up his professorship at the University of Berlin and left Germany. In contrast Heisenberg, the "favorite of international Jewry," wanted to continue "behind the mask of the politically harmless" to "champion of Jewish spirit and influence" and, in a thinly veiled warning to Himmler, "enjoy the protection and if possible even the support of leading National Socialists."[79]

Himmler replied to Heisenberg in November of 1937 by passing on the charges Stark had sent the editor of *Das Schwarze Korps*. Heisenberg replied immediately as best he could. He had let the German assistant go because he was not interested in modern physics. The two men he had hired to replace him were very good physicists but also Jews. Heisenberg and others had refused to sign Stark's appeal because they did not trust the latter and believed that they should demonstrate their loyalty in scientific, not political terms. The memorandum had been expressly requested by a REM official, Rudolf Mentzel. Finally, Heisenberg suggested that the way to settle the dispute would be a face-to-face meeting between himself and Stark.[80]

Investigations

Himmler passed the Heisenberg case on to the cultural division of the SD attached to his personal staff. Heisenberg never discussed this investigation in any of his memoirs and did not even mention it to his wife at the time. The SD made Heisenberg endure long and exhausting interrogations, planted spies in his classroom and throughout his institute, and had the Gestapo bug his home. But perhaps the most dangerous tactic it regularly used was to bring an even more serious charge against the victim, who would then confess to the lesser charge. In Heisenberg's case we can catch glimpses of this tactic in a letter from Hermann Beuthe, physicist and Stark's right-hand man at the PTR, to Ludwig Wesch, who had done his Ph.D. and *Habilitation* under Lenard in Heidelberg: Not everything was in the *Das Schwarze Korps* article; Heisenberg had married quickly in order to cover something up. Section 175 of the old Weimar criminal code made male homosexuality a crime. If convicted of this crime in

204   Living with the Bomb

1937, the offender usually landed immediately in a concentration camp. In fact the SS often used section 175 in order to extract confessions to lesser crimes but although Heisenberg did marry rather precipitously for various reasons, there is no indication that concealing homosexuality was one of them.

It is striking that both sides had physicists in the SD. Both Beuthe and Wesch were members. On Heisenberg's side was Johannes Juilfs, who was just finishing his Ph.D. in mathematics and theoretical physics under Laue. Fortunately for Heisenberg, it was Juilfs, not Beuthe or Wesch, who became part of the investigation. All three of the known SS investigators assigned to Heisenberg's case had some training in physics, one had Heisenberg as an examiner for his doctoral exam in physics at Leipzig, and Juilfs was working with Stark's staunchest academic opponent. In early 1938, a member of Himmler's personal staff asked Juilfs to prepare a comprehensive report on Heisenberg and theoretical physics.[81]

At around the same time Heisenberg was becoming more pessimistic about his chances. He wrote to Sommerfeld in February that "If my transfer [from Leipzig to Munich] does not happen, then Stark will certainly begin making a stink again.... It is really unfortunate, that at a time when physics is making such wonderful advances and it is really fun to work on it, that over and over again we have to deal with these political things." In a subsequent letter Heisenberg added: "Sometimes I lose all hope that the decent people will win out in Germany." Heisenberg complained again to his dean, including the example of a student who had received a stipend to study with Heisenberg but had turned it down because he was afraid that it could be politically damaging to him. But the officials in REM were not sympathetic. Heisenberg had no right to push for a decision, rather he would have to wait patiently until the time for a decision was right. Although Stark had gone too far with his attacks, Heisenberg "had himself brought on such attacks through his politically unacceptable conduct," in particular his refusal to sign the appeal for the Leader. However, Heisenberg would not be disciplined by REM for this.[82]

In the spring of 1938 Heisenberg received more bad news. A low-level SS officer, probably Juilfs, told Heisenberg that he had been unable to achieve anything on his behalf. The decision lay with Himmler, and Juilfs thought that the SS Leader would probably do nothing. Heisenberg now told Sommerfeld that: "You know that it will be very painful for me to leave Germany. I do not want to do this unless it is absolutely necessary. But I have no desire to live here as a second-class person."[83] By the following November, Heisenberg was more resigned. In a letter he sent to Walther Gerlach, thanking him for his support, Heisenberg wrote that he had a "thick skin" and would not be depressed if he lost the Munich professorship. Of course that would be aggravating but "we are still living in the middle of a revolution" and in any case one should not take "their own private fate too seriously."[84]

Compromising with Hitler

Ludwig Prandtl's Intervention

In November 1937 Heisenberg enlisted an important ally in his efforts to influence the SD investigation: the respected and influential aerodynamic engineer Ludwig Prandtl, someone who had excellent connections to the Reich Aviation Ministry and through it to influential National Socialists like Hermann Göring. Political assessments of Prandtl noted that he did not belong to any NS organizations and portrayed him as the

> unworldly scientific type. He is only interested in his scientific work, for which he enjoys an international reputation.... Prandtl is the type of honorable, conscientious scholar from a past age, concerned about his integrity and decency, whom because of his extraordinarily valuable scientific achievements we cannot, and do not want to do without in building up the air force.

As Heisenberg explained the problem to Prandtl: "Secret threads lead from our scientific circles into the circles of the SS. If through your connections to aviation you have any access to SS circles, you could do a lot of good." Prandtl responded that up until then he had no contact with the SS leadership but saw reasons for optimism because Alfred Rosenberg had formally and publicly declared that the NSDAP did not take an "ideologically dogmatic stance" towards "problems of experimental and theoretical science" and had advocated for the "freedom of research."[85]

In March of 1938 Prandtl unexpectedly had his chance when he found himself seated next to Himmler at a banquet of the German Academy for Aeronautical research. When Prandtl used this opportunity to advocate for Heisenberg, Himmler responded that if Heisenberg was convinced of the correctness of Einstein's theory, then there was no objection to Heisenberg using it. But Heisenberg should also distance himself sufficiently from Einstein as a person and politician, for the latter in fact stood in sharp contrast to the "Germany of today." Prandtl had promised Himmler that he would pass this advice on to Heisenberg.[86]

Heisenberg responded immediately, thanking Prandtl. Even though he had not received it, Heisenberg had been following Himmler's advice in private conversations, etc., because he had "never been sympathetic to Einstein's public stance." However, in lectures he had always only spoken about purely scientific questions and therefore had no opportunity to say something about Einstein as a person--or for that matter, about Stark. But Heisenberg was glad to follow Himmler's advice. When he spoke about the theory of relativity, Heisenberg would at the same time emphasize that he took a different political and ideological position than Einstein. Moreover Himmler could see that Heisenberg was different from Einstein because he had no intention of leaving Germany.[87]

Prandtl waited until after Germany's annexation of Austria, the subsequent plebiscite, the celebration of Hitler's birthday, and the Leader's trip to Rome had

206   Living with the Bomb

passed before following up his dinner conversation. Prandtl passed on a copy of Heisenberg's letter in which he agreed to follow Himmler's suggested guidelines but also added a few words about theoretical physics. Like Heisenberg, Prandtl argued that a small group of experimental physicists who "could not keep up with the theoretical research" had rejected the most recent developments because a considerable portion of it came from non-Aryan researchers.

But unlike Heisenberg, Prandtl was willing to use anti-Semitic rhetoric. Among the non-Aryan researchers there were those "of inferior rank who trumped their talmud-wares with the peculiar activity of their race. It was only right and fair that such products disappear." But there were also non-Aryan researchers of the very first rank who were ardently trying to advance science and in the past had truly advanced it. As far as Einstein was concerned, one had to distinguish between the man and the physicist. "The physicist is first class through and through but his early fame appears to have gone to his head, so that as a person he has become intolerable." But science could not concern itself with such personal characteristics. Scientific laws had been discovered that had in turn led to new discoveries and could not be left out without destroying the body of knowledge that had been erected on top of them.

Getting back to Heisenberg, Prandtl argued that it was urgently necessary that the stigma be effectively removed from him and both the central authorities and the highest Party offices make clear they do not share Stark's opinion. Otherwise the effectiveness of Heisenberg as an academic teacher will be severely inhibited because students would get the message that what they could learn from him was worthless, perhaps even harmful. Prandtl suggested specifically that Heisenberg be allowed to publish an essay in the journal *Zeitschrift für die gesamte Naturwissenschaft* (*Journal for the Entirety of Science*), which was controlled and edited by scientists loyal to Lenard and Stark. Prandtl closed by saying that the whole thing was less about Heisenberg personally and more about not allowing theoretical physics, which was so important for the further development of our understanding of nature, to "become deserted."[88]

The SS Rehabilitation of Heisenberg

Nine days after Prandtl's letter, Himmler sent letters to Prandtl, Heisenberg, and his second-in-command in the SS, Reinhard Heydrich. Like Prandtl, Himmler had come to the conclusion that Heisenberg was a "forthright man with integrity" and the SS leader found Prandtl's suggestion that Heisenberg publish in the *Zeitschrift* "very worth considering" and passed it on. When Himmler wrote Heisenberg, he noted that, precisely because he had been recommended to the SS Leader by his family, he had Heisenberg's case investigated in a "particularly correct and particularly thorough manner." Himmler was pleased to be able to tell Heisenberg that he did not support the attacks in *Das Schwarze*

Compromising with Hitler

Korps and had forbidden any further attacks. Himmler offered to meet with Heisenberg personally, so that they could have an in-depth discussion "man to man." Finally, in a "PS.," Himmler added: "I think it is right, however, if in the future you clearly separate for your audience the recognition of scientific research results from the personal and political attitude of the researcher."[89]

Himmler sent Heydrich copies of the SS report on Heisenberg, Prandtl's "very proper" letter to Himmler, and the SS Leader's own letter to Heisenberg. Heydrich was instructed to arrange a publication by Heisenberg in the *Zeitschrift* and to explain to Franz Six, the SS official in charge of the office overseeing matters of ideology, as well as to the leadership of the National Socialist University Students Organization, that Himmler believed Heisenberg to be "decent, and we cannot afford to lose or silence this man, who is relatively young and can train the next generation."[90]

The SS report itself, presumably authored by Juilfs, tells us more about how Heisenberg was defended, or defended himself, than what Heisenberg actually believed. To put it another way, we do not know whether Heisenberg said these things during his interrogations, whether this is how Juilfs chose to interpret Heisenberg's statements, or whether the report is a mixture of both. The report began by noting that Heisenberg had an outstanding scientific reputation and had already trained a number of good younger theoretical physicists. Heisenberg rejected the conflict between experimental and theoretical physics, because both branches needed each other, and instead made a sharp distinction within theoretical physics between good and poor scientists. Here he included physicists "who divorce themselves from descriptive experience" or were "alien thinkers" in the category of poor. In particular, Heisenberg included some of the Jewish and Aryan researchers from Jewish schools of physics who were strongly attacked by his opponents Lenard and Stark in the category of poor. Although Heisenberg had been trained in a school of "Jewish conception and methodology" that was divorced from nature, and his first great achievements therefore had an "alien character," in the meantime the physicist had developed a more and more "racially appropriate" way of working.

Heisenberg was described as personally "decent" and an "apolitical scholar." He was ready at any time to "defend Germany without reservation" because, as the report quoted Heisenberg, you are either "born a good German or not." He had been a member of the Freikorp Lützow paramilitary force immediately after the First World War and had volunteered for the armed forces during the Third Reich, serving in September 1938 when war with Czechoslovakia appeared likely. The report also addressed Stark's 1934 appeal for Hitler. Heisenberg had refused to participate because this would have been misunderstood by foreign colleagues. "However, over the years Heisenberg has become more and more convinced by the successes of National Socialism and today has a positive attitude towards it." Heisenberg still thought that, aside from the

208   Living with the Bomb

occasional participation in a political camp or something similar, active political activity was not appropriate for a university professor. The report closed with an anti-Semitic statement: "Heisenberg also rejects as a matter of principle the foreign infiltration of German living space by Jews." Heisenberg himself, of course, did not know what was in this report, rather just that he had been rehabilitated.[91]

Heisenberg thanked Himmler for his "friendly letter" that "freed me from a great concern." The physicist looked forward to meeting with Himmler because this would "contribute to clearing up the misunderstandings that exist between politics and science." Heisenberg also hoped that "some form could be found to publicly make clear that the attacks on my honor were unjustified." Initially Heisenberg hoped that the SS rehabilitation meant that he would be called to Munich but in fact Rudolf Hess, Hitler's personal representative in the NSDAP, had definitively rejected Heisenberg's call to Munich the year before. Himmler had taken Heisenberg's side but failed to persuade Hess to change his mind. Juilfs told Heisenberg that since the Party had decided against Heisenberg, it would now lose face if he came to Munich. Himmler had little desire to press for Heisenberg because the physicist could turn out to be a "bad National Socialist" in Munich, and the SS Leader would take the blame.[92]

The SS and Himmler had other plans for Heisenberg. When Heydrich sent the SS report on Heisenberg to Rudolf Mentzel, he attached a cover letter suggesting something else for Heisenberg. In Vienna, the professionally respected physicists at the University, who had mostly already belonged to the NSDAP when it was illegal in Austria, were politically and ideologically reliable. This appeared to offer a guarantee that, if Heisenberg were appointed there, the local circle of physicists would "draw him into interest in political events and the National Socialist worldview." The National Socialist officials in Vienna very much wanted Heisenberg to come.[93]

Himmler, who of course was very busy with what he undoubtedly considered more important matters, now told Heisenberg that, since it was planned to call him to Vienna, there was no need for a personal meeting. Heisenberg replied with a little ambivalence, saying that he would be happy to go to Vienna if the other professorships related to his subject were filled so that a "fruitful collaboration on a large scale was possible," but nevertheless still hoped for a personal meeting. In fact the two never met. Heisenberg's involvement in the wartime uranium project, with his regular commute from Leipzig to Berlin, then his move to the Reich capital, effectively ended any attempt to bring him to Vienna.[94]

Shortly after his article in *Das Schwarze Korps*, REM asked Stark to propose candidates for Munich. Ironically he struggled to do so. There were very few politically and ideologically acceptable candidates, and they were fairly old because younger theorists "either are Sommerfeld students or stand under his influence." Stark eventually recommended Wilhelm Müller, an engineer who taught applied mechanics and had published a small anti-Semitic book on "Science and Judaism" (*Wissenschaft und Judentum*). Although Müller's scientific limitations were clear to all, he probably appeared to be the lesser evil to the followers of Lenard and Stark in Munich.[95] Müller succeeded Sommerfeld as Professor of Theoretical Physics in Munich on December 1, 1939 and subsequently gave a job to Ludwig Glaser, a student of Stark and one of the earliest public opponents of Einstein. When a colleague told Heisenberg that Glaser had been "mentally ill for a long time," Heisenberg told his wife that: "on the whole I am amused by this entire monkey theater."[96]

Counterattack

The Munich Theological Dialogue

The appointment in Munich of the incompetent Wilhelm Müller was a pyrrhic victory for Lenard, Stark, and their few followers and supporters. In response, physicists mounted a counterattack spearheaded by Wolfgang Finkelnburg, a respected experimental physicist who had become politically active in the National Socialist University Lecturers League (*Nationalsozialistischer Deutscher Dozentenbund*, NSDB) at the Technical University of Darmstadt. In November of 1940, the Reich NSDB leadership organized a discussion between fourteen physicists from the two sides, Aryan Physics and the established physics community, that soon was dubbed the "theological dialogue" (*Religionsgespräch*). The seven physicists representing the physics of Lenard and Stark included Tomaschek, Wesch, Bruno Thüring, and Müller. The latter two left early after Gustav Borger, a physician and head of the Science Office in NSDB, who had been impartially chairing the meeting, criticized their conduct. The seven representatives of the other side included Finkelnburg and Weizsäcker.[97]

The followers of Lenard and Stark were forced to discuss physics instead of politics.[98] By the end of the meeting, there was a five-point agreement that included both the special theory of relativity and quantum mechanics as integral parts of physics. In practice, modern physics had now been officially sanctioned by the NSDB. The Aryan Physics movement quickly thereafter began to splinter. Tomaschek was an experimental physicist at the Technical University in Munich, which was now also searching for a theoretical physicist. Heisenberg noted to Sommerfeld: "Tomaschek is now only proposing capable theoreticians for the Technical University, in contrast to his previous stance, which confirms my past view that Tomaschek is the only capable but personally by far the most unpleasant man on the opposing side. By the way, during the last week I have not heard anything more about 'Aryan Physics.'"[99]

210   Living with the Bomb

The Ramsauer Petition

Ludwig Prandtl was outraged by Müller's appointment and complained directly to Hermann Göring: "A group of physicists, who unfortunately have the ear of the Leader, rage against theoretical physics and vilify the most respected theoretical physicists, push through completely unacceptable appointments for professorships, etc., on the grounds that modern theoretical physics is a Jewish creation that cannot be eradicated quickly enough and replaced by an 'Aryan Physics.'" Since winning this struggle was hopeless without winning over Hitler, Prandtl wanted Göring personally to intervene. A high-ranking official on Göring's staff responded that the Reich Marshall could not possibly deal with this matter at this time – unbeknownst to Prandtl, Göring was overseeing preparations for the German air force to invade the Soviet Union – and instead Prandtl should contact the Reich Minister of Education. Prandtl replied that bringing the matter to Rust was hopeless, since the latter had been forced by "more powerful Party influences" to make appointments he did not support.[100]

Prandtl now turned to Carl Ramsauer, the industrial physicist who as president of the German Physical Society could formally petition to Rust. Ramsauer took up the cause with enthusiasm and immediately enlisted high-ranking leaders in the army, navy, and air force. On January 20, 1942, Ramsauer submitted a twenty-nine-page memorandum, including a five-page cover letter, to Minister Rust arguing that: American physics had overtaken German; modern theoretical physics, which was decisively important for education, technology, and the ability to wage war, had been attacked unjustly as a product of Jewish spirit; and, quoting Prandtl, appointments like Müller's were "sabotage."

Like his colleague Prandtl before him, Ramsauer enthusiastically indulged in anti-Semitic rhetoric: "The justified struggle against the Jew Einstein and against the excesses of his speculative physics has been carried over to the whole of modern theoretical physics, which has largely been portrayed as a product of Jewish spirit." After the war, when Ramsauer published his memorandum in an effort to argue that physicists had resisted National Socialism, he excised this anti-Semitic remark without comment.[101]

Ramsauer's memorandum, which was immediately circulated widely among political and military leaders, should be seen in the context of the recognition that the lightning war was over and the war economy needed to become more efficient and productive. Heisenberg was impressed with how thoroughly Admiral Karl Witzell had read Ramsauer's memorandum, which had praised nuclear physics as: "The only area from which we can hope to make significant advances in energy-production and explosives." A month after Ramsauer submitted his memorandum, Heisenberg and colleagues from the uranium project gave talks before the Reich Research Council, including many invited military

Compromising with Hitler 211

leaders. In June of 1942, Heisenberg, together with colleagues from the KWG, again gave a talk on uranium before Albert Speer, Erhard Milch, and their respective staffs.[102]

Indeed by the summer of 1942, the leaders of Germany's armaments economy, including General Emil Leeb, head of Army Ordnance; General Friedrich Fromm, chief of Army Armaments and Commander of the Reserve Army; Admiral Witzell, director of the Naval Weapons Main Office in the Naval High Command; Field Marshal Erhard Milch, State Secretary in the Reich Aviation Ministry and Inspector General of the Air Force; and of course Minister of Armaments and Munitions Albert Speer, had all been briefed about the military potential of uranium. As Heisenberg wrote to Finkelnburg: "In general the highest positions now have a great interest in modern physics."[103]

Writing Einstein out of the History

In early November 1942 the NSDB sponsored a "physicists' retreat" (*Physikerlager*) in Seefeld, a city in the Tyrol region of what had been Austria. The thirty participants included three representatives of the NSDB. The few remaining followers of Lenard and Stark were overwhelmed and agreed to accept quantum mechanics and the theory of relativity. Although the invitation explicitly said that the goal of the retreat was not to find a compromise between the two camps, rather to "strengthen the connections among the physicists," a compromise mainly authored by the theoretical physicist Fritz Sauter and Weizsäcker was the most important result of the meeting. Einstein was thrown under the bus: the physicists agreed that the basis of the special theory of relativity had been created by Aryans and the theory would have been developed further even if Einstein had not participated.[104]

In the May of 1943 Laue, who was not at Seefeld, was criticized by Rudolf Mentzel for mentioning the theory of relativity in a lecture given in Sweden without also making clear that: "German research has explicitly distanced itself from Einstein's theory." Laue passed Mentzel's letter on to Weizsäcker, who urged him not to accept the criticism, mentioning the NSBD physics retreat and its recognition of special relativity as an integral part of physics. Weizsäcker summed up the debate at the retreat in a phrase: "The theory of relativity would have been developed without Einstein but it was not developed without him." Since Laue had been reprimanded by REM in the past without serious consequences, the physicist probably was not worried by Mentzel's scolding. Laue responded that he had sent a technical manuscript employing relativity to a journal, and that would be his answer.[105]

Even though the fight against Aryan Physics had clearly been won by the end of 1942, Heisenberg still insisted on publishing an article in the *Zeitschrift für die gesamte Naturwissenschaft*. When it became clear that there was resistance,

212   Living with the Bomb

apparently from some SS officials and definitely from Bruno Thüring, an unrepentant ally of Stark and editor of the journal, Heisenberg wrote directly to Himmler. After thanking the SS Leader for his appointment as Kaiser Wilhelm Institute for Physics (KWIfP) director in Berlin and the "restoration of my honor it represents," Heisenberg told Himmler that he had submitted his manuscript via SS officials but the journal claimed it had never received it and the SS officials were not responding to Heisenberg's inquiries. An official from Himmler's personal staff quickly promised to look into the matter. The article, "The Evaluation of 'Modern Theoretical Physics,'" subsequently appeared in the autumn of 1943.[106]

In the first section of the article, entitled "The Scientific Problem," Heisenberg clearly relished the opportunity to get even with his tormentors, beginning with an uncompromising rejection of "Aryan Physics." Instead of distinguishing between "pragmatic or dogmatic," "close to reality or alien to reality," and "clear or formalistic" physics, Heisenberg wanted to make another distinction: between "right and wrong." As he, Weizsäcker, and their allies had consistently done, Heisenberg excluded the general theory of relativity, which was much harder to separate from Einstein, with the excuse it was not as empirically established as special relativity. Both quantum mechanics and special relativity had made predictions that were verified by experiment. Because of the success of these two theories, critics needed to provide contradictory experimental results, not philosophical arguments or political attacks. "For this decisive point it truly has to be: The experiment to the front!"

The second section was devoted to "The Ideological and Political Struggle over Theoretical Physics." There was no reason, Heisenberg emphasized, why a National Socialist should see a contradiction between his ideological stance and modern theoretical physics or its conception of nature. Moreover, the struggle against modern theoretical physics had a very "unpleasant effect" on the reputation of German science and Germany's science and technology. The advocates of Aryan Physics had emphasized as much as possible the share of Jewish scientists in the theory of relativity and quantum theory, reduced as much as possible the share of German researchers, and presented the latter as mere "appendages" or "propagandizers" of Jews. Of course this was not done in order to emphasize the Jewish achievement, rather to discredit the two theories. But Heisenberg argued that reducing the achievements of German scholars like Max Planck was unacceptable and "un-German." Indeed "using anything other than scientific arguments or resources in a scientific argument does not correspond to the dignity of German research."

Heisenberg also followed the Seefeld guidelines and wrote Einstein out of the history. Aside from a reference in a footnote designed to discredit a supporter of Lenard and Stark, Einstein's name only appears once in the article.

A physical theory makes statements about reality, that is its only content. Reality is independent of theories, no matter how they came about. America would have been discovered if Columbus had never lived; the theory of electrical phenomena would have been found without Maxwell, electric waves without Hertz; for the discoverer can change nothing about the facts. In the same way the theory of relativity would undoubtedly have been developed without Einstein; precisely here it can be shown in detail that other scholars had already turned their thoughts in the same direction; the work of Voigt, Lorentz, and Poincaré already came very close to the complete formulation of the special theory of relativity. Therefore regarding the question of the *correctness* of a theory, the history of its discovery is best completely left aside.[107]

There is no doubt about Heisenberg's intentions here: he described his then forthcoming article to Theodor Vahlen, mathematician, long-standing NSDAP member, and President of the Prussian Academy of Sciences as follows: "In this article I have taken the position that the so-called special theory of relativity ... would also have been developed without Einstein."[108]

Conclusion

For Samuel Goudsmit, Weizsäcker's compromises at the Munich theological dialogue and Seefeld physicists' retreat were his greatest crimes. Indeed, writing Einstein out of the history of special relativity went further than the clear distinction between politics and science that SS Leader Heinrich Himmler had demanded. It was fortunate for Heisenberg that Goudsmit and other foreign colleagues apparently never learned about his 1943 article. Publicly renouncing Einstein was arguably the greatest professional compromise Heisenberg made with National Socialism. On the other hand, it is notable what Heisenberg and Weizsäcker did not do. Unlike Prandtl and Ramsauer, there was no anti-Semitism or attacks on Einstein as a person in either Weizsäcker's Seefeld text or Heisenberg's article. But even though Heisenberg and Weizsäcker never embraced anti-Semitism, they did accommodate themselves and their science in other ways to NS ideology.

But did Heisenberg compromise with the Nazis? Heisenberg did not oppose National Socialism but he also did not embrace it or withdraw into inner emigration. As he described in his Active and Passive Opposition manuscript, he chose to stay in a position of authority, indeed progressively taking on more authority, making what he subsequently argued were necessary compromises along the way. In the language of the postwar period, he was a fellow traveler. Fighting for the Munich professorship and defending modern physics, both because Heisenberg wanted and deserved the position, and in order to deny Johannes Stark and Aryan Physics a victory, meant engaging with some powerful and influential National Socialists in order to sideline or silence others or, to put it another way, navigating the complex, tortuous, and sometimes dangerous terrain of life and work under Hitler.

214   Living with the Bomb

It is also clear that Heisenberg went further than just demanding an end to the public attacks by Stark and others and his professional rehabilitation. The tone of his first letter to Himmler, his insistence on a personal meeting with the SS Leader, and his determination to have the article published in the *Zeitschrift* all went far beyond that. Heisenberg's fight to get the Munich professorship was not a fight against the National Socialists – all sides had National Socialists, indeed all sides had allies in the SS. It is not surprising that Hess and the Party Chancellery sided with Stark against Heisenberg, rather that some of the most powerful individuals in the NS leadership, including Hess and Himmler, devoted so much time and effort to deciding whether a particular scientist would be appointed to a particular university chair. In the end, this was because of Hitler's loyalty to his long-time supporters Lenard and Stark and the peculiar structure of the NS state.

After the war, Heisenberg and Weizsäcker could not defend their compromises against the criticism of their foreign and émigré colleagues. But the two German physicists must have found Goudsmit's conception of life and work under National Socialism and of the options open to them breathtakingly simplistic, black-and-white, and naive. Weizsäcker and Heisenberg, who had just lived through the Third Reich, knew better. Just as the story of compromising with Hitler began with Einstein, so it also ends with him. Heisenberg and Einstein had met several times during Weimar. In 1954, a year before Einstein's death, he invited Heisenberg, who was in the United States giving lectures, to visit him at his home in Princeton. As in all of their previous conversations, they only discussed physics.[109]

9 Rehabilitation

Weizsäcker assumes that it is no longer possible to act as if the atomic bomb did not exist, that is, in a sense to hush it up or conjure it away, rather it is necessary to create a political order that enables both parts of the world to live despite and with the bomb.

From the editor's introduction to the first part of Carl Friedrich von Weizsäcker's essay, "Living with the Bomb."[1]

Nobel Tales

In the summer of 1945 the news of Hiroshima refocused attention on the discovery of nuclear fission. At Farm Hall Otto Hahn was confronted with accounts in the British press with titles like "A Jewess Finds the Clue" that did not mention him and instead portrayed Lise Meitner as the discoverer.[2] When the German scientists responded to the news of Hiroshima with a memorandum two days later (which the British authorities suppressed), they asserted Hahn's priority: "Shortly after its publication Hahn's discovery was checked in many laboratories, especially in the United States. Many researchers, certainly first Meitner and [Otto] Frisch, demonstrated the great energies liberated by uranium fission. However, Professor Meitner had already left Berlin a half year before the discovery and personally did not participate in the discovery."[3]

On November 16, 1945, when the Farm Hall scientists were weary of their detainment and had begun to despair of ever returning to Germany, their spirits were raised by the unexpected announcement in the British press that Hahn had won the 1944 Nobel Prize for Chemistry. Hahn's Nobel Prize became a surrogate for their efforts to return home and the perceived failure of their wartime work. This was of course a great honor for Hahn but the scientists also saw this as a way to put pressure on their captors. When the British suggested that Hahn write a letter to Sweden accepting the Nobel Prize but regretting that he could not come to Stockholm to pick it up himself, Hahn insisted on mentioning that he could not attend because he was detained in England. In that case, The British officer replied, the letter would not be delivered: "You are Germans, you have lost the war."[4]

216 Living with the Bomb

When Hahn finally went to Sweden in December 1946 to receive his prize, he was warmly received: "Our stay in Stockholm and the welcome given to my wife and myself were entirely wonderful. We continually had the feeling that people were going out of their way to treat us well as Germans. Naturally the interest came mainly from the circumstances that for the past year I was not available, and that I am connected to the atom bomb."[5] Hahn came to Sweden determined to use his Nobel publicity as a platform to make a political statement and plead for Germany.[6] He also appeared to have "forgotten" or repressed both Meitner's role in the discovery of nuclear fission as well as German war crimes and the Holocaust.

In January 1947, Meitner wrote to her friend and colleague James Franck that Hahn had said that the Allies were doing in Germany what the Germans had done in Poland and Russia, a gross exaggeration and distortion of the facts: "Hahn ... absolutely did not respond to our objections; he suppresses the past with all his might, even though he always truly hated and despised the Nazis. As one of his main motives is to gain international respect for Germany once again ... he deceives himself about the facts, or belittles their importance."[7]

The Swedish Academy of Sciences decides who receives Nobel Prizes. In the case of nuclear fission, a committee of five Swedish chemists, in practice a voting majority of three, first decided in 1944 that Hahn alone would receive a Nobel Prize for Chemistry. The following year, a committee of five Swedish physicists, again via a voting majority of three, decided that Meitner and Frisch would not receive a Nobel Prize for Physics.[8]

One can ask how Hahn reacted to the exclusion of Meitner from a Nobel Prize, especially when it quickly became clear that this was controversial. After Hahn won his Nobel Prize, he then could nominate others. In the two years immediately following his award, when it probably would have counted most, he did not nominate Meitner for a Nobel Prize in physics but did nominate a German colleague for the chemistry prize. Eventually he did nominate Meitner in 1948.[9] Interestingly this is not what Hahn told the physicist, fellow Nobel laureate, and former émigré Max Born in 1954: "As far as Lise Meitner is concerned, I nominated her immediately after I received the prize."[10] Hahn no doubt thought that Meitner had suffered many injustices and deserved help and support, and he wanted to remain her friend and colleague. The one thing he was unwilling to do was to agree that the decision to give the Nobel Prize to him alone was wrong or unjust.

Repression

Otto Hahn returned to Germany from Sweden in triumph as a Nobel laureate, the newly elected president of the Kaiser Wilhelm Society, soon to be renamed after Max Planck, and, in the judgment of the British military government, a

Rehabilitation | 217

"known opponent of National Socialism."[11] After the war Hahn systematically carried out or oversaw the repression of three aspects of German science during the Third Reich: its nazification; its application to the war effort; and its participation in war crimes. This took place at three different levels: Hahn's own research and that of the Kaiser Wilhelm Institute for Chemistry (*Kaiser Wilhelm Institut für Chemie*, KWIfC) he directed; the Kaiser Wilhelm/Max Planck Society (*Max-Planck-Gesellschaft*, MPG); and German science as a whole.

Beginning at the very start of the Third Reich, there was a far-reaching and consequential nazification of the KWIfC, with many of its members openly embracing National Socialism,[12] although Hahn and Strassmann were exceptions to this. A secret report from Hahn to Army Ordnance in 1940 makes clear that during the war practically his entire institute was engaged with research directly relevant to the development of nuclear reactors and fissionable materials like uranium 235 and plutonium. For example, Fritz Strassmann did a comparative analysis of the uranium from various sources, including that from the Belgian Union Minière Company.[13] Three years later, when Hahn was speaking to the Academy for Aeronautical Research, he explained why the work he and Strassmann were personally conducting supported military research. The fission waste products produced in a uranium machine could hinder the fission process, so it was important to know which substances were produced, in what amounts, and how effective they were in absorbing neutrons.[14] Indeed these were all difficult problems that the Americans had to overcome to build the first atomic bombs. After the war, Hahn systematically portrayed all of this as basic research.[15]

From the beginning of National Socialist rule, the KWG voluntarily accommodated itself to the sometimes radical new policies of Hitler's movement. An important step in this process was the appointment of the chemist Ernst Telschow as general secretary of the KWG. Telschow was a NSDAP member who deeply integrated the KWG into an evolving military-industrial-academic complex, first into the rearmament effort, then the subsequent war economy.[16] Thanks in large part to Telschow's efforts, many if not most of the KWG institutes actively supported the war effort, including in particular the Institutes for Metals Research, Aeronautics, and Medical Research, with scientists working at the latter creating the first nerve gasses.[17] In 1945, Telschow admitted privately that:

After Max Planck and Friedrich Glum left, under the influence of the [National Socialist] party and the presidents [Carl] Bosch and [his successor Albert] Vögler a large number of institutes were added in the area of applied science, whereby the character of the society was greatly changed. We should try to get rid of some of these institutes and reestablish the purely scientific character of the society.[18]

Other institutes played an important role in the attempted colonization and germanization of Eastern Europe via the General Plan East, with sometimes murderous consequences. A series of biologically oriented institutes were set

218   Living with the Bomb

up to take advantage of German hegemony over Eastern Europe and territory conquered in the western Soviet Union.[19] Researchers from the Kaiser Wilhelm Institutes for Anthropology, Brain Research, and Psychiatry played roles in the inhuman medical experiments in German concentration camps and health-care institutions.[20] Perhaps most damaging was the connection between the Kaiser Wilhelm Institute for Anthropology led by Otmar von Verschuer and his former student Josef Mengele, the chief physician at Auschwitz and the human specimens Mengele sent to the Institute.[21]

After the war Verschuer refused to go quietly, demanding that his institute be reopened as part of the MPG. Desperate to distance itself from Verschuer but unwilling to admit any wrongdoing by the Society or one of its institutes, a commission was set up including a professor at the University of Berlin and three prominent MPG scientists and institute directors: Boris Rajewsky, Max Hartmann, and Adolf Butenandt. The clear goal was to rehabilitate Verschuer, not to bring him back into the MPG, rather to shift him somewhere else. As part of their argument, they fiercely "rejected the suggestion that Verschuer had been aware of the mass extermination in Auschwitz at the time the specimens were received." The MPG strategy worked when Verschuer was subsequently called to a professorship in Münster in 1951.[22] The Society's efforts on behalf of Verschuer contrasted starkly with its systematic opposition to the official Federal German policy of restitution and compensation (*Wiedergutmachung*). Although many scientists who had been forced to leave the KWG for racial or political reasons attempted to get compensation, the Society resolutely used bureaucratic and legalistic methods to obstruct and deny their claims. Since the Society was now publicly funded, this was not really about the money. Instead the MPG resisted admitting any responsibility for injustice done by the KWG or its officials during the Third Reich.[23]

When the four victorious Allied powers decided to dissolve the KWG because it had "performed war work to a large extent," Hahn replied that: "During the war and corresponding to its tradition, the KWG continued to nurture basic research to the furthest extent. Naturally to a certain extent work was carried out that was significant for the war economy. However, it was always of scientific significance." Telschow similarly claimed that: "As objective observers outside of Germany have admitted, the scientific standards of the KWG were maintained under National Socialist rule."[24] Thus if the Kaiser Wilhelm Institutes had done military research, at least it had been good science.

Hahn was now one of the most influential spokespersons for German science in general. Together with Hermann Rein, the Rector of the University of Göttingen and an expert in aviation medicine – which of course had been tainted by lethal low-pressure and low-temperature experiments on

Rehabilitation

concentration camp inmates – Hahn published an article in the *Göttinger Universitäts-Zeitung* under the title "Invitation to America."[25] Juxtaposing a denazification they described as unfair with the exploitation of German scientists, engineers, and patents by the victorious Allies, Hahn and Rein noted that: "Centuries ago the princes shipped peasants abroad as plantation workers or soldiers. Today the scientists are shipped abroad.... We do not comprehend why it obviously takes so long to distinguish "criminality" from "political mistake".... What is the purpose of driving people systematically into desperation and apathy? The result cannot be peace for Europe." This newspaper article encapsulates Hahn's postwar message: Germans and German science were the real victims. In contrast, Hahn said very little in public about the victims of National Socialism and the role German science had played in it.[26]

Otto Hahn did a great deal for German science after the fall of National Socialism but his unwillingness to face the Faustian pact that his own KWI for Chemistry, the KWG, and German science in general made with the NS regime is perhaps his most unfortunate legacy. Of course, Hahn was hardly alone in his refusal to confront the past, indeed one can argue that this was typical of German society on a whole,[27] but as the first President of the MPG, his words and actions carried particular weight. More than half a century passed before the Society began in earnest to examine what the KWG and its scientists had done during the Third Reich.[28] Otto Hahn set the tone for this long denial and repression of the Society's past.

While Hahn was still interned in Farm Hall, Meitner wrote him a deeply personal and powerful letter:

I have written many letters to you in my thoughts in the last few months, because it was clear to me that even people like you and Laue have not comprehended the reality of the situation.... That is indeed the misfortune of Germany, that you have lost all your standards of justice and fairness....

You all also worked for Nazi Germany and you did not even try passive resistance. Granted, to absolve your consciences you helped some oppressed person here and there but millions of innocent people were murdered and there was no protest.[29]

It is not clear that Hahn ever got the letter, or if he did, when he read it. But wittingly or unwittingly he did eventually respond to Meitner's reproach. Hahn knew what the Third Reich had been like and what he had done:

Would you, if you had been in our place, have acted differently from so many of us, namely to make forced concessions and to be inwardly very unhappy about them?. Think of the concessions made by Planck, so revered by you and by us all!.... One cannot do anything to counteract a terror regime.... How can one constantly reproach an entire people for their behavior during such times?.... We all know that Hitler was responsible for the war and the unspeakable misery all over the world but there must also be some sort of world understanding ... for the German people.[30]

220   Living with the Bomb

The Legend of Copenhagen

After the news of Hiroshima, Weizsäcker and Heisenberg recognized that their wartime work and future scientific research had to be decoupled from nuclear weapons. The two physicists pursued a careful and nuanced strategy. First of all they argued that the decision whether to give nuclear weapons to Hitler had been taken out of their hands, which allowed them to both emphasize that they had not made atomic bombs but also had not betrayed the German war effort. Next they claimed that they had tried to arrange an international agreement among all physicists to forestall all such weapons – not just German or Nazi. The apparent evidence for such a proposed arrangement was provided by a visit the two German physicists paid in 1941 to Heisenberg's mentor Niels Bohr in German-occupied Denmark. Eventually this visit and the legend that grew up around it came to dominate the story of the German wartime work on nuclear fission.

In 1946 the physicist Rudolf Ladenburg wrote to Goudsmit: "Thank you very much for your illuminating letter. It confirms in some respects, what Niels Bohr told us: Heisenberg and Weizsäcker visited Bohr in 1941 and expressed their hope and belief that if the war would last long enough, the atomic bomb would bring the decision for Germany." When the Dutch mathematician Bartel van der Waerden asked Heisenberg in 1948 about Copenhagen, the physicist responded that: "When I spoke with Bohr in Copenhagen in the autumn of 1941, I asked him the question whether a physicist had the moral right to work on atomic problems during wartime. Bohr asked in reply, whether I believed that the military use of atomic energy was possible, and I answered: yes, I knew it."[31]

Thus from the very beginning the different postwar accounts of Heisenberg's and Weizsäcker's visit were difficult to reconcile. Heisenberg's reply to van der Waerden also fit well with the arguments he made around the same time in his manuscript on Active and Passive Opposition[32]: staying in the system was opposition; because Heisenberg and Weizsäcker were in the system, not only could they help Bohr and his colleagues, they could also (at least attempt) to forestall all nuclear weapons on all sides.

In 1955 Weizsäcker presented a more differentiated version of this argument. After stating that German nuclear physicists had not needed to decide whether or not to make atomic bombs, he added that if they had faced this decision, then different scientists might have reacted differently. "Some would have certainly wanted to make bombs, others just as certainly not." What Weizsäcker regretted most, in a thinly veiled allusion to Heisenberg's conversation with Bohr in 1941, was that they had not made clear to their Allied colleagues that the Germans were not making atomic bombs, which might have forestalled nuclear weapons.[33]

Rehabilitation 221

Brighter Than a Thousand Suns

In early 1955 the writer Robert Jungk asked to meet with Heisenberg about a book he was planning on how scientists and especially physicists had grappled with the problem of political power during the previous three decades. Heisenberg turned him down. The subject was, as Jungk himself knew, "exceptionally difficult and delicate." The physicist had learned through experience that someone else, "even if he is so good an author," could not really express Heisenberg's own views.[34]

In contrast, Weizsäcker met in the summer of 1955 with Jungk and encouraged his project. "The longer I think it over, the more important it appears to me that something carefully considered be written about the themes we discussed, and you have the ability to do so and find resonance." Apparently one of the themes they discussed was the 1941 visit Heisenberg and Weizsäcker had with Niels Bohr. Jungk's 1956 book, *Heller als Tausend Sonnen. Das Schicksal der Atomforscher* (subsequently published in English as *Brighter than a Thousand Suns: A Personal History of the Atomic Scientists*), suggests that he was influenced by Weizsäcker. While interned at Farm Hall the physicist had said:

History will record that the Americans and the English made a bomb, and that at the same time the Germans, under the Hitler regime, produced a workable engine. In other words, the peaceful development of the uranium engine was made in Germany under the Hitler regime, whereas the Americans and the English developed this ghastly weapon of war.

This was very similar to the striking and controversial juxtaposition Jungk made in his book:

It appears paradoxical that the German physicists living in a saber-rattling dictatorship followed their consciences and wanted to hinder the construction of atomic bombs, while their professional colleagues in the democracies, who had no coercion to fear, with very few exceptions invested all their energy for the new weapon.[35]

Although stories or rumors about the visit to Copenhagen had circulated inside and outside of Germany throughout the first decade of the postwar period, *Brighter than a Thousand Suns* publicized the 1941 conversation between Niels Bohr and Werner Heisenberg in occupied Denmark. According to Jungk, Heisenberg and Weizsäcker traveled to Copenhagen in order to ask Bohr to help them contact their British and American counterparts and thereby forestall all nuclear weapons. Alone with Bohr, Jungk wrote, Heisenberg cautiously steered their conversation towards atomic bombs. "But unfortunately he never reached the stage of declaring frankly that he and his group would do everything in their power to impede the construction of such a weapon if the other side would consent to do likewise."

222   Living with the Bomb

Instead Jungk described the two men as talking past each other. Heisenberg asked Bohr if he thought atomic bombs were possible and his Danish mentor answered no. When Heisenberg asserted that such weapons were indeed possible, Bohr became so preoccupied that he did not pay attention to Heisenberg's subsequent remarks about "the dubious moral aspect of such a weapon." and instead became convinced that the Germans were "working intensively and successfully on an uranium bomb."[36]

Jungk's book made a great impression on the German-speaking world, including Lise Meitner in Sweden. In early 1957 she told to Otto Hahn that the book was: "a mixture of amusing anecdotes, sensational, exaggerated, and half-correct depiction of science, and definitely untrue personal claims." Jungk had painted a false picture of Weizsäcker and Heisenberg, "in this case in their favor." An English colleague had told Meitner that Jungk's book "had made him sick" and had been written in order to "wash Weizsäcker clean of Nazism." In contrast, Hahn told an American colleague that he had read it with "very great interest." Most of his German colleagues agreed with him, although everyone would have an objection to certain things written in the book. "The book actually reads almost like a novel and takes poetic liberties that the experts naturally notice and can criticize."[37]

Weizsäcker's reaction to Jungk's book was complex. He wrote to Jungk in the late autumn of 1956, during "one of the most terrible moments since 1945," referring to the overlapping Suez Crisis, when Israel, France, and Britain invaded Egypt, and the abortive Hungarian Revolution against the Stalinist government. Jungk's book was closely connected to the situation in which the Great Powers found themselves. Weizsäcker had to admit that he was "actually not happy" with Jungk's book but began by listing its merits. The book was well-written and presented very difficult material so that the layman could follow it. The seriousness of the matter was made clear to the reader early on, while some of the anecdotal passages were "really very amusing." More intensely than any other writer known to Weizsäcker, Jungk had tried to write the history of the atomic bomb as a history of real people.

It was "important and probably necessary" that Jungk had portrayed the role played by German scientists "to the best of my knowledge as it really was." Two points were most important: (1) the German physicists, "to say it a little more cautiously than you do, were very happy that they were never in the position to be able to make atomic bombs"; (2) the Americans' fallacy that the Germans were zealously making atomic bombs was the main reason why the bombs were completed during the Second World War. Here Weizsäcker added a third point: "We Germans failed to give the Americans a clear message that we were not making atomic bombs" and "considered it very unlikely that the Americans could make [such] bombs."

Jungk was correct to argue that the German physicists had never wanted to discuss this publicly. There were several reasons for this but one of the most

Rehabilitation

important was the "exceptional complexity" of the "moral and political problems." As far as Weizsäcker himself was concerned: "I do not and did not feel that I conducted myself correctly during the Third Reich. Here a consciousness of guilt cannot be eradicated. On the other hand, I can only find most people, who imagine that they would have done the right thing, to be naive."

Regarding the atomic bomb and everything that Goudsmit had criticized Weizsäcker about: "I actually feel that I did nothing wrong. Goudsmit's book, which to be frank I find unusually foolish, indicated to me that it was probably ten years or more too early to talk to Americans about these problems and have a hope of really coming to an understanding. I find it very much easier to not talk about the past and to support the obvious good will of most American friends and colleagues regarding the acute problems of today." Many years later, Weizsäcker told his friend and colleague in America, Edward Teller, that Goudsmit was the only person from his former circle of colleagues who "did us an injustice" because he should have "informed himself more carefully than he did."[38]

As far as Weizsäcker was concerned, by far the most important thing about Jungk's book was its "moral passion." Jungk understood that one "cannot be neutral about these questions." Although the physicist did not always find Jungk's solutions to these problems convincing and sometimes, "if I may use the word, also find them a little naive," Jungk was right to point out that, because of the nuclear arms race, the world was facing an "unrelenting judgment."

Turning to negative comments, Weizsäcker summed them up in one sentence: the level of Jungk's answers did not reach the level of the questions he asked. Jungk had exposed scientists to public scrutiny but "nobody wants to see themself naked on the market square." Some of Jungk's descriptions were dramatically exaggerated. "Real life is no less mysterious than a painting by Rembrandt, and sometimes your description seems to me to be like someone tracing the outlines of a Rembrandt painting with a red marker in order to make things clearer."

Weizsäcker again addressed the question of whether the German scientists had wanted to make atomic bombs, now in a more differentiated way. During the war there was neither a precise verbal agreement among the German physicists not to make the bomb, or to keep it secret. There was complete agreement in not desiring atomic bombs.

What we would have done if we would have discovered that we were in a position to make bombs, I cannot say afterwards, because this case did not occur. But here there was less verbal arrangement and more natural understanding than appears in your account. I would like to say explicitly that I am not completely certain that this understanding would have survived the moment in which we could have made a bomb. I believe that the majority of German physicists would also have then remained united but I do not dare say more.

They had told the National Socialist government, including Albert Speer, that "we were not making bombs, rather what today one calls a reactor." As they understood, there was the danger that he would have said that reactors

224   Living with the Bomb

were not important for the war and canceled the research. "We in fact did mention the possibility of an explosive but consciously in a way that this did not appear to be a goal that could be reached during the war." In this way they enjoyed the protection of an armaments project and "naturally no one who was not participating in our work knew with certainty that we were not making bombs." It simply appeared tactically smarter not to deceive the government and Weizsäcker admitted that he had also preferred not to do so.

But Weizsäcker left no doubt in Jungk's mind that "none of our close circle of friends would have hesitated to commit high treason against this government if we could thereby have achieved a clearly defined goal that we recognized as necessary." This suggests the question: Why at that time did Heisenberg not tell Bohr the complete truth? Weizsäcker explained that, during the Third Reich, he and Heisenberg had often had the experience that "where there was an essential unshakable human trust, it was superfluous to mention secret things because people understood each other anyway." In such circumstances, one refrained from telling secrets if possible, because if you did, then you might incriminate yourself and the other person if you were questioned by the Gestapo. Heisenberg naively assumed that he could speak with Bohr in the same way. When it became clear that Bohr no longer had complete confidence in Heisenberg, it would have been very risky to be completely open with him. Bohr was certainly a very admirable person but Weizsäcker was not certain that he "would have been able to avoid every step that could have endangered Heisenberg."[39]

Jungk took Weizsäcker's thorough and nuanced mixture of praise and criticism well. In fact the physicist had struck his "most vulnerable point." Jungk was aware of his tendency to "record and dramatize" and had been "fighting against it for years." Yes, he understood the argument that "if you want to reach ten thousands of people, then you must be effective" and "if you want to be effective, then you must exaggerate," but rejected the suggestion that his book was the result of economic necessity. Instead "the matter is deeper." Jungk was trying to give an overview of very specialized, technical material but every time he dug a little deeper, he asked himself, where does it end? He rejected the charge of not being conscientious. Jungk made his notes after the conversations. If errors arose, then they were the result of an imprecise recording of the protocol, not ill will or frivolity. Weizsäcker had written Jungk that he had not really given the subjects of his story any way out, and where he had tried, he had been naive. Jungk accepted this but replied that this was not his responsibility. Instead he referred the physicist to the simplest ethical commandments: "You should not kill (and not aid in this). You should protect your fellow men and not betray them. You should not allow any use of force, even in the name of something that appears justified to you." Here Jungk argued that most of the atomic scientists had failed. "If they had only been more naïve."[40]

Rehabilitation

When Heisenberg wrote Jungk about his book, he had two main concerns. The first "fairly important" point was Jungk's description of Weizsäcker's political conduct. Jungk had written: "He [Edward Teller] had to assume that his old student friend would remain loyal to Hitler." This was a "completely false picture" of Weizsäcker's political conduct, Heisenberg argued. "Just like every other decent person," at first Weizsäcker had "loathed the personality of Hitler and the crimes committed by his movement." Although this repugnance never diminished, it may have subsequently been mixed with admiration as Weizsäcker watched Hitler accumulate a monopoly on political power inside of Germany and practically without resistance forced other countries to make concessions. When the war began, all German physicists were faced with the dilemma that they either had to work for Hitler's victory or the defeat of Germany, and "naturally both alternatives appeared horrible." Most German physicists then attempted to "preserve what was valuable and wait for the end of the catastrophe, so long as one was lucky enough to experience that." Along with a defense of Weizsäcker's actions, this passage in Heisenberg's letter to Jungk reads as if it was consciously or unconsciously also autobiographical.

Heisenberg also took exception to a passage in Jungk's book describing "active resistance to Hitler," that betrayed a "complete misunderstanding of a totalitarian dictatorship." Echoing the argument he made in his manuscript on Active and Passive Opposition, Heisenberg argued that in a dictatorship only someone who pretends to participate in the system can actively resist, while anyone who openly opposes the system loses any possibility of active resistance. For example if a professor occasionally expresses criticism in a politically harmless form, Heisenberg told Jungk, then his political influence can easily be sealed off by telling the students that: "Old Professor X is a nice old man but he naturally has no understanding for the enthusiasm of youth." In contrast, if the professor tries to mobilize the students politically, then "naturally within a few days he would end up in a concentration camp and even his sacrificial death would remain practically unknown." This did not mean that Heisenberg himself had resisted Hitler. On the contrary, the physicist "felt ashamed" when compared to the men who tried to assassinate Hitler, some of whom had been his friends. They had sacrificed their lives to offer truly serious resistance. "But this example also shows that true resistance can only come from people who appear to be playing along."[41]

Jungk responded that Weizsäcker himself had admitted that, despite all the disgust he felt for individual National Socialists, he nevertheless had felt a "certain sympathy or let us say understanding" for National Socialism in the beginning of the Third Reich because it appeared that "deeper forces had broken through." Heisenberg responded that such an "understanding for National Socialism at the beginning" was very different from the phrase "loyalty to Hitler" Jungk had used. One could connect "understanding for National Socialism" with antipathy towards Hitler, for example by perceiving a "truly

226   Living with the Bomb

idealistic aspiration of the German people" was being "abused by such an unpleasant person as Hitler." Although the slogan "Hitler equals National Socialism" proved true in the years that followed, Heisenberg argued that this was not clear to many Germans in the beginning.[42]

Jungk was most interested in the visit to Copenhagen and asked Heisenberg for more detail. When Heisenberg obliged, Jungk published long excerpts from his letter in the second edition of *Brighter*, which was now translated into several languages, including Danish and English. These included a fleshed-out version of what Heisenberg had written van der Waerden in 1948.

My visit to Copenhagen took place in autumn 1941, actually I think it was at the end of October. At this time we in the "Uranverein" [uranium club], as a result of our experiments with uranium and heavy water, had come to the following conclusion: "It will definitely be possible to build a reactor from uranium and heavy water which will provide energy."

This talk took place on an evening walk in a district near Ny-Carlsberg. Being aware that Bohr was under the surveillance of the German political authorities and that his assertions about me would probably be reported to Germany, I tried to conduct this talk in such a way as to preclude putting my life into immediate danger. This talk probably started with my question as to whether or not it was right for physicists to devote themselves in wartime to the uranium problem – as there was the possibility that progress in this sphere could lead to grave consequences in the technique of war. Bohr understood the meaning of this question immediately, as I realized from his slightly frightened reaction. He replied as far as I can remember with a counterquestion. "Do you really think that uranium fission could be utilized for the construction of weapons?" I may have replied: "I know that this is in principle possible but it would require a terrific technical effort, which, one can only hope, cannot be realized in this war." Bohr was shocked by my reply, obviously assuming that I had intended to convey to him that Germany had made great progress in the direction of manufacturing atomic weapons. Although I tried subsequently to correct this false impression I probably did not succeed in winning Bohr's complete trust, especially as I only dared to speak guardedly (which was definitely a mistake on my part), being afraid that some phrase or other could later be held against me … [There should be an ellipsis here but it was not included in Jungk's book.] I was very unhappy about the result of this conversation.[43]

Heisenberg had written more about Copenhagen in his letter to Jungk, a passage very similar to one in his 1948 letter to Bartel van der Waerden but either Jungk chose not to reproduce it, or Heisenberg did not want it published:

I then asked Bohr once more, whether given the obvious moral misgivings, it might be possible that all physicists agree that the work on atomic bombs, which in any case could only be manufactured with an enormous technical effort, should not be attempted.

But Bohr said that it would be hopeless to try and influence what happens in the individual countries, and that it would be so to speak the natural course of events for physicists to work on the production of weapons in their countries.[44]

Cathryn Carson has made an important distinction between Jungk's bold claim that Heisenberg, Weizsäcker, and their colleagues would have sabotaged the German work on uranium if their Allied colleagues had agreed to do

Rehabilitation

the same, and Heisenberg's much more guarded statement that all physicists might have agreed not to make nuclear weapons. In fact neither Heisenberg nor Weizsäcker ever spoke about sabotage and they knew that it had not been possible for Germany to make nuclear weapons during the war. Carson interprets Heisenberg as talking about "less collusion than consensus."[45] However, this does suggest a question: if Allied physicists had wanted to work with Heisenberg and Weizsäcker to stop the atomic bomb, what did the two German physicists expect their colleagues to do?

While Heisenberg and Weizsäcker clearly had mixed feelings about *Brighter than a Thousand Suns* and wrote Jungk separately in order to correct and clarify things, it is important to note what they did not question, critique, or correct: (1) Jungk's juxtaposition of morally superior Germans with morally inferior Americans and émigrés; (2) his claim that in 1941 the two physicists went to Copenhagen in order to solicit Bohr's help as an intermediary with Allied physicists in order to forestall the creation of all nuclear weapons. As far as Jungk was concerned, he may have simply read between the lines of the suggestive juxtaposition that Heisenberg and Weizsäcker had been propagating since they had returned to Germany: We could not make atomic bombs and were happy about that; we tried to stop the Americans from making them as well.

Niels Bohr's Response to *Brighter*

When the second edition of *Brighter than a Thousand Suns* was published, both in Germany and translated into Danish, English, and many other languages, the long excerpt from Heisenberg's letter to Jungk about Copenhagen appeared to make very clear that the physicist stood behind Jungk's interpretation. Niels Bohr was evidently disturbed both by Heisenberg's account of their 1941 conversation and its publication. Between 1957 and 1962 he drafted several letters to Heisenberg in response.

Bohr had been in: "such a difficult and dangerous position during the German occupation, the visit was an event that had to make a quite extraordinary impression on us all, and I therefore carefully noted every word uttered in our conversation, during which, constantly threatened as we were by the surveillance of the German police, I had to assume a very cautious position."[46] However, Bohr also recognized that: "at that time and ever since, I have always had the definite impression that you and Weizsäcker had arranged the symposium at the German [Cultural] Institute [*Deutsches Wissenschaftliches Institut*, DWI], in which I did not take part myself as a matter of principle, and the visit to us in order to assure yourselves that we suffered no harm and to try in every way to help us in our dangerous situation."[47]

Most of all, Bohr wanted to know why Heisenberg and Weizsäcker had been allowed to come to Copenhagen. Indeed this is what he had been asked

228   Living with the Bomb

after he fled Denmark in 1943. "The question of how far Germany had come occupied not only the physicists but especially the government and the secret intelligence service [who wanted to know] how the visit had been arranged and what purpose lay behind it, as one has wondered in particular how and with what authorization such a dangerous matter, of such great political importance, could be taken up with someone in an occupied and hostile country."[48] Bohr may also have had a troubled conscience, fearing that his transmission of the information that Heisenberg and the Germans were working on atomic bombs may have made the Allies more determined to build them.[49]

In his draft responses to Heisenberg, Bohr emphasized the theme of cultural collaboration: while in Denmark, Heisenberg and Weizsäcker had urged Bohr and his colleagues to cooperate with the German occupation authorities.

It made a strong impression both on Margrethe and me, and on everyone at the Institute that the two of you spoke to, that you and Weizsäcker expressed your definite conviction that Germany would win and that it was therefore quite foolish for us to maintain the hope of a different outcome of the war and to be reticent as regards all German offers of cooperation....[50]

During conversations with [Christian] Møller, Heisenberg and Weizsäcker sought to explain that the attitude of the Danish people towards Germany, and that of the Danish physicists in particular, was unreasonable and indefensible since a German victory was already guaranteed and that any resistance against cooperation could only bring disaster to Denmark.[51]

My alarm was not lessened by hearing from the others at the Institute that Weizsäcker had stated how fortunate it would be for the position of science in Germany after the victory that you could help so significantly towards this end.[52]

Bohr's memory of their conversation about nuclear weapons differed from Heisenberg's in significant ways. First of all, whereas Heisenberg said that they had been taking an evening stroll in order to avoid being overheard, Bohr wrote: "I also remember quite clearly our conversation in my room at the Institute, where in vague terms you spoke in a manner that could only give me the firm impression that, under your leadership, everything was being done in Germany to develop atomic weapons."[53] Heisenberg told Jungk that Bohr had responded to him by asking whether he really believed that nuclear fission could be used as a weapon but Bohr remembered "quite clearly the impression it made on me when, at the beginning of the conversation, you told me without preparation that you were certain that the war, if it lasted long enough, would be decided with atomic weapons. I did not respond to this at all but as you perhaps regarded this as an expression of doubt, you related how in the preceding years you had devoted yourself almost exclusively to the question."[54]

Bohr may have objected to the suggestion that he was startled to learn that a bomb was technically feasible and had not grasped the physics.[55] Heisenberg's colleague insightfully suggested that his perception of the war had probably

Rehabilitation

changed over time. "I am thinking not only of the strong conviction that you and Weizsäcker expressed concerning German victory, which did not correspond to our hopes but more of how, during the course of the war, your conviction had to become less strong and finally end with the certainty of Germany's defeat."[56]

Although the German physicist Johannes Jensen had subsequently come to Copenhagen and "described the efforts to increase the production of heavy water in Norway and mentioned in this connection that, for him and other German physicists, it was only a matter of an industrial application of atomic energy,"[57] this had happened in 1942 or 1943, when "the war had already at that time taken a course quite different from what you and Weizsäcker expressed as your conviction in 1941."[58] When Bohr subsequently came to the United States, he brought with him a drawing of a nuclear reactor based on Jensen's information.[59] Finally, Bohr wrote that, because Heisenberg had told him that "he was working on the release of atomic energy and expressed his conviction that the war, if it did not end with a German victory, would be decided by such means,"[60] it was "quite incomprehensible to me that you should think that you hinted to me that the German physicists would do all they could to prevent such an application of atomic science."[61]

Niels Bohr never sent the letter to Heisenberg.[62]

The Göttingen Declaration

During the National Socialist period, Heisenberg's main opponents had been nonscientists, politically opportunistic second-rank scientists, and a few politicized scientists who had once been first-rank, all of whom tried to dictate what type of science would be supported, if not practiced. Heisenberg had been able first of all to overcome the advocates of Aryan Physics, and then pursue uranium research by impressing and gaining the personal support of the powerful National Socialists like SS Leader Heinrich Himmler and Minister of Armaments Albert Speer. After the shock of Hiroshima, both Heisenberg and Weizsäcker recognized that the atomic bomb had cast a deep shadow over their wartime work. Heisenberg had learned some important lessons under National Socialism and its immediate aftermath: (1) science policy should be determined by an elite circle of researchers who had made fundamental contributions to scientific knowledge; (2) support for such policy could come from politically powerful individuals; and (3) nuclear research, and in particular its public image, had to be separated from its military applications in nuclear weapons.

Heisenberg's fundamentally elitist conception of science policy was clearly embodied in the short-lived German Research Council (*Deutscher Forschungsrat*, DFR) for which he advocated. Composed of outstanding researchers and excluding administrators, politicians, or representatives of other groups, its self-proclaimed central task was to provide high-level policy

230   Living with the Bomb

advice to government leaders.[63] Although the DFR aspired to determine science policy in a very broad sense, in practice the scientists involved only represented the interests of basic, not applied research, and of the natural sciences, not the social sciences or humanities. For some observers, the DFR appeared undemocratic and reminded them of the Reich Research Council, a vehicle for the mobilization of academic science for the war effort by the National Socialist government. Heisenberg and other advocates for the DFR rejected this criticism, perhaps because their own politics of the past made it difficult for them to admit any wrongdoing during the Third Reich.

The science policy competitor of the DFR in postwar West Germany was the refounded Emergency Foundation for German Science (*Notgemeinschaft der Deutschen Wissenschaft*, NDW), an institution for dispensing government funds in support of scientific research established during the Weimar Republic and renamed the German Research Foundation during the Third Reich. The NDW had the support of the different West German states and promised to support a much broader definition of scholarship and research than the DFR. In the end, the DFR merged with the NDW to form the postwar German Research Foundation, so Heisenberg's efforts bore some fruit.[64]

Reestablishing nuclear research in postwar West Germany was inextricably linked to questions surrounding nuclear weapons. The American Atoms for Peace program, which promised to support civilian applications of nuclear energy, was complicated by shifting national security policies. The military doctrines of New Look, replacing large numbers of American troops and conventional weapons stationed in western Europe with less expensive nuclear weapons, and Massive Retaliation, whereby a Soviet attack on western Europe with conventional forces would be deterred by the threat of an American nuclear attack on the Soviet Union, begged the question of whether they would provide adequate protection for the West German Federal Republic.[65]

Chancellor Konrad Adenauer's government had to decide whether to join the European Defense Community (*Europäische Verteidigungsgemeinschaft*), which might include the joint development of nuclear weapons by European countries, and the American-led North Atlantic Treaty Organization (NATO), that promised the stationing of American nuclear weapons in the country. Membership in these organizations was intertwined with the question of whether and when the Allies would loosen their postwar control over West German nuclear research. As an internationally known and well-respected scientist, Heisenberg became an important advisor and agent for Adenauer, participating in the negotiations over membership by the Federal Republic in the European Defense Community and the new European Organization for Nuclear Research (*Conseil européenne pour la recherche nucléaire*).

The relationship between Adenauer and Heisenberg was one-sided. When Heisenberg was useful to Adenauer, the Chancellor was happy to employ his

Rehabilitation 231

services. But when it came to what Heisenberg wanted most, Adenauer disappointed him. Both men wanted to establish a nuclear reactor station in the Federal Republic. Heisenberg, who had been denied a professorship in Munich during the Third Reich by Johannes Stark, desperately wanted the new research center to come to the Bavarian capital, where he was planning to move his Max Planck Institute for Physics. Adenauer shocked Heisenberg, who had done so much for him, by placing the Reactor Station instead in Karlsruhe, at least in part for party-political reasons.[66] By 1957, Heisenberg was alienated from Adenauer.

The Ministry for Atomic Questions (*Bundesministerium für Atomfragen*) was established in 1955 with the ambitious and energetic Franz Josef Strauss as Minister. Shortly thereafter the German Atomic Commission (*Deutsche Atomkommission*) was created as its advisory board. By 1956 Strauss had become Minister of Defense, and his obvious flirtation with nuclear weapons disconcerted the members of the Atomic Commission, including Hahn, Walther Gerlach, Heisenberg, and Weizsäcker. They were afraid that the Karlsruhe Reactor Station could become a military research center with the result that other countries would oppose the resumption of nuclear research in West Germany. The scientists sent Strauss a letter setting out their concerns and threatened to go public with their criticism if Adenauer's government tried to get nuclear weapons. In response, Strauss assured the scientists at the start of 1957 that he was only interested in nuclear weapons within a European multinational alliance.[67]

The USA had begun stationing nuclear weapons in West Germany in 1953. When NATO announced in the spring of 1957 that it would equip its forces stationed in the Federal Republic with additional nuclear weapons, Adenauer's government decided that the time was right to push for their own.[68] In a news conference on April 5, 1957, Adenauer played down nuclear weapons as just a "further development of artillery." Strauss followed this up three days later by publicly arguing that the Federal German army needed modern weapons and the fact that all NATO states shared their defense meant that they all had to be armed with nuclear weapons. This so shocked the scientists that they agreed to set aside their collective reservations and differences and issued what came to be called the Göttingen Declaration.[69]

The Declaration was signed by eighteen prominent West German scientists – three chemists and fifteen physicists – none of whom could be accused of having communist or socialist sympathies. Weizsäcker was the driving force behind the declaration, writing and editing the text. It began with the sentence: "The plans for arming the Federal Army with atomic weapons fill the undersigned atomic researchers with deep concern" and proceeded to correct the misinformation being spread by Adenauer and Strauss. Every "tactical" nuclear weapon had the destructive effect of the atomic bomb that destroyed Hiroshima. While a tactical nuclear weapon could destroy a city, a hydrogen bomb would make an area as large as the Ruhr region uninhabitable. The

232   Living with the Bomb

radioactivity released from hydrogen bombs could exterminate the population of the Federal Republic. Moreover, there was no technical way to protect large numbers of people from this danger.

Admitting that they were not politicians, rather scientists, they insisted that, because they shared responsibility for the consequences of scientific research, they could not remain silent about nuclear weapons. Taking care to denounce communism, they admitted that the mutual fear of hydrogen bombs had helped keep the peace but insisted that in the long run this was an unreliable way to ensure peace. A "small country" like the Federal Republic would best protect itself and promote world peace by "explicitly and voluntarily renouncing the possession of nuclear weapons of any kind," they argued. Perhaps the most important part of the Declaration was the clear juxtaposition it ended with:

In any case none of the undersigned would be willing to participate in the manufacture, testing, or use of nuclear weapons in any way. At the same time we emphasize that it is extremely important to promote the peaceful applications of atomic energy with all means, and we want to continue to contribute to this goal.[70]

The resonance in the media to the Declaration was profound and positive, portraying the declaration as a morally courageous step. At first Adenauer attacked the scientists as "unreal" and argued that the "eighteen professors" should instead have aimed their declaration at the Soviet Union. Weizsäcker responded that they had addressed themselves to the West German government because they were citizens of the Federal German Republic and now accused Adenauer by name of downplaying the destructive force of tactical nuclear weapons. Adenauer then switched tactics and met with Gerlach, Hahn, and Weizsäcker in order to make it appear as if there really was no disagreement between what the scientists wanted and what his government was doing.[71]

Adenauer's strong reaction was in part due to the fact that there would be national elections in five months' time. Fighting fire with fire, the Chancellor enlisted a prominent and politically very conservative physicist, Pascual Jordan, to attack the credibility of what now came to be known as the Göttingen Eighteen. One hundred thousand copies of Jordan's pamphlet "We have to save the peace!" were printed and distributed. He argued that as far as politics were concerned, the Göttingen Eighteen scientists were naive and unwilling dupes of the Soviet Union. The "extremely unworldly" Declaration was simply "an appeal to the population of the Federal Republic to commit collective suicide."[72] In fact there were few political consequences of the Göttingen Declaration. By emphasizing the threat of Soviet aggression, Adenauer's party won the subsequent election handily. The Federal Republic's neighbors rejected the idea of West German nuclear weapons. The Americans were willing to see nuclear weapons in West Germany but only controlled and limited as part of NATO.

Rehabilitation

A timely popular history series in the influential German weekly magazine *Der Spiegel* (*The Mirror*) on the atomic bomb published shortly after the Göttingen Declaration also scrutinized the German wartime work on uranium. When asked about their research, Weizsäcker said that they had wanted to know whether chain reactions were possible. "No matter what we would do with this knowledge, we wanted to know." Echoing what he had privately said to Jungk, "If we had been under direct orders to build a bomb that was scientifically and technically recognized as possible," the physicist told *Der Spiegel*, "who knows whether we could have evaded this order." The *Spiegel* author connected Jungk's account of Heisenberg's discussion with Bohr in Copenhagen with the Göttingen Declaration, suggesting that Heisenberg had learned a lesson from his failure to clearly tell Bohr that "if you do not build it, then we will also not build it." Some of the Göttingen Eighteen had now spoken out in opposition to West German nuclear weapons because they had not wanted "to remain silent a second time."

Just like Samuel Goudsmit had done, the *Spiegel* article portrayed Weizsäcker's conduct during the Third Reich as flexible but now in a positive way. When describing the three physicists who went to meet Adenauer after the Declaration, Weizsäcker was the "militant comrade" who during the Third Reich had learned "maneuverability when confronted with greater force." When Weizäcker was asked why he had not defended himself when Goudsmit had accused him of "going along" during the Third Reich, he gave an answer that "would apply to millions of Germans." Weizsäcker "was not innocent enough to be able to acquit" himself, and "not guilty enough in order to have to justify" himself.[73]

The 1957 Göttingen Declaration and the 1956/1958 book *Brighter than a Thousand Suns* reinforced each other. After the publication of Jungk's book, even Franz Josef Strauss said that "to the credit of the German atomic researchers it must be said that they would have refused to build an atomic bomb for the dictators."[74] The public refusal by the eighteen scientists to help Adenauer's government to acquire nuclear weapons made more plausible Jungk's claim that, during the Third Reich, Heisenberg, Weizsäcker, and their colleagues had not wanted to build atomic bombs. In turn the book made these scientists appear consistent: both under National Socialism and in the new West German Federal Republic they supported civilian research on nuclear fission, not military. If one read between the lines of this juxtaposition, as very many people did, the connections became clearer: these scientists would have denied nuclear weapons to Hitler, during the war they wanted to deny nuclear weapons to the rulers of every government, and they were now trying to deny West German nuclear weapons to Konrad Adenauer and Franz Josef Strauss.

Living with the Bomb

Although Weizsäcker had drafted the Göttingen Declaration, it represented the minimum upon which the eighteen signatories could agree. By this time Weizsäcker had already developed a more differentiated analysis of nuclear weapons and what might be done about them. In his correspondence with Jungk, the physicist both agreed that, at the moment, the hydrogen bomb might be the strongest guarantee against a third world war, and defended his friend Edward Teller and his "admittedly passionate opinion that his colleagues were sticking their heads in the sand by thinking that the world would be all right if only they themselves stopped making weapons."[75]

In a radio lecture delivered in March of 1957, a month before the Göttingen Declaration, Weizsäcker asked whether humanity would have the strength to renounce large-scale war. There appeared to be three different answers to this question:

(1) A third world war would happen and either bring humanity's culture and therefore the atomic age to an end, or lead to a world domination that guarantees the peace;
(2) Another total war will not happen but there will always be wars fought with limited means and goals;
(3) All war will be abolished, either by tacit or explicit agreement.

Weizsäcker considered a third world war unlikely at that time but in the long run might well happen. For the foreseeable future, there probably would be limited wars but he doubted that they would help forestall another world war. As far as the third option was concerned, Weizsäcker was unsure. He thought that it was possible that "humanity will learn to avoid war," but added that this would require just as great an effort as in the past had been made in war: "Peace is not cheaper than war."

Weizäcker made clear in his lecture, as he did in the Göttingen Declaration, that he personally would not have anything to do with West German nuclear weapons. But the physicist went on to make a distinction between nuclear armament on the basis of national sovereignty and as part of a larger, transnational alliance. For small countries like West Germany, beginning to arm themselves with nuclear weapons was "criminal and suicidal nonesense." However, the nuclear armament of NATO, which would include the Federal Republic, was a "well thought out measure." Tactical nuclear weapons stationed in West Germany for the defense of its population made sense to Weizsäcker but acquiring sovereign nuclear weapons for the Federal Republic, which was precisely what Adenauer and Strauss wanted, did not.[76]

Just a few weeks after the Göttingen Declaration, Weizsäcker gave a lecture on the "Responsibility of Science in the Atomic Age" to a national university

Rehabilitation 235

student organization. After discussing both the wartime German and American atomic bomb research, and explicitly emphasizing that he was not passing any moral judgment on his American and émigré colleagues, he introduced the concept of the "simpler path." America waged war for freedom but took the simpler path of building the atomic bomb and then deciding to use it. Weizsäcker obviously did not mean simpler in the sense of science, technology, or industrial effort, rather that it would have been more difficult to have chosen not to build such a powerful weapon, or having built it, to not use it. After the war both the United States and the Soviet Union had again taken the simpler path and developed the hydrogen bomb, so that now for the first time in history "there is a weapon that can exterminate whole peoples." It was clear to Weizsäcker that humanity should stop taking the simpler path. First of all, nuclear weapons tests should stop. Physicists and engineers should work out how this could be verified and controlled, perhaps under the authority of the United Nations.[77]

After reading about the Declaration in a newspaper, an American and émigré colleague who had previously sharply criticized Weizsäcker's conduct under National Socialism, the physicist Victor Weisskopf, contacted Weizsäcker and asked for more information. Weizsäcker responded by sending his colleague the full text of the Declaration and describing the talks a few of the Göttingen Eighteen had in the meantime had with Adenauer and members of his government. Adenauer clearly wanted to shift the focus from what his government was doing to the international community, something with which Weizsäcker himself agreed.

Weizsäcker suggested to Weisskopf that the physicists of the world should hold an international conference on the theme: how can nuclear disarmament be effectively controlled? The initiative for the conference would come from physicists in smaller countries that did not possess nuclear weapons. Such a conference could not really fail, Weizsäcker argued, because whether or not the results were useful, the simple fact that it took place would relieve the political tension. However, this would only make sense if physicists from both America and the Soviet Union attended and Weizsäcker hoped that Weisskopf would help with this. Their Declaration had unexpectedly had a "very great resonance" in Germany and Weizsäcker hoped that it would encourage Adenauer to push harder for nuclear disarmament.[78]

Weisskopf responded that he was "much more in agreement than you think," and noted that the Göttingen Declaration had been very well received in the US. Everyone welcomed the fact that an important and responsible group of physicists had taken up the problem of nuclear disarmament. Weisskopf did note that the paragraph stating that the German scientists refused to work on nuclear weapons had "naturally caused some difficulties here," in part because it was usually all that the newspapers mentioned. While Weisskopf was in

236   Living with the Bomb

complete agreement and had refused to work on the hydrogen bomb, some physicists "took it a little too personally." The complete text, which Weisskopf had now received from Weizsäcker, made it clear that the Göttingen Eighteen "in no way (at least not directly) wanted to convict the US physicists who had worked on the bomb." Weisskopf was very much in favor of the conference Weizsäcker proposed and promised to help realize it. In fact their efforts were superseded by the first Pugwash Conference held in Nova Scotia in July of 1957. Although no Germans attended this meeting, Weizsäcker did participate in the second Pugwash Conference in April 1958.[79]

Weizsäcker had recognized that the nuclear arms race was one of the most important issues for humanity and decided to devote himself to it. Although he continued to organize meetings of the Göttingen Eighteen, the group never again issued a collective statement on nuclear weapons. Some members like Karl Wirtz, now the director of the Institute of Neutron Physics and Reactor Technology in Karlsruhe, were clearly unwilling to criticize Adenauer's government again. Others simply disagreed that any further statement would be necessary or helpful, and still others wanted the group to take a much stronger stand. However, this lack of agreement did not hinder Weizsäcker, who traveled to the USA in March and April of 1958, where he assimilated the discourse on nuclear weapons there by meeting with scientific and strategic experts and learning the new terminology and concepts, all of which he then brought back to Germany.[80]

In May and June of 1958 Weizsäcker published a four-part essay in the influential newspaper *Die Zeit* (*The Times*) with the title "Living with the Bomb."[81] The tone and content of the public discussion of nuclear weapons Weizsäcker found when he returned to Germany alarmed him. On both sides, people were arguing on the basis of emotions, not facts. The debate was simplistic, with one side saying that "so that no atomic bombs fall on us, we must not have them ourselves" and the other saying that "so that no atomic bombs fall on us, we must have them ourselves." Only one side could be right but both might be wrong.[82]

Using seven theses, Weizsäcker introduced his readers to the concept of graduated deterrence:

(1) Large-scale disarmament is not to be expected for the foreseeable future.
(2) The existence of thermonuclear weapons makes large-scale war very unlikely.
(3) However, these weapons do not protect from smaller-scale aggression and therefore not from gradual defeat in the Cold War.
(4) The West must be armed for fighting limited wars with limited weapons.
(5) This very preparation for limited war also makes these wars increasingly improbable.

Rehabilitation 237

(6) The abolition of war is the desired goal. It is a prerequisite for, not a consequence of disarmament.

(7) Along with graduated deterrence, the abolition of war will require multiple other political and moral commitments.[83]

Large-scale disarmament would require restrictions on the sovereignty of the superpowers and all other nations. Moreover, as more nations got nuclear weapons, the situation became less stable, something Weizsäcker called the problem of atomic chaos. This led Weizsäcker to carefully qualify something he had written in the Göttingen Declaration. The belief that the Federal Republic would be better protected if it did not contain nuclear weapons was "correct only to a limited extent." If all small countries renounced nuclear weapons, then this would greatly reduce the danger for all the countries. But they had never claimed that, if Germany was surrounded by nuclear-armed countries, then it would be spared.[84]

Perhaps the harshest critic of "Living with the Bomb" was Hedwig Born, the wife of the physicist Max Born. When the National Socialists purged the civil service in 1933, Born lost his professorship and took up a position in Scotland. After the war when he retired Born was one of the few émigrés to return to Germany, where he signed the Göttingen Declaration. As Quakers, the Borns were committed to peace and appalled by the nuclear arms race and the prospect of bringing such weapons to Germany. Apparently completely independent from Goudsmit's criticism, Hedwig Born brought up the question of compromise by asking whether, for a Christian like Weizsäcker, "conviction and compromise are compatible." Quoting from the Bible, Born told Weizsäcker:

Samuel says to God: "Speak, Lord, your servant hears" – he does not say: "Hear, God, your servant speaks." The first corresponds to conviction; it comes to us, it happens to us. The second is the compromise, the human objection. But we cannot hear and talk AT THE SAME TIME....

You have "heard" – in the manifest AND "talked" – "Living with the bomb" – and now because you have tried to combine the incompatible, none of the statements have any meaning....

One cannot publicly, following an inner conviction of conscience, testify – here I am speaking as a Quaker who stands by her peace testimony – and then, as it were, PUBLICLY "deal with the devil," and in doing so, whether YOU WANT TO OR NOT, become the Devil's advocate.[85]

Weizsäcker was visiting the Borns in July of 1958 when Hedwig Born gave him a letter spelling out her criticism after dinner. After reading it in private, he came back down for coffee with "deeply disturbed eyes" and said that her letter was "the most profound criticism I have received so far." They talked for the rest of the day and the next morning, with Max Born mostly listening.

238   Living with the Bomb

When Weizsäcker left, the Borns were still "deeply unsatisfied." As Hedwig Born wrote to a friend, her distinction between "conviction" and "compromise" was like "hitting the bull's eye while sleepwalking." Weizsäcker was "looking back after he had put his hand on the plow," but forward towards "political success."[86]

A month later, Weizsäcker, in a published reply to continued criticism from Pascual Jordan, explained his apparent intellectual transition from the Göttingen Declaration to "Living with the Bomb." At the time of the Declaration, they had to "scream loudly" in order to make everyone aware of the dangers associated with nuclear weapons. Now it was time to carefully consider the political pros and cons. In the meantime, Weizsäcker understood two things much better: (1) the nuclear policies of the superpowers; and (2) how the Göttingen Declaration had been interpreted "(in my eyes mostly misunderstood)." One of Weizsäcker's central points in "Living with the Bomb" was avoiding the threat of "atomic chaos," what subsequently was called nuclear proliferation. "None of us should imagine that once several European nation-states have atomic bombs, it will be possible in the long term to prevent Red China, Egypt or any dictatorship in the whole world from possessing these bombs." The world was more likely to see atomic chaos than complete nuclear disarmament and then the "balance of terror," that was precariously guaranteeing the peace, would become unstable. It would be easier to create an international order to prevent such chaos than to disarm the superpowers but "we certainly will not achieve this if we sabotage it through our own actions."[87]

For people like Max and Hedwig Born, Weizsäcker had compromised on his principles and had reneged on the Göttingen Declaration but this was not really true. The Declaration was directed against the Federal German government, despite Adenauer's efforts to deny this: West Germany should not create and have its own nuclear weapons. This dovetailed nicely with the imperative that Hahn, Heisenberg, and others shared: nuclear research in West Germany should be separated from the odium of nuclear weapons. Weizsäcker certainly supported this goal but had higher intellectual, personal, and political ambitions than the "just say no" message of the Göttingen Declaration. In contrast to some of the scientists who signed the Göttingen Declaration, Weizsäcker developed a much more sophisticated analysis of the admittedly dire situation the world was in and accepted that nuclear weapons from NATO or some other international force should be stationed in Germany. Indeed in a sense Weizsäcker advocated for this.

The Göttingen Declaration helped rehabilitate Weizsäcker in the eyes of some of his foreign colleagues. Although Goudsmit never forgave him, other scientists like Weisskopf did. "Living with the Bomb" rehabilitated Weizsäcker as far as Adenauer's government was concerned and represented the beginning of decades of work Weizsäcker dedicated to studying the interaction between

Rehabilitation 239

science and technology on one hand and the world political order on the other. He played a dominant role in the German Pugwash group, the Federation of German Scientists (*Vereinigung Deutscher Wissenschaftler*, VDW) founded in 1959. After Adenauer, the physicist became an important advisor to politicians, including Chancellors Willy Brandt and Helmut Schmidt.[88] In 1970 he received his own Max Planck Institute "Max Planck Institute for Research into the Living Conditions of the Scientific and Technical World."[89] Through his membership in the East German Leopoldina Academy of Sciences he regularly visited communist East Germany and inspired intellectuals there. When he died in 2007 at the end of a long life, Carl Friedrich von Weizsäcker had become one of the most influential and respected intellectuals in postwar Germany.

Conclusion

Otto Hahn, Werner Heisenberg, and Carl Friedrich von Weizsäcker were all rehabilitated in the postwar era. For Hahn, his Nobel Prize and, thanks to the support of the British occupation authorities, his powerful and influential position as president of the Max Planck Society obscured both the research he had overseen and carried out during the war and the concessions that he, like almost every German scientist, made to National Socialism. Heisenberg and Weizsäcker found it much harder to cleanse themselves from the lingering stench of the Third Reich but were aided first by Robert Jungk's dissemination of the legend of Copenhagen and their participation along with Hahn in the Göttingen Declaration. Finally Weizsäcker, who after the war was associated much more closely with National Socialism than either Hahn or Heisenberg, rehabilitated himself through his work on nuclear disarmament. Each in their own way, they had learned to live with the bomb.

10 Copenhagen

> What we have heard these days about the incomprehensible horrors in the concentration camps exceeds everything we had been afraid of. As I heard a very objective report in English radio from the English and Americans about Belsen and Buchenwald, I began to cry aloud and could not sleep all night. And if you would have seen the people who came out of the camp. A man like Heisenberg and many millions with him should be forced to see these camps and the martyred people. His appearance in Denmark in 1941 is unforgettable.
>
> Lise Meitner to Otto Hahn (June 27, 1945).[1]

In September of 1941 Werner Heisenberg and Carl Friedrich von Weizsäcker visited Heisenberg's mentor Niels Bohr in occupied Denmark.[2] Portrayals of Heisenberg during his stay in Copenhagen range from an obtuse German nationalist[3] to a resistance fighter against Hitler, determined to forestall all nuclear weapons,[4] and include an influential dramatization.[5] The contexts of this encounter are important. These include the course of World War II and particularly the invasion of the Soviet Union, the scientific progress made by the nuclear physics working group, and the ideological struggle within German physics. But perhaps the most important context was German cultural propaganda during the NS period, which included cultural exchanges and often served foreign policy and other broader political concerns.

Germany invaded Denmark in April of 1940. Until 1943 the Danish government cooperated with the German occupation forces in an uneasy political relationship, maintaining the fiction that the Germans were not hostile conquerors. Heisenberg and Weizsäcker undoubtedly went to Copenhagen in part to check up on Bohr and if possible to help him. However, there is more to this visit. While in Copenhagen, they contributed to official propaganda by participating in a workshop at a German Cultural Institute (*Deutsches Wissenschaftliches Institut*, DWI).[6] In his postwar manuscript on active and passive opposition, Heisenberg argued that in order to be in a position where one could actively oppose National Socialist policies, one had to stay and work within the system, even if that meant making compromises. His guest lectures in foreign

240

Copenhagen 241

countries and resulting participation in cultural propaganda should be seen in this context and provide an excellent example of how ambiguous and ambivalent cooperation with the NS state could be. Both inside and outside of the scientific community, the visit to Copenhagen has taken on a legendary status. Instead of the legend of Copenhagen, this chapter will investigate its history.

Foreign Lectures as Cultural Propaganda

The outbreak of war in September 1939 did not stop Heisenberg from giving talks abroad. In November 1940, Heisenberg was asked by the Hungarian Union for Cultural Cooperation to come to Budapest in early 1941. The Leipzig representative of the University Teachers League supported the request, noting that Heisenberg was suitable in every respect to represent German science in foreign countries.[7] Both the dean and the rector agreed that Heisenberg was an appropriate candidate as well.[8] The Reich Ministry of Science, Education, and Culture approved the lecture in Budapest.[9]

As he described it to his wife Elisabeth, Heisenberg enjoyed a stimulating and pleasant week in Hungary. Saturday he was taken first to the opera, where he did not understand the dialogue but enjoyed the music and stage scenery. Afterward a young local physicist took Heisenberg to a "night bar" where there were "unbelievable amounts of good food." It was 2 a.m. when Heisenberg went to bed. The next day a Hungarian colleague took him for an automobile ride in the neighboring countryside. They climbed a mountain to have a view of Budapest, enjoying the bright sun and a clear sky. Next they took a walk through Margaret Island in the Danube. Everything there was in full bloom. "How nice it would have been," if Elisabeth could have been there too.

Monday was a strenuous day. In the morning Heisenberg visited a lightbulb factory, followed by lunch. Heisenberg spent all day talking with people, followed by a talk for a general audience in the large lecture hall of the physics institute.

The hall was completely overflowing and I was celebrated like a prima donna. I cannot say that I always want it this way but it is much more fun to speak to 400 people who are pleased to be there than to lecture to six bored Saxon faces day after day.

Afterward was a formal dinner in a hotel in the city. Heisenberg bragged that "every day I consume at least one, often two half roast chickens," something hardly conceivable in Germany, where food had been rationed since the beginning of the war. On Tuesday, Heisenberg's last day in Budapest, he visited the physics institute early in the morning, had a late breakfast with a countess in a palace, in the afternoon went shopping in the city, and finished with his second talk. Although this was a more technical physics lecture, the lecture hall was again overflowing. The day ended with a banquet in the most elegant hotel in Budapest.[10]

242   Living with the Bomb

In May 1941, Heisenberg received an invitation to speak at the German Institute for Eastern Work (*Institut für deutsche Ostarbeit*, IDO), located in the General Government, the part of occupied Poland that was not planned to be annexed to Germany.[11] The Germans had set up the institute at the site of the former University of Cracow. With very few exceptions, the Polish faculty had been arrested by the German occupation forces and had been sent to the concentration camp in Sachsenhausen. The IDO's research supported the NS occupation policies of germanization: exploiting and eliminating non-Aryans and acquiring living space and resources for Germans at the expense of these peoples. The Institute's section for astronomy and mathematics employed the forced labor of Russian prisoners of war and concentration camp inmates for mathematical research.[12] Wilhelm Coblitz, the institute director, described their work as preparation for the final postwar solution of the European Jewish question.[13]

The founder and promoter of the IDO was Hans Frank, the powerful National Socialist leader in charge of the General Government and Heisenberg's childhood schoolmate. The two men were *Duzfreunde* (they used the familiar form of "you" in German).[14] Frank had personally invited Heisenberg to come and lecture in Cracow.[15] Heisenberg responded by requesting permission to travel to Cracow and asking Coblitz to schedule his talk when Frank could attend. The rector, dean, leader of the National Socialist Lecturers League from the University of Leipzig, and the High Command of the Army all supported Heisenberg's request.[16]

But REM said no. Rudolf Mentzel, a high-ranking official in the Ministry, carefully explained his decision in a letter to Frank himself.

The German Institute for Eastern Work has invited Professor Heisenberg from Leipzig to give a talk in Cracow. I did not grant Professor Heisenberg leave. The director of this institute has now told me that it was your personal wish to invite Professor Heisenberg.

The reason for my refusal to grant Heisenberg leave lies in his politically controversial personality. Heisenberg's connections to Jewish physicists and their supporters in foreign countries are so extensive, that the Party Chancellery has up until now been unable to approve appointments of this very talented scholar in Vienna and Munich. I can understand the reservations of the Party Chancellery, especially after the Jewish-influenced physics community recently again demonstrated enthusiastically for Heisenberg in Budapest. A letter from the Reich Ministry of Propaganda, which I recently received, also considers the talk Heisenberg gave in Budapest as unacceptable from the standpoint of National Socialism.

I am of course prepared to help you with cultural reconstruction with all my strength and request that you transmit your wishes to me in this regard.[17]

At this point in the war, the NSDAP was not able to control what went on in Germany's ally Hungary, which as far as the National Socialist leadership was concerned, was dragging its feet with regard to its treatment of Jews, who had not yet been completely excluded from public life. Some Jewish physicists

Copenhagen 243

may have attended Heisenberg's lectures, which no doubt would have embarrassed the NS officials who were also present. It is not clear that Heisenberg ever learned why his request had not been approved.

Copenhagen

Prehistory

The meeting between Bohr and Heisenberg in September of 1941 has a prehistory. In March of that year, Weizsäcker traveled to Copenhagen and gave talks at scientific institutions, including Bohr's institute. Weizsäcker's visit had strong support, both because his father Ernst was State Secretary in the Foreign Office and because the trip was serving German interests. Since Bohr's mother was Jewish, the German occupation officials considered him a non-Aryan. However, Bohr and the other scientists at his institute had been able to continue work because during the first few years of the war Germany treated both Denmark and the Danish Jews relatively gently while the Danish government was cooperating with the Third Reich. Weizsäcker undoubtedly wanted to check up on Bohr but also had other motivations.

The official purpose of Weizsäcker's visit was to give talks. The chief German official in Denmark was impressed by Weizsäcker's performance and reported to the Foreign Office that the physicist was able to make his lecture in Danish before the Physical and Astronomical Society, "Is the World Infinite in Time and Space," so interesting that "most of the audience, including the commander of the German troops in Denmark, could easily follow him." Weizsäcker also visited Bohr's Institute for Theoretical Physics, where he spoke on: "The Relationship of Quantum Mechanics to Kantian Philosophy." Weizäcker's talks had been "exceptionally effective, both for lay audiences as well as scientific Danish circles." The German authorities in Denmark wanted to invite Weizsäcker back to Copenhagen in the fall, this time together with Heisenberg, as part of a week-long conference on mathematics, astronomy, and theoretical physics at the newly founded DWI. The German Foreign Office forwarded the request to REM with its approval.[18]

Weizsäcker also used his trip to gather intelligence about any Allied work on nuclear weapons. In his official report submitted after this visit, Weizsäcker noted:

I was able to study the experimental and theoretical work at Bohr's institute, investigations of uranium and thorium fission by fast neutrons and deuterons. I have brought back copies and manuscripts of the work that is of great interest for our current investigations.

The technical production of energy from uranium fission is not being worked on in Copenhagen. They know that such investigations are being done in America, especially

244   Living with the Bomb

by [Enrico] Fermi. However, since the beginning of the war, no clear news has come from America. Bohr clearly did not know that we are working on these questions. Of course I encouraged this belief. Bohr himself brought the conversation to this point....

The American journal *Physical Review* was available in Copenhagen up until the issue from January 15, 1941. I have made photocopies of the most important publications. Arrangements have been made for the German Embassy to photocopy the journal for us as it arrives.[19]

Weizsäcker continued to be concerned about the prospect of American nuclear weapons. In July of 1941, he met with Minister of Education Bernhard Rust to discuss the status of physics in Germany, including America's advantage over Germany in nuclear physics.[20] On September 4, just before the trip to Copenhagen with Heisenberg, Weizsäcker passed on an article from a Swedish newspaper that he had received from the press division of the Foreign Office to the Army High Command. This reported that the Americans were working on a new bomb of unprecedented power.[21]

Planning

In June an REM official agreed that von Weiszäcker should return to Copenhagen but ignored Heisenberg. The Kaiser Wilhelm Society, von Weiszäcker's employer, told the Minister that von Weiszäcker would be happy to take part in the Copenhagen conference.[22] The Ministry of Education, in turn, informed the Foreign Office in early June that Weiszäcker would come.[23] But the DWI wanted Heisenberg too.[24]

On July 14 Weiszäcker met with an official from the German Academic Exchange Service in order to plan the Copenhagen conference. A week later he submitted a written proposal. Three German astronomers, Hans Kienle, Albrecht Unsold, and Ludwig Biermann, should be invited along with Weiszäcker and Heisenberg. The common theme of the conference could be the composition of the atmospheres of stars, a subject for which Kienle had done the best German empirical work, Unsold and Biermann the best theoretical. In addition – and probably the main reason for the choice – the subject was also the main field of research for the director of the Copenhagen observatory, Bengt Strömgren. Heisenberg would present his own work on cosmic radiation, while Weiszäcker would discuss the transformation of elements in stars.

Weizsäcker also made the case for Heisenberg: "Heisenberg's participation is important because, on one hand, as the leading German theoretical physicist he is difficult to surpass with regard to cultural propaganda effect, and on the other hand, because of his many years living in Denmark he is especially suited for Copenhagen and completely commands the Danish language."[25] The Foreign Office informed REM in early August that both Heisenberg and Weiszäcker had been consulted, and asked whether the authorities in

Copenhagen   245

Copenhagen could count on the participation of Kienle, Biermann, and Unsold as well.[26] Weiszäcker wrote to Bohr, informed him that he and Heisenberg were going to speak at the astrophysics conference at the DWI, and invited all of the Danish scientists to attend.[27]

When REM, which had just turned down Frank, resisted the idea of sending Heisenberg to Copenhagen, the Foreign Office requested a meeting with REM.[28] An official from the Foreign Office, the director of the Copenhagen DWI, and two REM officials got together on September 2. The director pointed out that

> the planning for the event has already been completed and a cancellation would be very harmful for the interests of the DWI, which has just begun its work. The DWI does not care about the disciplinary composition of the German group. It was emphasized that the event is only a scientific colloquium without any official character. The astronomers were consulted mainly in order to keep the event from having a one-sided physical character.... Heisenberg would only be in Copenhagen for 2 to 3 days.

There was also political pressure.

> Moreover, it is desirable for tactical reasons to carry out [Carl Friedrich von] Weizsäcker's event, because otherwise it is expected that the matter will not remain at the divisional level. The fact that the cultural political section of the Foreign Office has shown such special interest in carrying out this event ... is no doubt because the cultural political section fears an intervention from State Secretary [Ernst] von Weizsäcker.[29]

After some discussion, a proposal was cleared with Mentzel, the head of the science section in REM, to pass the buck. The Ministry would approve the conference if the Party Chancellery approved Heisenberg's participation. REM pointed out that the workshop would take place in the DWI without being advertised to the greater public. In other words, in contrast to Heisenberg's recent trip to Budapest, this visit would be carefully controlled and there would be no embarrassing pro-Jewish demonstrations.[30]

The Party Chancellery responded that there was no objection to Heisenberg's going to Copenhagen, provided that he kept a low profile and stayed only a few days. Denmark was certainly a less sensitive area than the General Government. The NSDAP did take care to emphasize once again that a high profile visit from Heisenberg was undesirable. When Heisenberg told Elisabeth that the trip had been approved, he said: "I am really looking forward to seeing Bohr, as well as the city, which I like very much. I feel a little bit at home there as well. Maybe I can also bring something home from there."[31]

The Visit

By the time Heisenberg and Weizsäcker traveled to Copenhagen in September of 1941, the former saw a clear path to the atomic bomb. The research had reached a point where nuclear weapons appeared feasible but nevertheless years

246   Living with the Bomb

away. Isotope separation via an ultracentrifuge had made significant progress with other compounds but had not yet worked with uranium. A nuclear reactor design in Leipzig developed under Heisenberg's direction had achieved significant neutron increase. As a result, in a report on model nuclear reactor experiments written for an internal conference in March of 1941, Heisenberg concluded that energy production via a chain reaction in a uranium machine was definitely possible.[32] Just a few weeks before the German invasion of the Soviet Union in June, Weizsäcker submitted his patent application for producing element 94 (plutonium) in a uranium machine.[33]

By this time the fighting in the East had taken on an unprecedented scale and quality. It was now a ruthless war between races and ideologies: National Socialism against the "Jewish-Bolshevist" Soviet Union. Although Germany was dominating Europe, Britain was under siege, the USA was remaining neutral, and the Lightning War (*Blitzkrieg*) against the Soviet Union still appeared to be going well, it is clear from his letters to his wife that Heisenberg nevertheless felt increasingly apprehensive about Germany's prospects in the war.

The available primary sources for the visit to Copenhagen include letters Heisenberg wrote to his wife while in Denmark and the official reports submitted after the workshop by Heisenberg, Weizsäcker, and the German occupation government in Denmark. While these latter documents clearly have to be scrutinized critically, it is important to note that, with so many different people observing what was done and said, the reports had to address the significant things that happened. In other words, the two physicists could not afford to remain silent about potentially controversial or important things.

On Monday, September 15, Heisenberg traveled to Copenhagen. "Late in the evening I walked under a clear and starry sky through the city, darkened, to Bohr." As he wrote to his wife, their conversation immediately turned to difficult issues: "The conversation quickly veered to the human concerns and unhappy events of these times; about the human affairs the consensus is a given; in questions of politics I find it difficult that even a great man like Bohr cannot separate out thinking, feeling, and hating entirely. But probably one ought never separate these."[34] The next day Heisenberg paid a visit to the local scientist who was cooperating with the workshop and worked out the details of the program. Later Heisenberg visited Bohr's institute.[35]

The rest of the German participants arrived in Copenhagen on Wednesday, while Heisenberg spent the entire evening with Bohr. A young Englishwoman stranded in Copenhagen was staying with the Bohrs: "During the unavoidable political conversations, where it naturally and automatically became my assigned part to defend our system, she retired, and I thought that was actually quite nice of her." While it is hardly surprising that Heisenberg could not avoid political discussions, this quotation does suggest that, in Copenhagen, both publicly and privately, Heisenberg defended German policies and the war.

Copenhagen 247

The postwar accounts of this visit all agree that Heisenberg told Bohr both that the Germans were working on the potential military applications of nuclear fission, and that atomic bombs should work. Despite Heisenberg's postwar account there is no contemporary evidence of Heisenberg and Bohr taking a walk, and Heisenberg appeared to be quite careful what he said in Bohr's home. Bohr in turn remembered having the conversation at his institute, whereas Heisenberg told his wife, he and Weizsäcker "had some scientific discussions, the Copenhagen group, however, does not know much more than we do either."[36] Wherever it took place, Bohr must have been alienated by the revelation that Weizsäcker, who in March had encouraged Bohr to believe that the Germans were not working on the military applications of nuclear fission, had deceived him. However, this also clearly did not stop Bohr, Heisenberg, and Weizsäcker from interacting in a friendly way.

The visit to Bohr's institute and discussions with the scientists there were definitely disappointing. As Heisenberg told Elisabeth:

Tomorrow the talks in the German Cultural Institute [DWI] begin; the first official talk is mine tomorrow night. Sadly, the members of Bohr's institute will not attend for political reasons. It is amazing, given that the Danes are living totally unrestricted and are doing so well, how much hatred or fear has been galvanized here, so that even a rapprochement in the cultural arena –where it used to be automatic in earlier times – has become almost impossible. In Bohr's institute I gave a short talk in Danish. Of course this was just like in the olden days (the people from the DWI had explicitly approved) but nobody wants to go to the German Institute on principle, because during and after its founding a number of brisk militarist speeches on the New Order in Europe were given.

When Heisenberg submitted his report on the workshop, he was quite clear about the fact that the Danes had refused to cooperate, and what he felt about it:

From being together with Danish colleagues, I have the impression that our relations with scientific circles in Scandinavia are now very difficult. Everywhere one encountered a very reserved, often even negative attitude. In the current situation only a few Danish colleagues are willing to work together scientifically in more or less official spaces, which is how they perceive the DWI. The Danes take this position, although almost all of the colleagues emphasized to me that they had no complaints about the behavior of the German armed forces.[37]

At the end of the war, Danish scientists explained that they perceived the workshop at the DWI as an attempt to coerce Bohr and his colleagues into cultural collaboration. Although pressed to attend the lectures – indeed Weiszäcker told the Danes that if they did not come to the DWI, then the SS would open their own cultural institute – the Danes refused. During the conference, Weiszäcker brought the director of the DWI into the Institute of Theoretical Physics and pushed him without an appointment past Bohr's secretary. Weiszäcker thereby forced Bohr into a confrontation he had taken pains

248   Living with the Bomb

to avoid, in part because he feared that the Danish resistance would believe that he was collaborating with the Germans.

The Danish scientists also recalled that Heisenberg had callously offended them by remarking that war was a "biological necessity," expressing pleasure at the successful German campaign in the East, and behaving as an "intense nationalist."[38] Immediately after the war, Lise Meitner wrote the Swiss physicist Paul Scherrer describing the "very peculiar things" she had heard from younger Danish colleagues about Heisenberg's visit: "He was completely infatuated with the chimera of a German victory and set forth a theory of superior men and nations over which Germany was meant to rule, even though he did describe the occupation of Denmark and Norway as 'regrettable.'"[39] Whether out of conviction or opportunism, the strikingly social darwinist comments Heisenberg made while visiting Denmark in 1941 consciously or unconsciously reflected the NS propaganda line about the war at that time.

Weizsäcker and Heisenberg probably did advise Bohr and his colleagues to cooperate with the German officials in Copenhagen, and in turn Bohr and his colleagues probably refused. For the Danes, participating in either the workshop or evening lectures would have been a morally objectionable and political act with unforeseen consequences. But for Heisenberg and Weizsäcker, such participation was simply the price for German officials, including representatives of the Foreign Office, to look out for Bohr. Perhaps most important, Heisenberg and Weizsäcker were merely advising their Danish colleagues to do what they themselves were doing, in Heisenberg's words, performing active opposition: working within the National Socialist system and being willing to make concessions in the hope of surviving, or perhaps even prospering.

The workshop proper began on Friday. In theory, it was run by Bengt Strömgren from the Copenhagen Observatory and his father Elis, which was an overt act of collaboration with the DWI. Whereas Heisenberg reported that, from the Danish side, only the two Strömgrens and the members of the Observatory participated,[40] the DWI described this in a more favorable light, noting that "the important Danish astronomers and a few theoretical physicists were present." In any case, it is important to note that, whereas Bohr, perhaps the most prestigious scientist in the country, and his immediate colleagues boycotted the DWI, other prominent Danes did not.

On the German side, along with Heisenberg and Weizsäcker, two astrophysicists, Hans Kienle and Ludwig Biermann participated and introduced the individual sections of the workshop devoted to their specialties. The workshop continued on into Saturday with morning and afternoon sessions interrupted by what Heisenberg called: "a big reception at the German embassy, with the meal being by far the best part of it." Indeed, in his report, Weizsäcker gushed with praise about the hospitality. The DWI had provided exceptionally pleasant space for the workshop. Weizsäcker was especially grateful for "the

Copenhagen 249

convivial reception on one hand from the director of the institute, Dr. Domes, the Plenipotentiary of the German Reich, and the members of the Foreign Office delegation, and on the other from the Danish scholars, with whom the German participants have old scientific and personal connections."[41]

The DWI was not content with a specialized scientific workshop, rather took advantage of the opportunity to have Heisenberg give a lecture for a more general audience made up on one hand of people Heisenberg described as the German colony in Copenhagen, including representatives of the Plenipotentiary of the German Reich and the NSDAP, and on the other prominent Danish representatives such as the rector and dean of the mathematical-scientific faculty from the University of Copenhagen, the president of the Rask-Ørsted Foundation, and colleagues from the Technical University. Heisenberg's lecture on "The Current State of Our Knowledge of Cosmic Radiation" used a "clear and simple presentation," which the DWI noted "educated lay listeners could easily follow" and was "very well received by the Danish and German listeners."[42]

On Saturday, the last full day Heisenberg was in Copenhagen, he once more visited Bohr at home, this time with Weizsäcker. "In many ways this was especially nice, the conversation revolved for a large part of the evening around purely human concerns, Bohr was reading aloud, I played a Mozart sonata (A-Major)." In contrast, as Heisenberg wrote to his wife: "The return to Germany from free Denmark made me quite gloomy. There people's lives are still so carefree; here everything is so extremely tense."[43]

While Heisenberg was clearly disappointed that the scientists at Bohr's institute had boycotted the workshop and Heisenberg's evening lecture, Weizsäcker's report had a more defensive tone: "The living proof that, even during the war, science is being carried on successfully in Germany, and the opportunity, in personal conversations to correct a series of inconsistent judgments about Germany, was certainly not without significance." As far as the DWI was concerned, the event was a success. Any cultural collaboration was a good start: "Both the colloquia as well as the lectures during the workshop by excellent German scientists helped lead new Danish researchers to the DWI and thereby expand the circle of the institute." A few months later, the Foreign Office told REM that "from the standpoint of cultural politics, a further accentuation of Professor Heisenberg is extremely desirable."[44]

The Goodwill Ambassador

Switzerland, Hungary, and Slovakia

Heisenberg's visit with Bohr in occupied Denmark in September of 1941 was merely one of many foreign lecture trips Heisenberg took abroad during the war. He spoke in Holland, Slovakia, Poland, and twice in Denmark, Hungary,

250   Living with the Bomb

and Switzerland. Taken together these foreign trips by Heisenberg help put the September 1941 visit to Copenhagen into context.

In the autumn of 1942, Heisenberg received an invitation to speak before the Swiss League of Students. Switzerland was one of the few countries in Europe to remain neutral during the war. Scherrer, who had invited Heisenberg, asked his German colleague to give a talk before the physicists at the Zurich Technical University as well.[45] Heisenberg was subsequently inundated with offers for speaking engagements. In the end, he agreed to lecture before the Science Faculty of the University of Geneva, the Swiss Physical Society, and the student organizations of Bern and Basel as well.[46] Heisenberg's invitation to lecture in neutral Switzerland was approved as a matter of course. The rector at the University of Leipzig noted as usual that the dean considered Heisenberg suitable for the trip and that the University Teachers League representative had no objections. He asked REM for its approval,[47] which was granted in late October.[48] The NSDAP merely reminded him of his obligation to call upon its foreign branch while in Switzerland.[49]

On November 17, 1942, Heisenberg arrived in Zurich and was met by the head of the Swiss Students League. The next day, he spoke at the university colloquium on observable variables in the theory of elementary particles. Although this was difficult material, he told Elisabeth that the audience "listened so intensely and I had such hearty, demonstrative applause afterward that our officials will be reasonably satisfied too." Afterward he visited Scherrer at the Technical University. Heisenberg's next lecture came before the Swiss Physical Society on November 19, which included dinner afterward as the guest of the president of the society. The next day he went to Basel, paid a courtesy call on the physicists there, and in the evening spoke before the local student organization on the current goals of physical research. Two days later, he gave an evening lecture before the Zurich student organization on changes in the foundation of the exact sciences, selling out the largest auditorium at the university. On November 24, he visited the German ambassador to Switzerland and the NSDAP representative in Bern and lectured to the Bern student organization.[50]

Heisenberg enjoyed Switzerland, even if the contrasts with Germany were sometimes depressing. On his first day in the country, he reported to Elisabeth that

you had feared that, as a German, I would encounter much hatred. But the first impression, which is so deeply moving, is just the opposite: a measure of friendliness we have not seen in years. And this comes not just from the people, who were friends from way back in peacetime.... Although I am immediately recognizable as a German when I speak, I encountered only friendly and happy faces, no hint at all of any hatred toward the individual German.... After the first surprise, I am gradually getting used to life among calm, always friendly and contented people.

Heisenberg was "spoiled" by his two physics colleagues, Gregor Wentzel and Scherrer, "like one can hardly imagine." He felt guilty that Elisabeth could not be there with him but "it is war" and that was out of the question.

Heisenberg also visited Scherrer at home but although the conversation turned to modern art, which was not to Heisenberg's taste, "fortunately politics is not discussed very much." The two physicists had "agreed in the most friendly way that they would not agree on everything." Heisenberg enjoyed the fact that "here such discussions do not hurt sacrosanct feelings." Heisenberg's official report noted that he was treated throughout in a very friendly fashion in Switzerland, and not just by old colleagues. Although he encountered frequent political condemnation of the "German re-ordering of Europe," this ill will did not carry over to personal relationships. His lectures had attracted great interest.[51]

Despite the displeasure of some NSDAP Party officials with how Heisenberg's 1941 visit to Hungary had gone, Hans Freyer, the president of the Budapest DWI wanted him to return. "Professor Heisenberg is so well known here because of his Nobel Prize and recent appointment at the Kaiser Wilhelm Society that a lecture from him will insure a cultural-political success" However, Freyer did agree that, because of the controversy Heisenberg's previous trip to Hungary had caused, other public lectures in Budapest would not be a good idea.[52]

REM was unenthusiastic but the Budapest DWI managed to get around the recalcitrant ministry by joining forces with the Kaiser Wilhelm Society. In early November the Society informed REM that a joint scientific meeting had been planned with the Budapest DWI, including talks not only by Heisenberg but also from Max Planck and Weizsäcker.[53] REM reacted angrily. Another talk by Heisenberg in Budapest would undoubtedly attract scholars of Jewish origin or liberal political views, including some of Heisenberg's former students and colleagues. The ministry was afraid that some members of the audience would see the affair as a political demonstration for Jewish scientists. However, the request by the Budapest DWI was very much strengthened by the Kaiser Wilhelm Society's participation.[54] REM informed the Foreign Office that they considered German initiatives for sending Heisenberg abroad (as opposed to invitations from other countries) inappropriate because his visits always ended up being so controversial. But since the KWG General Secretary Ernst Telschow had gone so far ahead with preparations for the lectures without consulting either the ministry or the Foreign Office, REM agreed to go along – this time.[55] At the end of November 1941, Heisenberg, Planck, Telschow, and Weizsäcker all traveled to Hungary as representatives of the KWG. A NS safe space was created inside the DWI where no Jewish or liberal scientists could attend.

Planck gave his standard talk on the "Senses and Boundaries of the Exact Sciences." The president of the DWI, who as Planck noted approvingly had

252   Living with the Bomb

set himself the task of cultivating the cultural relations between Germany and Hungary, met Planck and his wife at the train station and looked after them throughout their stay. Planck's talk was held on December 1 in the cozy atmosphere of the DWI. Guests included representatives of the NSDAP, and many Hungarian dignitaries, including Archduke Joseph, the president of the Hungarian Academy of Sciences, and the Archduchess Anna. Following Planck's talk, an official reception was accompanied by pleasant personal conversation. Planck was impressed both by the good will towards Germans expressed by the Hungarians and especially by Freyer's ability to awaken and maintain interest in German culture among the educated circles in Hungary. As Planck wrote in his report: "The entire event ran very satisfactorily and completely fulfilled its goal of supporting the intellectual connections between Germany and Hungary."[56]

The next day Weizsäcker spoke on "Atomic Theory and Philosophy" before invited guests, including "officials and the representatives of physics and neighboring fields from Budapest and other Hungarian universities." Afterward, he enjoyed meeting with Hungarian colleagues. That same day Heisenberg had lunch with the director of the DWI, tea with the German ambassador to Hungary, and lectured that evening on the "Current Goals of Physical Research." The talks by Heisenberg and Weizsäcker were followed by a concert of Mozart and Bach. An informal party at the institute brought the activities of the day to a congenial close. The three German physicists met the physics professor at the University of Budapest for lunch on the following day and Heisenberg joined his counterpart at the local technical university for dinner. He returned to Germany on December 4.[57]

The German foreign service stressed the value of the collaboration of the KWG. The Budapest DWI previously had sponsored only lectures in the humanities; they decided to try physics in order to attract Hungarians interested in science. The KWG was happy to send a few scientists. At first its president, Albert Vogler, planned to attend as well and provide a brief survey of the society. Telschow went instead. As Freyer noted approvingly, Telschow's talk provoked great interest among the Hungarian scientists and the representatives of the Ministry of Culture. The Hungarians had lost the research funds they previously had received from America; Freyer believed that Germany could fill the gap.

Freyer was effusive in his praise for the speakers. Planck demonstrated "astonishing freshness, inner dignity and intellectual elegance." Weizsäcker's lecture, given without text, was simply brilliant: "certainly today no one else is able to connect the research fields of modern physics and problems of modern philosophy as productively as this young scholar." The discussion provoked by Weizsäcker's talk lasted until midnight. Finally, Heisenberg had provided a "carefully balanced overview of the problems facing physics and

Copenhagen 253

the directions the current research is taking. The lecture had a clarity and maturity that only a researcher working at the cutting edge of science can provide." For his part, Heisenberg reported that: "The lectures in the DWI were heard by many Hungarians and I had the impression that the DWI there has succeeded in a very fortunate way to hold the interest of Hungarians."[58]

From the perspective of the president of the Budapest DWI, the lectures were a complete success. The audience had been hand-picked, and almost no invitations were declined. Along with the Archduke and Archduchess, the guests included the ambassadors or representatives of Italy, Finland, Croatia, and Slovakia, the Hungarian Minister of Culture, all the relevant professors from the University of Budapest, and representatives of other Hungarian universities. Best of all, great interest had already been expressed from the Hungarian side for more such cultural events, which was what Freyer wanted to hear.[59]

The trip to Budapest in 1942 was the last time Heisenberg experienced difficulty in traveling abroad. Henceforth, if he did not give a talk, then it was his own decision. Heisenberg received two invitations to France in 1943. The German Embassy in Paris was sponsoring a lecture series at the College de France, and wanted Heisenberg to deliver a strictly scientific talk in French.[60] The dean at the University of Berlin forwarded the invitation to Heisenberg with the remark that he, the rector, and the representative of the University Teachers League naturally would support the trip.[61] The German Institute in France also wanted a lecture from Heisenberg.[62] He turned down both offers, saying that his French was not good enough for lecturing.[63] In contrast, Weizsäcker did give a lecture in Paris but both his talk and the lunch given in his honor were boycotted by his French colleagues. When the French physicist Frédéric Joliot criticized his German colleague for the bad taste he had shown by accepting an invitation from the German occupation authorities, Weizsäcker replied that he had been forced to accept.[64]

Like Heisenberg, Weizsäcker traveled widely during the war to give talks, including occupied countries like Denmark, France, and Latvia, German allies like Italy, Finland, Rumania, and Bulgaria, and in 1944 two neutral but German-leaning countries, Spain and Portugal. In these last two countries he was impressed by the interest in German philosophy and the greater sympathy for Germany that he encountered when compared with the other European countries he had visited during the war and advocated closer cultural relations between them and Germany.[65]

In February 1943, the Slovakian University in Pressburg (Bratislava) sent an invitation by way of REM for Heisenberg to lecture in the Slovakian Protectorate, a puppet state that Germany had carved out of Czechoslovakia. The REM official told Heisenberg that they wanted him to accept the invitation and Heisenberg agreed to go.[66] Between March and October 1942, Slovak Jews had been concentrated into labor and concentration camps, although it

254   Living with the Bomb

is not clear that Heisenberg would have noticed any trace of this. On March 28 Heisenberg met the president of the local technical university, the dean of the Slovakian University, and a representative of the German Academic Exchange Service. That afternoon Heisenberg was the guest of the president, who took him to the opera in the evening. The next day, Heisenberg had an audience with the German ambassador, lunch with the dean and the president, an evening lecture on the state of atomic physics, and a late dinner with some Pressburg scientists. The following day brought more of the same: a walk through the old town hall with the mayor of Pressburg, lunch with the dean, the president, the local head of the German Academic Exchange Service, and the German ambassador, an evening lecture on cosmic radiation to a small group of scientists and students, and dinner with Pressburg scientists and a visiting Italian mathematician. The Pressburg scientists were very friendly. Heisenberg reported that the relations between Germans and their Slovakian colleagues were very good.[67]

The Netherlands

In June 1943, the collaborationist Dutch Ministry of Education sent Heisenberg an invitation to visit the Netherlands. Instead of public lectures, the officials wanted Heisenberg to make personal contacts and have discussions in small groups. The Reich Commissioner for the Occupied Dutch Territories, the highest German official in Holland, encouraged Heisenberg's acceptance.[68] REM welcomed the proposal, especially since the invitation had come from the Dutch Ministry.[69] Heisenberg responded that he was willing to visit Holland in principle but only under certain conditions, asking the Dutch officials to tell him which of his Dutch colleagues wanted to see him and what the exact details of his itinerary would be. Perhaps because of his experiences in Copenhagen two years earlier, Heisenberg wanted to know what his Dutch colleagues – including friends and former students – thought of the idea before he committed himself.[70] At this time, the Dutch universities and most of the research institutes were closed because many Dutch intellectuals had been reluctant to collaborate with the German occupation authorities.

A Dutch official in the ministry collaborating with the German authorities called in the Dutch physicist Hans Kramers and showed him Heisenberg's letter. Kramers wrote directly to Heisenberg to describe the poor working conditions of Dutch academics. The adverse working conditions that Kramers mentioned were illustrated by the state of the physical laboratory at the University of Leyden, where Kramers was professor of theoretical physics. German authorities had seized and closed the laboratory, which Dutch scientists were prohibited from entering. The scientific equipment was to be shipped to Germany as war booty.[71] An official of the Dutch Ministry of Education

Copenhagen 255

had hinted that this situation might be improved by reestablishing personal scientific contacts between Dutch and "foreign" – in other words, German – colleagues. The Dutch and German authorities wanted Heisenberg to spend a week in Holland. He would visit all the physics institutes, meet with his Dutch colleagues, and give talks drawn from his own research before small groups of Dutch physicists. Kramers added that he had discussed this matter with Hendrik Casimir and other Dutch scientists. All would welcome a visit by Heisenberg – which was exactly what Heisenberg wanted to hear.[72]

As soon as he received the letter from Kramers, Heisenberg told REM that he would visit Holland and implied that the personal invitation he had received from his Dutch colleague had been a crucial factor in his decision. Heisenberg simultaneously wrote to Kramers and expressed his pleasure in the upcoming visit. Kramers replied in kind. The German officials were pleased that Heisenberg was coming but also displeased that Kramers, who was not cooperating with the occupation authorities, had become involved. They informed Heisenberg that although he was free to see Kramers informally, Kramers would not be an official participant in the program for Heisenberg's visit. Furthermore, Heisenberg was ordered to visit the German occupation authorities at the very beginning of his visit in order to be briefed on the political state of the Dutch universities. Heisenberg now wrote to his wife: "I will go to Holland after all; I am looking forward to being together with old acquaintances a little, hopefully it will not be too politically difficult."[73]

Heisenberg traveled to Holland in October 1943, following a summer of protests by students and professors at Dutch universities over German occupation policies, including the persecution of Dutch Jews. The Germans responded with harsh repression and deportations of Dutch Jews to the death camps. Heisenberg's visit came a few months after he wrote a letter to his Dutch colleague Dirk Coster on behalf of Samuel Goudsmit's parents, who had already been deported to Auschwitz.[74]

As soon as Heisenberg arrived in the Netherlands, he met with collaborating officials from the Dutch Ministry of Education and with representatives of the German occupation authorities. The following day he paid a courtesy call on the physics institute in Utrecht and dined with the theoretical physicist Leon Rosenfeld. In the morning Heisenberg journeyed to Leyden, visited the famous Kamerlingh Onnes Laboratory, and met Kramers. On October 21, Heisenberg gave the first talk of his trip, a lecture on the theory of elementary particles, at a small colloquium at the Leyden physics institute. Heisenberg spent the next few days in Delft, where he visited his colleague Ralph Kronig as well as the nearby technical university. On October 24, Heisenberg and the physicists from the Philips Company and from the University of Leyden attended an informal colloquium presented by Kramers at Rosenfeld's house. The next day Heisenberg traveled to Amsterdam, where the physicist participated in

256   Living with the Bomb

some experiments on cosmic radiation. On October 26, Heisenberg discussed his visit with Dr. Arthur Seyss-Inquart, the German Commissioner in Holland.

According to Heisenberg's subsequent report, everywhere he went he met a most cordial reception. "The political theme was avoided as much as possible. However, when this theme was nevertheless touched, in most cases a brusque rejection of the German standpoint was expressed. But collaboration with the Dutch colleagues will certainly be possible on a purely scientific basis."[75]

Shortly after the end of the war, the physicist Casimir was questioned by the astronomer Gerard Kuiper, a former countryman and now a member of the American Armed Forces. Kuiper wrote a report that vividly captured the impression of callous nationalism that Heisenberg had made on his Dutch colleagues. Casimir reported that Heisenberg had been aware of the German concentration camps and the looting of other countries but he nevertheless wanted his country to control Europe. Indeed the German physicist said:

History legitimizes Germany to rule Europe (and later the world).... Only a nation which rules ruthlessly can maintain itself. Democracy cannot develop sufficient energy to rule Europe. There are, therefore, only two possibilities: Germany and Russia.... And then perhaps a Europe under German leadership would be the lesser evil.

Here Heisenberg was repeating an argument commonly used in NS propaganda after the catastrophe of Stalingrad. A letter from his wife from around the same time as his visit to Holland places Heisenberg's comment in perspective: "You can tell – all my thoughts are about the war again, I find it difficult to free my inner self from all the horrors that are happening. I am too depleted to concentrate on scientific work anymore."[76]

Heisenberg had been asked by his Dutch colleagues to visit their country in order to improve their working conditions. This is exactly what he did. On Heisenberg's intervention, Rosenfeld received permission to visit his mother in Belgium. After Heisenberg's visit, the German occupation authorities suddenly announced that the Dutch scientists might be allowed to retain some scientific instruments vital to their research. Kramers and his colleagues immediately submitted a modest list of apparatus they wished to keep. A German official visited Kramers, mentioned that he had spoken with Heisenberg in Berlin, and expressed surprise that the Leyden Laboratory was still closed. This official ostentatiously lifted the ban on research and promised that the Dutch physicists would be told as soon as possible what equipment would not be removed. Heisenberg's Dutch colleagues were sincerely grateful to him. As Kramers wrote: "You have done us a great service, and I am glad to give you our hearty thanks for that."[77]

The German occupation authorities had asked Heisenberg how his visit might be extended and the cultural cooperation between Dutch and German scientists increased. For a long time, he felt unable to answer but at last gave

Copenhagen 257

an apolitical response. Given the state of the war, which of course was steadily deteriorating for Germany, further visits did not appear to him to be a good idea. He counseled the occupation authorities to wait patiently. But Heisenberg also noted that he considered his trip to have been a success, since it had reopened channels of scientific communication between Dutch physicists and him. His recent correspondence with Kramers had been very valuable. Heisenberg was "convinced that scientific relations between the Germans and the Dutch will resume very quickly once the war has come to a happy end." Indeed Heisenberg also told a German colleague that his visit to Holland had gone well, despite all the politics.[78]

Cracow, General Government (Poland)

Although Heisenberg had considered emigration during the 1930s when he came under political attack, beginning with his rehabilitation by the SS in 1939 his star in the Third Reich steadily rose. His 1942 appointment as director at the Kaiser Wilhelm Institute for Physics was followed by a call to a professorship at the University of Berlin that same year.[79] Both positions were approved by several different agencies in the NS state. The Ministry of Education stressed the importance of Heisenberg's appointment for the national defense. Both Albert Speer's Ministry of Armaments and the Armed Forces had great interest in Heisenberg's research.[80] Alfred Rosenberg's office echoed Ramsauer's memorandum[81] and argued that the NSDAP should not take sides in the conflict between Philipp Lenard's and Heisenberg's schools of theoretical physics.[82] The National Socialist University Lecturers League merely repeated some of the positive statements made about Heisenberg in the SS report and added pointedly that Himmler had personally called a halt to political attacks on Heisenberg.[83] The contrast with the failed attempts to bring him to Munich and Vienna is stark. The Berlin appointments were arguably more prestigious than the professorships he had been denied in Munich and Vienna, although Heisenberg undoubtedly would have preferred a return to Bavaria.

The honors continued, with election to the Prussian Academy of Sciences in March of 1942,[84] selection as a corresponding member of the German Academy for Aviation Research in September,[85] and the award of the Copernicus Prize in June. Gustav Borger, director of the Science Department in the Reich Office of the National Socialist Lecturers League and the official who had overseen the meetings and physics camp that had marginalized Aryan Physics, congratulated Heisenberg on this award: "I am especially pleased because this is another satisfying recognition of your work and therefore theoretical physics from an official body." The physicist responded that this was especially gratifying because it could be seen as "an official rehabilitation of theoretical physics." The prize was worth two-and-a-half times Heisenberg's annual

258   Living with the Bomb

salary. "From Königsberg I hear that the Copernicus Prize this year is 20,000 Marks (but the wheelbarrow does not come with it)," Heisenberg joked with Elisabeth. "I really do not know what I should do with it, perhaps pay off the last Leipzig loan. Or do you have a good idea for it?"[86]

In December of 1943, Hitler followed Minister of Armaments Speer's recommendation and awarded Heisenberg the War Service Cross, First Class. Heisenberg responded with thanks, noting that he was "very pleased at the high recognition thereby expressed for my modest efforts in nuclear physics." The following May Heisenberg was featured in a front-page article in Josef Goebbels' most prestigious propaganda magazine, *Das Reich*. But as Heisenberg's personal fortunes rose, the prospects for Germany fell. Heisenberg described war-torn Berlin in early December of 1943: "Here the war is so close that it is difficult to stop thinking about it. So I am doubly happy about Christmas and you all [his family]. Perhaps I will still travel in the next few weeks for two nights and one day to Cracow."[87]

Two years after REM had denied Heisenberg permission to lecture in Cracow, the IDO director Coblitz contacted Heisenberg again. Frank would "greatly appreciate it" if Heisenberg would come and speak in Cracow, and this time the Ministry of Education approved the trip before Coblitz' letter to Heisenberg even arrived. The physicist immediately responded: "I am very willing to make up the talk planned for two years ago.... Please let me know which date would work for General Governor Frank." Coblitz replied: "Just like you, it is important to the General Governor to be at the talk." Coblitz also passed on Frank's invitation for Heisenberg and his wife to stay at Frank's residence, Castle Wartenberg. Although Elisabeth could not come because of "familial duties," Heisenberg accepted the invitation with thanks.

When Coblitz asked the physicist working at the IDO to attend Heisenberg's talk, he emphasized that "the General Governor, who is a close friend of Prof. Heisenberg, has invited him and will be at the lecture."[88] Heisenberg's host Hans Frank was, of course, one of the most ruthless and murderous of the NS elite. For example, on August 2, 1943, he gave an infamous speech to his staff and other officials, which he recorded in his diary: "With us things are very clear. If someone asks, what will happen to the NSDAP, we can retort: the NSDAP will certainly survive the Jews. Here we began with three-and-a-half million Jews, from which only a few work companies are still around, everyone else has – shall we say – emigrated."[89]

The physicist delivered his lecture in the second week of December, several months after the German authorities had begun to annihilate the Jewish ghettos in Cracow, Warsaw, and Lodz. But it is important to remember that Heisenberg would not have perceived Frank as a ruthless murderer. Similarly, although Cracow during the Third Reich today is synonymous with Schindler's factory and the nearby death camp Auschwitz, the very symbol of the Holocaust,

Heisenberg would not have seen it in this light. Instead Heisenberg probably experienced a pleasant city, not yet ravaged by the war, with the Jews gone and Poles only visible as servants or menial laborers. He would not have gone to nearby Auschwitz or learned much about it if he had asked. Like many Germans, he would have found out as little about the fate of Jews and Poles as he wanted.

Trips by German scholars to the General Government in occupied Poland were placed under especially stringent restrictions. Any and all contact between German scientists and Polish colleagues was forbidden.[90] Indeed his talk at IDO was very different from his trips to Denmark, Hungary, Slovakia, and the Netherlands precisely because no native Poles were present.[91] But this may not have seemed incongruous to Heisenberg, for Cracow was, at least temporarily, a German city.

The only information we have about Heisenberg's time in Cracow is a newspaper article describing his talk.

The smallest building blocks of matter.
Professor Dr Heisenberg on atomic physics
Prof. Dr. Werner Heisenberg, Director of the Kaiser-Wilhelm-Institut für Physik, Berlin-Dahlem, lectured to a large audience of interested listeners in the great lecture hall of the German Institute for Eastern Work about the central problems of scientific progress: contemporary research aims in physics....

After the enthusiastically received lecture, General Governor Dr. Frank spoke personally as the president of the German Institute for Eastern Work and praised the work of the lecturer, who is one of the most eminent personalities in the internationally recognised German science. Heisenberg, a Nobel Prize winner at the age of thirty, belongs to the ranks of great German physicists, whose investigations in theoretical physics have led to landmark discoveries.[92]

Copenhagen Again

During the winter of 1943–1944 the war entered its last, and for the majority of Germans, most hopeless phase. The steady deterioration of German society, including the destruction of cities from the air, interruptions in the transportation system, and increasing shortages of basic necessities, hampered but did not stop the invitations Heisenberg received to do guest lectures. He did not go to the DWI in Bucharest[93] or to the German Academy in the Austrian city of Klagenfurt.[94] Instead he stayed in Berlin for the 1944 summer semester to lecture at the university.[95] But one of Heisenberg's last foreign trips reprised his 1941 visit to Copenhagen.

During September and October of 1943 most of the Danes that the Germans considered Jews, including Niels Bohr, escaped deportation to the death camps by fleeing to Sweden. Bohr now shared his news regarding the German uranium work with officials in Britain and the United States. Early in 1944 Heisenberg learned from Hans Suess, a German scientist who had passed

260   Living with the Bomb

through Copenhagen, and a Swedish colleague, Hans von Euler-Chelpin, that the German authorities had closed the Bohr Institute and imprisoned the acting director Jørgen Bøggild.[96] Weizsäcker found out to his dismay that the German officials in Copenhagen were considering making him the new director of Bohr's old institute. He did not want to confront his Danish colleagues as a conqueror and asked Heisenberg to use his influence to kill the plan.[97] In the company of Army Ordnance physicist Kurt Diebner and others, Heisenberg traveled to Denmark on January 24 and met with the plenipotentiary of the German Reich in Copenhagen.[98] The German authorities were debating whether to staff the Bohr Institute with German physicists, to force the Danish scientists at this institute to contribute to the German war effort, or to strip the institute of all equipment needed in Germany.[99]

Heisenberg obviously wanted to arrange as beneficial a settlement as possible for the Danes. He toured the high-voltage equipment and the cyclotron at the institution with some occupation officials, emphasizing how complicated the equipment was and how difficult to move. The next day, the German authorities informed the Danish Foreign Office that the Bohr Institute would be reopened without conditions and released Bøggild.[100] Heisenberg subsequently told Johannes Jensen, a colleague who had many friends and acquaintances at the Bohr Institute, that the Danes were very happy about this outcome.[101]

Shortly after Heisenberg returned to Berlin, the bombing war intensified. As he told Elisabeth "the work can now continue but for how long?" The city was still brightly burning at nine in the evening. The following Sunday evening Heisenberg watched another attack "of unimaginable violence, the whole city center seems to be on fire." Heisenberg took solace in "a decent cup of hot chocolate" and "a few cookies that I brought back from Copenhagen." A few days later Heisenberg remarked that the fact that in the meantime it had been quiet only made him more anxious. He found it "almost impossible to concentrate on any sort of mental work."[102]

A month after his visit to Denmark, Heisenberg received an invitation by way of the Foreign Office and the German occupation officials to speak again at the Copenhagen DWI.[103] Heisenberg accordingly spent four days in Denmark, April 18 to 22, as a guest of Otto Höfler, the new director of the DWI. Höfler, whose specialty was Germanic philology, may have been typical of the scholars sent as cultural emissaries to foreign countries by the National Socialist state. He had spent many years in Scandinavia and had taught at the University of Uppsala. Höfler had connections with Scandinavian colleagues, knew the countries, and spoke the languages.[104]

In 1938, the SS helped Höfler trade his professorship at Kiel for a more prestigious one at Munich, and in return he placed his expertise in Germanic philology and close connections in Scandinavia at the service of the efforts of the SS to use the field of Germanic prehistory in order to justify the dominance

Copenhagen 261

of the Aryan race.[105] In 1942, before moving from the University of Munich to the Copenhagen DWI, Höfler visited Denmark to do intelligence work for the SS.[106] Once he became DWI director, he secretly used language courses at the DWI to train Danish Gestapo agents.[107]

On the evening of April 19, Heisenberg gave his talk, "The Smallest Building Blocks of Matter," before an audience made up almost completely of Germans. Heisenberg's Danish colleagues refused to attend, including the scientists who had attended the 1941 astrophysics conference and who, until the resignation of the Danish government, had participated in the programs of the DWI. The following day Heisenberg had lunch with the plenipotentiary of the Reich, Dr. Werner Best,[108] and spent the evening as Höfler's guest.

Also on April 19, Heisenberg paid a visit to Bohr's old institute, whereupon Heisenberg's Danish colleagues invited him to give them a talk on his own work. Heisenberg subsequently met with several Danish colleagues and their wives as the guest of Professor Christian Møller. On April 21 Heisenberg lectured on the "Theory of Elementary Particles" in Danish, preceded by a brief institute tea. When Heisenberg asked the Danes why they had not come to his talk at the DWI, they replied that, because of the tense political relationship that had existed between Germany and Denmark since the Danish government resigned in 1943, they wanted nothing to do with a "political institution" like the DWI.

In his subsequent report, Heisenberg energetically supported the plans of Höfler to focus for the time being more on scientific and scholarly work: "The Danes can probably only be won for the institute [DWI] if first of all it is restricted to purely scientific work and leaves the more propaganda side of the activity, like lectures and similar things, for a later more favorable time. The scientific collaboration with the Danes will certainly not encounter any difficulties once the war has come to a happy end."[109]

The Final Trip to Switzerland

Heisenberg's last foreign lectures took place in Geneva and Zurich in the autumn of 1944. Weizsäcker, his Swiss wife, and their children all accompanied Heisenberg to Zurich, with Weizsäcker's family staying in Switzerland when he returned to Germany.[110] An American spy, Moe Berg, was in the audience of Heisenberg's Zurich talks. After the war, a second-hand account claimed that Berg was carrying a revolver and had been prepared to kill the physicist. If this is true, it does not reflect very positively on American intelligence. The mere fact that Heisenberg had been allowed to travel to Switzerland should have made it obvious that he was not a key scientist in an atomic bomb project close to fruition. Moreover, Heisenberg would hardly have divulged any information about secret war work in a public lecture in a

262   Living with the Bomb

neutral country – he did not even do that inside of Germany. This may well be a story that is too good to be true.[111]

When he met with his Swiss colleagues, Heisenberg repeated what he had told their Dutch counterparts a year before: only Germany stood between Russia and European civilization.[112] This was one of the dominant tropes of National Socialist propaganda after Stalingrad. As demonstrated in Denmark in 1941 and the Netherlands in 1943, and indeed throughout his foreign lectures, Heisenberg's comments while abroad closely mirrored the prevailing propaganda message at that stage of the war. Moreover Heisenberg had consistently been anti-Marxist and antagonistic towards the Soviet Union throughout his adult life. Therefore there are reasons to believe that he was simply repeating the propaganda line, or had internalized it, or perhaps both.

Many of the émigrés and foreign colleagues both during and after the war appear not to have taken into account that Heisenberg, who had a family to protect, was not free to speak his mind in situations where he might be overheard and his comments then reported to the Gestapo. This does not necessarily mean that Heisenberg did not say what he believed, rather that we should not expect him to have made defeatist comments, contradicted NS policy, or admitted to knowing about atrocities. In other words, his statements need to be placed in context and not simply taken at face value. Whether out of conviction or caution, he generally said the right thing to avoid problems with the Gestapo and other German officials.

After the war, witnesses claimed that when Heisenberg was asked in Switzerland about the prospects for a German victory in Europe, he said "how fine would it have been if we had won this war." Heisenberg himself denied using this phrase.[113] This answer would not have pleased either his Swiss colleagues or the German authorities. The former would assume that Heisenberg wanted National Socialism to dominate Europe, if not the world. The latter would consider Heisenberg's comment defeatism, something that became a serious offense during the last, terrible months of the war. Perhaps in part for this reason, Heisenberg never got around to sending in a report on his 1944 trip to Switzerland. In late March 1945 REM reminded him of his omission,[114] but by this time Heisenberg was in southwestern Germany, more concerned about the advancing American forces than the bureaucrats in Berlin.

Conclusion

The legend of Copenhagen claims that, in the autumn of 1941, when German troops were still advancing deep into the Soviet Union, Heisenberg and Weizsäcker traveled to occupied Denmark. There they tried to enlist Bohr's help in an effort to forestall the creation of all nuclear weapons. What does history tell us about the legend?

Copenhagen 263

Context

Foreign visits like the one to Copenhagen in September of 1941 were only possible because they served the interests of the Third Reich. Heisenberg was an effective goodwill ambassador precisely because he did not spread obvious propaganda, rather gave both technical and popular scientific talks while playing his assigned role in defending the National Socialist system. German officials wanted Heisenberg because he drew natives into the DWIs or comparable institutions and facilitated cultural collaboration, or at least the appearance of it. Heisenberg went, not only to the Copenhagen astrophysics workshop, rather also to many other similar and sometimes, from our perspective, much more problematic places, gave comparable talks, and behaved in a similar fashion. This suggests that he did not go to Copenhagen only to look after and speak with Bohr, rather also for reasons of his own prestige and to support the German cultural mission. Similarly Heisenberg and Weizsäcker probably did make the nationalistic and militaristic comments their Danish colleagues remembered, because they made them elsewhere.

The active participation by Heisenberg and Weizsäcker in NS cultural propaganda and their exhortations to the Danes that they should collaborate with the German authorities made mistrust inevitable and compromised any other message the two physicists were trying to send. This is something that Heisenberg and Weizsäcker appeared unable to accept, both in 1941 and after the war, perhaps because of Heisenberg's own postwar defense of his conduct during the Third Reich. Going to Copenhagen, working with German officials on the propaganda, and participating in the workshop at the DWI were all working within the system, making compromises in the hope that one would have the authority and opportunity at some point to do good, conduct Heisenberg described after the war as active opposition. Such cultural propaganda also fell under what Samuel Goudsmit called compromising with the Nazis. Thus Copenhagen demonstrates that compromising and active opposition were two sides of the same coin.

Politics of the Past

In 1956 Heisenberg wrote Jungk that: "I then asked Bohr once more, whether given the obvious moral misgivings, it might be possible that all physicists agree that the work on atomic bombs, which in any case could only be manufactured with an enormous technical effort, should not be attempted."[115] There is no primary evidence for this claim, which was also directly contradicted by Bohr after he saw the Danish edition of *Brighter than a Thousand Suns*. Postwar statements by Heisenberg about his 1944 trip to Copenhagen and 1943 visit to Cracow can help shed light on this dispute.

264   Living with the Bomb

In 1947 Höfler wrote to Heisenberg and reminded him of his 1944 visit to the Copenhagen DWI. Like many other scholars who had been members of the SS or had held leadership positions in the NSDAP, Höfler encountered difficulties when he tried to return to academia after the war. When in 1949 Höfler applied for a teaching position at the University of Munich, a university official asked Heisenberg whether the Germanist had "strictly limited himself to scholarship while in Copenhagen, or had engaged in political cultural propaganda?" Heisenberg surprisingly responded that he had never met Höfler personally. According to Heisenberg, the Copenhagen DWI had not had "an entirely bad reputation" and that it had not spread "explicit National Socialist propaganda." It was not Höfler's fault that the Danes stopped frequenting the DWI, rather the Danes "no longer expected a German victory and did not want to bet on the wrong side." Heisenberg said that he had never heard harsh criticism of Höfler by his Danish colleagues, although he did admit that they would not have expressed such complaints to him. Heisenberg closed his report on Höfler by noting that even if the latter had not been as successful as Freyer in Budapest, Höfler had not "left behind very negative impressions in Denmark."[116]

In October of 1965, two decades after the end of the Third Reich, David Irving interviewed Heisenberg. While discussing the German wartime work on nuclear fission, Heisenberg volunteered the following account of his 1943 visit to Cracow.

Here in Munich I went to school with a few people who later became powerful Nazis, including the General Governor of Poland – [Hans] Frank. Frank was in the same class as my brother, so we naturally knew each other and used the informal "Du" address. I had completely lost touch with him and thought it was good that I had nothing to do with him. Then he wrote to me in September 1943 that, if I remember correctly, I should visit him in Cracow and give a scientific talk there. I thought that was a stupid idea, why would I want to go to Cracow, I want nothing to do with Frank. But his letter was so friendly, My dear friend! Could you ... so I wrote to him: Dear Frank! I have so much to do here that unfortunately it is not possible for me to come. Then he wrote to me again and made it so urgent, using turns of phrase that did not sound very pleasant, and I thought that I also did not want to make him an enemy. Okay, I will give a talk in Cracow.[117]

In fact there are no known letters from Frank to Heisenberg about the Cracow visit, rather several from the Director of the Institute for German Work in the East, Wilhelm Coblitz. Heisenberg appears to have been very willing to give a talk in Cracow as Frank's guest. There is no evidence that he had misgivings about it or felt pressured to do so. However, there is also no evidence that Heisenberg tried to enlist Frank, as he did Ernst von Weizsäcker and SS leader Heinrich Himmler, to help him with his political troubles. Of course the Cracow trip did not make Heisenberg complicit in the genocide being carried out in nearby Auschwitz, rather just made him, like many others, a bystander to it.

Copenhagen 265

When Heisenberg's postwar justifications for some of his most controversial visits abroad are checked against primary evidence, they are revealed to be neither accurate nor truthful, which also calls into question what he said after the war about the 1941 Copenhagen visit. In other words, Heisenberg's statements after the war, when he was free to say whatever he wanted about his conduct during National Socialism, were tailored, whether consciously or unconsciously, to help him in the postwar period, what Norbert Frei has called the Politics of the Past (*Vergangenheitspolitik*).[118] In the end, Heisenberg's claim that he suggested to Bohr that if the American scientists would not make an atomic bomb, then the German scientists would not do it either, cannot be proven either way. But along with the lack of evidence, the context of cultural propaganda, and the problematic nature of Heisenberg's postwar defense of other foreign trips, there are other reasons why this claim is implausible.

Key evidence is provided by Heisenberg's November 1941 report for Army Ordnance on the status of the working group, his February 1942 talk before the Reich Research Council, and the June 1942 talk for Albert Speer and Erhard Milch. In November 1941 Heisenberg made crystal clear to German officials that it would not be economically feasible to build atomic bombs in Germany during the war. If it appeared clear to Heisenberg that nuclear weapons would not be feasible in Germany, then two months earlier in Copenhagen, when German troops were advancing deep into the Soviet Union and eventual war between Germany and America appeared likely, he was not trying to forestall all nuclear weapons, just American ones.

In February of 1942, he revealed the potential of building bombs of unimaginable destructive force to influential political and military figures, both noting that this would be very difficult to do and mentioning that the Americans were probably working on it as well. Four months later he dangled the possibility of powerful new bombs in front of Speer, Milch, and others, again juxtaposed with an emphasis on the threat represented by American science and technology. This does not sound like a man who wanted to stop all nuclear weapons. It is difficult to believe that Heisenberg and Weizsäcker went to Copenhagen determined to forestall all atomic bombs but when this did not work out with Bohr, then abruptly changed their minds and decided to tempt National Socialist leaders with the terrible potential of nuclear weapons in order to get support.

Finally, by the autumn of 1941 these two men had already successfully weathered the dangerous and sometimes murderous shoals of the Third Reich and its politics, including dealing directly with some of the most powerful and sinister people in the regime. Heisenberg and Weizsäcker were not so naive as to believe that with Bohr's help they could arrange an international strike of physicists and thereby stop the atomic bomb. This is also a story that is too good to be true.

266 Living with the Bomb

Fear

Why did Heisenberg reveal to Niels Bohr that atomic bombs appeared feasible and the Germans were working on this? It was a treasonous act for Heisenberg to pass on this information, and doing so actually endangered the lives of both men. Heisenberg must have had good reasons. In fact, when Bohr passed on Heisenberg's revelations to the Allies, they became more concerned about German nuclear weapons; Heisenberg had unintentionally made atomic bombs more likely, not less.

Primary sources tell us that during the spring and summer of 1941 Heisenberg and Weizsäcker were actively gathering information about a possible American atomic bomb project.[119] This is the simplest, most straightforward, and most plausible explanation why Heisenberg, over the course of a conversation with Bohr, mentioned that he believed that atomic bombs could be built. Once Heisenberg became convinced that nuclear weapons were possible, he naturally started thinking about the other side getting them, and he knew that the scientific and industrial potential of the United States was incomparably greater than that of Germany.[120] In the autumn of 1941, when a future conflict with the United States appeared on the horizon,[121] Heisenberg did see a clear path to the atomic bomb – but in America, not in Germany.

After the war Heisenberg and especially Weizsäcker said that they had not thought that the Americans were working on nuclear weapons. That may well have eventually been true, and certainly was the case in the spring of 1945 after Goudsmit provided misinformation but from the summer of 1941 to the summer of 1942 they appeared to have been very concerned about the prospects of an American atomic bomb. There are two slightly different accounts of Heisenberg connecting the outcome of the war with atomic bombs, both directly or indirectly from Niels Bohr. In 1946 Rudolf Ladenburg reported that, when Bohr came to the US in 1943, he warned that Heisenberg had said that if the war lasted long enough, then German atomic bombs would win it. In one of the drafts of his unsent letters to Heisenberg from the 1950s, Bohr remembered Heisenberg saying he was certain that, if the war lasted long enough, then it "would be decided by such means."[122] Both of these accounts are compatible with a belief that whichever side first built atomic bombs would then use them in order to win the war.

When the texts of Bohr's unsent letters to Heisenberg were released in 2002, Weizsäcker was asked about them. It is remarkable that Weizsäcker, near the end of his long life, apparently for the first time publicly echoed Elisabeth Heisenberg's claim that Heisenberg had been afraid of Allied atomic bombs falling on Germany. Indeed she had gone so far as to say that: "This vision tormented him constantly."[123] In an interview in a German newspaper, Weizsäcker explained that:

Copenhagen 267

We came ... to the conclusion that we would not be finished, in any case not in the time that we thought was available. We then became afraid that the English or Americans could build atomic bombs quicker. Therefore we traveled together to Bohr. Heisenberg wanted to ask him to persuade the physicists in England and America not to build the atomic bomb.... But we knew that if we asked the Americans this directly, they would think that we wanted to build the bomb alone, we wanted to deceive them. Heisenberg thought that Bohr would be more likely to persuade his colleagues in America and England.

When asked in a different newspaper interview about Heisenberg's motive for trying to get Bohr to help him stop Allied physicists from working on nuclear weapons, he responded: "Well, so that a bomb would not fall on us."[124]

Conclusion

The Bomb

Why did the National Socialist regime fail to build atomic bombs during the Second World War? Many historians, scientists, and others have provided simple answers: Walther Bothe made an error when he measured the neutron absorption in carbon;[1] the Norwegian resistance and Allied bombing of the Norsk Hydro stopped the flow of heavy water;[2] Werner Heisenberg did not understand how nuclear weapons would work and thought that an atomic bomb was a nuclear reactor gone out of control;[3] the Germans were not led by a strong military leader;[4] Heisenberg, Carl Friedrich von Weizsäcker, and Fritz Houtermans withheld information about plutonium from the German authorities;[5] Heisenberg and Weizsäcker wanted to enlist Niels Bohr to help them forestall all nuclear weapons.[6] As this book has argued, these explanations are either flawed or at best only part of the story.

Since the Americans, with the help of émigrés, built an atomic bomb, it makes sense to judge the German work according to this yardstick or standard. But one cannot simply juxtapose the end results – rather a nuanced comparison during the different phases of the war is needed. When this is done, it is clear that the German scientists did some excellent work, a lot of good work, made some mistakes, and had some setbacks, just like the scientists working on the Manhattan Project in the United States. During the Lightning War phase, when powerful new weapons like the atomic bomb did not appear needed in Germany, preliminary measurements and model uranium machine experiments suggested that nuclear reactors could be built.

After the war against the Soviet Union had faltered and the United States had entered the war, during the period of Selling Uranium, it became clear that, because of the limitations of the German war economy, nuclear weapons could not possibly be made in time to help Germany. Here it is worth noting the obvious: the war in Europe had ended before the Americans managed to test an atomic bomb. In the summer of 1942 the German understanding of how isotope separation, uranium machines, and atomic bombs might work was not as deep and refined as that of their counterparts in America but they were also

Conclusion 269

not that far behind. In part because it was recognized that the Americans might also be investigating the military applications of nuclear fission, all stakeholders in Germany agreed that the research should continue.

In the period of Total War, the destructive effects of the war, including bombing, sabotage, shortages, and evacuations, severely affected the research. Perhaps the best examples for this were the large-scale uranium machine experiments with an arrangement of cast metal uranium plates and heavy water. In June of 1942 Heisenberg expected the experiments to begin the following autumn and hoped that they might lead to a self-sustaining uranium burner; Karl Wirtz finally began setting up this uranium machine in early 1944. Here the contrast with the United States is stark: Precisely when the encroaching war started to seriously hamper research in Germany, the American government began making massive investments in industrial facilities and created a new secret laboratory in Los Alamos, New Mexico. Finally, during the last desperate years of the war, these scientists, like very many other Germans, were mainly focused on saving themselves and their families.

Contrast Heisenberg's experiences with those of a scientist like J. Robert Oppenheimer, who spent the first part of the war as an academic in Berkeley, occasionally traveling to other American cities, and moved to Los Alamos in the spring of 1943. There he and the other scientists, mathematicians, engineers, and technicians, many times the total number of uranium researchers in Germany, could work undisturbed with generous financial support from the United States government and draw upon the logistical and technical support of the US Army and several industries. There simply is no comparison between the scale of the two projects from 1943 onwards, even though the two respective core groups of scientists initially did very similar things and had comparable understandings.

In fact, the German scientists were never in the position where they could have helped build nuclear weapons but what if they could have? The American Manhattan Project suggests some answers to this question. Originally the threat of Nazi nuclear weapons was overpowering and justified a herculean effort by scientists, some of whom otherwise would have not participated. Victory in Europe finally came in May of 1945, months before the first successful American test of an atomic bomb. Surprisingly few of the scientists who had been working to beat Hitler to the bomb now even questioned whether or not they should keep working. Only the Polish physicist Joseph Rotblat left the Manhattan Project.

Several influential scientists, including James Franck and Leo Szilard, did try to forestall the use of the atomic bomb against the Japanese but their petitions and arguments were listened to politely, then set aside. On June 16, 1945, the advisory Science Panel consisting of the scientists Arthur Holly Compton, Enrico Fermi, Ernest Lawrence, and J. Robert Oppenheimer concluded that

270   Living with the Bomb

there was "no technical demonstration likely to bring an end to the war ... no acceptable alternative to direct military use ... [and scientists had] no claim to special competence in solving the political, social, and military problems which are presented by the advent of atomic power."[7] If American and émigré scientists could not stop the American government from dropping atomic bombs on Japan, is there any reason to believe that, if nuclear weapons had been available to Hitler's government, Heisenberg, Weizsäcker, or anyone else could have stopped the Nazis from using them?

However, the answer to the question, did the Germans try to build atomic bombs, depends on the meaning of "try." If trying required making the enormous industrial-scale effort that was obviously going to be necessary, then the National Socialist state did not try; if trying meant working as hard as they could with the materials and resources that were available in order to make as much progress as quickly as possible towards centrifuges that could enrich or produce pure uranium 235 or nuclear reactors that could produce energy and manufacture plutonium, then these scientists did try. Readers will have to answer this question for themselves.

Living with the Bomb

When Carl Friedrich von Weizsäcker chose the title "Living with the Bomb" for his essay in *Die Zeit*, he meant living with the existential threat posed by the already large stockpiles of nuclear weapons arrayed on both sides of the Cold War. However, this phrase also describes very well the process of German scientists finding a way during the postwar period to deal with the fact that they had been working for a genocidal regime towards the same weapons that had instantaneously destroyed two Japanese cities. Heisenberg, Weizsäcker, and others needed a way to distance themselves from both National Socialism and the bombs that fell on Hiroshima and Nagasaki but without appearing to have betrayed Germany. The juxtaposition Heisenberg used in his 1946 article on the German wartime work, first stating that a German atomic bomb had been impossible but then implying that the scientists had kept control over the research, should be read in this light.

When Samuel Goudsmit, who was also aware of similar statements by Weizsäcker at Farm Hall, read Heisenberg's article as tacitly claiming moral superiority over their Allied colleagues, something that Robert Jungk subsequently made explicit, he challenged German scientists by condemning their willingness to compromise with Nazism. This criticism alienated Heisenberg and Weizsäcker from many of their colleagues outside of Germany. Heisenberg and Goudsmit tried to come to an understanding but where the latter saw concessions, the former claimed to have been actively opposing Hitler's regime. An examination of how and why Heisenberg interacted with leading National

Conclusion   271

Socialists both demonstrates that the compromises Heisenberg and his supporters made were more extensive and profound than Goudsmit knew, and
calls into question Heisenberg's postwar claim that such compromises were
only made in order to be in a position where one could do good.

According to the legend of Copenhagen, after Heisenberg and Weizsäcker
recognized that it would not be possible for Germany to make atomic bombs
during the war, they traveled to Denmark in order to enlist Niels Bohr in
their efforts to forestall all nuclear weapons. Thus they had neither betrayed
Germany, nor tried to make atomic bombs for Hitler; they had not compromised with Nazism, rather resisted it. However, when the September 1941
visit is scrutinized within the context of Heisenberg's foreign lectures during the Third Reich, the most plausible motivation appears to be the fear of
an American atomic bomb rather than a desire to forestall all nuclear weapons. The legend nevertheless helped the two physicists live with the bomb in
the postwar era. Publicly and privately, it dovetailed easily with the genuine
ambivalence they felt towards the prospect of West German nuclear weapons
in the postwar period, articulated by the Göttingen Declaration. Weizsäcker's
undoubtedly sincere commitment to working against the threats of nuclear proliferation and war finally allowed him to overcome what remained of his postwar ostracism.

Hitler's Atomic Bomb remains controversial because it is a specter that cannot be put to rest. Michael Frayn's play *Copenhagen*, which consists of conversations between the ghosts of Niels Bohr, Margarethe Bohr, and Werner
Heisenberg, is a perhaps unintentional metaphor for this.[8] Even though the
German atomic bomb never existed, it has profoundly affected many lives,
meaning very different things to different people, with this meaning also
changing over time. Hitler's atomic bomb is still influential today, not really
because of what happened but instead because of what might have been. It
blurs the line between history and legend, between hero and villain, and perhaps even between good and evil.

Epilogue
The Historian as Historical Actor

History is something that perhaps cannot be written until everything is so far in the past that no one still alive has a current interest in how it *should* have been.

Carl Friedrich von Weizsäcker from an interview in 1993.[1]

Historians strive to be as objective as possible, and this includes standing outside of the history they are writing. I certainly thought that I was doing this in 1984 when I asked Carl Friedrich von Weizsäcker for an interview to complement my archival research.[2] I was not interested in the conspiracy to resist Hitler by denying him atomic bombs, since I was already convinced that this was a legend, or at least part of a legend, so I did not ask Weizsäcker about it. By the end of our interview, he seemed surprised that I had not. When my dissertation was finished in 1987,[3] I sent him a copy, with no response.

I had the good fortune to spend the 1989–1990 academic year in Berlin and experienced the fall of the Berlin Wall and the abrupt transition that the Germans call *die Wende* firsthand. My book appeared in December of 1989, and the German translation shortly thereafter in early 1990.[4] The German version of my book brought me into contact with Robert Jungk, whom I met once at the offices of my German publisher, Siedler Verlag. My editor Thomas Karlauf had persuaded him to write a forward to my book. Jungk revealed to me that it had been Weizsäcker who had told him that German scientists had deliberately denied nuclear weapons to Hitler. He hinted this in the foreword, without naming names, but was quite explicit in the memoir that appeared two years later, entitled *Trotzdem* (*Nevertheless*), that Weizsäcker had misled him.

The years 1953 to 1955, in which I researched my book *Brighter than a Thousand Suns*, were dominated by the American Senator McCarthy, whose suspicions and interrogations made many American scientists act as politically docile as if they were living under a dictatorship. A shameful and disheartening theater! Now German physicists shared with me the surprising revelation that not even the dictatorship of the Third Reich had succeeded in forcing its researchers to collaborate on a project they had rejected. For, as I thought I had understood Carl Friedrich von Weizsäcker, as I spoke with him in his Göttingen apartment about these events, they had very consciously tried

Epilogue: The Historian as Historical Actor 273

to hinder the construction of a German atomic bomb. They had been, as he literally expressed it, in this respect not "activists," rather "pacifists."

That was the kernel of Weizsäcker's statement and later also Heisenbergs, which I remember and which I used shortly after my interviews with them to describe the race to build atomic bombs.

When my book, *Brighter Than a Thousand Suns* appeared in the autumn of 1956 in Scherz-Goverts-Verlag and worldwide was immediately greeted with an overwhelmingly positive reaction, at first my two main witnesses did not protest, indeed I heard that they were very pleased to be liberated from any suspicion of complicity with Hitler's regime in the eyes of the world public through their secret resistance against the construction of a German atomic bomb.[5]

Decades after the publication of Jungk's book, Weizsäcker denied telling Jungk this, instead describing him as "naïve."[6] I was surprised when Jungk told me that he had known for a long time that the conspiracy theory he incorporated into *Brighter than a Thousand Suns* was false but had hesitated to admit this in public. Indeed he said that my book had given him the opportunity to do so. Of course at this time I had not read the correspondence between Jungk and Weizsäcker.

When I contacted Weizsäcker to apologize for an error in the English version of my book (his first name had a hyphen that should have been omitted), he responded. We proceeded to have a long exchange of letters, including a request that I interview him again. Although I realized at the time that I was probably one of the very few people who turned down such an invitation, I was reluctant to visit him because I was certain that I knew what he would say and that I would not be persuaded by it. He appeared convinced that, if he only explained it to me in person, then I would agree and understand; I did not want to put myself in a position where I had to contradict him to his face.

My book renewed interest in the German wartime nuclear fission work, including Weizsäcker's role. In 1991 the movie *Ende der Unschuld* (*The End of Innocence*) about the wartime German work on nuclear weapons was telecast on one of the main German television channels over Easter and attracted a great deal of attention.[7] The author, Wolfgang Menge, had visited me during my last year in graduate school in 1987 to check a few details about the script he described at that time as almost finished. After meeting with me and reading the copy of my dissertation I subsequently sent him, he rewrote the script in a much more critical form, following the outlines of my work. Shortly after the broadcast Weizsäcker attended the annual meeting of the Leopoldina Academy of Sciences and was clearly surprised to be confronted by young physicists who asked him whether or not he had tried to build nuclear weapons for Hitler.[8]

Probably as a response to the increasing public scrutiny, an interview with Weizsäcker was subsequently published in the influential magazine *Der Spiegel* with the title, "I Admit It, I Was Crazy." Now, thirty-five years after *Brighter than a Thousand Suns*, he effectively publicly renounced the suggestion that he

274   Living with the Bomb

had resisted Hitler by denying him nuclear weapons. Rather than downplaying or hiding his understanding of plutonium, he had reported it to the authorities.

I had simply realized that it is easy to fission the daughter products of uranium, which today one designates as plutonium....
Then came the question: Should I keep this to myself, or write a report? I wrote the report, and also delivered it.
If you ask me now, what was the reason for that, then I will answer: I thought that, if the construction of a bomb is possible in this way, then I will be one of the people with whom one will have to speak. And then I will see to it that I find a way to the true decision makers, in order to make them comprehend something that these primitive fellows in any case do not understand....

By reporting this, he hoped to become politically important.

What I did then, belongs to the actions during my life that after the fact I would not repeat. I made a mistake. The technical aspects [of nuclear fission] did not interest me at all, scientifically I found other subjects much more interesting. But I thought that politics is important. And I had the idea that I could gain political influence, if I was someone who even Adolf Hitler had to talk with....
I believed — and this was my great error — that it might be possible to move Hitler to the politics of peace. In this regard you can naturally say to me that I must have been crazy. And I am prepared to admit it: I was crazy.[9]

In retrospect, Weizsäcker's 1991 *Der Spiegel* interview and Jungk's revelations should have made clear to me that I had already stepped outside of the usual historian's role – but I did not see it. It was only at a conference in the spring of 2012, organized by my colleagues Klaus Hentschel and Dieter Hoffmann at the Leopoldina Academy in Halle, Germany to honor the centennial anniversary of Weizsäcker's birth,[10] that this became shockingly clear. My unease began when several colleagues came up to me and mentioned that they had looked through my correspondence with Weizsäcker, which was now in an archive. One remarked that it was "very interesting!"

The conference itself was a nice mix of historians and contemporary witnesses (*Zeitzeugen*) but I was taken aback when, at the end of my talk, I was asked, not about the history I had just analyzed but instead about my personal interactions with Weizsäcker. As I responded to the question, I thought to myself, "I am a historian, not a witness." This made me very uncomfortable, for I realized suddenly that I had stepped outside of the secure zone of objective historians and had become a participant in the very history I had helped write. The historian had become a historical actor. By writing this book, which has included finding and analyzing sources not available in the 1980s and 1990s, considering other interpretations from historians, scientists, playwrights, and other authors, extending the chronological scope far into the postwar period, and most of all being conscious of my own role, I hope that I have reached closure in my own efforts to live with the bomb.

Glossary

Adsorption The adhesion of atoms, ions, or molecules from a gas, liquid, or dissolved solid to a surface.

Catalyst A substance that speeds up a chemical reaction, or lowers the temperature or pressure needed to start one, without being itself consumed during the reaction.

Critical mass The minimum mass or size of material capable of undergoing nuclear fission required in a nuclear reactor or atomic bomb to sustain a steady chain reaction.

Cyclotron A device in which charged atomic particles are held in a spiral trajectory by a static magnetic field and accelerated by a rapidly varying electric field.

Desorption The physical process by which adsorbed atoms or molecules are released from a surface.

Distillation The process of separating the components or substances from a liquid mixture by using selective boiling and condensation.

Electrolysis Chemical decomposition produced by the passage of an electric current through a liquid containing ions.

Element 94 (plutonium) A transuranic element formed in a series of steps after uranium 238 has absorbed a neutron; a fissionable material used in atomic bombs.

Elutriation A process for separating particles based on their size, shape, and density, using a stream of gas or liquid usually flowing in a direction opposite to the direction of sedimentation.

Half-life The time required for one half of the atomic nuclei of a radioactive sample to decay into other elements by emitting particles and energy.

Heavy water Water composed of oxygen and deuterium, an isotope of hydrogen with an extra neutron.

Isotope Forms of a chemical element that have different numbers of neutrons and therefore different masses, but share the same chemical properties.

Nuclear fission A type of nuclear reaction in which the nucleus divides into two nuclei of smaller charges and masses with a release of energy and neutrons.

Resonance absorption The strong absorption by atomic nuclei of neutrons having certain energies.

Uranium 235 A rare isotope of uranium that can sustain a nuclear fission chain reaction and therefore be used in an atomic bomb.

Uranium 238 The most common isotope of uranium; after absorbing a neutron it can transmute into plutonium.

Uranium burner An operating nuclear reactor.

Uranium machine A model nuclear reactor experiment.

Notes

Preface

1. Mark Walker, *German National Socialism and the Quest for Nuclear Power, 1939–1949* (Cambridge: Cambridge University Press, 1989).

1 Farm Hall

1. Jeremy Bernstein, *Hitler's Uranium Club: The Secret Recordings at Farm Hall* (Woodbury: American Institute of Physics Press, 1996), 69.
2. For Farm Hall see: Charles Frank (ed.), *Operation Epsilon: The Farm Hall Transcripts* (Bristol: Institute of Physics, 1993); Bernstein, Uranium; Ryan Dahn, "The Farm Hall Transcripts: The Smoking Gun That Wasn't," *Berichte zur Wissenschaftsgeschichte*, 45 (2022), 202–218.
3. Bernstein, Uranium, 72–73.
4. Bernstein, Uranium, 80.
5. Bernstein, Uranium, 87.
6. Bernstein, Uranium, 99.
7. Bernstein, Uranium, 99.
8. Bernstein, Uranium, 96.
9. Bernstein, Uranium, 258.
10. Bernstein, Uranium, 63, 95.
11. Bernstein, Uranium, 235–236, 239.
12. Bernstein, Uranium, 308–309.
13. Bernstein, Uranium, 96, 102.
14. Max von Laue to Theodore von Laue (August 7, 1945), ADM, MLN.
15. Bernstein, Uranium, 119–120.
16. Bernstein, Uranium, 133–134, 147.
17. Bernstein, Uranium, 137.
18. Erich Bagge, Kurt Diebner, and Kenneth Jay, *Von der Uranspaltung bis Calder Hall* (Hamburg: Rowohlt, 1957), 58.
19. Bagge, Uranspaltung, 56.
20. Bernstein, Uranium, 121, 123, 138, 187–209.
21. Bagge, Uranspaltung, 56.
22. Announcement of Hiroshima on BBC (August 6, 1945), ADM, IMC 31 1295-1301.
23. Bernstein, Uranium, 145.
24. Bernstein, Uranium, 128–129.

Notes to pages 11–16 277

25. Bernstein, Uranium, 131–132, 135, 243.
26. Bernstein, Uranium, 122, 129–132, 137.
27. David C. Cassidy, *Beyond Uncertainty: Heisenberg, Quantum Physics, and The Bomb* (New York: Bellevue Literary Press, 2009), 377; Max von Laue to Theodore von Laue (August 7, 1945) ADM, MLN.
28. Bernstein, Uranium, 150.
29. Bagge, Uranspaltung, 58; Bernstein, Uranium, 161; the British officials did not release this statement.

2 Nuclear Fission

1. Otto Hahn to Lise Meitner (December 19, 1938), ADM, IMC 29-023; Lise Meitner to Otto Hahn (December 21, 1938), ADM, WGN NL 080/127-01.
2. See Spencer Weart, *The Rise of Nuclear Fear* (Cambridge, MA: Harvard University Press, 2012).
3. For the early history of nuclear physics, see Roger Stuewer, *The Age of Innocence: Nuclear Physics between the First and Second World Wars* (Oxford: Oxford University Press, 2018), especially 31–35 and 155–162.
4. Stuewer, Innocence, 278–282, 298–303, 317–322; Spencer Weart, *Scientists in Power* (Cambridge, MA: Harvard University Press, 1979), 53.
5. Stuewer, Innocence, 393.
6. Weart, Power, 53–54.
7. Ruth Lewin Sime, "The Search for Transuranium Elements and the Discovery of Nuclear Fission," *Physics in Perspective*, 2 (2000), 48–62, here 55, 59.
8. Louis Turner, "Nuclear Fission," *Reviews of Modern Physics*, 12/1 (1940), 1–29, here 4.
9. Weart, Power, 54.
10. Ruth Lewin Sime, *Lise Meitner: A Life in Physics* (Berkeley: University of California Press, 1996), 221–254; Ruth Lewin Sime, "An Inconvenient History: the Nuclear-Fission Display in the Deutsches Museum," *Physics in Perspective*, 12 (2010), 190–218.
11. Sime, Life, 228, 231; Sime, "Search," 59–60.
12. Otto Hahn to Lise Meitner (December 19, 1938), ADM, IMC 29-023; Lise Meitner to Otto Hahn (December 21, 1938), ADM, WGN NL 080/127-01.
13. Lise Meitner to Otto Hahn (January 1, 1939), ADM, WGN NL 080/127-01 and AMPG, III. Abt., Rep. 14 4876.
14. Otto Hahn and Fritz Strassmann, "Über den Nachweis und das Verhalten der bei der Bestrahlung des Urans mittels Neutronen entstehenden Erdalkalimetalle," in *Die Naturwissenschaften*, 27 (1939), 11–15, in Horst Wohlfarth (ed.), *40 Jahre Kernspaltung: eine Einführung in der Originalliteratur* (Darmstadt: Wissenschaftliche Buchgesellschaft, 1979), 65–76, here 75–76.
15. Otto Hahn and Fritz Strassmann, "Nachweis der Entstehung aktiver Bariumisotope aus Uran und Thorium durch Neutronenbestrahlung: Nachweis weiterer aktiver Bruchstücke bei der Uranspaltung," in *Die Naturwissenschaften*, 27 (1939), 89–95, in Wohlfarth, 78–96, here 95.
16. Lise Meitner and Otto Frisch, "Disintegration of Uranium by Neutrons: A New Type of Nuclear Reaction," in *Nature*, 143 (1939), 239–240, in Wohlfarth, 97–100, here 99.

278   Notes to pages 16–21

17. Otto Frisch, "Physical Evidence for the Division of Heavy Nuclei under Neutron Bombardment," *Nature* 143 (1939), 276, in Wohlfarth, 101–102, here 102.
18. Weart, Power, 63.
19. Hans von Halban, Frédéric Joliot, and Lew Kowarski, "Liberation of Neutrons in the Nuclear Explosion of Uranium," *Nature*, 143 (1939), 470–471, in Wohlfarth, 111–114, here 113–114; Hans von Halban, Frédéric Joliot, and Lew Kowarski, "Number of Neutrons Liberated in the Nuclear Fission of Uranium," *Nature*, 143 (1939), 680, in Wohlfarth, 115–118, here 117; Weart, Power, 91.
20. Turner, "Fission," 12.
21. Siegfried Flügge, "Kann der Energieinhalt der Atomkerne technisch nutzbar gemacht werden?" *Die Naturwissenschaften*, 27 (1939), 402–410, in Wohlfarth, 119–140, here 119, 121, and 140.
22. Niels Bohr and John Wheeler, "The Mechanism of Nuclear Fission," in *Physical Review*, 56 (1939), 426–450, in Wohlfarth, 141–190, here 143, 169, and 171.
23. Alfred Nier, Eugene Booth, John Dunning, and Astrid von Grosse, "Nuclear Fission of Separated Uranium Isotopes," *Physical Review*, 57 (1940), 546; Eugene Booth, John Dunning, Astrid von Grosse, and Alfred Nier, "Neutron Capture by Uranium (238)," *Physical Review*, 58 (1940), 475–476.
24. Louis Turner, "The Nonexistence of Transuranic Elements," *Physical Review*, 57 (1940), 157; Edwin McMillian and Philip Abelson, "Radioactive Element 93," *Physical Review*, 57 (1940), 1185–1186.
25. Sime, Life, 184.
26. Wilhelm Frick to Carl Bosch (June 16, 1938), quoted from Ruth Lewin Sime, *Lise Meitner. Ein Leben für die Physik* (Frankfurt am Main: Insel Verlag, 2001), 251.
27. Sime, Life, 184–220, 257–258.
28. Sime, Life, 234, 256–257.
29. Otto Hahn to Lise Meitner (December 19, 1938) in Sime, Leben, 297–298.
30. Lise Meitner and Otto Frisch to Otto Hahn (January 1, 1939), ADM, WGN NL 080/127-01.
31. Sime, Life, 242.
32. Sime, Life, 254.
33. Hahn and Strassmann, "Nachweis," 95–96.
34. Sime, Life, 143.
35. Otto Hahn to Lise Meitner (March 3, 1939), ADM, WGN NL 080/127-01.
36. Alex Wellerstein, *Restricted Data: The History of Nuclear Secrecy in the United States* (Chicago: University of Chicago Press, 2021), 15–29.
37. Weart, Power, 75, 146.
38. Albert Einstein to Franklin D. Roosevelt (August 2, 1939) in Philip L. Cantelon, Richard G. Hewlett, and Robert C. Williams (eds.), *The American Atom: A Documentary History of Nuclear Policies from the Discovery of Fission to the Present*, 2nd Ed. (Philadelphia: University of Pennsylvania Press, 1991), 9–11.

3 Lightning War

1. Paul Harteck and Wilhelm Groth to OKH (April 24, 1939), quoted in Samuel Goudsmit to R. Furman (May 25, 1945), ADM, IMC 29 058.
2. Werner Heisenberg to Niels Bohr (September 14, 1939), NBA.

Notes to pages 21–26   279

3. Werner Heisenberg to Elisabeth Heisenberg (September 15, 1939), in Werner Heisenberg and Elisabeth Heisenberg, *"Meine Liebe Li!" Der Briefwechsel 1937–1946* (St. Pölten: Residenz Verlag, 2011), 90.

4. Werner Heisenberg to Elisabeth Heisenberg (September 17, 1940), in Heisenberg and Heisenberg, Meine Liebe, 146.

5. Werner Heisenberg to Elisabeth Heisenberg (September 23, 1939), in Heisenberg and Heisenberg, Meine Liebe, 97.

6. *Meldungen aus dem Reich. Die geheimen Lageberichte des Sicherheitsdienstes der SS 1938–1945*, Volume 2 (Herrsching: Pawlak, 1984), 331.

7. Abraham Esau to Walther Bothe (April 24, 1939), AMPG, III. Abt., Rep 6; Abraham Esau to General? (November 13, 1939), ADM, IMC 29 098-101.

8. Mark Walker's interview with Nikolaus Riehl (1985).

9. Paul Harteck, Überblick über den Stand der Arbeiten im Institut für Physikalische Chemie, Hamburg (1941), ADM, FA 002 465.

10. Basche (HWA) to Paul Harteck (August 22, 1939), EBN; Paul Harteck to Werner Heisenberg (January 15, 1947), in Michael Schaaf, *Heisenberg, Hitler und die Bombe. Gespräche mit Zeitzeugen*, 2nd Ed. (Diepholz: GNT-Verlag, 2018), 293–294.

11. Werner Heisenberg, "Über die Arbeiten zur technischen Ausnutzung der Atomkernenergie in Deutschland," *Die Naturwissenschaften*, 33 (1946), 325–329, here 326; Abraham Esau to General? (November 13, 1939), ADM, IMC 29 098-101.

12. Abraham Esau to General? (November 13, 1939), ADM, IMC 29 098-101; Jeremy Bernstein, *Hitler's Uranium Club: The Secret Recordings at Farm Hall* (Woodbury: American Institute of Physics Press, 1996), 145.

13. Erich Bagge's diary (September 11, 1939), ADM, IMC 29 134; Paul Harteck to OKH (September 18, 1939), ADM, IMC 29 615; Werner Heisenberg to the Dean of the Philosophical Faculty, University of Leipzig, AHU, Uk. H185 III, 46; Werner Heisenberg to Elisabeth Heisenberg (September 21, 1939) in Heisenberg and Heisenberg, Meine Liebe, 94.

14. Werner Heisenberg to Elisabeth Heisenberg (September 15, 1939) in Heisenberg and Heisenberg, Meine Liebe, 90.

15. Werner Heisenberg, Die Möglichkeit der technischen Energiegewinnung aus der Uranspaltung (1939), 1, ADM, FA 002 461.

16. Heisenberg, "Möglichkeit," 24; David C. Cassidy, *Beyond Uncertainty: Heisenberg, Quantum Physics, and the Bomb* (New York: Bellevue Literary Press, 2009), 300.

17. Heisenberg, "Möglichkeit," 24.

18. Klaus Clusius and Gerhard Dickel, "Das Trennrohr," *Zeitschrift für physikalische Chemie B*, 44 (1939), 459.

19. Paul Harteck to Ruff (September 25, 1939), ADM, IMC 29 618; Paul Harteck, Arbeitsprogramm (November 23, 1939), ADM, IMC 29 618.

20. Paul Harteck to Kurt Diebner (October 9, 1939), ADM, IMC 29 617; Basche to Paul Harteck (October 19, 1939), EBN.

21. Wilhelm Groth and Paul Harteck, Stand der Arbeiten zur Trennung der Isotope ^{235}U und ^{238}U (June 5, 1940), ADM, FA 002 490; Paul Harteck to OKH (January 8, 1940), ADM, IMC 29 621.

22. Paul Harteck to OKH (December 4, 1939), EBN; Paul Harteck to the Vereinigte Deutsche Nickelwerke (February 3, 1940), EBN.

23. Firma Canzler to Paul Harteck (April 12, 1940), EBN; Paul Harteck to OKH (April 15, 1940), EBN.

280   Notes to pages 26–31

24. Paul Harteck, Überblick über den Stand der Arbeiten im Institut für Physikalische Chemie, Hamburg (1941), ADM, FA 002 465.
25. Paul Harteck to OKH (October 10, 1940), EBN.
26. Cassidy, Uncertainty, 301.
27. Paul Harteck, Bericht über Stand der Arbeiten und Arbeitsvorschläge (April 17, 1941), EBN.
28. Karl-Heinz Höcker, Berechnung der Energieerzeugung in der Uranmaschine. II. Kohle als Bremssubstanz (April 20, 1940), AMPG, I. Abt. Rep. 34.
29. Werner Heisenberg, Bericht über die Möglichkeit technischer Energiegewinnung aus der Uranspaltung (II) (February 29, 1940), ADM, FA 002 474.
30. Georg Joos, Betr.: Präp. 38. Herstellung äußerst reiner Kohle (March 29, 1940), ADM, FA 002 476.
31. Walther Bothe, Die Diffusionslänge für thermische Neutronen in Kohle, (June 5, 1940), ADM, FA 002 489; Walther Bothe and Peter Jensen, Die Absorption thermischer Neutronen in Elektrographit, (January 20, 1941), ADM, FA 002 544; Walther Bothe and Peter Jensen, "Die Absorption thermischer Neutronen in Elektrographit," *Zeitschrift für Physik*, 122 (1944), 749–755.
32. Werner Heisenberg to Walther Bothe (November 29, 1946), AMPG, III. Abt. Rep. 93; Walther Bothe to Werner Heisenberg (December 7, 1946), AMPG, III. Abt., Rep 6; Heisenberg, Ausnutzung, 327.
33. Werner Heisenberg, "Das Dritte Reich versuchte nicht, die Atombombe zu bauen," *Frankfurter Allgemeine Zeitung*, 286 (December 9, 1967), Beilage Bilder und Zeiten, 4.
34. Wilhelm Hanle, Über den Nachweis von Bor und Cadmium in Kohle (1941), ADM, FA 002 526; Wilhelm Hanle, Spektralanalytische Untersuchungen von Kohle, Aluminium und Beryllium (March 17, 1942), ADM, FA 002 736.
35. Spencer Weart, *Scientists in Power* (Cambridge, MA: Harvard University Press, 1979), 134–136.
36. Werner Heisenberg, Bericht über die Möglichkeit technischer Energiegewinnung aus der Uranspaltung (II) (February 29, 1940), 26, ADM, FA 002 474.
37. Paul Harteck to Werner Heisenberg (January 15, 1940), ADM, IMC 29 625.
38. Werner Heisenberg to Paul Harteck (January 18, 1940), ADM, IMC 29 626.
39. Paul Harteck to OKH (January 24, 1940), ADM, IMC 29 628-629; Basche (OKH) to Paul Harteck (February 1, 1940), ADM, IMC 29 629-630; Paul Harteck to OKH (February 8, 1940, written January 8, 1940), EBN.
40. Karl-Friedrich Bonhoeffer to Paul Harteck (January 28, 1940), RPI, PHP Box 1, Folder 6.
41. Paul Harteck to Karl-Friedrich Bonhoeffer (February 4, 1940), RPI, PHP Box 1, Folder 6; Paul Harteck to Karl-Friedrich Bonhoeffer (February 16, 1940), EBN.
42. Paul Harteck to Karl-Friedrich Bonhoeffer (April 14, 1940), RPI, PHP Box 1, Folder 6; Paul Harteck to Karl-Friedrich Bonhoeffer (May 21, 1940), RPI, PHP Box 1, Folder 6.
43. Paul Herold to Paul Harteck (May 28, 1940), ADM, FA 002 783; Paul Harteck to Paul Herold (June 4, 1940), ADM, FA 002 783.
44. Paul Herold to Paul Harteck (June 10, 1940), ADM, FA 002 783; Aktennotiz über eine Besprechung in Leuna (January 25, 1941), ADM, FA 002 783.
45. Karl Wirtz, Bericht II. Eine 10-stufige Elektrolyseanlage zur Gewinnung von schwerem Wasser (June 19, 1940), ADM, FA 002 494; Erika Cremer and

Notes to pages 31–36 281

Karl Wirtz, Untersuchung des Schweres-Wassergehalts einiger technischer Elektrolyseure in Deutschland (July 24, 1940), ADM, FA 002 502.

46. Paul Harteck, Bericht über Stand der Arbeiten und Arbeitsvorschläge (April 17, 1941), ADM, IMC 29 662.

47. Karl Wirtz, Vorschläge zur Beschaffung und Erzeugung von schwerem Wasser (March 31, 1941), AMPG, I. Abt. Rep. 34.

48. Paul Harteck to OKH (June 26, 1940), EBN; Paul Harteck to OKH (October 10, 1940), EBN.

49. Paul Harteck to OKH (May 5, 1941), EBN.

50. Karl-Friedrich Bonhoeffer to Paul Harteck (July 22, 1941), RPI, PHP Box 1, Folder 7; Paul Harteck to Karl-Friedrich Bonhoeffer (June 27, 1941), RPI, PHP Box 1, Folder 7.

51. Karl-Friedrich Bonhoeffer to Paul Harteck (July 22, 1941), RPI, PHP Box 1, Folder 7.

52. Basche (OKH) to Paul Harteck (January 5, 1940), ADM, IMC 29 620; Paul Harteck to OKH (January 15, 1940), EBN.

53. Paul Harteck to OKH (April 12, 1940), EBN; Paul Herold to Paul Harteck (April 15, 1940), ADM, FA 002 783.

54. Paul Harteck to OKH (April 19, 1940), EBN; Paul Harteck to Paul Herold (April 20, 1940), ADM, FA 002 783; Basche (OKH) to Paul Harteck (April 25, 1940), ADM, IMC 29 638; Werner Heisenberg to Paul Harteck (April 29, 1940), ADM, IMC 29 639.

55. Paul Harteck to Werner Heisenberg (April 30, 1940), ADM, IMC 29 640; Werner Heisenberg to Paul Harteck (May 4, 1940), in Schaaf, 289.

56. Paul Harteck to Kurt Diebner (May 9, 1940), ADM, IMC 29 644. Paul Harteck to Paul Herold (May 6, 1940), ADM, FA 002 783; Paul Herold to Paul Harteck (May 16, 1940), ADM, FA 002 783; Paul Harteck to Paul Herold (May 20, 1940), ADM, FA 002 783.

57. Heinz Pose to Paul Harteck (May 22, 1940), ADM, IMC 29 645; Basche (OKH) to Paul Harteck (May 27, 1940), ADM, IMC 29 646; Paul Harteck to OKH (June 3, 1940), EBN. Ammoniakwerk Merseburg to Paul Herold (May 25, 1940), ADM, FA 002 783; Paul Herold to Paul Harteck (June 10, 1940), ADM, FA 002 783; Paul Harteck, Überblick über den Stand der Arbeiten im Institute für physikalische Chemie, Hamburg (1941), ADM, FA 002 465.

58. *Meldungen*, Volume 4, Report No. 98, (June 20, 1940), 1274–1275.

59. Werner Heisenberg to Elisabeth Heisenberg (July 18, 1940), in Heisenberg and Heisenberg, Meine Liebe, 126.

60. Übernahme des KWI f. Physik durch das Heereswaffenamt (January 22, 1940), AMPG, I. Abt. Rep. 34; Erich Schumann to KWG (January 25, 1940), AMPG, I. Abt. Rep. 34.

61. Walther Bothe, Einige Eigenschaften des U und der Bremsstoffe. Zusammenfassender Bericht über die Arbeiten im Institut für Physik im K.W.I. für med. Forschg., Heidelberg (March 8, 1941), ADM, FA 002 550; Otto Hahn, Zur Arbeitstagung vom 13. Bis 14. März 1941 im Kaiser Wilhelm-Institut für Physik (March 14, 1941), ADM, FA 002 536; Otto Hahn and Fritz Strassmann, Zur Frage nach der Entstehung des 2,3 Tage-Isotops des Elementes 93 aus Uran (March 1942), ADM, FA 002 735.

62. Karl-Heinz Höcker, Berechnung der Energieerzeugung in der Uranmaschine. II. Kohle als Bremssubstanz (April 20, 1940), AMPG, I. Abt. Rep. 34.

282   Notes to pages 36–40

63. Paul Müller, Berechnung der Energieerzeugung in der Uranmaschine. III. D_2O als Bremssubstanz (April 29, 1940), AMPG, I. Abt. Rep. 34.

64. Karl-Heinz Höcker, Berechnung der Energieerzeugung in der Uranmaschine. IV. Wasser als Bremssubstanz (June 3, 1940), AMPG, I. Abt. Rep. 34.

65. Werner Heisenberg to Elisabeth Heisenberg (July 12, 1940), in Heisenberg and Heisenberg, Meine Liebe, 120; Werner Heisenberg to Elisabeth Heisenberg (October 10, 1940), in Heisenberg and Heisenberg, Meine Liebe, 156–157.

66. Aktenvermerk über die Besprechung mit der Degussa, Frankfurt/M, Gutleutstr. 215, am 4. 4. 1941, betreffend die Herstellung von Prap. 38-Metall (April 8, 1941), AMPG, I. Abt. Rep. 34; Otto Hahn, Zur Arbeitstagung vom 13. Bis 14. März 1941 im Kaiser Wilhelm-Institut für Physik (March 14, 1941), ADM, FA 002 536.

67. Paul Harteck to OKH (May 5, 1941), EBN.

68. Richtlinien für das Arbeiten mit Präp. 38 (October 1, 1940), AMPG, I. Abt. Rep. 34.

69. Werner Heisenberg, Bericht über die ersten Versuche an der im Kaiser Wilhelm-Institut f. Physik aufgebauten Apparatur (December 21, 1940), AMPG, I. Abt. Rep. 34; Werner Heisenberg, Bericht über Versuche mit Schichtenanordnungen von Präparat 38 und Paraffin am Kaiser Wilhelm-Institut f. Physik in Bln-Dahlen (March 1941), AMPG, I. Abt. Rep. 34.

70. Carl Friedrich von Weizsäcker and Karl Wirtz, Vorschläge für die Arbeiten über Präparat 38 im Kaiser Wihelm-Institut für Physik. Berlin-Dahlem (March 31, 1941), AMPG, I. Abt. Rep. 34; Aktenvermerk über die Besprechung mit der Degussa, Frankfurt/M, Gutleutstr. 215, am 4. 4. 1941, betreffend die Herstellung von Prap. 38-Metall (April 8, 1941), AMPG, I. Abt. Rep. 34.

71. Robert Döpel, Klara Döpel, and Werner Heisenberg, Bestimmungen der Diffusionslänge thermischer Neutronen in schwerem Wasser (August 7, 1940), ADM, FA 002 466.

72. Robert Döpel, Klara Döpel, and Werner Heisenberg, Versuche mit einer Schichtenanordnung von Wasser und Prap. 38 (April 28, 1941), ADM, FA 002 524; Werner Heisenberg to Elisabeth Heisenberg (June 15, 1941), in Heisenberg and Heisenberg, Meine Liebe, 167–168; Werner Heisenberg to Elisabeth Heisenberg (July 17, 1941), in Heisenberg and Heisenberg, Meine Liebe, 179–180; Robert Döpel, Klara Döpel, and Werner Heisenberg, Versuche mit einer Schichtenanordnung von D_2O und Prap. 38 (October 28, 1941), ADM, FA 002 524.

73. David Irving's interview with Werner Heisenberg in Munich (October 23, 1965), ADM, IMC 31 541.

74. See the chapter on Nuclear Fission.

75. Carl Friedrich von Weizsäcker, Eine Möglichkeit der Energiegewinnung aus ^{238}U (July 17, 1940), ADM, FA 002 501.

76. Otto Hahn, Bericht über die Arbeiten des Kaiser Wilhelm-Instituts für Chemie über "Präparat 38" (December 10, 1940), ADM, FA 002 514.

77. Otto Hahn, Zur Arbeitstagung vom 13. Bis 14. März 1941 im Kaiser Wilhelm-Institut für Physik (March 14, 1941), ADM, FA 002 536; Otto Hahn and Fritz Strassmann, Zur Frage nach der Entstehung des 2,3 Tage-Isotops des Elementes 93 aus Uran (March 1942), ADM, FA 002 735; Kurt Starke, Anreicherung des künstlich radioaktiven Uran-Isotope $^{239}U_{92}$ und seines Folgeproduktes $^{239}93$ (Element 93) (May 20, 1941), ADM, FA 002 555; Mark Walker's interview with Kurt Starke.

78. Karl Wirtz to Reichspatentamt (March 11, 1941), AMPG, I. Abt. Rep. 34.

Notes to pages 41–44

79. Carl Friedrich von Weizsäcker, Kernenergieerzeugung aus dem Uranisotop der Masse 238 und anderen schweren Elementen. (Herstellung und Verwendung des Elements 94) (June 6, 1941), AMPG, I. Abt. Rep. 34.

80. Carl Friedrich von Weizsäcker, Kurzer Bericht über die eventuelle praktische Auswirkung der Uranuntersuchungen auf Grund einer Rücksprache mit Dr. Diebner, AMPG, I. Abt. Rep. 34.

81. Klaus Hentschel, "'Der neue Weg': Mit 'interatomarer Energie' zum 'Herrn der Welt' werden. Zu einem bislang unbekannten Typoskript vom Oktober 1944," *NTM*, 28, (2020), 121–147.

82. Josef Schintlmeister and Friedrich Hernegger, Über ein bisher unbekanntes, alphastrahlendes chemisches Element (June 1940), ADM, FA 002 486; Josef Schintlmeister and Friedrich Hernegger, Weitere chemische Untersuchungen an dem Elemente mit Alphastrahlen von 1,8 cm Reichweite (May 1941), ADM, FA 002 552; Josef Schintlmeister, Die Stellung des Elementes mit Alphastrahlen von 1,8 cm Reichweite im periodischen System (May 20, 1941), ADM, FA 002 554; for Schintlmeister and the other Austrian members of the uranium project, see Christian Forstner, *Kernphysik, Forschungsreaktoren und Atomenergie: Transnationale Wissensströme und das Scheitern einer Innovation in Österreich* (Wiesbaden: Springer, 2019).

83. Dieter Hoffmann, "Ein Physiker zwischen Hitler und Stalin," *Spektrum der Wissenschaft* (2014), 62–70.

84. Fritz G. Houtermans, Zur Frage der Auslösung von Kern-Kettenreaktionen (August 1941 and August 1944), ADM, FA 002 743.

85. V. Weizel to Franz Moeller (August 31, 1941), NBL, SGP Box 27, Folder 35; Admiral Witzell to Rudolf Mentzel (March 13, 1942), NBL, SGP Box 27, Folder 35; Rudolf Mentzel to Admiral Witzell (March 31, 1942), NBL, SGP Box 27, Folder 35; Viktor Frenkel, "Professor Friedrich Houtermans – Arbeit, Leben, Schicksal. Biographie eines Physikers des zwanzigsten Jahrhunderts," *Max-Planck-Institut für Wissenschaftsgeschichte, Preprint 414* (2011).

86. Rudolf Ladenburg to Lyman Briggs (April 14, 1941), NARA Record Group 227, S-1 Briggs, Box 5, Ladenburg folder; Leo Szilard to Isidor Rabi (April 28, 1941), CUA, Isidor Rabi Papers, Box 7, Folder 16.

87. Thomas Powers, *Heisenberg's War: The Secret History of the German Bomb* (London, Jonathan Cape, 1993), 479, 101.

88. Manfred von Ardenne, *Die Erinnerungen* (München: Herbig, 1990), 165.

89. Powers, Heisenberg's, the first quotation is from pages 479, the next two from 101.

90. Werner Heisenberg to Elisabeth Heisenberg (July 15, 1940), in Heisenberg and Heisenberg, 122–123; Werner Heisenberg to Elisabeth Heisenberg (September 3, 1940), in Heisenberg and Heisenberg, 132; Werner Heisenberg to Elisabeth Heisenberg (September 13, 1940), in Heisenberg and Heisenberg, Meine Liebe, 139.

91. Werner Heisenberg to Elisabeth Heisenberg (September 17, 1940), in Heisenberg and Heisenberg, Meine Liebe, 146; Werner Heisenberg to Elisabeth Heisenberg (October 4, 1940), in Heisenberg and Heisenberg, Meine Liebe, 152.

92. Werner Heisenberg to Elisabeth Heisenberg (October 10, 1940), in Heisenberg and Heisenberg, Meine Liebe, 158; Karl-Friedrich Bonhoeffer to Paul Harteck (September 10, 1940), RPI, PHP Box 1, Folder 6; Karl-Friedrich Bonhoeffer to Paul Harteck (November 13, 1940), RPI, PHP Box 1, Folder 6.

93. Adam Tooze, *The Wages of Destruction: The Making and Breaking of the Nazi Economy* (New York: Viking, 2007), 486.

284 Notes to pages 44–50

94. Werner Heisenberg to Elisabeth Heisenberg (June 15, 1941), in Heisenberg and Heisenberg, Meine Liebe, 167–168; Werner Heisenberg to Elisabeth Heisenberg (June 22, 1941), in Heisenberg and Heisenberg, Meine Liebe, 170.

95. Werner Heisenberg to Elisabeth Heisenberg (July 9, 1941), in Heisenberg and Heisenberg, Meine Liebe, 174–175.

96. Werner Heisenberg to Elisabeth Heisenberg (July 15, 1941), in Heisenberg and Heisenberg, Meine Liebe, 179; Werner Heisenberg to Elisabeth Heisenberg (July 24, 1941), in Heisenberg and Heisenberg, Meine Liebe, 183.

97. Omer Bartov, *Hitler's Army: Soldiers, Nazis, and War in the Third Reich* (New York: Oxford University Press, 1992), 106.

98. Werner Heisenberg to Elisabeth Heisenberg (July 19, 1941), in Heisenberg and Heisenberg, Meine Liebe, 180–181.

99. Werner Heisenberg to Elisabeth Heisenberg (July 21, 1941), in Heisenberg and Heisenberg, Meine Liebe, 181; Werner Heisenberg to Elisabeth Heisenberg (September 22, 1941), in Heisenberg and Heisenberg, Meine Liebe, 197.

100. Christian Streit, *Keine Kameraden. Die Wehrmacht und die sowjetischen Kriegsgefangenen, 1941–1945* (Bonn: Dietz, 1991).

101. Ian Kershaw, *Hitler 1937–1945: Nemesis* (New York: Norton, 2000), 409, 417.

102. Werner Heisenberg to Elisabeth Heisenberg (July 17, 1941), in Heisenberg and Heisenberg, Meine Liebe, 179–180.

103. Henry Smyth, *Atomic Energy for Military Purposes: The Official Report on the Development of the Atomic Bomb under the Auspices of the United States Government* (Princeton: Princeton University Press, 1945), 45–74, especially 64–66; Richard Rhodes, *The Making of the Atomic Bomb* (New York: Simon and Schuster, 1986), 332–333, 339–340, 343, 346–354, 360, 366–267, 380–381.

104. Smyth, Atomic, 55–56, 68–69, 73; Weart, Power, 144–146.

105. Smyth, Atomic, 59.

106. Philip Cantelon, Richard Hewlett, and Robert Williams (eds.), *The American Atom: A Documentary History of Nuclear Policies from the Discovery of Fission to the Present,* 2nd Ed. (Philadelphia: University of Pennsylvania Press, 1991), 11–15; Weart, Power, 147; Rhodes, 321–325.

107. This report is reprinted in Margaret Gowing, *Britain and Atomic Energy, 1939–1945* (St. Martins: London, 1964), 394–436.

108. Gowing, Britain, 396, 405–407, 412–414; Rhodes, Making, 368–369.

109. Gowing, Britain, 394–395, 398; Smyth, Atomic, 72; Rhodes, Making, 386–387.

110. Smyth, Atomic, 73–74.

4 Selling Uranium

1. Josef Goebbels, *Tagebücher aus den Jahren 1942–1943* (Zürich: Atlantis Verlag, 1948), 136 (March 21, 1942).

2. Werner Heisenberg, Zur Durchführung der Arbeiten an der Uranmaschine (November 27, 1941), AMPG, I. Abt. Rep. 34.

3. Jeremy Noakes and Geoffrey Pridham (ed.), *Nazism: A History in Documents and Eyewitness Accounts, 1919–1945, Volume III* (Exeter: University of Exeter Press, 1988), 826; Erich Schumann to Paul Harteck (December 5, 1941), ADM, IMC 29 687; Samuel Goudsmit, *Alsos* 2nd Ed. (Los Angeles: Tomash 1983), 142–145.

Notes to pages 51–59 285

4. Erich Schumann to Paul Harteck (December 5, 1941), ADM, IMC 29 687.
5. Karl-Friedrich Bonhoeffer to Paul Harteck (January 9, 1942), RPI, PHP Box 1, Folder 7; Karl-Friedrich Bonhoeffer to Paul Harteck (January 24, 1942), RPI, PHP Box 1, Folder 7.
6. Heereswaffenamt, Die Energiegewinnung aus Uran (February 1942), 12, 21, 126, 15, 87–88 EBN; Werner Heisenberg, "Über die Arbeiten zur technischen Ausnutzung der Atomkernenergie in Deutschland," *Die Naturwissenschaften*, 33 (1946), 325–329, here 327.
7. Energiegewinnung aus Uran (February 1942) 8, 13, 16–17 EBN.
8. Energiegewinnung aus Uran (February 1942), 9 EBN.
9. Energiegewinnung aus Uran (February 1942), 8, 12–13, 47 EBN.
10. Energiegewinnung aus Uran (February 1942), 13 EBN.
11. Energiegewinnung aus Uran (February 1942), 132 EBN.
12. Energiegewinnung aus Uran (February 1942), 134, 133 EBN.
13. Albert Vögler to General Leeb (Army Ordnance) (February 27, 1942), AMPG, I. Abt., Rep 1A.
14. Niederschrift über die Sitzung des Senats der Kaiser-Wilhelm Gesellschaft zur Förderung der Wissenschaften (April 24, 1942), BAK, R26 III 701; Albert Vögler (KWG) to General Leeb (HWA) (May 11, 1942), AMPG, I. Abt., Rep 1A; Ernst Telschow (KWG) to Werner Heisenberg (May 12, 1942), AMPG, I. Abt., Rep 1A; Albert Vögler (KWG) to General Leeb (HWA) (May 27, 1942), AMPG, I. Abt., Rep 1A; Ernst Telschow to Kurt Diebner (June 2, 1942), AMPG, I. Abt., Rep 1A.
15. Arbeitstagung Kaiser Wilhelm-Institut für Physik (February 16, 1942), AMPG, I. Abt. Rep. 34.
16. Bernhard Rust to Lorenz (February 12, 1942), ADM, IMC 29 993.
17. Vortragsfolge der 2. wissenschaftlichen Tagung der Arbeitsgemeinschaft "Kernphysik" (Reichsforschungsrat – Heereswaffenamt), ADM, IMC 29 998.
18. Otto Hahn, Die Spaltung des Urankerns, ADM, FA 002 606.
19. Paul Harteck, Die Gewinnung von schwerem Wasser (February 26, 1942), ADM, FA 002 591.
20. Jeremy Bernstein, *Hitler's Uranium Club: The Secret Recordings at Farm Hall* (Woodbury: American Institute of Physics Press, 1996), 123, 138.
21. Bernstein, Uranium, 139, 187–210, the quotation is on 146.
22. Werner Heisenberg to Samuel Goudsmit (January 5, 1948), NBL, SGP B11 F98.
23. Werner Heisenberg, Die theoretischen Grundlagen für die Energiegewinnung aus der Uranspaltung (February 26, 1942), ADM, IMC 29 1005-1013.
24. Heisenberg, Grundlagen.
25. Heisenberg, Grundlagen.
26. Heisenberg, Grundlagen.
27. Otto Hahn's diary (February 26, 1942), ADM, IMC 29 997; "Physik und Landesverteidigung. Vollsitzung des Reichsforschungsrates," *Berliner Börsenzeitung* (February 27, 1942), AMPG, I. Abt., Rep 1A 203; Wolfgang Finkelnburg to Werner Heisenberg (May 6, 1942), AMPG, III. Abt. Rep. 93; Goebbels, Tagebücher, 136 (March 21, 1942).
28. Albert Vögler to General Leeb (Army Ordnance) (February 27, 1942), AMPG, I. Abt., Rep 1A; Albert Vögler to General Leeb (Army Ordnance) (February 27, 1942), AMPG, I. Abt., Rep 1A; Albert Vögler (KWG) to General Leeb (HWA) (March 6, 1942), AMPG, I. Abt., Rep 1A.

286 Notes to pages 59-62

29. Paul Harteck to Karl-Friedrich Bonhoeffer (September 26, 1941), RPI, PHP Box 1, Folder 7; Betr.: Vorbesprechung des Besuches der Herren Dr. Weil, Professor Dr. Harteck, und Dr. Wirtz von OKH, Berlin, im Werk Vermork der Norsk Hydro (October 1, 1941), ADM, FA 002 785; Ergebnisse der Besprechungen zwischen den Herren Ing Braun, Prof. Harteck, und Dr. Wirtz. (October 4, 1941), ADM, FA 002 785.

30. Bericht über die Reise zur Fa. Norsk Hydro in Oslo und Rjukan, Norwegen, betreffend die Steigerung der Produktion von schwerem Wasser (October 20, 1941), ADM, FA 002 785.

31. Protokoll über die Sitzung im Heereswaffenamt am 22.11.41. (November 22, 1941), ADM, IMC 29 668-669.

32. Karl Wirtz, Entwurf für Wa Fa W Stab N. (October ~8, 1941), ADM, FA 002 785; Karl Wirtz to Norsk Hydro (November 1941), ADM, FA 002 785; Betr.: Entwurf des K.W.Inst.f.Physik für die Antwort an den Wehrmachtsbefehlshaber Norwegen. Abt. W Stb H (January 7, 1942), ADM, FA 002 785.

33. Norsk Hydro to Paul Harteck and Karl Wirtz (February 9, 1942), ADM, FA 002 785; Norsk Hydro to Wehrwirtschaftstab (March 14, 1942), ADM, FA 002 785; Norsk Hydro to Wehrwirtschaftsstab Norwegen (February 19, 1942), ADM, FA 002 785.

34. Norsk Hydro to Wehrwirtschaftstab Norwegen (April 23, 1942), ADM, FA 002 785; Niederschrift über die Besprechung bei Norsk Hydro am 27.5.42 ADM, FA 002 785; Paul Harteck to Paul Herold (June 4, 1942), ADM, FA 002 783; Paul Herold to Heimatstab Übersee WGM (June 15, 1942), ADM, FA 002 783.

35. Aktennotiz über Besprechung über Anreicherung von Wasser am 22.10.1941 in Leuna (October 30, 1941), ADM, FA 002 783. Paul Herold to Paul Harteck (March 23, 1942), ADM, FA 002 783. Aktennotiz Besprechung am 17.4.1942 in Leuna über D-Anreicherung im Wasser. (April 20, 1942), ADM, FA 002 783.

36. Heinrich Bütefisch to Paul Harteck (April 20, 1942), ADM, FA 002 783; Besprechung: Heranziehung der I.G.-Farbenindustrie zur Herstellung von schwerem Wasser in Deutschland (April 30, 1942), ADM, FA 002 783; Paul Harteck to Heinrich Bütefisch (April 22, 1942), ADM, FA 002 783.

37. Über die Besprechung am 30.04.1942 in der Physikal. Techn. Reichsanstalt Berlin betr.: weiter Mitarbeit des Ammoniakwerkes am D_2O-Beschaffungsproblem. (May 4, 1942), ADM, FA 002 783.

38. Heisenberg, Durchführung; Paul Harteck, Die Trennung der Uranisotope, (December 1941), ADM, FA 002 533.

39. Paul Harteck, Die Trennung der Uranisotope, (December 1941), ADM, FA 002 533. Für die Planung von Grossanlagen fehlen zur Zeit die Voraussetzungen. Wilhelm Groth, Die Trennung der Uranisotope nach dem Trennrohr- und dem Ultrazentrifugenverfahren, (March 23, 1942), ADM, FA 002 735.

40. Paul Harteck to the Military High Command (November 1, 1941), EBN; Betr.: Arbeitsbesprechung zum Ultrazentrifugenbau in Hamburg am 12. und 13. November 1941, ADM, FA 002 792; Wilhelm Groth, Stand der Arbeiten zur Herstellung einer Ultrazentrifuge (December 14, 1941), ADM, FA 002 579; Anschütz to Paul Harteck (January 3, 1942), ADM, FA 002 792.

41. Walther Groth's diary (April 15, 1942), ADM, IMC 29 814; Wilhelm Groth, Trennung der Uranisotope nach dem Ultrazentrifugenverfahren (May 1942), ADM, FA 002 590.

42. Paul Harteck to OKH (June 26, 1942), ADM, IMC 29 719-720.

Notes to pages 63–69

43. Fritz Bopp, Erich Fischer, Werner Heisenberg, Carl Friedrich von Weizsäcker, and Karl Wirtz, Untersuchungen mit neuen Schichtenanordnung aus 38-Metall und Paraffin (February 26, 1942), ADM, FA 002 735.

44. Robert Döpel, Klara Döpel, and Werner Heisenberg, Die Neutronenvermehrung in einem D_2O-38-Metallschichtensystem (March 1942), ADM, FA 002 735; Robert Döpel, Klara Döpel, and Werner Heisenberg, Der experimentelle Nachweis der effektiven Neutronenvermehrung in einem Kugel-Schichten-System aus D_2O und Uran-Metall (April 1942); the image of L-IV is from Robert Döpel, Bericht über zwei Unfälle beim Umgang mit Uranmetall (July 9, 1942), ADM, FA 002 587.

45. Adam Tooze, *The Wages of Destruction: The Making and Breaking of the Nazi Economy* (New York: Viking, 2007), 553–554.

46. Helmut Maier, *Forschung als Waffe. Rüstungsforschung in der Kaiser-Wilhelm-Gesellschaft und das Kaiser-Wilhelm-Institut für Metallforschung 1900–1945/48, Volume 2* (Göttingen: Wallstein, 2007), 742; Albert Speer, *Erinnerungen* (Berlin: Propyläen Verlag, 1969), 239.

47. Maier, Forschung, 742, footnote 373.

48. Speer, Erinnerungen, 239.

49. See the chapter below on Compromising with Hitler.

50. David Irving, *The German Atomic Bomb* (New York: Simon and Schuster, 1967), 120.

51. Maier, Forschung, 743–744.

52. David Irving's Interview with Werner Heisenberg (October 23, 1965), ADM, IMC 31 526-567, here 546.

53. Speer, Erinnerungen, 240.

54. Werner Heisenberg, Die Arbeiten am Uranproblem (June 4, 1942), AMPG, I. Abt. Rep. 34.

55. Heisenberg, Uranproblem.

56. David Irving's Interview with Werner Heisenberg (October 23, 1965), ADM, IMC 31 526-567, here 547.

57. Werner Heisenberg to Samuel Goudsmit (October 3, 1948), NBL, SGP B10 F93.

58. David Irving's Interview with Werner Heisenberg (October 23, 1965), ADM, IMC 31 546; Werner Heisenberg to David Irving (June 10, 1966), AMPG, III. Abt. Rep. 93 1743.

59. Henry DeWolf Smyth, *Atomic Energy for Military Purposes: The Official Report on the Development of the Atomic Bomb under the Auspices of the United States Government, 1940–1945* (Princeton: Princeton University Press, 1945).

60. Speer, Erinnerungen, 240–241.

61. Speer, Erinnerungen, 240.

62. Willi Boelcke (ed.), *Deutschlands Rüstung im Zweiten Weltkrieg. Hitlers Konferenzen mit Albert Speer 1942–1945* (Frankfurt am Main: Akademische Verlagsgesellschaft Athenaion, 1969), 137.

63. David Irving's Interview with Werner Heisenberg (October 23, 1965), ADM, ICM 31 526-567, here 558–559.

64. Werner Heisenberg to Elisabeth Heisenberg (June 5, 1942) in Werner Heisenberg and Elisabeth Heisenberg, *"Meine Liebe Li!" Der Briefwechsel 1937–1946* (St. Pölten: Residenz Verlag, 2011), 201–202; (June 11, 1942), 204.

65. Forstmann (KWG) to Heisenberg (October 13, 1942), AMPG, I. Abt. Rep. 34.

66. Thomas Powers, *Heisenberg's War: The Secret History of the German Bomb* (London: Jonathan Cape, 1993), 99–102, 147; Michael Frayn, *Copenhagen* (New York: Anchor, 1998), 75.

288   Notes to pages 70–78

67. David Irving's Interview with Werner Heisenberg (October 23, 1965), ADM, ICM 31 526-567, here 548.
68. Speer, Erinnerungen, 241–242.
69. Werner Heisenberg, Betr.: Bauvorhaben am Kaiser Wilhelm-Institut für Physik (June 5, 1942), AMPG, I. Abt. Rep. 34. Werner Heisenberg, Bemerkungen zu dem geplanten halbtechnischen Versuch mit 1,5 to D_2O und 5 to 38-Metall (July 31, 1942), ADM, FA 002 620; Werner Heisenberg to Ernst Telschow (June 11, 1942), AMPG, III. Abt. Rep. 93; Heisenberg and Heisenberg, Meine Liebe, 204.
70. Smyth, Atomic, 54, 75–76, 78.
71. Smyth, Atomic, 79–81; Richard Rhodes, *The Making of the Atomic Bomb* (New York: Simon and Schuster, 1986), 406.
72. Smyth, Atomic, 80, 94.
73. Smyth, Atomic, 92–94.
74. Smyth, Atomic, 95–96; Rhodes, Making, 395–397, 400–401.
75. Smyth, Atomic, 179–180; Rhodes, Making, 405–406.
76. Smyth, Atomic, 189–194.
77. Smyth, Atomic, 193–194.
78. Smyth, Atomic, 72, 103–104; Lillian Hoddeson, Paul Henriksen, Roger Meade, and Catherine Westfall, *Critical Assembly: A Technical History of Los Alamos during the Oppenheimer Years, 1943–1945* (Cambridge: Cambridge University Press, 1993), 43; Rhodes, 415–421.
79. Tooze, Wages, 510.
80. Smyth, Atomic, 82.
81. Bernstein, Uranium, the quotations are from 197 and 209.
82. Manfred Popp, "Misinterpreted Documents and Ignored Physical Facts: The History of 'Hitler's Atomic Bomb' Needs to Be Corrected," *Berichte zur Wissenschaftsgeschichte*, 39 (2016), 265–282, here 274; also see Manfred Popp, "Hitlers Atombombe. Störfall der Wissenschaftsgeschichte," *Spektrum der Wissenschaft*, 12/16 (2016), 12–21; Manfred Popp, "Why Hitler Did Not Have Atomic Bombs," Journal of Nuclear Engineering, 2 (2021), 9–27; My response to Popp's critique of my work includes a more technical and detailed analysis of Heisenberg's science than provided here, see Mark Walker, "Physics, History, and the German Atomic Bomb," *Berichte zur Wissenschaftsgeschichte*, 40 (2017), 271–288.
83. Heisenberg, Grundlagen.
84. Werner Heisenberg, Die Möglichkeit der technischen Energiegewinnung aus der Uranspaltung (1939), 1, ADM, FA 002 461.

5 Total War

1. Werner Heisenberg to Elisabeth Heisenberg (13 and 22 September 1942), in Werner Heisenberg and Elisabeth Heisenberg, *"Meine Liebe Li!" Der Briefwechsel 1937–1946* (St. Pölten: Residenz Verlag, 2011), 207–209.
2. Jeremy Noakes and Geoffrey Pridham (eds.), *Nazism: A History in Documents and Eyewitness Accounts, 1919–1945, Volume III* (Exeter: University of Exeter Press, 1988), 841–845.
3. Jeremy Noakes and Geoffrey Pridham (eds.), *Nazism: A History in Documents and Eyewitness Accounts, 1919–1945, Volume IV* (Exeter: University of Exeter Press, 1998), 487–488, 495.

Notes to pages 78–84 289

4. Noakes and Pridham, Nazism IV, 490.
5. Noakes and Pridham, Nazism IV, 491.
6. Noakes and Pridham, Nazism IV, 542.
7. Paul Harteck to Karl-Friedrich Bonhoeffer (January 11, 1943), RPI, PHP B1 F7.
8. Noakes and Pridham, Nazism IV, 543.
9. Noakes and Pridham, Nazism IV, 543.
10. Noakes and Pridham, Nazism IV, 543–544.
11. Noakes and Pridham, Nazism IV, 545–546.
12. Telegram, Wilhelm Groth to Paul Harteck (August 13, 1942), RPI, PHP B2 F7; Wilhelm Groth and A. Suhr, Trennung der Uranisotope nach dem Ultrazentrifugenverfahren. II. Anreicherung der Uranisotope U^{234} und U^{235} in einer einstufigen Ultrazentrifuge (August 17, 1942), ADM, FA 002 621.
13. Konrad Beyerle (Anschütz) to Wilhelm Groth (July 13, 1942), ADM, FA 002 792; Konrad Beyerle to Paul Harteck (August 8, 1942), ADM, FA 002 792.
14. Abraham Esau to Rudolf Mentzel (November 24, 1942), ADM, IMC 29 1035-1943.
15. Wilhelm Groth, Paul Harteck, A. Suhr, Trennung der Uranisotope nach dem Ultrazentrifugenverfahren III. Anreicherung des Xenon- und der Uranisotope nach dem Schaukelverfahren (February 1943), ADM, FA 002 635; Paul Harteck and Johannes Jensen, Berechnung des Trenneffektes und der Ausbeute verschiedener Zentrifugenanordnungen zur Erhöhung des Wirkungsgrades einer einzelnen Zentrifuge (February 1943), ADM, FA 002 592.
16. Abraham Esau to Rudolf Mentzel (RFR) (April 5, 1943), ADM, IMC 29 1060-1061. Abraham Esau, Einleitung (May 6, 1943), ADM, FA 002 173; Klaus Clusius, Isotopentrennung (May 6, 1943), ADM, FA 002 737.
17. Abraham Esau to Paul Harteck (July 15, 1943), ADM, FA 002 796; Paul Harteck to Abraham Esau (July 21, 1943), ADM, FA 002 796.
18. Noakes and Pridham, Nazism IV, 554–557.
19. Max von Laue to Otto Hahn (August 5, 1943), AMPG, III. Abt., Rep. 14 2461; Max von Laue to Werner Heisenberg (August 20, 1943), AMPG, III. Abt. Rep. 93.
20. Karl-Friedrich Bonhoeffer to Paul Harteck (August 30, 1943), RPI, PHP B1 F7.
21. Paul Harteck to Konrad Beyerle (June 15, 1943), ADM, FA 002 792; Beuthe to Paul Harteck (August 3, 1943), ADM, FA 002 796.
22. Paul Harteck to Kurt Diebner (September 16, 1943), ADM, FA 002 796.
23. Heinrich Grobbrügge to Paul Harteck (June 25, 1948), HSA, HSWD- and PA 1206 B.1; Paul Harteck to Heinrich Grobbrügge (July 29, 1948), HSA, HSWD- and PA 1206 B.1.
24. Auszug aus dem Protokoll des Universitätssenats (June 26, 1945), HSA, Universität 1- D.10.10 Bd. I; Paul Harteck to Johannes Jensen (August 15, 1944), ADM, FA 002 798; Koch's betrayal of Harteck was common knowledge after the war, for example, see Robert Jungk, *Brighter than a Thousand Suns: A Personal History of the Atomic Scientists* (New York: Harcourt, Brace, and Company, 1958), 96; Harteck to Jensen (15 August 1944), ADM, FA 002 797.
25. Mark Walker's interview with Paul Harteck.
26. Niederschrift über die Besprechungen am 24. und 25.7.42 in Rjukan und Vemork, ADM, FA 002 786.
27. Ammoniakwerk Merseburg to IG Farben (August 24, 1942), ADM, FA 002 783.
28. Paul Herold to Paul Harteck (December 10, 1942), ADM, FA 002 783; W Stab N to Ammoniakwerk Merseburg (December 19, 1942), ADM, FA 002 783.

290   Notes to pages 84–89

29. W Stab N to OKH (March 2, 1943), ADM, FA 002 803.
30. Niederschrift über die Besprechungen am 24. und 25.7.42 in Rjukan und Vemork, ADM, FA 002 786.
31. Wehrwirtschaftsstab Norwegen to Norsk Hydro (October 6, 1942), ADM, IMC 31 436.
32. Norsk Hydro to W Stab N (October 20, 1942), ADM, FA 002 786.
33. Per Dahl, *Heavy Water and the Wartime Race for Nuclear Energy* (Bristol: Institute of Physics Publishing, 2009), 158.
34. Major General George V. Strong to General Eisenhower (September 8, 1942), NARA, M1109 File 7E.
35. David Irving, *The German Atomic Bomb* (New York: Simon and Schuster, 1967), 136–142, here 136.
36. Bericht über Besuch Konsul Ing. Schöpke von 6.-8.1.43 bei Norsk Hydro-Elektrisk Kvaelstofaktieselskab in Rjukan, Vemork, Såheim, Notodden und Oslo (January 11, 1943), ADM, FA 002 786.
37. Irving, German, 156–170, here 156.
38. W Stab N to OKH (March 2, 1943), ADM, FA 002 803 and 786.
39. Bericht über Konsul Ing E. Schoepkes Reise und Besprechungen v. 10.-12.3.1943 (March 13, 1943), ADM, FA 002 786.
40. Bericht von Konsul Ing. Schöpke über die Besprechungen am 17. und 18.6.43 in Rjukan, Vemork und Såheim betr. den weiteren Ausbau und Betrieb der SH 200-Anlagen (June 21, 1943), ADM, FA 002 786.
41. Paul Harteck to Kurt Diebner (April 14, 1943), ADM, FA 002 796.
42. Abraham Esau, Einleitung (May 6, 1943), ADM, FA 002 173.
43. Paraphrase of a Telegram Just Received from a Reliable Source (August 13, 1943), NARA, M1109 File 7E; Memo, Major General Strong to Army Chief of Staff (August 13, 1943), NARA, M1109 File 7E.
44. Abraham Esau to Rudolf Mentzel (November 24, 1942), ADM, IMC 29 1035-1943.
45. Heinrich Bütefisch to Abraham Esau (August 5, 1942), ADM, FA 002 783.
46. Paul Harteck to Heinrich Bütefisch (Ammoniakwerk Merseburg) (December 19, 1942), ADM, FA 002 783.
47. Paul Herold to Paul Harteck (September 11, 1942), ADM, FA 002 783.
48. Paul Harteck to Heinrich Bütefisch (December 19, 1942), ADM, FA 002 783.
49. Paul Herold to Paul Harteck (December 22, 1942), ADM, FA 002 783.
50. Besprechung über die Produktion von schwerem Wasser, insbes. über das Clusius/Llnde-Verfahren (July 16, 1942), ADM, IMC 29 723-724; Paul Harteck to HWA Draft (December 1, 1942), ADM, IMC 29 759; Abraham Esau, Einleitung (May 6, 1943), ADM, FA 002 173; Paul Harteck to Heinrich Bütefisch (Ammoniakwerk Merseburg) (December 19, 1942), ADM, FA 002 783.
51. Bericht über den Besuch bei der Montecatini in Meran und die sich hieraus ergebende Möglichkeit für eine zusätzliche SH 200-Produktion (May 27, 1943), ADM, FA 200 796.
52. Paul Harteck, Bericht über die Besprechungen in Berlin am 27.9.43 und in Leuna am 28.9.43 (October 2, 1943), ADM, FA 002 796.
53. Die Hauptarbeiter des Uranproblems (June 12, 1942), AMPG, I. Abt. Rep. 34; Werner Heisenberg to OKH (July 18, 1942), AMPG, I. Abt. Rep. 34.
54. Ernst Telschow to Albert Vögler (July 24, 1942), AMPG, I. Abt., Rep 1A; Aktennotiz: Besprechung mit Dr. Diebner am 1.8.42. (August 3, 1942), AMPG, I. Abt., Rep 1A.

Notes to pages 90–95

55. Robert Döpel, Bericht über zwei Unfälle beim Umgang mit Uranmetall (July 9, 1942), ADM, FA 002 587.
56. Walther Bothe to Werner Heisenberg (June 30, 1942), AMPG, I. Abt. Rep. 34; Werner Heisenberg to Walther Bothe (July 9, 1942), AMPG, I. Abt. Rep. 34; Walther Bothe to Werner Heisenberg (September 1, 1942), AMPG, III. Abt. Rep. 93; Werner Heisenberg to OKH (October 7, 1942), AMPG, I. Abt. Rep. 34; Werner Heisenberg to Walther Bothe (October 23, 1942), AMPG, III. Abt. Rep. 93.
57. Forstman to Walther Bothe (November 12, 1942), AMPG, III. Abt., Rep 6 62; Werner Heisenberg, Bericht über die mit dem Uranproblem zusammenhängenden Arbeiten des Kaiser Wilhelm-Instituts für Physik im zweiten Halbjahr 1942 (December 19, 1942), AMPG, I. Abt. Rep. 34.
58. Ernst Telschow to Albert Vögler (July 24, 1942), AMPG, I. Abt., Rep 1A; Karl Wirtz to Ernst Telschow (Gen, Verw. KWG) (August 28, 1942), AMPG Heisenberg; Heisenberg, Halbjahr (December 19, 1942), AMPG, I. Abt. Rep. 34; Werner Heisenberg to Ernst Telschow (KWG) (January 11, 1943), AMPG, III. Abt. Rep. 93.
59. Abraham Esau to Rudolf Mentzel (November 24, 1942), ADM, IMC 29 1035-1943; Erich Bagge's Diary (December 4, 1942), ADM, IMC 29 138-139.
60. Abraham Esau to Rudolf Mentzel (November 24, 1942), ADM, IMC 29 1035-1943.
61. Ernst Telschow, Memo (January 22, 1942), AMPG, III. Abt., Rep. 19.
62. Walther Bothe to Werner Heisenberg (June 30, 1942), AMPG, I. Abt. Rep. 34; Werner Heisenberg to Walther Bothe (July 9, 1942), AMPG, I. Abt. Rep. 34; Ernst Telschow to Albert Vögler (July 24, 1942), AMPG, I. Abt., Rep 1A; Werner Heisenberg, Bemerkungen zu dem geplanten halbtechnischen Versuch mit 1,5 to D_2O und 5 to 38-Metall. (July 31, 1942), ADM, FA 002 620.
63. Werner Heisenberg to Carl Friedrich von Weizsäcker (December 16, 1942), AMPG, III. Abt. Rep. 93.
64. F. Berkei, W. Borrmann, W. Czulius, K. Diebner, G. Hartwig, W. Herrmann K. Höcker, H. Pose, and W. Rexer, Bericht über einen Würfelversuch mit Uranoxyd und Paraffin in der Versuchsstelle Gottow des Heereswaffenamtes (November 26, 1942), ADM, FA 002 629; Karl-Heinz Höcker, Auswertung des Würfelversuchs mit Uranoxyd und Paraffin in der Versuohsstelle Gottow des Heereswaffenamts. (November 26, 1942), ADM, FA 002 638; K.-H. Höcker, Über die Anordnung von Uran und Streusubstanz in der U-Maschine. (January 25, 1943), AMPG, III. Abt. Rep. 93.
65. Hermann Göring to Abraham Esau (December 8, 1942), ADM, IMC 29 1044-1045; Rudolf Mentzel to Görnnert (Göring) (December 8, 1942), ADM, IMC 29 1046-1048.
66. Ernst Telscow, Aktennotiz (February 8, 1943), ADM, IMC 291049-1050.
67. Ernst Telschow to Rudolf Mentzel (March 1, 1943), ADM, IMC 29 1052-1053; Mentzel to Telschow (March 4, 1943), ADM, IMC 29 1054; Albert Vögler to Rudolf Mentzel (March 4, 1943), ADM, IMC 29 1049; Rudolf Mentzel to Albert Vögler (March 9, 1943), ADM, IMC 29 1049.
68. Erich Schumann to Werner Heisenberg (January 18, 1943), AMPG, III. Abt. Rep. 93; Erich Schumann to Paul Harteck (March 8, 1943), ADM, FA 002 796.
69. Abraham Esau to Paul Harteck (and others) (March 19, 1943), ADM, FA 002 796.
70. Werner Heisenberg to Ernst Telschow (March 25, 1943), AMPG, III. Abt. Rep. 93.
71. Kurt Diebner, Georg Hartwig, W. Herrmann, H. Westmeyer, Werner Czulius, F. Berkei, and Karl-Heinz Höcker, Vorläufige Mitteilung über einen Versuch mit Uranwürfeln und Schwerem Eis als Bremssubstanz (April 1943), ADM, FA 002 648.

292   Notes to pages 95–102

72. K. Diebner, G. Hartwig, W. Herrmann, H. Westmeyer, W. Czulius, F. Berkei, and K.-H. Höcker, Bericht über einen Versuch mit Würfeln aus Uran-Metall und Schwerem Eis (July 1943), ADM, FA 002 651.

73. Werner Heisenberg to Abraham Esau (May 4, 1943), AMPG, I. Abt. Rep. 34.

74. Werner Heisenberg to OKH (January 13, 1943), AMPG, III. Abt. Rep. 93; Walther Bothe to Werner Heisenberg (February 10, 1943), AMPG, III. Abt. Rep. 93; Probleme der Kernphysik, Schriften der Deutschen Akademie der Luftfahrtforschung (May 6, 1943), ADM, FA 002 737; Abraham Esau, Einleitung (May 6, 1943), ADM, FA 002 173.

75. Esau, Einleitung, ADM, FA 002 173.

76. Esau, Einleitung, ADM, FA 002 173.

77. Werner Heisenberg, Die Energiegewinnung aus der Atomkernspaltung (May 6, 1943), ADM, FA 002 737.

78. Heisenberg, Atomkernspaltung.

79. Niederschrift über die Besprechung am 7.5.1943 i. D. PTR. (May 7, 1943), ADM, FA 002 796.

80. Abraham Esau to Paul Harteck (May 29, 1943), ADM, FA 002 796.

81. Werner Heisenberg to Abraham Esau (June 4, 1943), AMPG, I. Abt. Rep. 34.

82. Heinz Pose and Ernst Rexer, Versuche mit verschiedenen geometrischen Anordnungen von Uranoxyd und Paraffin (October 12, 1943), ADM, IMC 30 453-456.

83. K. Diebner, W. Czulius, W. Heremann, G. Hartwig, E. Kamin, and F. Berkei, Bericht über die Neutronenvermehrung einer Anordnung von Uranwürfeln und Schwerem Wasser (G III) (December 1943), ADM, FA 002 634; Karl Wirtz to Werner Heisenberg (November 22, 1943), AMPG, III. Abt. Rep. 93.

84. Forstmann to Werner Heisenberg (April 13, 1943), AMPG, III. Abt. Rep. 93.

85. Werner Heisenberg to Ernst Telschow (March 5, 1943), AMPG, III. Abt. Rep. 93; Werner Heisenberg to Ernst Telschow (April 1, 1943), AMPG, III. Abt. Rep. 93; Werner Heisenberg to Walther Bothe (April 7, 1943), AMPG, I. Abt. Rep. 34.

86. Abraham Esau to Paul Harteck (May 29, 1943), ADM, FA002 796; Werner Heisenberg to Albert Vögler (June 1, 1943), AMPG, I. Abt. Rep. 34.

87. Werner Heisenberg to Albert Vögler (June 1, 1943), AMPG, I. Abt. Rep. 34; Auergesellschaft to Werner Heisenberg (July 15, 1943), AMPG, III. Abt. Rep. 93; Werner Heisenberg to Albert Vögler (August 11, 1943), AMPG, I. Abt. Rep. 34.

88. Auergesellschaft (Riehl) to Werner Heisenberg (August 19, 1943), AMPG, III. Abt. Rep. 93; Werner Heisenberg to Albert Vögler (August 23, 1943), AMPG, I. Abt. Rep. 34.

89. Ernst Telschow to Werner Heisenberg (September 4, 1943), AMPG, I. Abt. Rep. 34; Fischer to Heisenberg (September 9, 1943), AMPG, III. Abt. Rep. 93; Karl Wirtz to Werner Heisenberg (November 22, 1943), AMPG, III. Abt. Rep. 93.

90. Werner Heisenberg to Abraham Esau (July 24, 1943), AMPG, I. Abt. Rep. 34.

91. Werner Heisenberg to Walther Bothe (July 24, 1943), AMPG, I. Abt. Rep. 34; Walther Bothe to Werner Heisenberg (July 30, 1943), AMPG, III. Abt. Rep. 93; Erich Fischer to Walther Bothe (August 26, 1943), AMPG, III. Abt. Rep. 93.

92. Rudolf Mentzel to Görnnert (Göring) (July 8, 1943), ADM, IMC 29 1077.

93. Albert Vögler to Werner Heisenberg (July 28, 1943), AMPG, I. Abt. Rep. 34.

94. Werner Heisenberg to Albert Vögler (June 1, 1943), AMPG, I. Abt. Rep. 34; Auergesellschaft to Werner Heisenberg (July 15, 1943), AMPG, III. Abt. Rep. 93; Werner Heisenberg to Albert Vögler (August 11, 1943), AMPG, I. Abt. Rep. 34.

Notes to pages 102–106 293

95. Werner Heisenberg to Elisabeth Heisenberg (16 and 24 May 1943) in Heisenberg and Heisenberg, *Meine Liebe*, 216–217.
96. Werner Heisenberg to Elisabeth Heisenberg (20 May and 21 July 1943), in Heisenberg and Heisenberg, *Meine Liebe*, 217 and 223.
97. Werner Heisenberg to Elisabeth Heisenberg (July 21, 1943), in Heisenberg and Heisenberg, *Meine Liebe*, 222.
98. Werner Heisenberg to Elisabeth Heisenberg (May 30, 1943), in Heisenberg and Heisenberg, *Meine Liebe*, 220.
99. Werner Heisenberg to Elisabeth Heisenberg (December 9, 1943), in Heisenberg and Heisenberg, *Meine Liebe*, 213; in fact some copies of the book survived.
100. Ian Kershaw, *Hitler 1937–1945: Nemesis* (New York: Norton, 2000), 604–606.
101. Heinrich Himmler, Rede Reichsführer-SS Himmler vor den Gauleitern am 6.Okt.43 in Posen (October 6, 1943), Bradley Smith and Agnes Peterson (eds.), *Geheimreden 1933 bis 1945 und andere Ansprachen* (Frankfurt/Main: Propyläen, 1974), 162–183, here 169–171.
102. Albert Speer, Rede Reichminister Speer vor den Gauleitern am 6.Okt.43 in Posen (October 6, 1943) at www.nuremberg.law.harvard.edu/documents/3441-transcript-of-a-speech?q=Posen#p.1 (accessed July 1, 2022).
103. Adam Tooze, *The Wages of Destruction: The Making and Breaking of the Nazi Economy* (New York: Viking, 2007), 605–607, 611–612; Speer's postwar claims that he had not heard Himmler talk about genocide are improbable.
104. Albert Speer, Rede Reichminister Speer vor den Gauleitern am 6.Okt.43 in Posen, (October 6, 1943) at www.nuremberg.law.harvard.edu/documents/3441-transcript-of-a-speech?q=Posen#p.1 (accessed July 1, 2022).
105. Heinrich Himmler, Rede Reichsführer-SS Himmler vor den Gauleitern am 6.Okt.43 in Posen (October 6, 1943), Smith and Peterson, 169–171.
106. Albert Speer, Rede Reichminister Speer vor den Gauleitern am 6.Okt.43 in Posen, (October 6, 1943) at www.nuremberg.law.harvard.edu/documents/3441-transcript-of-a-speech?q=Posen#p.1 (accessed July 1, 2022).
107. See the chapter on Copenhagen.
108. David Irving's interview with Werner Heisenberg (October 23, 1965) in ADM, IMC 31 557.
109. Niederschrift über die Direktorenbesprechung am 9.11.1943 im Harnack-Haus AMPG, I. Abt. Rep. 34.
110. Werner Heisenberg to Hornung (August 20, 1943), AMPG, III. Abt. Rep. 93; Erich Bagge's Diary (September 8, 1943), ADM, IMC 29 106; Werner Heisenberg to Dekan der Universität Berlin (October 2, 1943), AMPG, III. Abt. Rep. 93; Julius Hiby to Werner Heisenberg and Karl Wirtz (January 20, 1944), AMPG, III. Abt. Rep. 93; www.mpic.de/4469999/umzuege (accessed July 2, 2022).
111. Niederschrift über die Direktorenbesprechung am 9.11.1943 im Harnack-Haus AMPG, I. Abt. Rep. 34.
112. Henry Smyth, *Atomic Energy for Military Purposes: The Official Report on the Development of the Atomic Bomb under the Auspices of the United States Government, 1940–1945* (Princeton: Princeton University Press, 1945), 83–86.
113. Smyth, Atomic, 91, 147–148, 169; *Manhattan District History Book III: The P-9 Project*, 5.9. www.hsdl.org/c/the-manhattan-district-history-full-text-now-available-online/ (accessed May 16, 2020).
114. Smyth, Atomic, 93–94.

294   Notes to pages 106–111

115. Smyth, Atomic, 98; Richard Rhodes, *The Making of the Atomic Bomb* (New York: Simon and Schuster, 1986), 428–430, 432–442.
116. Enrico Fermi, "Experimental Production of a Divergent Chain Reaction," in Horst Wohlfarth (ed.), *40 Jahre Kernspaltung: eine Einführung in der Originalliteratur* (Darmstadt: Wissenschaftliche Buchgesellschaft, 1979), 322–370, here 322–324.
117. Smyth, Atomic, 141–143.
118. Lillian Hoddeson, Paul W. Henriksen, Roger A. Meade, and Catherine Westfall, *Critical Assembly: A Technical History of Los Alamos during the Oppenheimer Years, 1943–1945* (Cambridge: Cambridge University Press, 1993), 38.
119. Smyth, Atomic, 101, 129; Rhodes, Making, 457–458.
120. Smyth, Atomic, 175–176, 184, 194, 200–201; Rhodes, Making, 486–496.
121. Smyth, Atomic, 103, 210.
122. Smyth, Atomic, 213.
123. Robert Serber, *The Los Alamos Primer: The First Lectures on How to Build an Atomic Bomb* (Berkeley: University of California Press, 1992), 27; Hoddeson, Critical, 69–77; Rhodes, Making, 460–464.
124. Jeremy Bernstein, *Hitler's Uranium Club: The Secret Recordings at Farm Hall* (Woodbury: American Institute of Physics Press, 1996), 197 and 209; see most recently Manfred Popp, "Misinterpreted Documents and Ignored Physical Facts: The History of 'Hitler's Atomic Bomb' Needs to Be Corrected," *Berichte zur Wissenschaftsgeschichte*, 39 (2016), 265–282.

6 The War is Lost

1. Werner Heisenberg, "Das Dritte Reich versuchte nicht, die Atombombe zu bauen," *Frankfurter Allgemeine Zeitung*, 286 (December 9, 1967), Beilage Bilder und Zeiten, 4.
2. Kernphyslkalische Tagung 1943 (beschränkter Teilnehmerkreis) in der Physikalisch-Technische Reichsanstalt (October 14–16, 1943), ADM, IMC 29 1078-1080; Abraham Esau to Rudolf Mentzel (October 28, 1943), NBL, SGP Box 27, Folder 30.
3. Rudolf Mentzel to Görnnert (November 12, 1943), NBL, SGP Box 27, Folder 30; Rudolf Mentzel to Görnnert (December 3, 1943), NBL, SGP Box 27, Folder 30.
4. Rudolf Mentzel to Goerner (November 6, 1943), ADM, IMC 29 1084; Albert Speer to Görnnert (November 17, 1943), NBL, SGP Box 27, Folder 30; Hermann Göring to Walther Gerlach (December 2, 1943), NBL, SGP Box 27, Folder 30; Hermann Göring to Walther Gerlach (December 2, 1943), NBL, SGP Box 27, Folder 30; Klaus Clusius to Werner Heisenberg (January 18, 1944), AMPG, III. Abt. Rep. 93; Hentschel, Klaus (ed.), *Physics and National Socialism: An Anthology of Primary Sources* (Basel: Birkhäuser, 1996), XXVIII; Walther Gerlach to Paul Harteck (January 24, 1944), ADM, FA 002 803.
5. Lage-Bericht Vemork den 13. Dezember 1943 (December 13, 1943), ADM, FA 002 785; David Irving, *The German Atomic Bomb* (New York: Simon and Schuster, 1967), 193–194.
6. Protokoll über die in der Norsk Hydro Büro, Oslo, am 10.Dezember 1943 abgehaltene Sitzung (December 11, 1943), ADM, FA 002 786.
7. Paul Harteck to Kurt Diebner (February 16, 1944), ADM, FA 002 803; Aktennotiz. Betr.: Schlussbesprechung anlässlich des Besuches der Herren Professor Harteck und Dr. Seeger, SH 200 (January 9, 1945), ADM, FA 002 786.

Notes to pages 111–116

8. Werner Heisenberg to Albert Vögler (January 21, 1944), AMPG, I. Abt. Rep. 34; Albert Vögler to Werner Heisenberg (January 27, 1944), AMPG, III. Abt. Rep. 93.

9. Irving, German, 200–211. For the number of casualties, see WIkipedia, www.en.wikipedia.org/wiki/Norwegian_heavy_water_sabotage (accessed July 25, 2020).

10. Heinrich Bütefisch to Abraham Esau (December 8, 1943), ADM, IMC 29 759; IG Farben to Paul Harteck (June 1, 1944), ADM, FA 002 802.

11. Hans Suess to Walther Gerlach (June 29, 1944), ADM, FA 002 803; Paul Harteck to OKH (July 20, 1944), ADM, FA 002 799; Hans Suess, Entwurf für eine Patentanmeldung. Verfahren zur Gewinnung von schwerem Wasser oder schwerem Wasserstoff. (July 21, 1944), ADM, FA 002 804.

12. Paul Harteck, Bericht über den Stand der SH 200-Gewinnung (April 15, 1944); Anlage zum Bericht über den Stand der SH 200-Gewinnung (April 15, 1944), ADM, IMC 29 762-771.

13. Harteck, Stand; Paul Harteck, Erwägungen und zu diskutierende Gesichtspunkte für eine SH 200 – Produktion nach dem Clusius-Linde-Verfahren, das gekoppelt ist an einen Wasserstoffregenerator nach Harteck und Suess (May 9, 1944), ADM, FA 002 803; Paul Harteck to Klaus Clusius (April 1, 1944), ADM, FA 002 797.

14. Harteck, Stand.

15. Paul Harteck, Termine (May 23, 1944), ADM, FA 002 803.

16. Paul Harteck to Paul Herold (March 10, 1944), ADM, FA 002 803.

17. Harteck, Termine.

18. Walther Gerlach, Bericht über die Arbeiten auf kernphysikalischen Gebiet vom 1. Febr. bis 31 Mai 1944 (May 30, 1944), ADM, FA 002 796.

19. Walther Gerlach to Paul Herold (July 28, 1944), ADM, FA 002 804; Irving, German, 239; Paul Herold to Walther Gerlach (August 23, 1944), ADM, FA 002 802.

20. Besprechung in Berlin am Sonnabend, dem 28.10.1944 (November 15, 1944), ADM, FA 002 804; Leuna to Paul Harteck (January 6, 1945), ADM, FA 002 802; Paul Harteck to Paul Herold (March 9, 1945), ADM, FA 002 802.

21. Paul Harteck to Walther Gerlach (February 5, 1944), ADM, FA 002 803; Paul Harteck to Abraham Esau (December 15, 1943), ADM, FA 002 796; Paul Harteck to Kurt Diebner (Februar 16, 1944), ADM, FA 002 803; Paul Harteck to Kurt Diebner (March 25, 1944), ADM, FA 002 799; Friedrich Berkei to Paul Harteck (April 26, 1944), ADM, FA 002 803.

22. Paul Harteck to Kurt Diebner (March 25, 1944), ADM FA 002 803; Walther Gerlach to Paul Harteck (April 18, 1944), ADM, FA 002 803; Paul Harteck to Karl-Friedrich Bonhoeffer (August 15, 1944), ADM, FA 002 797; Paul Harteck to Walther Gerlach (September 29, 1944), ADM, FA 002 804; Aktennotiz (October 18, 1944), ADM, FA 002 804.

23. Paul Harteck to Werner Osenberg (July 19, 1944), ADM, FA 002 799; Karl-Heinz Ludwig, *Technik und Ingenieure im Dritten Reich* (Königstein/Ts: Athenäum-Verlag, 1979), 243–245, 251–253.

24. Paul Harteck to Kurt Diebner (July 28, 1944), ADM, FA 002 804; Konrad Beyerle, Niederschrift über meine Reise nach Freiburg und Kandern in der Zeit von 2.8 bis 13.8.44 (August 17, 1944), ADM, IMC 29 776-779; Konrad Beyerle, Ergebnis einer Besprechung zwischen Herrn Prof. Harteck (RFR/Inst. F. phys. Chem. Hambg.) und Herrn Dr. Beyerle (Anschütz and Co.) über Maßnahmen zur Sicherstellung von Einrichtungen für das UZ-Vorhaben. (September 9, 1944), ADM, IMC 29

296   Notes to pages 116–120

784-787; Paul Harteck to Walther Gerlach (September 29, 1944), ADM, FA 002 804; Paul Harteck to Kurt Diebner (January 9, 1945), ADM, FA 002 804; Paul Harteck to Walther Gerlach (February 7, 1945), ADM, FA 002 804.

25. Foreign Intelligence Supplement No. 1 to Manhattan District History. Book 1 -- General. Volume 14 -- Intelligence and Security (1947); www.osti.gov/opennet/manhattan_district (accessed July 30, 2020).

26. Werner Heisenberg to Walther Gerlach (February 15, 1944), AMPG, I. Abt. Rep. 34; Abraham Esau, Bericht über den Stand der Arbeiten auf dem Gebiete der Kernphysik am 31.3.44 (July 21, 1944), ADM, IMC 29 1102-1108; Kurt Diebner to Werner Heisenberg (November 10, 1944), AMPG, I. Abt. Rep. 34.

27. Nikolaus Riehl and Karl Zimmer to Werner Heisenberg (December 21, 1943), AMPG, I. Abt. Rep. 34; Hermann Beuthe to Rudolf Mentzel (December 22, 1943), NBL, SGP Box 27, Folder 41.

28. Werner Heisenberg, Bericht über den gegenwärtigen Stand der Uran-Arbeiten am Kaiser Wilhelm-Institut für Physik (January 6, 1944). AMPG, I. Abt. Rep. 34; Albert Vögler to Werner Heisenberg (January 18, 1944), AMPG, I. Abt. Rep. 34; Werner Heisenberg to Albert Vögler (January 21, 1944), AMPG, I. Abt. Rep. 34; Werner Heisenberg to Walther Gerlach (February 15, 1944), AMPG, I. Abt. Rep. 34; Werner Heisenberg to Walther Gerlach (February 15, 1944), AMPG, I. Abt. Rep. 34; Werner Heisenberg to KWG (June 26, 1944), AMPG I. Abt. Rep. 34.

29. Werner Heisenberg and Karl Wirtz, "Großversuche zur Vorbereitung der Konstruktion eines Uranbrenners," in Walther Bothe and Siegfried Flügge (eds.), *Naturforschung und Medizin in Deutschland 1939–1946. Volume 14: Kernphysik und kosmische Strahlen.* Part II (Weinheim: Verlag Chemie, 1949), 143–165, here 153.

30. Karl Wirtz to Werner Heisenberg (March 15, 1944), AMPG, III. Abt. Rep. 93; Werner Heisenberg to Karl Wirtz (March 18, 1944), AMPG, I. Abt. Rep. 34; Karl Wirtz, Einrichtung der Elektrolyse zur Aufarbeitung von schwerem Wasser (August 8, 1944), AMPG, I. Abt. Rep. 34.

31. Werner Heisenberg to Paul Harteck (May 22, 1944), ADM, FA 002 798; Paul Harteck to Karl-Friedrich Bonhoeffer (May 31, 1944), ADM, FA 002 797; Karl-Friedrich Bonhoeffer to Paul Harteck (June 7, 1944), ADM, FA 002 797; Karl Wirtz to Paul Harteck (June 27, 1944), ADM, FA 002 799.

32. Karl Wirtz to Gerhard Borrmann (September 26, 1944), AMPG, I. Abt. Rep. 34; Walther Gerlach to Werner Heisenberg (Oktober 30, 1944), AMPG, I. Abt. Rep. 34; Paul Harteck to Walther Gerlach (November 10, 1944), ADM, FA 002 804; Karl Wirtz to Werner Heisenberg (January 26, 1945), AMPG, I. Abt. Rep. 34; Heisenberg and Wirtz, 157.

33. Walther Gerlach to Werner Heisenberg (June 7, 1944), AMPG, I. Abt. Rep. 34; Werner Heisenberg, Bericht über den Fortgang der Arbeiten am Kaiser Wilhelm Institut für Physik (June 26, 1944), AMPG, I. Abt. Rep. 34; also see Fritz Bopp, Walther Bothe, Erich Fischer, Erwin Fünfer, Werner Heisenberg, Ritter, Karl Wirtz, Bericht über einen Versuch mit 1,5 to D_2O und U und 40 cm Kohlerückstreumantel (January 3, 1945), ADM, FA 002 705.

34. Jeremy Bernstein, *Hitler's Uranium Club: The Secret Recordings at Farm Hall* (Woodbury: American Institute of Physics Press, 1996), 211; Werner Heisenberg, Theoretische Auswertung der Dahlemer Großversuche (September 1944) Karl Heinz Höcker Papers; Werner Heisenberg, Bericht über den Stand der kernphysikalischen

Notes to pages 120–126   297

Arbeiten am Kaiser-Wilhelm-Institut für Physik, Berllin-Dahlem (October 16, 1944), AMPG, I. Abt. Rep. 34.

35. Werner Heisenberg to Elisabeth Heisenberg (October 27, 1944) in Werner Heisenberg and Elisabeth Heisenberg, *"Meine Liebe Li!" Der Briefwechsel 1937–1946* (St. Pölten: Residenz Verlag, 2011), 263–264; Walther Gerlach to Werner Heisenberg (30. Oktober 1944), AMPG, I. Abt. Rep. 34.

36. Karl Wirtz to Werner Heisenberg (January 26, 1945), AMPG, I. Abt. Rep. 34; Karl Wirtz to Werner Heisenberg (January 29, 1945), AMPG, I. Abt. Rep. 34.

37. Irving, German, 268–269.

38. Werner Heisenberg to Elisabeth Heisenberg (February 1, 1945) in Heisenberg and Heisenberg, Meine Liebe, 273–274.

39. Irving, German, 269.

40. Erich Bagge's Diary (February 23, 1945), ADM, IMC 29 141; Werner Heisenberg, "Über die Arbeiten zur technischen Ausnutzung der Atomkernenergie in Deutschland," *Die Naturwissenschaften*, 33 (1946), 325–329, here 328; Werner Heisenberg to Friedrich Hund (February 28, 1945), AMPG, I. Abt. Rep. 34.

41. Bernstein, Uranium, 211; Heisenberg and Wirtz, Großversuche, 158–160.

42. Cameron Reed, "An Inter-Country Comparison of Nuclear Pile Development during World War II," *European Physical Journal H*, 46/15 (2021); David C. Cassidy, *Beyond Uncertainty: Heisenberg, Quantum Physics, and The Bomb* (New York: Bellevue Literary Press, 2009), 364; Irving, German, 270.

43. *Manhattan District History*, 4.29. Heisenberg and Wirtz, Großversuche, 162 and 164; the image is on page 159; Heisenberg, Ausnutzung, 328.

44. Werner Heisenberg's Diary (April 17, 1945), in Heisenberg and Heisenberg, Meine Liebe, 287.

45. Rainer Karlsch, "Was geschah im März 1945? Dokumente und Zeugenaussagen zu den Tests auf dem Truppenübungsplatz Ohrdruf," in Rainer Karlsch and Heiko Petermann (eds.), *Für und Wider "Hitlers Bombe" Studien zur Atomforschung in Deutschland* (Münster: Waxmann, 2007), 15–48, here 21.

46. Rainer Karlsch, *Hitlers Bombe: Die geheime Geschichte der deutschen Kernwaffenversuche* (Munich: Deutsche Verlags-Anstalt, 2005), 24, 232.

47. Rainer Karlsch, "Vorwort," in Karlsch and Petermann, Für, 10.

48. GRU Bericht (November 15, 1944), in Karlsch, geschah, 22.

49. GRU Report (March 23, 1945) in Karlsch, geschah, 25–26.

50. Karlsch, geschah, 15–48, here 18, 34–37, 47.

51. GRU Report (March 23, 1945) in Karlsch, geschah, 25–26.

52. I. V. Kurchatov, Stellungnahme zu Unterlagen "Über eine deutsche Atombombe" (March 30, 1945), in Karlsch, geheime, 342–343.

53. Herbert Janßen and Dirk Arnold, "In Bodenprobem keine Spur von 'Hitlers Bombe.'" (February 15, 2006); www.ptb.de/cms/en/gateways/press/press-releases/press-release.html?tx_news_pi1%5Bnews%5D=321&cHash=19ceb389eb977cdd 14f86fab0a1e109f (accessed June 25, 2020).

54. Erich Schumann to Ernst Telschow (April 2, 1948) in Karlsch, geheime, 334–337.

55. Erich Schumann to Ernst Telschow (April 2, 1948) in Karlsch, geheime, 334–337.

56. W. Hermann, G. Hartwig, H. Rackwitz, W. Trinks, and H. Schaub, Versuche über die Einleitung von Kernreaktionen durch die Wirkung explodierender Stoffe (1944?), ADM, FA 002 721; Kurt Diebner, "Fusionsprozesse mit Hilfe konvergenter Stoßwellen – Einige ältere und neuere Versuche und Überlegungen," *Kerntechnik* 3, (1962), 89–93.

298   Notes to pages 127–132

57. www.merriam-webster.com/dictionary/Occam%27s%20razor (accessed August 7, 2020).
58. Adam Tooze, *The Wages of Destruction: The Making and Breaking of the Nazi Economy* (New York: Viking, 2007), 653.
59. Paul Harteck to Klaus Clusius (January 18, 1944), ADM, FA 002 797; Paul Harteck to Karl-Friedrich Bonhoeffer (May 9, 1944), ADM, FA 002 797; Paul Harteck to Karl-Friedrich Bonhoeffer (June 26, 1944), ADM, FA 002 797.
60. Paul Harteck to Klaus Clusius (July 31, 1944), ADM, FA 002 797; Werner Heisenberg to Arnold Sommerfeld (August 8, 1944), ADM, ASN.
61. Karl-Friedrich Bonhoeffer to Paul Harteck (May 2, 1944), ADM, FA 002 797; Werner Heisenberg to Elisabeth Heisenberg (May 24, 1943) in Heisenberg and Heisenberg, Meine Liebe, 217–218; Werner Heisenberg to Elisabeth Heisenberg (January 28, 1944) in Heisenberg and Heisenberg, Meine Liebe, 230–231.
62. Reichsministerium für Bewaffnung und Munition to Kaiser Wilhelm Gesellschaft (August 24, 1943), AMPG, I. Abt. Rep. 34; Forstmann to Karl Weber (September 18, 1943), AMPG, I. Abt. Rep. 34; Gestapo (Berlin) to Werner Heisenberg (July 14, 1944), AMPG, I. Abt. Rep. 34; Werner Heisenberg to Meyer (Gestapo) (July 26, 1944), AMPG, I. Abt. Rep. 34.
63. Otto Hahn, Bericht über den Angriff vom 15.2.44 (Brand und Volltreffer im Kaiser Wilhelm-Institute für Chemie), AMPG, I. Abt. Rep. 11; Forstmann, Bericht über die Fliegerschäden in Dahlem nach dem Angriff am 15. Februar 1944, AMPG, I. Abt. Rep. 11.
64. Werner Heisenberg to Elisabeth Heisenberg (January 1944), in Heisenberg and Heisenberg, Meine Liebe, 229; Werner Heisenberg to Elisabeth Heisenberg (July 11, 1944) in Heisenberg and Heisenberg, Meine Liebe, 248; Max von Laue to Otto Hahn (April 28, 1944), AMPG, III. Abt., Rep. 14 2461.
65. Thomas Pegelow, "Determining 'People of German Blood,' 'Jews' and 'Mischlinge': The Reich Kinship Office and the Competing Discourses and Powers of Nazism, 1941–1943," *Contemporary European History*, 15/1 (2006), 43–65, here 46.
66. TH Berlin to REM (June 2, 1943), BABL, Riehl Research Wi; TH Berlin to REM (December 18, 1943), BABL, Riehl Research Wi; TH Berlin to REM (July 26, 1944), BABL, Riehl Research Wi.
67. See Klaus Scholder, *Die Mittwochsgesellschaft. Protokolle aus dem geistigen Deutschland 1932–1944*, 2. Ed. (Berlin: Severin und Siedler, 1982).
68. Werner Heisenberg, *Der Teil und das Ganze: Gespräche im Umkreis der Atomphysik* (Munich: DTV, 1973), 222; Werner Heisenberg to Elisabeth Heisenberg (July 11, 1944) in Heisenberg and Heisenberg, Meine Liebe, 248.
69. Heisenberg, *Teil*, 223; Werner Heisenberg to Elisabeth Heisenberg (August 10, 1944) in Heisenberg and Heisenberg, Meine Liebe, 252.
70. Karl-Friedrich Bonhoeffer to Paul Harteck (February 2, 1945), RPI, PHP Harteck B1 F7.
71. Karl-Friedrich Bonhoeffer to Paul Harteck (February 2, 1945), RPI, PHP Harteck B1 F7; Paul Harteck to Karl-Friedrich Bonhoeffer (February 19, 1945), RPI, PHP Harteck B1 F7; Karl-Friedrich Bonhoeffer to Paul Harteck (March 20, 1945), RPI, PHP Harteck B1 F8.
72. Werner Heisenberg to Elisabeth Heisenberg (October 14, 1943) in Heisenberg and Heisenberg, Meine Liebe, 224–225; Borger (Hauptamt Wissenschaft, NSDAP) to Parteikanzlei (October 2, 1942), IZG, MA 612 59823.

Notes to pages 132–135 299

73. Albert Vögler to Werner Heisenberg (April 12, 1944), AMPG, I. Abt. Rep. 34; Alsos Report on Gerlach Summary of Nuclear Reports (May 2, 1945), ADM, IMC 29 1320-1323; Bernstein, Uranium, 134–135.

74. Kurt Diebner to Paul Harteck (November 19, 1943), ADM, FA 002 796; Ernst Telschow to Werner Heisenberg (November 26, 1943), AMPG, III. Abt. Rep. 93; Ernst Telschow to Otto Hahn (November 26, 1943), AMPG, III. Abt., Rep. 14 5604; Goerner to Werner Heisenberg (December 17, 1943), AMPG, III. Abt. Rep. 93; Werner Heisenberg to Goerner (Speer's Ministry) (January 12, 1944), AMPG, III. Abt. Rep. 93.

75. Josef Goebbels, "Der Totale Krieg wird praktische Wirklichkeit," *Völkischer Beobachter* (July 28, 1944), quoted in Karlsch, geheime, 163.

76. Rudolf Mentzel to Walther Gerlach (September 2, 1944), BAK, R26 III 515; Walther Gerlach an Werner Heisenberg (30. Oktober 1944), AMPG, I. Abt. Rep. 34; Walther Gerlach to RFR (February 26, 1945), ADM, IMC 29 1158-1159.

77. SS-Obergruppenführers Hossmann to the Gauleiter Murr and Wagner (22 June1944), BABL, Berlin-Lichterfelde, NS 19/317, quoted in Karlsch, geheime, 193; Heinrich Himmler to Befehlshaber des Ersatzheeres, Obergruppenführer Jüttner (July 23, 1944), ADM, IMC 31 1062; Leon Poliakov and Joseph Wulf, *Das Dritte Reich und seine Denker*, 2nd Ed. (Frankfurt am Main: Ullstein, 1983), 319, 321.

78. Martin Bormann, Rundschreiben to the Gauleiter. Betrifft: Sicherstellung der für Forschungsaufgaben freigestellten Kräfte (September 3, 1944), ADM, IMC 29 1062; Werner Osenberg, Rundschreiben. Betreff: Bildung einer Wehrforschungs-Gemeinschaft (September 7, 1944), AMPG, I. Abt. Rep. 34; Walther Gerlach to Martin Bormann (December 16, 1944), AMPG, I. Abt. Rep. 34.

79. Albert Vögler to Werner Heisenberg (October 31, 1944), AMPG, I. Abt. Rep. 34; Albert Speer to Walther Gerlach (December 19, 1944), BAK, R3/1579.

80. Werner Heisenberg to Arnold Sommerfeld (August 8, 1944) SN; Werner Heisenberg to Elisabeth Heisenberg (August 25, 1944) in Heisenberg and Heisenberg, Meine Liebe, 254–255; Werner Heisenberg to Elisabeth Heisenberg (September 1, 1944) in Heisenberg and Heisenberg, Meine Liebe, 255–256; Werner Heisenberg to Elisabeth Heisenberg (January 21, 1945) in Heisenberg and Heisenberg, Meine Liebe, 272; Werner Heisenberg to Elisabeth Heisenberg (March 9, 1945) in Heisenberg and Heisenberg, Meine Liebe, 279–280; Werner Heisenberg to Elisabeth Heisenberg (March 16, 1945), in Heisenberg and Heisenberg, Meine Liebe, 282–283.

81. Werner Heisenberg to Elisabeth Heisenberg (October 10, 1944) in Heisenberg and Heisenberg, Meine Liebe, 261; Werner Heisenberg to Elisabeth Heisenberg (March 1, 1945) in Heisenberg and Heisenberg, Meine Liebe, 277–278.

82. Werner Heisenberg to Elisabeth Heisenberg (August 25, 1944) in Heisenberg and Heisenberg, Meine Liebe, 254–255; Werner Heisenberg to Elisabeth Heisenberg (January 21, 1945) in Heisenberg and Heisenberg, Meine Liebe, 272.

83. Werner Heisenberg to Elisabeth Heisenberg (February 23, 1945) in Heisenberg and Heisenberg, Meine Liebe, 276; Werner Heisenberg to Elisabeth Heisenberg (March 1, 1945) in Heisenberg and Heisenberg, Meine Liebe, 277–278; Elisabeth Heisenberg to Werner Heisenberg (March 12, 1945) in Heisenberg and Heisenberg, Meine Liebe, 280–281.

84. Werner Heisenberg to Elisabeth Heisenberg (September 26, 1944) in Heisenberg and Heisenberg, Meine Liebe, 256–257; Werner Heisenberg to Elisabeth

300 Notes to pages 136–140

Heisenberg (October 3, 1944) in Heisenberg and Heisenberg, Meine Liebe, 258; Werner Heisenberg to Elisabeth Heisenberg (October 12, 1944) in Heisenberg and Heisenberg, Meine Liebe, 262; Werner Heisenberg to Elisabeth Heisenberg (October 22, 1944) in Heisenberg and Heisenberg, Meine Liebe, 263.

85. For the *Volksturm* see Ian Kershaw, *Hitler. 1936–45: Nemesis* (New York: Norton, 2000), 714–715; Erich Bagge, Tagebuch ADM, IMC 29 141; Max von Laue to Werner Heisenberg (November 7, 1944), AMPG, I. Abt. Rep. 34; Werner Heisenberg to Elisabeth Heisenberg (October 27, 1944) in Heisenberg and Heisenberg, Meine Liebe, 263–264; Walther Gerlach to Martin Bormann (December 16, 1944), AMPG, I. Abt. Rep. 34.

86. Werner Heisenberg to Elisabeth Heisenberg (January 11, 1945) in Heisenberg and Heisenberg, Meine Liebe, 270–271; Werner Heisenberg to Elisabeth Heisenberg (January 14, 1945) in Heisenberg and Heisenberg, Meine Liebe, 271–272.

87. Werner Heisenberg to Elisabeth Heisenberg (January 11, 1945) in Heisenberg and Heisenberg, Meine Liebe, 270–271; Werner Heisenberg to Elisabeth Heisenberg (January 28, 1945) in Heisenberg and Heisenberg, Meine Liebe, 272–273.

88. Werner Heisenberg to Elisabeth Heisenberg (January 28, 1945) in Heisenberg and Heisenberg, Meine Liebe, 272–273; Werner Heisenberg to Elisabeth Heisenberg (February 15, 1945) in Heisenberg and Heisenberg, Meine Liebe, 274–275.

89. Werner Heisenberg to Elisabeth Heisenberg (March 9, 1945) in Heisenberg and Heisenberg, Meine Liebe, 279–280; Werner Heisenberg to Elisabeth Heisenberg (March 16, 1945), in Heisenberg and Heisenberg, Meine Liebe, 282–283; Werner Heisenberg to Elisabeth Heisenberg (April 11, 1945), in Heisenberg and Heisenberg, Meine Liebe, 284–285.

90. Werner Heisenberg to Elisabeth Heisenberg (March 9, 1945) in Heisenberg and Heisenberg, Meine Liebe, 279–280; Werner Heisenberg to Elisabeth Heisenberg (April 11, 1945), in Heisenberg and Heisenberg, Meine Liebe, 284–285.

91. Siegfried Hülsmann, Bericht (November 4, 1945), AMPG, I. Abt. Rep. 34; Irving, German, 275.

92. Werner Heisenberg's Diary (April 15, to May 3, 1945), in Heisenberg and Heisenberg, Meine Liebe, 286–299, here 288–290; Werner Heisenberg to Robert Jungk (November 17, 1956), AMPG Heisenberg III. Abt. Rep. 93.

93. Werner Heisenberg's Diary (April 15, to May 3, 1945), in Heisenberg and Heisenberg, Meine Liebe, 286–299, here 290–292.

94. Werner Heisenberg's Diary (April 15, to May 3, 1945), in Heisenberg and Heisenberg, Meine Liebe, 286–299, here 291–293.

95. Werner Heisenberg's Diary (April 15, to May 3, 1945), in Heisenberg and Heisenberg, Meine Liebe, 286–299, here 292–294.

96. Werner Heisenberg's Diary (April 15, to May 3, 1945), in Heisenberg and Heisenberg, Meine Liebe, 286–299, here 290–296.

97. Werner Heisenberg's Diary (April 15, to May 3, 1945), in Heisenberg and Heisenberg, Meine Liebe, 286–299, here 296.

98. Werner Heisenberg's Diary (April 15, to May 3, 1945), in Heisenberg and Heisenberg, Meine Liebe, 286–299, here 297.

99. Werner Heisenberg's Diary (April 15, to May 3, 1945), in Heisenberg and Heisenberg, Meine Liebe, 286–299, here 298–299.

100. Werner Heisenberg's Diary (April 15, to May 3, 1945), in Heisenberg and Heisenberg, Meine Liebe, 286–299, here 299; David Irving's Interview with

Notes to pages 141–149 301

Werner Heisenberg and Carl Friedrich von Weizsäcker (July 19, 1966), ADM, IMC 31 617.

101. Henry Smyth, *Atomic Energy for Military Purposes: The Official Report on the Development of the Atomic Bomb under the Auspices of the United States Government, 1940–1945* (Princeton: Princeton University Press, 1945), 168–169; Manhattan District History Book III: The P-9 Project (1947), 5.9 and 5.27. www.osti.gov/opennet/manhattan_district (accessed September 12, 2020).

102. Smyth, Atomic, 148–149.

103. Jesse Beams, Report on the Use of the Centrifuge Method for the Concentration of U^{235} by the Germans (April 9, 1946), ADM, FA 002 769.

104. Lilian Hoddeson, Paul Henriksen, Roger Meade, and Catherine Westfall, *Critical Assembly: A Technical History of Los Alamos during the Oppenheimer Years, 1943–1945* (Cambridge: Cambridge University Press, 1993), 39, 251, 263.

105. Hoddeson, Critical, 265.

106. Smyth, Atomic, 142–147; Hoddeson, Critical, 38.

107. Hoddeson, Critical, 3, 129, 162, 228, 312, 330–331.

108. Alvin Weinberg and Lothar Nordheim to Arthur Compton (November 8, 1945), ADM, IMC 31 1182-1184.

7 Oversimplifications

1. Samuel Goudsmit, "Secrecy or Science," *Science Illustrated*, 1 (1946), 97–99, here 98–99.

2. Samuel Goudsmit to Major Frank Smith (January 31, 1945), NARA, Foreign Intelligence Supplement No. 1 to Manhattan District History Book I – General. Volume 14 – Intelligence and Security; www.osti.gov/opennet/manhattan_district (accessed July 16, 2023).

3. Rudolf Fleischmann, Notes on Report by Alsos (May 22, 1942), ADM, FA 002 396; Alsos Report on Gerlach Summary of Nuclear Reports (May 2, 1945), ADM, IMC 29 1320-1323. Manfred Popp has recently taken up Goudsmit's arguments; Manfred Popp, "Misinterpreted Documents and Ignored Physical Facts: The History of 'Hitler's Atomic Bomb' Needs to Be Corrected," *Berichte zur Wissenschaftsgeschichte*, 39 (2016), 265–282; Manfred Popp, "Hitlers Atombombe. Störfall der Wissenschaftsgeschichte," *Spektrum der Wissenschaft*, 12/16 (2016), 12–21; Manfred Popp, "Why Hitler Did Not Have Atomic Bombs," *Journal of Nuclear Engineering*, 2 (2021), 9–27.

4. Fred Wardenburg to Samuel Goudsmit (April 12, 1945), ADM, IMC 31 1153; Erich Bagge, Tagebuch IMC 29 134-159; Landsdale to Groves (May 5, 1945), NARA, M1109 File 7B; David Irving's Interview with Werner Heisenberg and Carl Friedrich von Weizsäcker (July 19, 1966), ADM, IMC 31 616-617.

5. R.C. Ham, Munich Operation: Report to Boris Pash (May 12, 1945), NARA, RG 160 Box 93 Folder 334.

6. Werner Heisenberg to Elisabeth Heisenberg (May 4, 1945) in Werner Heisenberg and Elisabeth Heisenberg, *"Meine Liebe Li!" Der Briefwechsel 1937–1946* (St. Pölten: Residenz Verlag, 2011), 299–300; Werner Heisenberg to Fritz Schumacher (Oxford) (May 6, 1945 [never delivered]), ADM, IMC 31 1085.

7. Werner Heisenberg to Elisabeth Heisenberg (May 7, 1945) in Heisenberg and Heisenberg, Meine Liebe, 300–301.

302 Notes to pages 149–154

8. David Irving's Interview with Werner Heisenberg and Carl Friedrich von Weizsäcker (July 19, 1966), ADM, IMC 31 616-617; Werner Heisenberg to David Irving (May 23, 1966) AMPG, III. Abt. Rep. 93 1743.
9. Elisabeth Heisenberg, *Das politische Leben eines Unpolitischen. Erinnerungen an Werner Heisenberg* (Munich: Piper, 1983), 133.
10. Samuel Goudsmit, "Nazis' Atomic Secrets," *Life*, 23 (October 20, 1947), 123–134.
11. David Irving's Interview with Werner Heisenberg and Carl Friedrich von Weizsäcker (July 19, 1966), ADM, IMC 31 616-617; Carl Friedrich von Weizsäcker to Robert Jungk (November 6, 1956), AMPG, III. Abt., Rep. 111, 250.
12. Jeremy Bernstein, *Hitler's Uranium Club: The Secret Recordings at Farm Hall* (Woodbury: American Institute of Physics Press, 1996), 144.
13. Werner Heisenberg to Elisabeth Heisenberg (August 6, 1945) in Heisenberg and Heisenberg, Meine Liebe, 304.
14. Elisabeth Heisenberg to Werner Heisenberg (August 20, 1945) in Heisenberg and Heisenberg, Meine Liebe, 304–306.
15. Bernstein, Uranium, 294, 348, 352.
16. Werner Heisenberg to Elisabeth Heisenberg (January 9, 1946), in Heisenberg and Heisenberg, Meine Liebe, 316.
17. Werner Heisenberg to Elisabeth Heisenberg (January 20, 1946), in Heisenberg and Heisenberg, Meine Liebe, 321–322; Elisabeth Heisenberg to Werner Heisenberg (January 23, 1946), in Heisenberg and Heisenberg, Meine Liebe, 323.
18. Werner Heisenberg to Elisabeth Heisenberg (January 25, 1946), in Heisenberg and Heisenberg, Meine Liebe, 325–326.
19. Werner Heisenberg to Elisabeth Heisenberg (June 5, 1946), in Heisenberg and Heisenberg, Meine Liebe, 340–341; Elisabeth Heisenberg to Werner Heisenberg (June 11, 1946), in Heisenberg and Heisenberg, Meine Liebe, 341–342.
20. Samuel Goudsmit to Vannevar Bush (August 23, 1945), NBL, SGP Box 25, Folder 4.
21. For example, Goudsmit, "Secrecy"; Samuel Goudsmit, "War Physics in Germany," *The Review of Scientific Instruments*, 17/1 (1946), 49–52; Samuel Goudsmit, "How Germany Lost the Race," *Bulletin of the Atomic Scientists*, 1/7 (1946), 4–5.
22. Samuel Goudsmit to Rudolf Ladenburg (October 14, 1946), NBL, SGP Box 14, Folder 138.
23. Goudsmit, "War," 50.
24. Goudsmit, "Lost," 5.
25. Samuel Goudsmit, "Heisenberg on the German Uranium Project," *Bulletin of the Atomic Scientists*, 3/11 (1947), 343; Samuel Goudsmit, "Germans Overrated on Atom," *Washington Post* (August 3, 1947), B8.
26. Goudsmit, "Lost," 4.
27. Goudsmit, "Secrecy," 98–99.
28. Ernst Brüche to Carl Friedrich von Weizsäcker (August 20, 1946), AMPG, III. Abt. Rep. 93.
29. Carl Friedrich von Weizsäcker to Ernst Brüche (August 27, 1946), AMPG, III. Abt. Rep. 93.
30. Carl Friedrich von Weizsäcker to Werner Heisenberg (August 27, 1946), AMPG, III. Abt. Rep. 93; Ernst Brüche, Introduction to Samuel Goudsmit, "Wissenschaft oder Geheimhaltung," *Physikalische Blätter*, 2 (1946), 203–207, here 203.
31. Werner Heisenberg to Walther Bothe, Klaus Clusius, Siegfried Flügge, Walther Gerlach, and Paul Harteck (November 29, 1946), AMPG, III. Abt., Rep 6.

Notes to pages 154–158 303

32. Walther Bothe to Werner Heisenberg (December 7, 1946), AMPG, III. Abt., Rep 6.
33. Werner Heisenberg, "Über die Arbeiten zur technischen Ausnutzung der Atomkernenergie in Deutschland," *Die Naturwissenschaften*, 33 (1946), 325–329, here 327; Werner Heisenberg, "Research in Germany on the Technical Application of Atomic Energy," *Nature*, 160/4059 (1947), 211–215.
34. Heisenberg, "Ausnutzung," 329.
35. This text is taken from the English version, Heisenberg, Research, 214; Heisenberg, Ausnutzung, 329.
36. Werner Heisenberg to Walther Bothe, Klaus Clusius, Siegfried Flügge, Walther Gerlach, and Paul Harteck (November 29, 1946), AMPG, III. Abt., Rep 6.
37. Heisenberg, Research, 214.
38. Goudsmit, Heisenberg, 343.
39. Samuel Goudsmit, *Alsos*, 2nd Ed. (Los Angeles: Tomash 1983), originally published in 1947.
40. Goudsmit, Alsos, 138–139. The text was italicized in the original. Heisenberg was quoted as saying: "Germany's uranium pile, which I was building up to create energy for machines and not for bombs … As the world now knows, the explosive, plutonium, is produced in such a uranium pile."
41. Goudsmit, Alsos, 176–177, 243,134; Goudsmit, Heisenberg; Goudsmit, Overrated; Goudsmit, Atomic; Samuel Goudsmit to Rudolf Ladenburg (October 14, 1946), NBL, SGP Box 14, Folder 138.
42. Werner Heisenberg, Die theoretischen Grundlagen für die Energiegewinnung aus der Uranspaltung (February 26, 1942), ADM, IMC 29 1005-1013; David Irving copied this manuscript from Goudsmit's files.
43. See Popp, Misinterpreted and Mark Walker, "Physics, History, and the German Atomic Bomb," *Berichte zur Wissenschaftsgeschichte*, 40 (2017), 271–288.
44. Philip Morrison, "Alsos: The Story of German Science," *Bulletin of the Atomic Scientists*, 3/12 (1947), 354, 365.
45. Morrison, "Alsos," 365.
46. Samuel Goudsmit to Vannevar Bush (August 23, 1945), NBL, SGP Box 25, Folder 4; see the chapters Compromising and Rehabilitation.
47. For Hahn, see Ruth Lewin Sime, "The Politics of Memory: Otto Hahn and the Third Reich," *Physics in Perspective*, 8 (2006), 3–51; for von Laue and Martius/ Franklin, see Gerhard Rammer, "Allied Control of Physics and the Collegial Self-Denazification of the Physicists," in Helmuth Trischler and Mark Walker (eds.), *Physics and Politics: Research and Research Support in Twentieth Century Germany in International Perspective* (Stuttgart: Franz Steiner Verlag, 2010), 61–84; Gerhard Rammer, "'Cleanliness among Our Circle of Colleagues': The German Physical Society's Policy toward its Past," in Dieter Hoffmann and Mark Walker (eds.), *The German Physical Society in the Third Reich: Physicists between Autonomy and Accommodation* (Cambridge: Cambridge University Press, 2012), 367–421; and Ursula Maria Martius, "Videant consules…" in Dieter Hoffmann und Mark Walker (eds.), *Physiker zwischen Autonomie und Anpassung. Die Deutsche Physikalische Gesellschaft im Dritten Reich* (Weinheim: Wiley-VCH, 2007), 636–640.
48. Max von Laue to Theodore von Laue (July 10, 1946?), ADM Gerlach Papers NL 080/097-01.
49. Max von Laue, "The Wartime Activities of German Scientists," *Bulletin of the Atomic Scientists*, 4/4 (1948), 103; Max von Laue, "Die Kriegstätigkeit der

304   Notes to pages 158–166

deutschen Physiker," *Physikalische Blätter*, 4 (1948), 424–425, reprinted in Hoffmann and Walker, *Autonomie*, 640–643.

50. Philip Morrison, "A Reply to Dr. von Laue," *Bulletin of the Atomic Scientists*, 4 (1948), 104.

51. "Comment by the Editor," *Bulletin of the Atomic Scientists*, 4 (1948), 104.

52. For the quotations see Waldemar Kaempffert, "Why the Germans Failed to Develop an Atomic Bomb Is Now Revealed in Two Reports," *New York Times* (October 26, 1947), B9 and "Mr. Kaempffert Replies" [to Samuel Goudsmit, "German Atom Research: Scientist Disputes Statement on Development of Bomb"], *New York Times* (November 9, 1947).

53. Waldemar Kaempffert to Samuel Goudsmit (November 3, 1947), NBL, SGP Box 12, Folder 121.

54. Samuel Goudsmit to the *New York Times* (October 29, 1947), NBL, SGP Box 12, Folder 121; for the quotation, see Samuel Goudsmit, "German Atom Research: Scientist Disputes Statement on Development of Bomb," *New York Times* (November 9, 1947).

55. See Goudsmit, Alsos, 113 and Samuel Goudsmit to Waldemar Kaempffert (October 29, 1947), NBL, SGP Box 12, Folder 121.

56. Werner Heisenberg to Samuel Goudsmit (September 23, 1947), NBL, SGP Box 10, Folder 96.

57. Samuel Goudsmit to Werner Heisenberg (December 1, 1947), NBL, SGP Box 10, Folder 96.

58. Samuel Goudsmit to Werner Heisenberg (December 1, 1947), NBL, SGP Box 10, Folder 96; Goudsmit, Alsos, 115–119; see the Compromising chapter below.

59. Goudsmit, Alsos, 113–115.

60. Samuel Goudsmit to Werner Heisenberg (December 1, 1947), NBL, SGP Box 10, Folder 96.

61. Werner Heisenberg to Samuel Goudsmit (January 5, 1948), NBL, SGP Box 11, Folder 98; the original German captions in the diagram have been translated; although Goudsmit already had the text of Heisenberg's February, 1942 talk, this apparently did not include the diagram.

62. See Reinhard Siegmund-Schultze, "Bartel Leendert van der Waerden (1903–1996) im Dritten Reich: Moderne Algebra im Dienste des Anti-Modernismus?" in Dieter Hoffmann and Mark Walker (eds.), *"Fremde" Wissenschaftler im Dritten Reich. Die Debye-Affäre im Kontext* (Göttingen: Wallstein, 2011), 200–229.

63. Bartel van der Waerden to Samuel Goudsmit (March 17, 1948), NBL, SGP Box 10, Folder 93; Samuel Goudsmit to Bartel van der Waerden (March 1948), NBL, SGP Box 11, Folder 98.

64. Bartel van der Waerden to Werner Heisenberg (March 18, 1948), AMPG, III. Abt. Rep. 93.

65. Bartel van der Waerden to Werner Heisenberg (April 20, 1948), AMPG, III. Abt. Rep. 93.

66. Werner Heisenberg to Bartel van der Waerden (April 28, 1948), NBL, SGP Box 10, Folder 93.

67. Samuel Goudsmit to Werner Heisenberg (September 20, 1948), NBL, SGP Box 10, Folder 95.

68. Werner Heisenberg to Samuel Goudsmit (October 3, 1948), NBL, SGP Box 10, Folder 93.

Notes to pages 167–174 305

69. Samuel Goudsmit to Viktor Weisskopf (September 29, 1948), NBL, SGP Box 24, Folder 257; Viktor Weisskopf to Samuel Goudsmit (October 6, 1948), NBL, SGP Box 24, Folder 257; Viktor Weisskopf to Samuel Goudsmit (December 13, 1948), NBL, SGP Box 24, Folder 257.
70. Werner Heisenberg (interview), "Nazis Spurned Idea of an Atomic Bomb," *New York Times* (December 28, 1948).
71. Samuel Goudsmit (letter to the editor), *New York Times* (January 9, 1949).
72. Werner Heisenberg (letter to the editor), "German Atom Research," *New York Times* (January 30, 1949).
73. Samuel Goudsmit to Werner Heisenberg (February 11, 1949), NBL, SGP Box 10, Folder 95; Werner Heisenberg to Samuel Goudsmit (April 20, 1949) SGP Box 10, Folder 95; Samuel Goudsmit to Werner Heisenberg (June 3, 1949), NBL, SGP Box 10, Folder 96; Werner Heisenberg to Samuel Goudsmit (June 22, 1949), NBL, SGP Box 10, Folder 96; Samuel Goudsmit to Werner Heisenberg (September 19, 1950), NBL, SGP Box 10, Folder 96; Samuel Goudsmit to Werner Heisenberg (October 9, 1950), NBL, SGP Box 10, Folder 96.
74. Gregory Breit to Samuel Goudsmit (June 16, 1951), NBL, SGP Box 6, Folder 29; Samuel Goudsmit to Gregory Breit (July 2, 1951), NBL, SGP Box 6, Folder 29.
75. Samuel Goudsmit to Vannevar Bush (August 23, 1945), NBL, SGP Box 25, Folder 4; Samuel Goudsmit to Gregory Breit (July 2, 1951), NBL, SGP Box 6, Folder 29; Gregory Breit to Werner Heisenberg (August 3, 1951), AMPG, III. Abt. Rep. 93; Werner Heisenberg to Gregory Breit (August 25, 1951), AMPG, III. Abt. Rep. 93.
76. Nevill Mott and Rudolf Peierls, "Werner Heisenberg. December 5, 1901–February 1, 1976," *Biographical Memoirs of Fellows of the Royal Society*, 23/11 (1977), 212–251, here 236; Lise Meitner to James Franck in Klaus Hentschel, *Die Mentalität deutscher Physiker in der frühen Nachkriegszeit (1945–1949)* (Heidelberg: Synchron, 2005), 155; Werner Heisenberg to Gregory Breit (August 25, 1951), AMPG, III. Abt. Rep. 93.
77. Goudsmit, Alsos, 48–49.
78. Waldemar Kaempffert to Samuel Goudsmit (November 3, 1947), NBL, SGP Box 12, Folder 121.
79. Laue, "Wartime," 103; Laue, "Kriegstätigkeit," 424–425.
80. Morrison, "Reply."
81. Dirk Coster to Max von Laue (June 7, 1943), ADM, IMC 29 1051; Werner Heisenberg to Dirk Coster (February 16, 1943), ADM, IMC 29 1051.
82. David C. Cassidy, *Beyond Uncertainty: Heisenberg, Quantum Physics, and The Bomb* (New York: Bellevue Literary Press, 2009), 355.
83. Eckart Conze, Norbert Frei, Peter Hayes, and Moshe Zimmermann, *Das Amt und die Vergangenheit. Deutsche Diplomaten im Dritten Reich und in der Bundesrepublik* (Munich: Blessing, 2010), 69, 30, 127.
84. Conze, Vergangenheit, 173, 187–198, 229, 397.
85. Werner Heisenberg to Elisabeth Heisenberg (March 17, 1946), in Heisenberg and Heisenberg, Meine Liebe, 331.
86. Werner Heisenberg, Die aktive und passive Opposition im Dritten Reich (November 12, 1947), AMPG, III. Abt. Rep. 93.
87. Norbert Frei, *Vergangenheitspolitik. Die Anfänge der Bundesrepublik und die NS-Vergangenheit* (Munich: Deutsche Taschenbuch Verlag, 1999), 178; Conze, Vergangenheit, 397, 433–434.

306   Notes to pages 174–180

88. Joseph Haberer, *Politics and the Community of Science* (New York: Van Nostrand Reinhold, 1969), 167–168; Herbert Mehrtens, "Das 'Dritte Reich' in der Naturwissenschaftsgeschichte: Literaturbericht und Problemskizze," in Herbert Mehrtens and Steffen Richter (eds.), *Naturwissenschaft, Technik und NS-Ideologie. Beiträge zur Wissenschaftsgeschichte des Dritten Reiches* (Frankfurt am Main: Suhrkamp, 1980), 15–87, here 34.
89. This was the second such meeting. For the theological dialogue see Alan Beyerchen, *Scientists under Hitler: Politics and the Physics Community in the Third Reich* (New Haven: Yale University Press, 1977), 177–192 and the Compromising chapter.
90. Goudsmit, Alsos, 105; Carl Friedrich von Weizsäcker to Max von Laue (June 2, 1943), ADM, IMC 29 1066; Max von Laue to Carl Friedrich von Weizsäcker (June 4, 1943), ADM, IMC 29 1067; see the chapter on Compromising.
91. Wolfgang Finkelnburg to Werner Heisenberg (February 6, 1948), AMPG, III. Abt. Rep. 93.
92. Carl Friedrich von Weizsäcker to Edward Teller (November 4, 1948), AMPG, III. Abt. Rep. 111 264; Edward Teller to Carl Friedrich von Weizsäcker (February 21, 1949), AMPG, III. Abt. Rep. 111 264.
93. Samuel Goudsmit to Robert Hutchins (September 15, 1949), NBL, SGP Box 24, Folder 258; Robert Hutchins to Samuel Goudsmit (September 20, 1949), NBL, SGP Box 24, Folder 258.
94. Samuel Goudsmit to Edward Teller (November 22, 1949), NBL, SGP Box 22, Folder 240.
95. Samuel Goudsmit to James Franck (January 23, 1950), NBL, SGP Box 9, Folder 75;
96. James Franck to Samuel Goudsmit (January 27, 1950), NBL, SGP Box 9, Folder 75; Carl Friedrich von Weizsäcker to James Franck (June 21, 1952), RLC, JFP Box 10, Folder 4.
97. Samuel Goudsmit to Viktor Weisskopf (February 20, 1950), NBL, SGP Box 24, Folder 257.
98. Viktor Weisskopf to Samuel Goudsmit (February 24, 1950), NBL, SGP Box 24, Folder 257; Samuel Goudsmit to Viktor Weisskopf (February 26, 1950), NBL, SGP Box 24, Folder 257.
99. Samuel Goudsmit to Vannevar Bush (August 23, 1945), NBL, SGP Box 25, Folder 4; Samuel Goudsmit, "Our Task in Germany," *Bulletin of the Atomic Scientists* (April 1948), 106.

8   Compromising with Hitler

1. Samuel Goudsmit to Werner Heisenberg (December 1, 1947), NBL, SGP Box 10, Folder 95.
2. Samuel Goudsmit to Werner Heisenberg (December 1, 1947), NBL, SGP Box 10, Folder 95.
3. For general relativity see Matthew Stanley, *Einstein's War* (New York: Dutton, 2019); for Einstein's politics during the war, Stanley and David Rowe and Robert Schulman (eds.), *Einstein on Politics* (Princeton: Princeton University Press, 2007), 61–92; for the nationalism of most German physicists during the war, see Stefan Wolff, "Physicists in the 'Krieg der Geister': Wilhelm Wien's 'Proclamation,'" *Historical Studies in the Physical and Biological Sciences*, 33/2 (2003). 337–368

Notes to pages 180–185 307

and Stefan Wolff, "Die Konstituierung eines Netzwerkes reaktionärer Physiker in der Weimarer Republik," *Berichte zur Wissenschaftsgeschichte*, 31 (2008), 372–392.

4. Albert Einstein, "Dialogue about Objections to the Theory of Relativity," *Die Naturwissenschaften*, 6/48 (November 29, 1918), 697–702, in David Rowe and Robert Schulman (eds.), *Einstein on Politics* (Princeton: Princeton University Press, 2007), 97–103.
5. For the story of Eddington and Einstein, see Stanley, Einstein's.
6. Albert Einstein, "Meine Antwort. Über die antirelativistische G.m.b.H," *Berliner Tageblatt und Handels-Zeitung* (August 27, 1920), 1.
7. Arnold Sommerfeld to Albert Einstein (September 3, 1920) in Armin Hermann (ed.), *Albert Einstein/Arnold Sommerfeld. Briefwechsel. Sechzig Briefe aus dem goldenen Zeitalter der modernen Physik* (Basel: Schwabe u. Co., 1968), 65, 68–69; Albert Einstein to Arnold Sommerfeld (September 6, 1920) in Hermann, Einstein, 69; Arnold Sommerfeld to Albert Einstein (September 11, 1920), in Hermann, Einstein, 71.
8. Philipp Lenard to Arnold Sommerfeld (September 14, 1920), in Charlotte Schönbeck, *Albert Einstein und Philipp Lenard. Antipoden im Spannungsfeld von Physik und Zeitgeschichte* (Heidelberg: Springer, 2000), 28; "Versammlung und Kurze," *Zeitschrift für mathematischen und naturwissenschaftlichen Unterricht aller Schulgattungen*, 52 (1921), 80–82; "Anschaulichkeit; Allgemeine Diskussion über Relativitätstheorie," *Physikalische Zeitschrift*, 21 (1920), 666–668.
9. Rowe and Schulmann, Einstein, 114.
10. Albert Einstein to Paul Langevin (February 27, 1922), in Rowe and Schulmann, Einstein, 114–115; Albert Einstein to Paul Langevin (March 6, 1922), in Rowe and Schulmann, Einstein, 116.
11. Johannes Stark, (letter to the editor) *Deutsche Tages Zeitung* (April 4, 1922) in Siegfried Grundmann, *Einsteins Akte*, 2nd Ed. (Berlin: Springer, 2004), 217.
12. Charles Nordmann, "Avec Einstein dans les régions dévastées," *L'Illustration* 80/4128 (April 15, 1922), 328–331, in Rowe and Schulmann, Einstein, 118–119; the photograph is reproduced between pages 268 and 269; Albert Einstein, "In Memoriam Walther Rathenau," (after June 24, 1922), in Rowe and Schulmann, Einstein, 123.
13. Alan Beyerchen, *Scientists under Hitler: Politics and the Physics Community in the Third Reich* (New Haven: Yale University Press, 1977), 93–95.
14. Rowe and Schulmann, Einstein, 124–125; Albert Einstein to Max Planck (July 6, 1922), in Grundmann, 176 and Rowe and Schulmann, Einstein, 125; Grundmann, Einsteins, 223.
15. Philipp Lenard, *Äther und Uräther,* 2nd Ed. (1922), in Schönbeck, Einstein, 36.
16. Beyerchen, Scientists, 91–93.
17. Schönbeck, Einstein, 39.
18. Beyerchen, Scientists, 111–113.
19. Johannes Stark, *Die gegenwärtige Krisis in der deutschen Physik* (Leipzig: Barth, 1922), 6, 11.
20. Beyerchen, Scientists, 106.
21. Schönbeck, Einstein, 39.
22. Völkischer Beobachter to Philipp Lenard (February 17, 1923), ADM, JN 7c; Alfred Rosenberg to Philipp Lenard (October 6, 1924), ADM, JN 7b.

308   Notes to pages 185–189

23. Ernst Gehrcke, *Die Massensuggestion der Relativitätstheorie. Kulturhistorisch-psychologische Dokumente* (Berlin: Meusser, 1924); Josef Goebbels, *Michael* (Munich: Franz-Eher Verlag, 1929), in Grundmann, 116.

24. Philipp Lenard und Johannes Stark, "Hitlergeist und Wissenschaft," *Großdeutsche Zeitung. Tageszeitung für nationale und soziale Politik und Wirtschaft* (May 8, 1924), 1–2, reprinted in *Nationalsozialistische Monatshefte*, 7/71 (February 1936), 110–111.

25. Alfred Rosenberg to Philipp Lenard (September 28, 1927), ADM, JN 7c; Alfred Rosenberg to Philipp Lenard (October 4, 1927), ADM, JN 7b; Alfred Rosenberg to Philipp Lenard (February 2, 1928), ADM, JN, 7b.

26. SS (Himmler) to Philipp Lenard (July 22, 1926), ADM, JN 7c; Adolf Hitler to Philipp Lenard (June 8, 1927), ADM, JN, 7a; SS to Philipp Lenard (August 2, 1927), ADM, JN 7c; NSDAP to Philipp Lenard (April 23, 1928), ADM, JN 7c; JF Lehmann to Philipp Lenard (May 15, 1929), ADM, JN 7a.

27. Beyerchen, Scientists, 97; Adolf Hitler to Philipp Lenard (October 23, 1926), ADM, JN 7a; Rudolf Hess to Philipp Lenard (May 2, 1928), ADM, JN 7a.

28. Andreas Kleinert, "Der Briefwechsel zwischen Philipp Lenard (1862–1947) und Johannes Stark (1874–1975)," *Jahrbuch 2000 der Deutschen Akademie der Naturforscher Leopoldina* (Halle/Saale) LEOPOLDINA (R. 3), 46 (2001), 243–261, here 254; Dieter Hoffmann, "Johannes Stark--eine Persönlichkeit im Spannungsfeld von wissenschaftlicher Forschung und faschistischer Ideologie," *Philosophie und Naturwissenschaften in Vergangenheit und Gegenwart*, 22 (1982), 90–101, here 91; Philipp Lenard to Johannes Stark (November 9, 1927), ADM, JN 7c.

29. Johannes Stark to Philipp Lenard (May 5, 1928), ADM, JN 7c.

30. Johannes Stark to Philipp Lenard (October 29, 1928), ADM, JN 7c; Johannes Stark to Philipp Lenard (December 28, 1928), ADM, JN 7c; Johannes Stark to Arnold Sommerfeld (January 30, 1929) in Michael Eckert and Karl Märker (eds.), *Arnold Sommerfeld, Wissenschaftlicher Briefwechsel. Band 2: 1919–1951* (Berlin: GNT Verlag, 2004), 296–297; Arnold Sommerfeld to Johannes Stark (February 18, 1929), in Sommerfeld, Briefwechsel, 298; Johannes Stark to Philipp Lenard (March 17, 1929), ADM, JN 7c.

31. Kurt Zierold, *Forschungsförderung in drei Epochen* (Wiesbaden: Steiner Verlag, 1968), 173–174; Johannes Stark to the Oberste Parteigericht (November 7, 1937), BABL, BDC Stark.

32. Johannes Stark to Phlipp Lenard (April 16, 1928), ADM, JN 7c; Johannes Stark to Philipp Lenard (Juli 10, 1929), ADM, JN 7c.

33. Zierold, Forschungsförderung 173–174. Johannes Stark to the Oberste Parteigericht (November 7, 1937), BABL, BDC Stark; Johannes Stark to Philipp Lenard (September 24, 1930) in Kleinert, Briefwechsel, 253–254; Johannes Stark to Philipp Lenard (October 1, 1931), ADM, JN 7c.

34. Max Planck to Albert Einstein (March 19, 1933) in Grundmann, 441; Rowe and Schulman, Einstein, 270; Albert Einstein to the Prussian Academy of Sciences, Berlin (March 28, 1933) in Grundmann, Einsteins, 442.

35. Albert Einstein, Statement on Conditions in Germany, (March 28, 1933) in Rowe and Schulmann, Einstein, 270–271 and Grundmann, Einsteins, 443; *Kölnische Zeitung* (March 30, 1933) in Grundmann, Einsteins, 443.

Notes to pages 189–193   309

36. Sitzung der Gesamt-Akademie vom 30. März 1933, BABL AdW II-IV, 102; Außerordentliche Sitzung der Gesamt-Akademie vom 6. April 1933, BABL, AdW, II-IV, 102; Press Release from the Prussian Academy of Sciences (April 1, 1933), in Grundmann, Einsteins, 444.
37. Albert Einstein to Heinrich Ficker (April 5, 1933), BABL, AdW II-III-57 and Albert Einstein, Response to the Declaration of the Prussian Academy (April 5, 1933), in HUJ, AEA 36–062 and Rowe and Schulmann, Einstein, 272–273; Albert Einstein to Max Planck (April 6, 1933), HUJ, AEA 19-391 and Rowe and Schulmann, Einstein, 273–275.
38. Max Planck's Speech to the Akademie (May 11, 1933) in Grundmann, 445–446.
39. Max von Laue to Albert Einstein (May 14, 1933), in Dieter Hoffmann and Mark Walker (eds.), *Physiker zwischen Autonomie und Anpassung. Die Deutsche Physikalische Gesellschaft im Dritten Reich* (Weinheim: Wiley-Verlag VCH, 2007), 531; Albert Einstein to Max von Laue (May 26, 1933), HUJ, AEA 16-089 and Rowe and Schulmann, Einstein, 277–278; Albert Einstein to Max von Laue (June 5, 1933), in Hoffmann and Walker, Autonomie, 532–533.
40. Fritz Haber to Reichsminister Bernhard Rust (April 30, 1933), in Hoffmann and Walker, Autonomie, 530–531; Max von Laue: Fritz Haber (February 16, 1934), in Klaus Hentschel (ed.), *Physics and National Socialism: An Anthology of Primary Sources* (Basel: Birkhäuser, 1996), 76–77.
41. Johannes Stark to the Vorstand der Deutschen Physikalischen Gesellschaft (March 1, 1934), in Hoffmann and Walker, Autonomie, 543; Max von Laue, Zum Brief von Herrn Johannes Stark an den Vorstand der Deutschen Physikalischen Gesellschaft vom 1. März 1934, in Hoffmann and Walker, Autonomie, 544; REM Vermerk (April 4, 1934), in Hoffmann and Walker, Autonomie, 544–545; Max von Laue to Albert Einstein (March 10, 1934), in Hoffmann and Walker, Autonomie, 545–546; Albert Einstein to Max von Laue (March 23, 1934), in Hoffmann and Walker, Autonomie, 546–547.
42. For the Haber Memorial, see Helmut Maier, *Chemiker in "Dritten Reich."* (Frankfurt a.M.: Wiley, 2015), 140–145; REM Decree (January 15, 1935) and Max Planck to Bernhard Rust (January 18, 1935) in Hoffmann and Walker, Autonomie, 557–559.
43. Bernhard Rust to Max Planck (January 24, 1935), BABL, AdW II-XIV, 23, 14; also see Maier, Chemiker, 140–145.
44. Johannes Stark to Philipp Lenard (February 3, 1933) in Andreas Kleinert, "Lenard, Stark und die Kaiser-Wilhelm-Gesellschaft. Auszüge aus der Korrespondenz der beiden Physiker zwischen 1933 und 1936," *Physikalische Blätter*, 36/2 (1980), 35–43, here 35; Philipp Lenard, Denkschrift, (March 21, 1933) in Grundmann, Einsteins, 436–437 and in Kleinert, Gesellschaft, 35; Wilhelm Frick to Philipp Lenard (April 22, 1933) in Grundmann, Einsteins, 437; Philipp Lenard to Johannes Stark (April 27, 1933) in Kleinert, Gesellschaft, 257; Professor Philipp Lenard, "Ein großer Tag für die Naturforschung," *Völkischer Beobachter* (May 13, 1933); Johannes Stark to Philipp Lenard (April 20, 1933) in Kleinert, Gesellschaft, 35–36.
45. Johannes Stark, "Organisation der physikalischen Forschung," in Hoffmann and Walker, Autonomie, 537–542.
46. Max von Laue, Ansprache bei Eröffnung der Physikertagung in Würzburg am September 18, 1933, in Hoffmann and Walker, Autonomie, 535–537.

310   Notes to pages 193–197

47. Max von Laue, "Bemerkung zu der vorstehenden Veröffentlichung von J. Stark," *Physikalische Blätter*, 3 (1947), 272–273; Stark, Nationalsozialismus und Wissenschaft, 8.

48. Sitzung der phys.-math. Kasse (PAW) (December 14, 1933), BABL, AdW II-IV, 137 228; Max von Laue, "Bemerkung zu der vorstehenden Veröffentlichung von J. Stark," *Physikalische Blätter*, 3 (1947), 272–273; Sitzung der phys.-math. Kasse (PAW) (Januar 11, 1934), BABL, AdW II-IV, 137 231.

49. Verzeichnis der Dozenten für Mathematik an der Universität Berlin und deren Beurteilung in politischer und wissenschaftlicher Hinsicht, BABL, BDC Bieberbach.

50. Moritz Föllmer, *"Ein Leben wie im Traum". Kultur in Dritten Reich* (Munich: Beck, 2016), 75–76. Also see Michael Kater, *Culture in Nazi Germany* (New Haven: Yale University Press, 2019), 151.

51. Patrick Wagner, *Notgemeinschaften der Wissenschaften. Die Deutsche Forschungsgemeinschaft (DFG) in drei politischen Systemen, 1920 bis 1973* (Stuttgart: Franz Steiner Verlag, 2021), 171–173.

52. Samuel Goudsmit, *Alsos*, 2nd Ed. (Los Angeles: Tomash Publishers, 1983), 6.

53. Zierold, Forschungsförderung, 188–189; Wagner, Notgemeinschaften, 177, 183.

54. Helmut Maier, *Forschung als Waffe. Rüstungsforschung in der Kaiser-Wilhelm-Gesellschaft und das Kaiser-Wilhelm-Institut für Metallforschung 1900–1945/48, Volume 1* (Göttingen: Wallstein, 2007), 312, 320, 340; Johannes Stark to Philipp Lenard (May 3, 1933) in Kleinert, Gesellschaft, 36; Philipp Lenard to Johannes Stark (May 8, 1933) in Kleinert, Gesellschaft, 36; Johannes Stark to Philipp Lenard (April 6, 1936) in Kleinert, Gesellschaft, 37.

55. Bernhard Rust to Adolf Hitler in Zierold, Forschungsförderung, 208; Johannes Stark to Philipp Lenard (February 3, 1936) in Kleinert, Gesellschaft, 36; Wagner 2021, 186.

56. Wagner, Notgemeinschaften, 174; Johannes Stark to Philipp Lenard (April 29, 1936) in Kleinert, Gesellschaft, 38.

57. Beyerchen, Scientists, 121.

58. Wagner, Notgemeinschaften, 186–189.

59. Wagner, Notgemeinschaften, 189; Rudolf Mentzel to Johannes Stark (January 4, 1937), BABL, 15,19 70/144; Johannes Stark to Philipp Lenard (November 12, 1936) in Kleinert, Gesellschaft, 38.

60. Franz Gürtner to Rudolf Hess (January 30, 1936), BABL, BDC Stark.

61. Nippold to Arthur Görlitzer (March 4, 1936), BABL, BDC Stark; Adolf Wagner to Oberstes Parteigericht (March 31, 1937), BABL, BDC Stark.

62. Johannes Stark to Oberste Parteigericht (July 1, 1936), BABL, BDC Stark; Johannes Stark to Oberste Parteigericht (February 4, 1937), BABL, BDC Stark; Adolf Wagner to Oberstes Parteigericht (March 31, 1937), BABL, BDC Stark;

63. Johannes Stark to Oberste Parteigericht (October 26, 1937), BABL, BDC Stark; Johannes Stark to Oberste Parteigericht (Nov 7, 1937), BABL, BDC Stark; Johannes Stark to Oberste Parteigericht (December 23, 1937), BABL, BDC Stark.

64. Schneider to Rudolf Hess (November 16, 1937), BABL, BDC Stark; Hansen to Oberste Parteigericht (January 11, 1938), BABL, BDC Stark; In Sachen des Prof. Dr. Johannes Stark, (January 17, 1938), BABL, BDC Stark; for Stark's fight with Wagner, see also Johannes Stark, *Erinnerungen eines deutschen Naturforschers* (Mannhein: Bionomica Verlag, 1987), 118–122.

Notes to pages 198–204 311

65. Frederick Saunders to Werner Heisenberg (May 9, 1934), AMPG, III. Abt. Rep. 93; Frederick Saunders to Werner Heisenberg (July 24, 1934), AMPG, III. Abt. Rep. 93; Werner Heisenberg to Arnold Sommerfeld (August 31, 1938) in Sommerfeld, Briefwechsel, 452–453.
66. Johannes Stark to H. Gall (July 7, 1934), BABL, 15.19 65/256; Theodor Vahlen (REM) to Johannes Stark (August 29, 1934), BABL, 15.19 67/188; Stark, Nationalsozialismus und Wissenschaft, 12; Johannes Stark, "Philipp Lenard als deutscher Naturforscher. Rede zur Einweihung des Philipp-Lenard-Instituts in Heidelberg am 13. Dezember 1935," *Nationalsozialistische Monatshefte*, 7/71 (February 1936), 106–111.
67. Willi Menzel, "Deutsche Physik und jüdische Physik," *Völkischer Beobachter*, 29, Ausgabe A, Norddeutsche Ausgabe (January 29, 1936); Werner Heisenberg, "Zum Artikel: Deutsche und Jüdische Physik," *Völkischer Beobachter*, Norddeutsche Ausgabe/Ausgabe A, No. 59 (February 28, 1936), 6; Johannes Stark, "Stellungnahme von Prof. Dr. J. Stark," *Völkischer Beobachter*, Norddeutsche Ausgabe/Ausgabe A, Nr. 59 (February 28, 1936), 6.
68. Werner Heisenberg to Heinrich Himmler (November 7, 1937) in Alan Beyerchen, *Wissenschaftler unter Hitler. Physiker im Dritten Reich* (Frankfurt a. M.: Ullstein, 1982), 204–205.
69. Beyerchen, Scientists, 150; Werner Heisenberg, Hans Geiger, and Max Wien, Petition to REM (September 1936) in Walter Blum, Hans-Peter Dürr, and Helmut Rechenberg (eds.), *Werner Heisenberg, Gesammelte Werke. Abteilung C Allgemeinverständliche Schriften. Band V Wissenschaft und Politik* (Munich: Piper, 1989), 12–13.
70. Philipp Lenard, *Deutsche Physik*, 4 vols. (Munich: Lehmann, 1925).
71. Philipp Lenard to REM (May 16, 1936), ADM, Lenard Papers 68; Rudolf Tomaschek to Bernhard Rust (May 14, 1936), ADM, JN 68; for Tomaschek, see Vanessa Osganian, "Rudolf Tomaschek – An Exponent of the 'Deutsche Physik' Movement," in Christian Forstner and Mark Walker (eds.), *Biographies in the History of Physics: Actors, Objects, Institutions* (Cham: Springer, 2020), 89–109.
72. Sommerfeld, Briefwechsel, 367; Werner Heisenberg to Niels Bohr (March 18, 1937) in Beyerchen, Wissenschaftler, 213.
73. Johannes Stark to the Reichsstatthalter Bayerns (May 21, 1937), ADM, JN 7a; Johannes Stark to Reichsminister Rust (REM) (June 11, 1937), ADM, JN 7c.
74. Beyerchen, Scientists, 118–119; Johannes Stark to Germany's Nobel Laureates (August 11, 1934) in Beyerchen, Wissenschaftler, 166; Johannes Stark to Max von Laue (August 21, 1934), in Hoffmann and Walker, Autonomie, 547; "'Weiße Juden' in der Wissenschaft," *Das Schwarze Korps* (July 15, 1937), 8; Johannes Stark to Josef Goebbels (August 23, 1934) BABL 15,19 65/276.
75. Johannes Stark to Philipp Lenard (June 2, 1937), ADM, JN 7a; Johannes Stark and Philipp Lenard (Juli 29, 1937), ADM, JN 7c.
76. Weiße Juden, 8.
77. Werner Heisenberg to Spektabilität, Universität Leipzig (July 17, 1937), AHU, Uk. H185IV, 45.
78. Werner Heisenberg to Heinrich Himmler (July 21, 1937), ADM, JN 7a.
79. Johannes Stark to Das Schwarze Korps (September 6, 1937) ADM, JN 7a.
80. Beyerchen, Scientists, 160–161.
81. David C. Cassidy, *Beyond Uncertainty: Heisenberg, Quantum Physics, and The Bomb* (New York: Bellevue Literary Press, 2009), 275–277.

312　　Notes to pages 204–209

82. Werner Heisenberg to Arnold Sommerfeld (February 12, 1938), in Sommerfeld, Briefwechsel, 446–447; Werner Heisenberg to Arnold Sommerfeld (February 23, 1938), in Sommerfeld, Briefwechsel, 448–449; Werner Heisenberg to Dekan der Philosophischen Fakultät Universität Leipzig (February 22, 1938), AHU, Uk. H185IV 42; Studentkowski (Sächsischen Ministeriums für Volksbildung) to Knick (Rector der Universität Leipzig) (December 22, 1938) HU Uk. H185 IV, 37.
83. Werner Heisenberg to Arnold Sommerfeld (April 14, 1938) in Sommerfeld, Briefwechsel, 449–450.
84. Werner Heisenberg to Walther Gerlach (November 16, 1938) in Michael Eckert, "Die Deutsche Physikalische Gesellschaft und die 'Deutsche Physik,'" in Hoffmann and Walker, Autonomie, 139–172, here 148.
85. Michael Eckert, *Ludwig Prandtl: Strömungsforscher und Wissenschaftsmanager. Ein unverstellter Blick auf sein Leben* (Berlin: Springer, 2017), 253–254; NSDAP (Süd-Hannover-Braunschweig) to NSDAP (München-Oberbayern) (April 28, 1941), BABL, BDC Prandtl; Göttingen Kreisleiter to das Amt für Technik Gauamtsleitung (May 28, 1937), AMPG, III. Abt. Rep. 61; Werner Heisenberg to Ludwig Prandtl (November 24, 1937) in Eckert 2017, 254; Ludwig Prandtl to Werner Heisenberg (December 18, 1937) in Eckert, Ludwig, 254.
86. Sommerfeld, Briefwechsel, 370; Ludwig Prandtl to Werner Heisenberg (March 5, 1938) in Eckert, Ludwig, 254–255.
87. Werner Heisenberg to Ludwig Prandtl (March 8, 1938), AMPG, IX 4 1935-1939.
88. Ludwig Prandtl to Heinrich Himmler (July 12, 1938), AMPG, Abt. 111, Rep. 61, 675.
89. Heinrich Himmler to Ludwig Prandtl (July 21, 1938), AMPG III. Abt. Rep. 61; Heinrich Himmler to Werner Heisenberg (July 21, 1938), NBL, SGP Box 11, Folder 98.
90. Heinrich Himmler to Reinhard Heydrich (July 21, 1938), NBL, SGP Box 11, Folder 98. Here the phrase "tot zu machen," which literally translates as "kill," has been interpreted as "silence."
91. SS Gutachten betr. Heisenberg (May 26, 1939), BABL, REM 2943, 370–372.
92. Werner Heisenberg to Heinrich Himmler (July 23, 1938), NBL, SGP Box 11 Folder 98; Werner Heisenberg to Arnold Sommerfeld (July 23, 1938) in Sommerfeld, Briefwechsel, 451–452; Faber, Dekan der naturwissenschaftlichen Fakultät Münchens to Rektorat München (December 29, 1938) in Freddy Litten, *Mechanik und Antisemitismus. Wilhelm Müller (1880–1968)* (Munich: Institut für Geschichte der Naturwissenschaften München, 2000), 83–84; Werner Heisenberg to Arnold Sommerfeld (February 15, 1939) in Sommerfeld, Briefwechsel, 460–461; Werner Heisenberg to Arnold Sommerfeld (May 13, 1939) in Sommerfeld, Briefwechsel, 465–466.
93. SS (Chef des Sicherheithauptamtes) to Rudolf Mentzel (May 26, 1939), BABL, REM 2943, 370–372; Rössner to Haertle (June 12, 1942), IZG, MA-116/5 HA Wissenschaft Heisenberg.
94. Heinrich Himmler to Werner Heisenberg (June 7, 1939), NBL, SGP Box 11 Folder 98; Werner Heisenberg to Heinrich Himmler (June 14, 1939), NBL, SGP Box 11 Folder 98.
95. Johannes Stark and Philipp Lenard (July 29, 1937), ADM, JN 7c; Johannes Stark to Bruno Thüring (January 27, 1938), BABL, 15,19 71/206; Bruno Thüring to Johannes Stark (February 1, 1938), BABL, 15,19 71/207; Litten, 101–104.
96. Werner Heisenberg to Arnold Sommerfeld (December 17, 1939) in Sommerfeld, Briefwechsel, 468–469; Werner Heisenberg to Elisabeth Heisenberg (October 4, 1940) in Heisenberg and Heisenberg, Meine Liebe, 152.

Notes to pages 209–214   313

97. Sommerfeld, Briefwechsel, 480–481; Carl Ramsauer to Bernhard Rust (January 1, 1942), Anlage VI Der Münchener Einigungs- und Befriedungsversuch in Hoffmann and Walker, Autonomie, 616–617.
98. Beyerchen, Scientists, 177–179.
99. Sommerfeld, Briefwechsel, 480–481; Carl Ramsauer to Bernhard Rust (January 1, 1942), Anlage VI Der Münchener Einigungs- und Befriedungsversuch in Hoffmann and Walker, Autonomie, 616–617; Werner Heisenberg to Arnold Sommerfeld (January 5, 1941) in Sommerfeld, Briefwechsel, 536–537.
100. Ludwig Prandtl to Hermann Göring (April 28, 1941), AMPG, III. Abt. Rep. 61; Rumann (Zweiter Staatssekretär Göring) to Ludwig Prandtl (May 19, 1941), AMPG, III. Abt. Rep. 61; Ludwig Prandtl to Rumann (Zweiter Staatssekretär Göring) (May 27, 1941), AMPG, III. Abt. Rep. 61.
101. Ludwig Prandtl to Carl Ramsauer (June 8, 1941), AMPG, III. Abt. Rep. 61; Carl Ramsauer to Ludwig Prandtl (October 31, 1941) in Hoffmann and Walker, Autonomie, 592–593; Ludwig Prandtl to Erhard Milch (November 13, 1941), AMPG, III. Abt. Rep. 61; Generalchefingenieur Lucht (Reichsluftfahrtministerium) to Ludwig Prandtl (December 3, 1941), in Hoffmann and Walker, Autonomie, 593; Carl Ramsauer to Bernhard Rust (January 20, 1942), in Hoffmann and Walker, Autonomie, 594–617; Carl Ramsauer, "Eingabe an Rust," Physikalische Blätter, 3 (1947), 43–44.
102. Ramsauer, "Eingabe."
103. Werner Heisenberg to Wolfgang Finkelnburg (May 22, 1942), AMPG, III. Abt. Rep. 93; also see the chapter on Selling Uranium.
104. Reichsdozentenführer Schultze to Werner Heisenberg (October 7, 1942), AMPG, III. Abt. Rep. 93; Teilnehmerliste (November 1–3, 1942), NBL, SGP Box 25, Folder 12; Carl Friedrich von Weizsäcker to Sauter (June 21, 1943), NBL, SGP Box 25, Folder 12; Vorläufiger Bericht über der Physlkerlager in Seefeld (Tirol) (November 1–3, 1942), NBL, SGP Box 25, Folder 12.
105. Rudolf Mentzel to Max von Laue (May 22, 1943), NBL, SGP Box 25, Folder 12; Max von Laue to Carl Friedrich von Weizsäcker (May 26, 1943), NBL, SGP Box 25, Folder 12; Carl Friedrich von Weizsäcker to Max von Laue (June 2, 1943), ADM, IMC 29 1066; Max von Laue to Carl Friedrich von Weizsäcker (June 4, 1943), ADM, IMC 29 1067.
106. Werner Heisenberg to Bosech (Reichssicherheitshauptamt) (June 26, 1942), AMPG, III. Abt. Rep. 93; Bruno Thüring to Johannes Stark (May 31, 1937), BABL, 15,19 71/204; Bruno Thüring to Werner Heisenberg (October 14, 1942), AMPG, III. Abt. Rep. 93; Werner Heisenberg to Dr. Bosech (Reichssicherheithauptamt) (December 10, 1942), AMPG, III. Abt. Rep. 93; Werner Heisenberg to Heinrich Himmler (February 4, 1943), AMPG, III. Abt. Rep. 93; Brandt (Persönlicher Stab des Reichsführers-SS) to Werner Heisenberg (February 15, 1943), AMPG, III. Abt. Rep. 93.
107. Werner Heisenberg, "Die Bewertung der 'modernen theoretischen Physik,'" Zeitschrift für die gesamte Naturwissenschaft, 9/10-12 (1943), 201–212, here 201, 211, 205.
108. Werner Heisenberg to Theodor Vahlen (September 10, 1942) AMPG, III. Abt. Rep. 93.
109. Werner Heisenberg, Encounters with Einstein (Princeton: Princeton University Press, 1989), 112–117, 121.

314 Notes to pages 215–217

9 Rehabilitation

1. Carl Friedrich von Weizsäcker, "Mit der Bombe leben (I)," *Die Zeit* (May 15, 1958).
2. Max von Laue to Theodore von Laue (August 7, 1945), ADM, MLN.
3. Jeremy Bernstein, *Hitler's Uranium Club: The Secret Recordings at Farm Hall* (Woodbury: American Institute of Physics Press, 1996), 161.
4. Erich Bagge, Kurt Diebner, and Kenneth Jay, *Von der Uranspaltung bis Calder Hall* (Hamburg: Rowohlt, 1957) 67, 69.
5. Otto Hahn to Fritz Strassmann (December 28, 1946), AMPG, III. Abt., Rep. 14, 4267 17.
6. Ruth Lewin Sime, *Lise Meitner: A Life in Physics* (Berkeley: University of California Press, 1996), 340.
7. Lise Meitner to James Franck (January 16, 1947) in Sime, Life, 345.
8. Elisabeth Crawford, Ruth Lewin Sime, and Mark Walker, "A Nobel Tale of Wartime Injustice," *Nature,* 382 (1996), 393–395; Elisabeth Crawford, Ruth Lewin Sime, and Mark Walker, "A Nobel Tale of Postwar Injustice," *Physics Today,* 50 (September 1997), 26–32; see also Robert Marc Friedman, *The Politics of Excellence: Behind the Nobel Prize in Science* (New York: W. H. Freeman, 2001), 225, 240–244, 246–249, 252–254, and Elisabeth Crawford, *The Nobel Population 1901–1950: A Census of the Nominators and Nominees for the Prizes in Physics and Chemistry* (Tokyo: Universal Academy Press, 2002).
9. Crawford, Population, 182–183, 323–324.
10. Otto Hahn to Max Born (January 14, 1954), ADM, WGN NL 080/127-02.
11. Otto Hahn, Unterredung mit Colonel Blount am 31. August 1946, AMPG, Gründungsakten 4(10).
12. Sime, Life, 143–144, 153–154.
13. Otto Hahn, Bericht über die Arbeiten des Kaiser Wilhelm-Instituts für Chemie über "Präparat 38." (Dezember 10, 1940), ADM, FA 002 514.
14. Otto Hahn, Künstliche Atomumwandlungen und die Spaltung des Urans (May 6, 1943), ADM, FA 002 737.
15. Otto Hahn, Die deutschen Arbeiten über Atomkernenergie, (February 2, 1946), AMPG, III. Abt., Rep. 14 G183, 5–8; also see Ruth Lewin Sime, "The Politics of Forgetting: Otto Hahn and the German Nuclear-Fission Project in World War II," *Physics in Perspective*, 14 (2012), 59–94.
16. Rüdiger Hachtmann, *Wissenschaftsmanagement im "Dritten Reich": Geschichte der Generalverwaltung der Kaiser-Wilhelm-Gesellschaft* (Göttingen: Wallstein Verlag, 2007); Rüdiger Hachtmann, "A Success Story? Highlighting the History of the Kaiser Wilhelm Society's General Administration in the Third Reich," in Susanne Heim, Carola Sachse, and Mark Walker (eds.), *The Kaiser Wilhelm Society under National Socialism* (Cambridge: Cambridge University Press, 2009), 19–46.
17. Helmuth Trischler, *Luft- und Raumfahrtforschung in Deutschland 1900–1970. Politische Geschichte einer Wissenschaft* (Frankfurt am Main: Campus, 1992); Helmuth Trischler, "Self-mobilization or Resistance? Aeronautical Research and National Socialism," in Monika Renneberg and Mark Walker (eds.), *Science, Technology, and National Socialism* (Cambridge: Cambridge University Press, 1994), 72–88, 356–358; Helmut Maier, *Forschung als Waffe. Rüstungsforschung in der Kaiser-Wilhelm-Gesellschaft und das Kaiser-Wilhelm-Institut für*

Notes to pages 217–219 315

Metallforschung: 1900–1945 2 Vols. (Göttingen: Wallstein Verlag, 2007). Helmut Maier (ed.), *Rüstungsforschung im Nationalsozialismus. Organisation, Mobilisierung und Entgrenzung der Technikwissenschaften* (Göttingen: Wallstein, 2002); Helmut Maier (ed.), *Gemeinschaftsforschung, Bevollmächtigte und der Wissentransfer. Die Rolle der Kaiser-Wilhelm-Gesellschaft im System kriegsrelevanter Forschung des Nationalsozialismus* (Göttingen: Wallstein Verlag, 2007); Moritz Epple, "Rechnen, Messen, Führen: Kriegsforschung am Kaiser-Wilhelm--Institut für Strömungsforschung 1937–1945," in Maier 2002, 305–356; Ulf Schmidt, *Secret Science: A Century of Poison Warfare and Human Experiments* (Oxford: Oxford University Press, 2015), 74–99, esp 97.

18. Ernst Telschow, "Ziele der KWG" (1945) AMPG Gründungsakten.

19. Susanne Heim, *Plant Breeding and Agrarian Research in Kaiser-Wilhelm-Institutes 1933–1945: Calories, Caoutchouc, Careers* (Dordrecht: Springer, 2008) and Susanne Heim (ed.), *Autarkie und Ostexpansion. Pflanzenzucht und Agrarforschung im Nationalsozialismus* (Göttingen: Wallstein Verlag, 2002).

20. Carola Sachse (ed.), *Die Verbindung nach Auschwitz: Biowissenschaften und Menschenversuche an Kaiser-Wilhelm-Instituten* (Göttingen: Wallstein, 2003); Hans Walter Schmuhl (ed.), *Rassenforschung an Kaiser-Wilhelm-Instituten vor und nach 1933* (Göttingen: Wallstein, 2003); Wolfgang Schieder and Achim Trunk (ed.), *Adolf Butenandt und die Kaiser-Wilhelm-Gesellschaft: Wissenschaft, Industrie und Politik im "Dritten Reich"* (Göttingen: Wallstein, 2004); Hans-Walter Schmuhl, *The Kaiser Wilhelm Institute for Anthropology, Human Heredity, and Eugenics, 1927–1945: Crossing Boundaries* (Dordrecht: Springer, 2008), 362–386. Hans-Walter Schmuhl, *Grenzüberschreitungen: das Kaiser-Wilhelm-Institut für Anthropologie, menschliche Erblehre und Eugenik 1927–1945* (Göttingen: Wallstein Verlag, 2005), 470–501.

21. Schmuhl, Boundaries, 362–386. Schmuhl, Grenzüberschreitungen, 470–501; Paul Julian Weindling, "Mengele at Auschwitz: Reconstructing the Twins," in Susan Bargett, Christine Schmidt, and Dan Stone (eds.), *Beyond Camps and Forced Labor* (Cham: Palgrave Macmillian, 2020), 11–30.

22. Carola Sachse, "'Whitewash Culture': How the Kaiser Wilhelm/Max Planck Society Dealt with the Nazi Past," in Heim, Sachse, and Walker, 373–399, here 388.

23. Michael Schüring, *Minervas verstoßene Kinder. Vertriebene Wissenschaftler und die Vergangenheitspolitik der Max-Planck-Gesellschaft* (Göttingen: Wallstein, 2006); Michael Schüring, "Expulsion, Compensation, and the Legacy of the Kaiser Wilhelm Society," *Minerva*, 44/3 (2006), 307–324.

24. Otto Hahn, Denkschrift (1946), AMPG, Gründingsakten 5; Ernst Telschow, Antwort auf die Fragen (May 18, 1947), AMPG, Gründungsakten 12.

25. Paul Julian Weindling, *Nazi Medicine and the Nuremberg Trials: From Medical War Crimes to Informed Consent* (Houndmills: Palgrave Macmillan, 2004), 66.

26. Republished by Otto Hahn and Hermann Rein, "Einladung nach USA," *Physikalische Blätter* 3/2 (1947), 33–35.

27. See Lutz Niethammer, *Die Mitläuferfabrik: die Entnazifizierung am Beispiel Bayerns* (Berlin: Dietz, 1982); Clemens Vollnhals, *Entnazifizierung: Politische Säuberung und Rehabilitierung in den vier Besatzungszonen 1945–1949* (Munich: Deutscher Taschenbuch Verlag, 1991); Norbert Frei, *Vergangenheitspolitik. Die Anfänge der Bundesrepublik und die NS-Vergangenheit* (Munich: Deutsche Taschenbuch Verlag, 1999).

316   Notes to pages 219–226

28. The Max Planck Society funded a project on the history of the Kaiser Wilhelm Society during National Socialism (Geschichte der Kaiser-Wilhelm-Gesellschaft während des Nationalsozialismus) that ran from 1998 to 2005, was overseen by Reinhard Rürup and Wolfgang Schieder, and was led in turn by Doris Kaufmann, Carola Sachse, Susanne Heim, and Rüdiger Hachtmann.

29. Lise Meitner to Otto Hahn (June 27, 1945), AMPG, III. Abt., Rep. 14, 4898; quoted and translated in Sime, Life, 309–310.

30. Otto Hahn to Lise Meitner (June 16, 1948), quoted and translated in Sime, Life, 356.

31. Rudolf Ladenburg to Samuel Goudsmit (October 23, 1946) NBL, SGP Box 14, Folder 138; Werner Heisenberg to Bartel van der Waerden (April 28, 1948), AMPG, III. Abt., Rep. 93, 1705.

32. Werner Heisenberg, Die aktive und die passive Opposition im Dritten Reich (Geschrieben im Zusammenhang mit Zeitungsberichten über die Kriegsverbrecherprozesse in Nürnberg) (November 12, 1947), AMPG, III. Abt., Rep. 93, 1705.

33. Carl Friedrich von Weizsäcker to Carl Seelig (October 14, 1955) in Carl Seelig (ed.), *Helle Zeit--Dunkle Zeit. In Memoriam Albert Einstein* (Zurich: Europa Verlag, 1955), 130–133, here 130–131.

34. Robert Jungk to Werner Heisenberg (February 10, 1955), AMPG, III. Abt. Rep. 93; Werner Heisenberg to Robert Jungk (February 14, 1955), AMPG, III. Abt. Rep. 93.

35. Carl Friedrich von Weizsäcker to Jungk (September 21, 1955), AMPG, III. Abt. Rep. 111 250; Bernstein, Uranium, 154; Robert Jungk, *Heller als tausend Sonnen. Das Schicksal der Atomforscher*, 2nd. Ed. (Stuttgart: Scherz and Goverts, 1958), 122.

36. Robert Jungk, *Brighter than a Thousand Suns: A Personal History of the Atomic Scientists* (New York: Harcourt, Brace, and Company, 1958), 101 – this is an English translation of the passage that appeared in Jungk, Heller, 120–121.

37. Lise Meitner to Otto Hahn (January 9, 1957), ADM, WGN NL 080/127-02; Lise Meitner to Otto Hahn (January 24, 1957), ADM, WGN NL 080/127-02; Otto Hahn to Moir (Bulletin of the Atomic Scientists) (November 23, 1957), AMPG, III. Abt., Rep. 14 5141.

38. Carl Friedrich von Weizsäcker to Robert Jungk (November 6, 1956), AMPG, III. Abt. Rep. 111 250; Carl Friedrich von Weizsäcker to Edward Teller (November 27, 1972), AMPG, III. Abt. Rep. 111 264.

39. Carl Friedrich von Weizsäcker to Robert Jungk (November 6, 1956), AMPG, III. Abt., Rep. 111, 250.

40. Robert Jungk to Carl Friedrich von Weizsäcker (December 26, 1956), AMPG, III. Abt., Rep. 111, 250.

41. Werner Heisenberg to Robert Jungk (November 17, 1956), AMPG, III. Abt., Rep. 93, 1705.

42. Robert Jungk to Werner Heisenberg (December 29, 1956), AMPG, III. Abt., Rep. 93, 1705; Werner Heisenberg to Robert Jungk (January 18, 1957), AMPG, III. Abt., Rep. 93, 1705.

43. Robert Jungk to Werner Heisenberg (December 29, 1956), AMPG, III. Abt., Rep. 93, 1705; Jungk, *Brighter*, 102–104; Jungk, Heller, 407–408; Werner Heisenberg to Robert Jungk (January 18, 1957), AMPG, III. Abt., Rep. 93, Nr. 1705.

44. Werner Heisenberg to Robert Jungk (January 18, 1957), AMPG, III. Abt., Rep. 93, Nr. 1705; Werner Heisenberg to Bartel van der Waerden (April 28, 1948) NBL, SGP Box 10, Folder 93.

Notes to pages 227–231

45. Cathryn Carson, "Reflections on Copenhagen," in Matthias Dörries (ed.), *Michael Frayn's Copenhagen in Debate: Historical Essays and Documents on the 1941 Meeting between Niels Bohr and Werner Heisenberg* (Berkeley: Office for History of Science and Technology, University of California, Berkeley, 2005), 7–17; Cathryn Carson, *Heisenberg in the Atomic Age: Science and the Public Sphere* (Cambridge: Cambridge University Press, 2010), 403–405.
46. Dörries, Frayn, 151.
47. Dörries, Frayn, 111 and 113; for this symposium and its context, see the chapter on Copenhagen.
48. Dörries, Frayn, 153, 155, and 157.
49. John Cornwell, *Hitler's Scientists: Science, War, and the Devil's Pact* (New York: Penguin, 2004), 308.
50. Dörries, Frayn, 109.
51. Dörries, Frayn, 131 and 133.
52. Dörries, Frayn, 163.
53. Dörries, Frayn, 109.
54. Dörries, Frayn, 153, 155, and 157.
55. Carson, Heisenberg, 410.
56. Dörries, Frayn, 153, 155, and 157.
57. Dörries, Frayn, 145.
58. Dörries, Frayn, 145; Jensen visited Bohr's institute in Copenhagen in 1942 and 1943.
59. In 1943 Jensen shared what he knew about the uranium project and in particular the experiments being carried out under Heisenberg's direction. Jeremy Bernstein, "The Drawing or Why History Is Not Mathematics," *Physics in Perspective*, 5 (2003), 243–261, here 256–257.
60. Dörries, Frayn, 131.
61. Dörries, Frayn, 163.
62. These unpublished letters were published on the internet in 2002.
63. Michael Eckert, "Primacy Doomed to Failure: Heisenberg's Role as Scientific Adviser for Nuclear Policy in the FRG," *Historical Studies in the Physical and Biological Sciences*, (1990) 21/1 (1990), 29–58, here 30; Arne Schirrmacher, "Physik und Politik in der frühen Bundesrepublik Deutschland. Max Born, Werner Heisenberg und Pascual Jordan als politische Grenzgänger," *Berichte zur Wissenschaftsgeschichte*, 30 (2007) 13–31, 16; also see Carson, Heisenberg, 193–205.
64. Carson, Heisenberg, 204.
65. Robert Lorenz, *Protest der Physiker. Die "Göttinger Erklärung" von 1957* (Bielefeld: Transcript Verlag, 2011), 37.
66. Eckert, "Primacy," 47; Lorenz, Protest, 256; Rolf-Jürgen Gleitsmann, *Im Widerstreit der Meinungen: zur Kontroverse um die Standortfindung für eine deutsche Reaktorstation (1950–1955): ein Beitrag zur Gründungsgeschichte des Kernforschungszentrums Karlsruhe und zu einem Kapitel deutscher Kernenergiegeschichte* (Karlsruhe: Kernforschungszentrum Karlsruhe, 1986).
67. Lorenz, Protest, 46, 208, 48; also see Carson, Heisenberg, 320–330.
68. Carola Sachse, "The Max Planck Society and Pugwash during the Cold War: An Uneasy Relationship," *Journal of Cold War Studies*, 20/1 (2018),170–209, here 180, 174.

318   Notes to pages 231–237

69. Lorenz, Protest, 50–51; Carola Sachse, *Wissenschaft und Diplomatie. Die Max-Planck-Gesellschaft im Feld der internationalen Politik (1945–2000)* (Göttingen: Vandenhoeck and Ruprecht, 2023), 389–392; "Strauß denkt an Änderung der Wehrpflicht," [unknown newspaper] (April 8, 1957), ADM, WGN NL 080/327/2-02.
70. Fritz Bopp, Max Born, Rudolf Fleischmann, Walther Gerlach, Otto Hahn, Otto Haxel, Werner Heisenberg, Hans Kopfermann, Max v. Laue, Heinz Maier-Leibnitz, Josef Mattauch, Friedrich-Adolf Paneth, Wolfgang Paul, Wolfgang Riezler, Fritz Strassmann, Wilhelm Walcher, Carl Friedrich Frhr. v. Weizsäcker, Karl Wirtz, "Die Göttinger Erklärung" (April 12, 1957), in Lorenz, 31–32.
71. Lorenz, 57, 61–62. "Heftiges Duell zwischen Kanzler und Professoren," *Welt am Sonntag* (April 13, 1957), 1, ADM, WGN NL 080/144-03.
72. Arne Schirrmacher, "Physik und Politik in der frühen Bundesrepublik Deutschland. Max Born, Werner Heisenberg und Pascual Jordan als politische Grenzgänger," *Berichte zur Wissenschaftsgeschichte*, 30 (2007), 19; Richard Beyler, "The Demon of Technology, Mass Society, and Atomic Physics in West Germany, 1945–1957," *History and Technology*, 19/3 (2003), 227–239, here 233.
73. "Und führe uns nicht in Versuchung. Vom gespaltenen Atom zu gespaltenen Gewissen – Die Geschichte einer menschheitsgefährdenden Waffe," *Der Spiegel* (May 8, 1957), 45–46, 48–53.
74. Gerta Tzschaschel to Werner Heisenberg (October 27, 1956) AMPG, III. Abt., Rep. 93, Nr. 1705.
75. Carl Friedrich von Weizsäcker to Robert Jungk (November 6, 1956), AMPG, III. Abt., Rep. 111, 250; Carl Friedrich von Weizsäcker to Robert Jungk (January 4, 1957), AMPG, III. Abt., Rep. 111, 250.
76. Carl Friedrich von Weizsäcker, Atomenergie und Atomzeitalter. Elfte Vorlesung: Politische Folgen, Dritten Programm des NDR (March 3, 1957), subsequently published as Carl Friedrich von Weizsäcker, *Atomenergie und Atomzeitalter* (Frankfurt am Main: Fischer, 1957).
77. Carl Friedrich von Weizsäcker, Die Verantwortung der Wissenschaft im Atomzeitalter, Opening Lecture at the 9th Meeting of the Verbandes Deutscher Studentenschaften (April 29, 1957), ADM, WGN NL 080/327/2-04.
78. Carl Friedrich von Weizsäcker to Viktor Weisskopf (April 25, 1957), AMPG, III. Abt. Rep. 111 245-264-267.
79. Viktor Weisskopf to Carl Friedrich von Weizsäcker (May 6, 1957), AMPG, III. Abt. Rep. 111 245-264-267; C. F. Powell to Werner Heisenberg (May 17, 1957), ADM, WGN NL 080/327/2-04; Sachse, Pugwash.
80. Carl Friedrich von Weizsäcker to the Göttingen 18 (May 9, 1958), ADM, WGN NL 080/347-1; Lorenz, 279.
81. Carl Friedrich von Weizsäcker, "Mit der Bombe leben (I)," *Die Zeit* (May 15, 1958); Carl Friedrich von Weizsäcker, "Mit der Bombe leben (II)," *Die Zeit* (May 22, 1958); Carl Friedrich von Weizsäcker, "Mit der Bombe leben (III)," *Die Zeit* (May 29, 1958); Carl Friedrich von Weizsäcker, "Mit der Bombe leben (IV)," *Die Zeit* (June 5, 1958).
82. Weizsäcker, Mit der Bombe leben (I).
83. Weizsäcker, Mit der Bombe leben (II).
84. Weizsäcker, Mit der Bombe leben (IV).
85. Hedwig Born to Carl Friedrich von Weizsäcker (July 15, 1958), ADM, WGN NL 080/347-2.

Notes to pages 238–242 319

86. Hedwig Born to Stauder (July 24, 1958), ADM, WGN NL 080/347-2.
87. Carl Friedrich von Weizsäcker, "Prof. Weizsäcker antwortet," *Die Weltwoche* (Zürich) (August 15, 1958), ADM, WGN NL 080/144-08.
88. Sachse, "Whitewash."
89. Sachse, Diplomatie, 110–124, 394–398, 416–438.

10 Copenhagen

1. Lise Meitner to Otto Hahn (June 27, 1945), ADM, WGN NL 080/127-02.
2. See Matthias Dörries (ed.), *Michael Frayn's Copenhagen in Debate: Historical Essays and Documents on the 1941 Meeting Between Niels Bohr and Werner Heisenberg* (Berkeley: Office for History of Science and Technology, University of California, Berkeley, 2005).
3. Paul Lawrence Rose, *Heisenberg and the Nazi Atomic Bomb Project* (Berkeley: University of California Press, 1998), 271–282.
4. Thomas Powers, *Heisenberg's War: The Secret History of the German Atomic Bomb* (London: Jonathan Cape, 1993), 120–128.
5. Michael Frayn, *Copenhagen* (New York: Anchor, 1998).
6. For a general history of the DWIs, see Frank-Rutger Hausmann, *"Auch im Krieg schweigen die Musen nicht"*. *Die Deutschen Wissenschaftlichen Institute im Zweiten Weltkrieg* (Göttingen: Vandenhoeck and Ruprecht, 2001).
7. Werner Heisenberg to the Rektor of the Uni Leipzig (December 4, 1940) HUB Uk.H185 IV, 23; Dozentenführer to Rektor Uni Leipzig (December 9, 1940), HUB, Uk. H185 IV, 23.
8. Rektor Uni Leipzig to REM (December 11, 1940), HUB, Uk. H185 IV, 22.
9. REM to Rektor Uni Leipzig (March 19, 1941), HUB, Uk. Hl85 IV, 20.
10. Werner Heisenberg to Elisabeth Heisenberg (April 28, 1941) in Werner Heisenberg and Elisabeth Heisenberg, *"Meine Liebe Li!" Der Briefwechsel 1937–1946* (St. Pölten: Residenz Verlag, 2011), 163–165.
11. Wilhelm Coblitz to Werner Heisenberg (May 20, 1941), AMPG, III. Abt. Rep. 93; for the IDO, see Götz Aly and Susanne Heim, *Vordenker der Vernichtung. Auschwitz und die deutschen Pläne für eine neue europäische Ordnung*, 2nd Ed. (Frankfurt am Main: Fischer, 2013).
12. Herbert Mehrtens, "Angewandte Mathematik und Anwendungen der Mathematik im nationalsozialistischen Deutschland," *Geschichte und Gesellschaft*, 12/3 (1986), 317–347, here 344.
13. Max Weinreich, *Hitler's Professors: The Part of Scholarship in Germany's Crimes against the Jewish People*, 2nd Ed. (New Haven: Yale University Press, 1999), 95–97.
14. Jeremy Bernstein, "Heisenberg in Poland," *American Journal of Physics*, 72 (2004), 300–304, here 300.
15. REM to Hans Frank (July 29, 1941), BABL, REM 690,67; Paul Rosbaud, Interview (August 12, 1945), NBL, SGP Box 27, Folder 41.
16. Wilhelm Coblitz to Heisenberg (May 20, 1941), AMPG, III. Abt. Rep. 93; Werner Heisenberg to Wilhelm Coblitz (June 6, 1941), AMPG, III. Abt. Rep. 93; Werner Heisenberg to Elisabeth Heisenberg (June 13?, 1941), in Heisenberg and Heisenberg, 166–167; Berne (Rektor der Universität Leipzig) an REM (June 23,

320   Notes to pages 242–248

1941), HUB, Uk. H185 IV, 16; Berne (Rektor der Universität Leipzig) an REM (Juli 23, 1941), HUB, Uk. H185 IV, 14.

17. REM to Rektor Uni Leipzig (September 9, 1941), HUB, Uk. H185IV, 13; REM (Rudolf Mentzel) to the General Governor in Cracow (Hans Frank) (July 29, 1941), BABL, REM 690-76.

18. Der Bevollmächtigte des Deutschen Reiches, Denmark to AA (Berlin) (March 27, 1941), BABL, REM 2943,524–25; AA, Vermerk (April 16, 1941), BABL, REM 2943,525.

19. Carl Friedrich von Weizsäcker, Bericht über die Vortragsreise nach Kopenhagen vom 19.-24.3.41 (March 26, 1941), AMPG, I. Abt. Rep. 34.

20. Carl Friedrich von Weizsäcker to Bernhard Rust (September 5, 1941), translation in Manhattan District History Volume 14: Intelligence and Security, www.osti .gov/opennet/manhattan_district.jsp (accessed August 18, 2017).

21. Carl Friedrich von Weizsäcker to the Oberkommando des Heeres (September 4, 1941), translation in Manhattan District History Volume 14: Intelligence and Security, www.osti.gov/opennet/manhattan_district.jsp (accessed August 18, 2017).

22. REM to KWG (May 8, 1941), BABL, REM 2943,528; KWG to REM (May 20, 1941), BABL, REM 2943,529.

23. REM to AA (June 3, 1941), BABL, REM 2943,530.

24. Der Bevollmächtigte des Deutschen Reiches, Denmark to AA (June 27, 1941), BABL, REM 2943,537.

25. Carl Friedrich von Weizsäcker to DAAD (July 22, 1941), BABL, REM 2943, 538.

26. AA to REM (August 2, 1941), BABL, REM 2943,531.

27. Carl Friedrich von Weizsäcker to Niels Bohr (August 15, 1941), NBA, Niels Bohrs General Correspondence.

28. REM, Vermerk, (August 21, 1941), BABL, REM 2943,532.

29. REM, Vermerk, (September 2, 1941), BABL, REM 2943,534–35.

30. REM to Parteikanzlei, (around September 2, 1941), BABL, REM 2943,535.

31. REM, Vermerk, (September 11, 1941), BABL, REM 2943,536; Werner Heisenberg to Elisabeth Heisenberg (September 9, 1941) in Heisenberg and Heisenberg, 190–191.

32. Werner Heisenberg, Bericht über Versuche mit Schichtenanordnungen von Präparat 38 und Paraffin am Kaiser Wilhelm-Institut f. Physik in Bln-Dahlem (March, 1941), AMPG, I. Abt. Rep. 34.

33. Carl Friedrich von Weizsäcker, Kernenergieerzeugung aus dem Uranisotop der Masse 238 und anderen schweren Elementen. (Herstellung und Verwendung des Elements 94) (June 6, 1941), AMPG, I. Abt. Rep. 34.

34. Werner Heisenberg to Elisabeth Heisenberg (September 16, 1941) in Heisenberg and Heisenberg, Meine Liebe, 193.

35. Werner Heisenberg, Bericht über die Teilnahme an einer astrophysikalischen Arbeitstagung im Deutschen Wissenschaftlichen Institut in Kopenhagen (September 23, 1941), BABL, REM 2943, 547.

36. Werner Heisenberg to Elisabeth Heisenberg (September 18, 1941) in Heisenberg and Heisenberg, Meine Liebe, 194–195.

37. Werner Heisenberg to Elisabeth Heisenberg (September 18, 1941) in Heisenberg and Heisenberg, Meine Liebe, 195; Heisenberg, Teilnahme.

38. J.G. Crowther, Science in Liberated Europe (London: Pilot, 1949), 106–108: Aage Bohr, "The War Years and the Prospects Raised by the Atomic Weapons," in Stefan Rozental (ed.), Niels Bohr (Amsterdam: North Holland, 1968), 193: Stefan

Notes to pages 248–253   321

Rozental, *NB. Erindringer om Niels Bohr*, (Copenhagen: Gyldendal, 1985), 44–45; Interview with Stefan Rozental.

39. Lise Meitner to Paul Scherrer (June 26, 1945), quoted in Dieter Hoffmann, "Copenhagen Was Not an Isolated Case," in Dörries, Frayn, 39–47, here 39.
40. Heisenberg, Teilnahme.
41. Der Bevollmächtigte des Deutschen Reiches to Auswärtiges Amt (September 26, 1941), BABL, REM 2943, 544–545; Werner Heisenberg to Elisabeth Heisenberg (September 20, 1941) in Heisenberg and Heisenberg, 195–196; Carl Friedrich von Weizsäcker, Zusammenfassender Bericht über die astrophysikalische Arbeitswoche in Kopenhagen vom 18.-24.9.41 (October 1, 1941), BABL REM 2943, 549–550.
42. Heisenberg, Teilnahme; Weizsäcker, Zusammenfassender; Der Bevollmächtigte des Deutschen Reiches to Auswärtiges Amt (September 26, 1941), BABL REM 2943, 544–545.
43. Werner Heisenberg to Elisabeth Heisenberg (September 22, 1941), in Heisenberg and Heisenberg, Meine Liebe, 196–197.
44. Weizsäcker, Zusammenfassender; Der Bevollmächtigte des Deutschen Reiches to Auswärtiges Amt (September 26, 1941), BABL, REM 2943, 544–545; Auswärtiges Amt (Roth) to REM (November 27, 1941), BABL, REM 2943, 557.
45. Paul Scherrer to Werner Heisenberg (May 26, 1942), AMPG, III. Abt. Rep. 93; Werner Heisenberg to Dekan phil. Fak. der Uni. Leipzig (June 10, 1942), AMPG, III. Abt. Rep. 93.
46. Stueckelberg to Werner Heisenberg (August 20, 1942), AMPG, III. Abt. Rep. 93; Studentenschaft der Universität Bern to Werner Heisenberg (September 7, 1942), AMPG, III. Abt. Rep. 93; Fischer to Werner Heisenberg (October 23, 1942), AMPG, III. Abt. Rep. 93; Studentenschaft der Universität Basel to Werner Heisenberg (November 2, 1942), AMPG, III. Abt. Rep. 93.
47. REM to Werner Heisenberg (October 21, 1942), AMPG, III. Abt. Rep. 93.
48. Rektor Uni Leipzig to REM (July 30, 1942), HUB, Uk. H185 IN, 7.
49. NSDAP to Werner Heisenberg (October 28, 1942), AMPG, III. Abt. Rep. 93.
50. Werner Heisenberg, Bericht (December 11, 1942), AMPG, III. Abt. Rep. 93; Werner Heisenberg to Elisabeth Heisenberg (November 17 and 19, 1941) in Heisenberg and Heisenberg, Meine Liebe, 211–212.
51. Werner Heisenberg to Elisabeth Heisenberg (November 17 and 19, 1941) in Heisenberg and Heisenberg, Meine Liebe, 209–211; Werner Heisenberg, Bericht (December 11, 1942), AMPG, III. Abt. Rep. 93.
52. Deutsche Gesandtschaft to AA (October 17, 1942), BABL, REM 2943,89.
53. KWG (Forstmann) to REM (November 4, 1942), BABL, REM 2943,86.
54. REM, Vermerk (November 19, 1942), BABL, REM 2943,90.
55. REM to AA (November 26, 1942), BABL, REM 2943,93.
56. Max Planck, Bericht über meine Vortragsreise nach Budapest (December 10, 1942), BABL, REM 2943, 94.
57. Carl Friedrich von Weizsäcker, Bericht (around December 10, 1942), BABL, REM 2943,97; Werner Heisenberg, Bericht (December 11, 1942), AMPG, III. Abt. Rep. 93.
58. Deutsche Gesandtschaft Prag to AA (January 6, 1943), BABL, REM 2943, 99–100; Werner Heisenberg, Bericht über die Reise nach Budapest vom 30.11.-4.12.42 (December 11, 1942), AMPG, III. Abt., Rep. 93, 1705.
59. Deutsche Gesandtschaft (Prag) to AA (January 6, 1943), BABL, REM 2943,99–100.
60. REM to Rektor der Uni Berlin (March 11, 1943), HUB, Uk. H185II, 8.

322 Notes to pages 253–257

61. Ludwig Bieberbach to Werner Heisenberg (March 22, 1943), HUB, Uk. H185II, 8; Dozentenführer to Rektor der Uni Berlin (March 17, 1943), HUB, Uk. H1851,18.
62. REM to Werner Heisenberg (July 17, 1943), AMPG, III. Abt. Rep. 93.
63. Werner Heisenberg to Ludwig Bieberbach (March 25, 1943), HUB, Uk. H185 1,20.
64. Samuel Goudsmit, Interview with "F.J." (August 31, 1944), NARA, Ml 108 File 26.
65. Samuel Goudsmit, *Alsos*, 2nd Ed. (Los Angeles: Tomash Publishers, 1983), 103; CIA Biographic Register Carl Friedrich von Weizsäcker (13 September 1948) www.theblackvault.com/documentarchive/files-on-german-physicist-walther-gerlach/ (accessed 19 November 2023).
66. REM to Werner Heisenberg (February 24, 1943), AMPG, III. Abt. Rep. 93; Werner Heisenberg to DAAD (March 9, 1943), AMPG, III. Abt. Rep. 93.
67. Werner Heisenberg to REM (April 9, 1943), AMPG, III. Abt. Rep. 93.
68. REM to Werner Heisenberg (June 15, 1943), AMPG, III. Abt. Rep. 93.
69. REM to Werner Heisenberg (July 31, 1943), AMPG, III. Abt. Rep. 93.
70. Werner Heisenberg to REM (August 11, 1943), AMPG, III. Abt. Rep. 93.
71. Hans Kramers to Werner Heisenberg (July 5, 1944), AMPG, III. Abt. Rep. 93.
72. Hans Kramers to Werner Heisenberg (July 29, 1943), AMPG, III. Abt. Rep. 93.
73. Werner Heisenberg to REM (August 20, 1943), AMPG, III. Abt. Rep. 93; Werner Heisenberg to Hans Kramers (August 20, 1943), AMPG, III. Abt. Rep. 93; Hans Kramers to Werner Heisenberg (September 1, 1943), AMPG, III. Abt. Rep. 93; REM to Werner Heisenberg (September 6, 1943), AMPG, III. Abt. Rep. 93; Reichskommissar für die besetzten niederländischen Gebiete to Werner Heisenberg (September 15, 1943), AMPG, III. Abt. Rep. 93; Werner Heisenberg to Elisabeth Heisenberg (October 14, 1943) in Heisenberg and Heisenberg, Meine Liebe, 224.
74. See the chapter on Oversimplifications.
75. Werner Heisenberg, Bericht über eine Reise nach Holland vom 18.-26.10.43 (November 10, 1943), AMPG, III. Abt., Rep. 93, Nr. 1705.
76. Gerard Kuiper to Manor Fisher (June 30, 1945) SCUA, GKP; Werner Heisenberg to Elisabeth Heisenberg (July 21, 1943) in Heisenberg and Heisenberg, Meine Liebe, 222.
77. Interview with Stefan Rosental; Stefan Rosenfeld to Werner Heisenberg (December 10, 1943), AMPG, III. Abt. Rep. 93; Rosenfeld to Werner Heisenberg (April 14, 1944), AMPG, III. Abt. Rep. 93; Hans Kramers to Werner Heisenberg (July 5, 1944), AMPG, III. Abt., Rep. 93, 1705.
78. Werner Heisenberg to Schwarz (February 14, 1944), AMPG, III. Abt. Rep. 93; Werner Heisenberg to Hiby (November 1, 1943), AMPG, III. Abt. Rep. 93.
79. Bernhard Rust to Werner Heisenberg (February 26, 1943), AMPG, III. Abt. Rep. 93.
80. Parteikanzlei to Hartle (July 8, 1942) MA 116/5 Wissenschaft Heisenberg IZG; Forstmann (KWG) to Werner Heisenberg (October 13, 1942), AMPG, III. Abt. Rep. 93; Ernst Telschow to Rudolf Mentzel (March 1, 1943), ADM, IMC 29 1052-1053.
81. See the chapter on Compromising.
82. Erxleben to Bechtold (Parteikanzlei) (September 9, 1942), IZG, MA 116/5 Wissenschaft Heisenberg.
83. Erxleben to Borger (July 10, 1942), IZG, MA 116/5 Wissenschaft Heisenberg; Erxleben to Parteikanzlei (September 9, 1942), IZG, MA 116/5 Wissenschaft Heisenberg.
84. Max von Laue to PAW (December 11, 1942), BABL, AdW II-HI, 66/7; BABL, AdW SGA II-V, 104; BABL, AdW REM to PAW (April 17, 1943) II–III, 66/7; Sitzung der Gesamt-Akademie vom 11. März 1943 BABL, AdW II-IV, 104.

Notes to pages 257–260 323

85. David C. Cassidy, *Beyond Uncertainty: Heisenberg, Quantum Physics, and The Bomb* (New York: Bellevue Literary Press, 2009), 334.
86. Gustav Borger to Werner Heisenberg (June 7, 1943), AMPG, III. Abt. Rep. 93; Werner Heisenberg an Borger (June 11, 1943), AMPG, III. Abt. Rep. 93; Werner Heisenberg to Elisabeth Heisenberg (June 6, 1943), in Heisenberg and Heisenberg, 221–222.
87. Goerner (Ministry Speer) to Werner Heisenberg (December 17, 1943), AMPG, III. Abt. Rep. 93; Werner Heisenberg to Goerner (Speer's Ministry) (January 12, 1944), AMPG, III. Abt. Rep. 93; Cassidy, 379; Werner Heisenberg to Elisabeth Heisenberg (December 9, 1943), in Heisenberg and Heisenberg, Meine Liebe, 213.
88. Wilhelm Coblitz to Werner Heisenberg (May 25, 1943), AMPG, III. Abt. Rep. 93; Werner Heisenberg to Wilhelm Coblitz (May 26, 1943), AMPG, III. Abt. Rep. 93; Werner Heisenberg to Wilhelm Coblitz (May 31, 1943), AMPG, III. Abt. Rep. 93; Wilhelm Coblitz to Werner Heisenberg (July 15, 1943), AMPG, III. Abt. Rep. 93; Wilhelm Coblitz to Werner Heisenberg (September 29, 1943), AMPG, III. Abt. Rep. 93; Werner Heisenberg to Wilhelm Coblitz (October 11, 1943), AMPG, III. Abt. Rep. 93; Werner Heisenberg to Wilhelm Coblitz (October 29, 1943), AMPG, III. Abt. Rep. 93; Wilhelm Coblitz to Dennhardt (December 8, 1943) BAK R521V/152.
89. Hans Frank's diary (August 2, 1943) NS-Archiv. Dokumente zum Nationalsozialismus www.ns-archiv.de/personen/frank/02-08-1943.php (accessed December 31, 2019).
90. REM to Rektor der Uni Berlin (July 2, 1941), HUB, PF 1483,107; REM, Merkblatt (June 1, 1942), AMPG, III. Abt. Rep. 93; REM to Rektor Uni. Berlin (July 6, 1942), HUB, PF 1484, 33.
91. Bernstein, Poland, 302.
92. *Krakauer Zeitung*, 302 (December 18, 1943).
93. REM to Werner Heisenberg (July 17, 1943), AMPG, III. Abt. Rep. 93; Werner Heisenberg to Deutsches Wissenschaftliches Institut Bucharest (December 18, 1943), AMPG, III. Abt. Rep. 93.
94. Deutsche Akademie to Werner Heisenberg (September 29, 1943), AMPG, III. Abt. Rep. 93; Deutsche Akademie to Werner Heisenberg (December 29, 1943), AMPG, III. Abt. Rep. 93.
95. REM to Rektor der Uni Berlin (December 29, 1944), HUB, Uk. H1851,12.
96. Hans von Euler-Chelpin to Werner Heisenberg (January 8, 1944), AMPG, III. Abt., Rep. 93, 1705; Rapport over Begivenhedeme under Besaettelsen af Universitetets Institut for teoretisk Fysik fra d.6.December 1943 til d.3.February 1944 (1944 or 1945), NBA; Stephan Schwarz, "The Occupation of Niels Bohr's Institute: December 6, 1943–February 3, 1944," *Physics in Perspective*, 23 (2021), 49–82.
97. Carl Friedrich von Weizsäcker to Werner Heisenberg (January 16, 1944) in Manhattan District History Volume 14: Intelligence and Security, www.osti.gov/opennet/manhattan_district.jsp (accessed August 18, 2017).
98. Rapport NBA.
99. Handwritten note by Werner Heisenberg on the back of Hans von Euler-Chelpin to Werner Heisenberg (January 8, 1944), AMPG, III. Abt. Rep. 93.
100. Rapport NBA.

324   Notes to pages 260–266

101. Werner Heisenberg to Johannes Jensen (1 February1944), AMPG, III. Abt. Rep. 93.
102. Werner Heisenberg to Elisabeth Heisenberg (January 29, and February 3, 1944) in Heisenberg and Heisenberg, Meine Liebe, 231–234.
103. REM to Werner Heisenberg (March 1, 1944), AMPG, III. Abt. Rep. 93; Deutsche Forschungsgemeinschaft to Werner Heisenberg (March 28, 1944). AMPG, III. Abt. Rep. 93.
104. Walther Wüst to Heinrich Himmler (October 15, 1937), BABL, BDC Otto Höfler.
105. Walther Wüst to Heinrich Himmler (October 15, 1937), BABL, BDC Otto Höfler.
106. SS-Brigadeführer und Generalmajor der Polizei to Reichsführer-SS im Hause (November 23, 1942), BABL, BDC Otto Höfler.
107. Frank-Rutger Hausmann, "The 'Third Front': German Cultural Policy in Occupied Europe, 1940–1945," in Ingo Haar and Michael Faulbusch (eds.), *German Scholars and Ethnic Cleansing 1919–1945* (New York: Berghahn Books, 2005), 213–235, here 224.
108. Werner Heisenberg, Bericht über eine Vortragsreise nach Kopenhagen (April 27, 1944), AHU, Uk. H185 I, 32; for Best see Ulrich Herbert, *Best. Biographische Studien über Radikalismus, Weltanschauung und Vernunft, 1903–1989* (Bonn: Dietz, 1996).
109. Werner Heisenberg, Bericht über eine Vortragsreise nach Kopenhagen (April 27, 1944), AHU, Uk. H185 I, 32.
110. Cassidy, Beyond, 361.
111. Louis Kaufman, Barbara Fitzgerald and Tom Sewell, *Moe Berg: Athlete, Scholar, Spy* (Boston: Little, Brown and Company, 1975), 195, 231; also see Powers, 395, 397, and 402.
112. Powers, Heisenberg's, 402.
113. Goudsmit, Alsos, 114; Bartel van der Waerden to Werner Heisenberg (April 28, 1948), AMPG, III. Abt. Rep. 93.
114. REM to Werner Heisenberg (March 27, 1945), HUB, Uk. H1851,36.
115. Werner Heisenberg to Robert Jungk (January 18, 1957), AMPG, III. Abt., Rep. 93, 1705.
116. Otto Höfler to Werner Heisenberg (January 12, 1947), AMPG, III. Abt. Rep. 93; Klinger to Werner Heisenberg (June 28, 1949), AMPG, III. Abt. Rep. 93; Werner Heisenberg to Klinger (July 4, 1944), AMPG, III. Abt. Rep. 93.
117. David Irving's interview with Werner Heisenberg (October 23, 1965), ADM, IMC 31 557.
118. Norbert Frei, *Vergangenheitspolitik. Die Anfänge der Bundesrepublik und die NS-Vergangenheit* (Munich: Deutsche Taschenbuch Verlag, 1999).
119. Arnold Kramish has argued that intelligence gathering was a major reason for the visit to Copenhagen; Heisenberg was not an agent for the NS government but did want to gather intelligence about any Allied atomic bomb; see Arnold Kramish, *The Griffin* (Boston: Houghton Mifflin, 1986), 120.
120. Werner Heisenberg, Die Arbeiten am Uranproblem (June 4, 1942), AMPG, I. Abt. Rep. 34.
121. Werner Heisenberg to Elisabeth Heisenberg (November 12, 1941) in Heisenberg and Heisenberg, Meine Liebe, 191.
122. Dörries, Frayn, 153, 131; Rudolf Ladenburg to Samuel Goudsmit (October 23, 1946) NBL, SGP Box 14, Folder 138.

Notes to pages 266–272 325

123. Elisabeth Heisenberg, *Das politische Leben eines Unpolitischen* (Munich: Piper, 1983),98; also see David Irving's interview with Werner Heisenberg (October 23, 1965), ADM, IMC 31 541.
124. Carl Friedrich von Weizsäcker, "Bohr hat Heisenberg nicht lange genug zugehört," *Die Welt* (February 8, 2002); Carl Friedrich von Weizsäcker, "Angst vor der Bombe. Carl Friedrich von Weizsäcker über die neuen Dokumente und sein Treffen mit Bohr und Heisenberg," *Süddeutsche Zeitung* (February 8, 2002).

Conclusion

1. Werner Heisenberg, "Das Dritte Reich versuchte nicht, die Atombombe zu bauen," *Frankfurter Allgemeine Zeitung*, 286 (December 9, 1967), Beilage "Bilder und Zeiten," 4; David Irving, *The German Atomic Bomb* (New York: Simon and Schuster, 1967), 84–85.
2. Irving, German, 156–169, 192–194, 200–211.
3. Samuel Goudsmit, Alsos, 2nd Ed. (Los Angeles: Tomash 1983), 176–177; Paul Lawrence Rose, *Heisenberg and the Nazi Atomic Bomb Project* (Berkeley: University of California Press, 1998), 115–122; Manfred Popp, "Misinterpreted Documents and Ignored Physical Facts: The History of 'Hitler's Atomic Bomb' Needs to Be Corrected," *Berichte zur Wissenschaftsgeschichte*, 39 (2016), 265–282.
4. Irving, German, 297.
5. Thomas Powers, *Heisenberg's War: The Secret History of the German Atomic Bomb* (London: Jonathan Cape, 1993), 101.
6. Robert Jungk, *Heller als tausend Sonnen. Das Schicksal der Atomforscher* (Stuttgart: Scherz & Goverts, 1958), 110.
7. Philip L. Cantelon, Richard G. Hewlett, and Robert C. Williams (eds.), *The American Atom: A Documentary History of Nuclear Policies from the Discovery of Fission to the Present*, 2nd Ed. (Philadelphia: University of Pennsylvania Press, 1991), 47–48.
8. Michael Frayn, *Copenhagen* (New York: Anchor, 1998).

Epilogue

1. Carl Friedrich von Weizsäcker, "Farm Hall und das deutsche Uranprojekt. Ein Gespräch," in Dieter Hoffmann (ed.), *Operation Epsilon. Die Farm-Hall-Protokolle erstmals vollständig, ergänzt um zeitgenössische Briefe und weitere Dokumente der 1945 in England internierten deutschen Atomforscher*, 2nd Ed. (Diepholz: GNT-Verlag, 2023), 519–549, here 538.
2. A transcript of this interview, in German, can be found at the Niels Bohr Library of the American Institute of Physics in College Park, MD USA.
3. Mark Walker, "Uranium Machines, Nuclear Explosives, and National Socialism: The German Quest for Nuclear Power, 1939–1949" (Princeton: Princeton University Ph.D., 1987).
4. Mark Walker, *German National Socialism and the Quest for Nuclear Power, 1939–1949* (Cambridge, Cambridge University Press, 1989); Mark Walker, *Die Uranmaschine. Mythos und Wirklichkeit der deutschen Atombombe* (Berlin, Siedler Verlag, 1990).

326 Notes to pages 273–274

5. See Robert Jungk, "Vorwort," in Walker, Uranmaschine, 7–10; Robert Jungk, *Trotzdem. Mein Leben für die Zukunft* (Munich: Carl Hanser Verlag, 1993), 297–298.
6. Carl Friedrich von Weizsäcker, *Bewusstseinswandel* (Munich: Hanser, 1988), 383; Jungk, Trotzdem, 299.
7. Wolfgang Menge, *Ende der Unschuld: die Deutschen und ihre Atombombe* (Berlin: Volk und Welt, 1991).
8. "Abend der Physiker über das 'Ende der Unschuld,'" *Die Zeit* (April 19, 1991), www.zeit.de/1991/17/abend-der-physiker-ueber-das-ende-der-unschuld (accessed June 20, 2017).
9. Carl Friedrich von Weizsäcker, "'Ich gebe zu, ich war verrückt' Carl Friedrich von Weizsäcker über die Chance der Deutschen im Zweiten Weltkrieg, die Atombombe zu bauen," *Der Spiegel*, 17 (1991), 227–238; also see Carl Friedrich von Weizsäcker, "Farm Hall und das deutsche Uranprojekt. Ein Gespräch," 525–530.
10. Klaus Hentschel and Dieter Hoffmann (eds.), *Carl Friedrich von Weizsäcker: Physik – Philosophie – Friedensforschung, Acta Historica Leopoldina*, 63, (2014).

Archives

ADM: Archives of the Deutsches Museum, Munich, Germany
ASN: Sommerfeld Nachlass
FA 002: Atomdokumente
IMC: David Irving Microfilm Collection
JN: Jung Nachlass
MLN: Max von Laue Nachlass
WGN: Walther Gerlach Nachlass
AdW: Akademie der Wissenschaften (Academy of Sciences)
AHU: Archives of the Humboldt University, Berlin, Germany
AMPG: Archives of the Max Planck Society, Berlin, Germany
I. Abt. Rep. 1A Generalverwaltung der KWG
I. Abt. Rep. 11 KWI für Chemie
I. Abt. Rep. 29 KWI für medizinische Forschung
I. Abt. Rep. 34 KWI für Physik
II. Abt. Rep. 23 MPI für medizinische Forschung
III. Abt. Rep 6 Nachlass Walther Bothe
III. Abt. Rep. 14 Nachlass Otto Hahn
III. Abt. Rep. 19 Nachlass Peter Debye
III. Abt. Rep. 50 Nachlass Max von Laue
III. Abt. Rep. 61 Ludwig Prandtl
III. Abt. Rep. 93 Nachlass Werner Heisenberg
III. Abt. Rep. 111 Nachlass Carl Friedrich von Weizsäcker
Gründungsakten: A collection of documents on the founding of the Max Planck
   Society available to researchers in the 1980s
BABL: Bundesarchiv (Federal German Archives) Berlin-Lichterfelde, Germany
BDC: Materials from the former Berlin Document Center
BAK: Bundesarchiv (Federal German Archives) Koblenz. Germany
CUA: Columbia University Archives, New York, NY, USA
IRP: Isidor Isaac Rabi Papers
EBN: Erich Bagge Nachlass
HSA: Staatsarchiv Hamburg (State Archives of Hamburg), Hamburg, Germany
HUB: Archives of the Humboldt University, Berlin, Germany
HUJ: Hebrew University of Jerusalem, Israel
AEA: Albert Einstein Archives
IZG: Institut für Zeitgeschichte, Munich, Germany
NARA: National Archives and Records Administration, College Park, MD USA

328   Archives

NBA: Niels Bohr Archive, Niels Bohr Institute, Copenhagen, Denmark
NBL: Niels Bohr Library & Archives, American Institute of Physics, College Park, Maryland USA
  SGP: Samuel Goudsmit Papers
RLC: Regenstein Library, University of Chicago, USA
  JFP: James Franck Papers
RPI: Institute Archives and Special Collections, Rensselaer Polytechnic Institute, Troy, NY, USA
  PHP: Paul Harteck Papers
SCUA: Special Collections, University of Arizona, Tucson, Arizona, USA
  GKP: Gerard Kuiper Papers

Bibliography

"Abend der Physiker über das Ende der Unschuld,'" *Die Zeit* (April 19, 1991).

Aly, Götz, and Susanne Heim, *Vordenker der Vernichtung. Auschwitz und die deutschen Pläne für eine neue europäische Ordnung*, 2nd Ed. (Frankfurt am Main: Fischer, 2013).

Bagge, Erich, Kurt Diebner, and Kenneth Jay, *Von der Uranspaltung bis Calder Hall* (Hamburg: Rowohlt, 1957).

Ball, Philip, *Serving the Reich: The Struggle for the Soul of Physics under Hitler* (Chicago: University of Chicago Press, 2014).

Bartov, Omer, *Hitler's Army: Soldiers, Nazis, and War in the Third Reich* (New York: Oxford University Press, 1992).

Bernstein, Jeremy, "The Drawing or Why History Is Not Mathematics," *Physics in Perspective*, 5 (2003), 243–261.

Bernstein, Jeremy, "Heisenberg in Poland," *American Journal of Physics*, 72 (2004), 300–304.

Bernstein, Jeremy (ed.), *Hitler's Uranium Club: The Secret Recordings at Farm Hall* (Woodbury: American Institute of Physics Press, 1996).

Beyerchen, Alan, *Scientists under Hitler: Politics and the Physics Community in the Third Reich* (New Haven: Yale University Press, 1977).

Beyerchen, Alan, *Wissenschaftler unter Hitler. Physiker im Dritten Reich* (Frankfurt: Ullstein, 1982).

Beyerle, Konrad, Wilhelm Groth, Paul Harteck, and Johannes Jensen, *Über Gaszentrifugen. Anreicherung der Xenon, Krypton, und der Selen-Isotope nach dem Zentrifugenverfahren* (Weinheim: Verlag Chemie, 1950).

Beyler, Richard, "The Demon of Technology, Mass Society, and Atomic Physics in West Germany, 1945–1957," *History and Technology*, 19/3 (2003), 227–239.

Bohr, Niels, and John Wheeler, "The Mechanism of Nuclear Fission," in *Physical Review*, 56 (1939), 426–450, in Horst Wohlfarth (ed.), *40 Jahre Kernspaltung: eine Einführung in der Originalliteratur* (Darmstadt: Wissenschaftliche Buchgesellschaft, 1979), 141–190.

Booth, Eugene, John Dunning, Astrid von Grosse, and Alfred Nier, "Neutron Capture by Uranium (238)," *Physical Review*, 58 (1940), 475–476.

Bothe, Walther, and Peter Jensen, "Die Absorption thermischer Neutronen in Elektrographit," *Zeitschrift für Physik*, 122 (1944), 749–755.

Browning, Christopher, *The Final Solution and the German Foreign Office: A Study of Referat D III of Abteilung Deutschland 1940–43* (New York: Holmes & Meier, 1978).

Brüche, Ernst, Introduction to Samuel Goudsmit, "Wissenschaft oder Geheimhaltung," *Physikalische Blätter*, 2 (1946), 203–207, here 203.

330   Bibliography

Cantelon, Philip L., Richard G. Hewlett, and Robert C. Williams (eds.), *The American Atom: A Documentary History of Nuclear Policies from the Discovery of Fission to the Present*, 2nd Ed. (Philadelphia: University of Pennsylvania Press, 1991).

Carson, Cathryn, *Heisenberg in the Atomic Age: Science and the Public Sphere* (Cambridge: Cambridge University Press, 2010).

Carson, Cathryn, "Reflections on Copenhagen," in Matthias Dörries (ed.), *Michael Frayn's Copenhagen in Debate: Historical Essays and Documents on the 1941 Meeting between Niels Bohr and Werner Heisenberg* (Berkeley: Office for History of Science and Technology, University of California, Berkeley, 2005), 7–17.

Cassidy, David C., *Beyond Uncertainty: Heisenberg, Quantum Physics, and The Bomb* (New York: Bellevue Literary Press, 2009).

Conze, Eckart, Norbert Frei, Peter Hayes, and Moshe Zimmermann, *Das Amt und die Vergangenheit. Deutsche Diplomaten im Dritten Reich und in der Bundesrepublik* (Munich: Blessing, 2010).

Cornwell, John, *Hitler's Scientists: Science, War, and the Devil's Pact* (New York: Penguin, 2004).

Crawford, Elisabeth, *The Nobel Population 1901–1950: A Census of the Nominators and Nominees for the Prizes in Physics and Chemistry* (Tokyo: Universal Academy Press, 2002).

Crawford, Elisabeth, Ruth Lewin Sime, and Mark Walker, "A Nobel Tale of Postwar Injustice," *Physics Today*, 50 (September 1997), 26–32.

Crawford, Elisabeth, Ruth Lewin Sime, and Mark Walker, "A Nobel Tale of Wartime Injustice," *Nature*, 382 (1996), 393–395.

Crowther, James Gerald, *Science in Liberated Europe* (London: Pilot, 1949).

Dahl, Per, *Heavy Water and the Wartime Race for Nuclear Energy* (Bristol: Institute of Physics Publishing, 2009).

Dahn, Ryan, "Big Science, Nazified? Pascual Jordan, Adolf Meyer-Abich, and the Abortive Scientific Journal Physis," *Isis*, 110/1 (2019), 68–90.

Dahn, Ryan, "The Farm Hall Transcripts: The Smoking Gun That Wasn't," *Berichte zur Wissenschaftsgeschichte*, 45 (2022), 202–218.

Deichmann, Ute, *Biologists under Hitler* (Cambridge, MA: Harvard University Press, 1996).

Dörries, Matthias (ed.), *Michael Frayn's Copenhagen in Debate: Historical Essays and Documents on the 1941 Meeting between Niels Bohr and Werner Heisenberg* (Berkeley: Office for History of Science and Technology, University of California, Berkeley, 2005).

Eckert, Michael, *Arnold Sommerfeld: Science, Life and Turbulent Times 1868–1951* (New York: Springer, 2013).

Eckert, Michael, "The German Physical Society and 'Aryan Physics,'" in Dieter Hoffmann and Mark Walker (eds.), *The German Physical Society in the Third Reich: Physicists between Autonomy and Accommodation* (Cambridge: Cambridge University Press, 2012), 96–125.

Eckert, Michael, *Ludwig Prandtl: A Life for Fluid Mechanics and Aeronautical Research* (Heidelberg: Springer, 2019).

Eckert, Michael, "Primacy Doomed to Failure: Heisenberg's Role as Scientific Adviser for Nuclear Policy in the FRG," *Historical Studies in the Physical and Biological Sciences*, 21/1 (1990), 29–58.

Eckert, Michael, and Karl Märker (eds.), *Arnold Sommerfeld, Wissenschaftlicher Briefwechsel. Band 2: 1919–1951* (Berlin: GNT Verlag, 2004).

Bibliography

Einstein, Albert, "Dialogue about Objections to the Theory of Relativity," *Die Naturwissenschaften*, 6/48 (November 29, 1918), 697–702.

Einstein, Albert, "Meine Antwort. Über die antirelativistische G.m.b.H," *Berliner Tageblatt und Handels-Zeitung* (August 27, 1920), 1.

Fermi, Enrico, "Experimental Production of a Divergent Chain Reaction," in Horst Wohlfarth (ed.), *40 Jahre Kernspaltung: eine Einführung in der Originalliteratur* (Darmstadt: Wissenschaftliche Buchgesellschaft, 1979), 322–370.

Flügge, Siegfried, "Kann der Energieinhalt der Atomkerne technisch nutzbar gemacht werden?" *Die Naturwissenschaften*, 27 (1939), 402–410, in Horst Wohlfarth (ed.), *40 Jahre Kernspaltung: eine Einführung in der Originalliteratur* (Darmstadt: Wissenschaftliche Buchgesellschaft, 1979), 119–140.

Föllmer, Moritz, *"Ein Leben wie im Traum"*. *Kultur in Dritten Reich* (Munich: Beck, 2016).

Forstner, Christian, *Kernphysik, Forschungsreaktoren und Atomenergie: Transnationale Wissensströme und das Scheitern einer Innovation in Österreich* (Wiesbaden: Springer, 2019).

Forstner, Christian, "Laboratory Life Instead of Nuclear Weapons: A New Perspective on the German Uranium Club," *Physics in Perspective*, 24 (2022), 181–227.

Frank, Charles (ed.), *Operation Epsilon: The Farm Hall Transcripts* (Bristol: Institute of Physics, 1993).

Frayn, Michael, *Copenhagen* (New York: Anchor, 1998).

Frei, Norbert, *Vergangenheitspolitik. Die Anfänge der Bundesrepublik und die NS-Vergangenheit* (Munich: Deutsche Taschenbuch Verlag, 1999).

Friedman, Robert Marc, *The Politics of Excellence: Behind the Nobel Prize in Science* (New York: W. H. Freeman, 2001).

Frisch, Otto, "Physical Evidence for the Division of Heavy Nuclei under Neutron Bombardment," *Nature* 143 (1939), 276.

Gehrcke, Ernst, *Die Massensuggestion der Relativitätstheorie. Kulturhistorisch-psychologische Dokumente* (Berlin: Meusser, 1924).

Goebbels, Josef, "Der Totale Krieg wird praktische Wirklichkeit," *Völkischer Beobachter* (July 28, 1944).

Goebbels, Josef, *Michael* (Munich: Franz-Eher Verlag, 1929).

Goebbels, Josef, *Tagebücher aus den Jahren 1942–1943* (Zurich: Atlantis Verlag, 1948).

Goudsmit, Samuel, *Alsos*, 2nd Ed. (Los Angeles: Tomash Publishers, 1983).

Goudsmit, Samuel, "Freedom of Science," *Proceedings of the American Philosophical Society*, 94/2 (1950), 111–113.

Goudsmit, Samuel, "German Atom Research," *New York Times* (November 9, 1947).

Goudsmit, Samuel, "Germans Overrated on Atom," *Washington Post* (August 3, 1947), B8.

Goudsmit, Samuel, "Heisenberg on the German Uranium Project," *Bulletin of the Atomic Scientists*, 3/11 (1947), 343.

Goudsmit, Samuel, "How Germany Lost the Race," *Bulletin of the Atomic Scientists*, 1/7 (1946), 4–5.

Goudsmit, Samuel, (letter to the editor), *New York Times* (January 9, 1949).

Goudsmit, Samuel, "Nazis' Atomic Secrets," *Life*, 23 (October 20, 1947), 123–134.

Goudsmit, Samuel, "Our Task in Germany," *Bulletin of the Atomic Scientists*, 4/4 (April 1948), 106.

Goudsmit, Samuel, "Secrecy or Science," *Science Illustrated*, 1 (1946), 97–99.

332   Bibliography

Goudsmit, Samuel, "War Physics in Germany," *The Review of Scientific Instruments*, 17/1 (1946), 49–52.

Gowing, Margaret, *Britain and Atomic Energy, 1939–1945* (London: St. Martin's Press, 1964).

Groves, Leslie, *Now It Can Be Told: The Story of the Manhattan Project*, 2nd Ed. (New York: Da Capo, 1983).

Grundmann, Siegfried, *Einsteins Akte*, 2nd Ed. (Berlin: Springer, 2004).

Haberer, Joseph, *Politics and the Community of Science* (New York: Van Nostrand Reinhold, 1969).

Hachtmann, Rüdiger, "A Success Story? Highlighting the History of the Kaiser Wilhelm Society's General Administration in the Third Reich," in Susanne Heim, Carola Sachse, and Mark Walker (eds.), *The Kaiser Wilhelm Society under National Socialism* (Cambridge: Cambridge University Press, 2009), 19–46.

Hachtmann, Rüdiger, *Wissenschaftsmanagement im "Dritten Reich": Geschichte der Generalverwaltung der Kaiser-Wilhelm-Gesellschaft* (Göttingen: Wallstein Verlag, 2007).

Hahn, Otto, and Fritz Strassmann, "Nachweis der Entstehung aktiver Bariumisotope aus Uran und Thorium durch Neutronenbestrahlung: Nachweis weiterer aktiver Bruchstücke bei der Uranspaltung," *Die Naturwissenschaften*, 27 (1939), 89–95.

Hahn, Otto, and Fritz Strassmann, "Über den Nachweis und das Verhalten der bei der Bestrahlung des Urans mittels Neutronen entstehenden Erdalkalimetalle," *Die Naturwissenschaften*, 27 (1939), 11–15.

Haupt, Heinz Dieter, *Deutschlands Weg zur Bombe. Chimäre oder Realität? Vom Dritten Reich bis zur Bundesrepublik. Die Geschichte alternativer Kernwaffenentwicklungen in Deutschland im Kontext der internationalen Forschung* (Munich: Literareon, 2022).

Hausmann, Frank-Rutger, *"Auch im Krieg schweigen die Musen nicht": Die Deutschen Wissenschaftlichen Institute im Zweiten Weltkrieg* (Göttingen: Vandenhoeck & Ruprecht, 2001).

Hausmann, Frank-Rutger, "The 'Third Front': German Cultural Policy in Occupied Europe, 1940–1945," in Ingo Haar and Michael Faulbusch (eds.), *German Scholars and Ethnic Cleansing 1919–1945* (New York: Berghahn Books, 2005), 213–235.

Heim, Susanne (ed.), *Autarkie und Ostexpansion. Pflanzenzucht und Agrarforschung im Nationalsozialismus* (Göttingen: Wallstein Verlag, 2002).

Heim, Susanne, *Plant Breeding and Agrarian Research in Kaiser-Wilhelm-Institutes 1933–1945: Calories, Caoutchouc, Careers* (Dordrecht: Springer, 2008).

Heim, Susanne, Carola Sachse, and Mark Walker (eds.), *The Kaiser Wilhelm Society under National Socialism* (Cambridge: Cambridge University Press, 2009).

Heisenberg, Elisabeth, *Das politische Leben eines Unpolitischen: Erinnerungen an Werner Heisenberg* (Munich: Piper, 1983).

Heisenberg, Werner, "Das Dritte Reich versuchte nicht, die Atombombe zu bauen," *Frankfurter Allgemeine Zeitung*, 286 (December 9, 1967), 4.

Heisenberg, Werner, *Der Teil und das Ganze: Gespräche im Umkreis der Atomphysik* (Munich: DTV, 1973).

Heisenberg, Werner, "Die Bewertung der 'modernen theoretischen Physik,'" *Zeitschrift für die gesamte Naturwissenschaft*, 9/10–12 (1943), 201–212.

Heisenberg, Werner, *Encounters with Einstein* (Princeton: Princeton University Press, 1989), 112–117, 121.

Heisenberg, Werner, "German Atom Research," *New York Times* (January 30, 1949).

Bibliography 333

Heisenberg, Werner, "Nazis Spurned Idea of an Atomic Bomb," *New York Times* (December 28, 1948).

Heisenberg, Werner, *Physics and Beyond: Encounters and Conversations* (New York: Harper and Row, 1971).

Heisenberg, Werner, "Research in Germany on the Technical Application of Atomic Energy," *Nature*, 160/4059 (1947), 211–215.

Heisenberg, Werner, "Über die Arbeiten zur technischen Ausnutzung der Atomkernenergie in Deutschland," *Die Naturwissenschaften*, 33 (1946), 325–329.

Heisenberg, Werner, "Zum Artikel: Deutsche und Jüdische Physik," *Völkischer Beobachter*, Norddeutsche Ausgabe/Ausgabe A, No. 59 (February 28, 1936), 6.

Heisenberg, Werner, and Elisabeth Heisenberg, *"Meine Liebe Li!" Der Briefwechsel 1937–1946* (St. Pölten: Residenz Verlag, 2011).

Heisenberg, Werner, and Elisabeth Heisenberg, *My Dear Li: Correspondence, 1937–1946* (New Haven: Yale University Press, 2017).

Heisenberg, Werner, and Karl Wirtz, "Großversuche zur Vorbereitung der Konstruktion eines Uranbrenners," in Walther Bothe and Siegfried Flügge (eds.), *Naturforschung und Medizin in Deutschland 1939–1946. Volume 14: Kernphysik und kosmische Strahlen. Teil II* (Weinheim: Verlag Chemie, 1949), 143–165.

Hentschel, Klaus, "'Der neue Weg': Mit 'interatomarer Energie' zum 'Herrn der Welt' werden. Zu einem bislang unbekannten Typoskript vom Oktober 1944," *NTM*, 28, (2020), 121–147.

Hentschel, Klaus, *The Mental Aftermath: The Mentality of German Physicists 1945–1949* (Oxford: Oxford University Press, 2009).

Hentschel, Klaus, *Die Mentalität deutscher Physiker in der frühen Nachkriegszeit (1945–1949)* (Heidelberg: Synchron, 2005).

Hentschel, Klaus (ed.), *Physics and National Socialism: An Anthology of Primary Sources* (Basel: Birkhäuser, 1996).

Hentschel, Klaus, and Dieter Hoffmann (eds.), "Carl Friedrich von Weizsäcker: Physik – Philosophie – Friedensforschung," *Acta Historica Leopoldina*, 63, (2014).

Herbert, Ulrich, *Best. Biographische Studien über Radikalismus, Weltanschauung und Vernunft, 1903–1989* (Bonn: Dietz, 1996).

Hermann, Armin (ed.), *Albert Einstein/Arnold Sommerfeld. Briefwechsel. Sechzig Briefe aus dem goldenen Zeitalter der modernen Physik* (Basel: Schwabe u. Co., 1968).

Himmler, Heinrich, "Speech at the Gauleiter Conference in Posen (6 October 1943)," in Bradley Smith and Agnes Peterson (eds.), *Geheimreden 1933 bis 1945 und andere Ansprachen* (Frankfurt: Propyläen, 1974), 162–183.

Hoddeson, Lillian, Paul Henriksen, Roger Meade, and Catherine Westfall, *Critical Assembly: A Technical History of Los Alamos during the Oppenheimer Years, 1943–1945* (Cambridge: Cambridge University Press, 1993).

Hoffmann, Dieter, "Copenhagen Was Not an Isolated Case," in Matthias Dörries (ed.), *Michael Frayn's Copenhagen in Debate: Historical Essays and Documents on the 1941 Meeting Between Niels Bohr and Werner Heisenberg* (Berkeley: Office for History of Science and Technology, University of California, Berkeley, 2005), 39–47.

Hoffmann, Dieter, "Friedrich Houtermans (1903–1966): ein Physiker zwischen Hitler und Stalin," *Spektrum der Wissenschaft*, 2 (2014), 62–70.

Hoffmann, Dieter (ed.), *Operation Epsilon. Die Farm-Hall-Protokolle erstmals vollständig, ergänzt um zeitgenössische Briefe und weitere Dokumente der 1945*

334   Bibliography

in England internierten deutschen Atomforscher, 2nd Ed. (Diepholz: GNT-Verlag, 2023).

Hoffmann, Dieter, and Mark Walker (eds.), *"Fremde" Wissenschaftler im Dritten Reich. Die Debye-Affäre im Kontext* (Göttingen: Wallstein, 2011).

Hoffmann, Dieter, and Mark Walker (eds.), *The German Physical Society in the Third Reich: Physicists between Autonomy and Accommodation* (Cambridge: Cambridge University Press, 2012).

Hoffmann, Dieter and Mark Walker (eds.), *Physiker zwischen Autonomie und Anpassung. Die Deutsche Physikalische Gesellschaft im Dritten Reich* (Weinheim: Wiley-Verlag VCH, 2007).

Irving, David, *The German Atomic Bomb* (New York: Simon & Schuster, 1967).

Jungk, Robert, *Brighter than a Thousand Suns: A Personal History of the Atomic Scientists* (New York: Harcourt, Brace, and Company, 1958).

Jungk, Robert, *Heller als tausend Sonnen. Das Schicksal der Atomforscher* (Stuttgart: Scherz & Goverts, 1958).

Jungk, Robert, *Trotzdem. Mein Leben für die Zukunft* (Munich: Carl Hanser Verlag, 1993).

Jungk, Robert, "Vorwort," in Mark Walker, *Die Uranmaschine. Mythos und Wirklichkeit der deutschen Atombombe* (Berlin: Siedler Verlag, 1990), 7–10.

Kant, Horst, "Die Erforschung und Nutzung der Kernenergie – ihre Ambivalenz(en) im historischen Kontext," in Klaus Fischer and Heinrich Parthey (eds.), *Ambivalenz der Wissenschaft* (Berlin: Wissenschaftlicher Verlag, 2019), 135–172.

Karlsch, Rainer, *Hitlers Bombe: Die geheime Geschichte der deutschen Kernwaffenversuche* (Munich: Deutsche Verlags-Anstalt, 2005).

Karlsch, Rainer, and Heiko Petermann (eds.), *Für und Wider "Hitlers Bombe" Studien zur Atomforschung in Deutschland* (Münster: Waxmann, 2007).

Karlsch, Rainer, and Mark Walker, "New Light on Hitler's Bomb," *Physics World* (2005), 15–18.

Kater, Michael, *Culture in Nazi Germany* (New Haven: Yale University Press, 2019).

Kaufman, Louis, Barbara Fitzgerald, and Tom Sewell, *Moe Berg: Athlete, Scholar, Spy* (Boston: Little, Brown and Company, 1975).

Kershaw, Ian, *Hitler 1889–1936: Hubris* (New York: W. W. Norton & Company, 1998).

Kershaw, Ian, *Hitler 1937–1945: Nemesis* (New York: W. W. Norton & Company, 2000).

Kleinert, Andreas, "Der Briefwechsel zwischen Philipp Lenard (1862–1947) und Johannes Stark (1874–1975)," *Jahrbuch 2000 der Deutschen Akademie der Naturforscher Leopoldina (Halle/Saale) LEOPOLDINA* (R. 3), 46 (2001), 243–261.

Kleinert, Andreas, "Lenard, Stark und die Kaiser-Wilhelm-Gesellschaft. Auszüge aus der Korrespondenz der beiden Physiker zwischen 1933 und 1936," *Physikalische Blätter*, 36/2 (1980), 35–43.

Kramish, Arnold, *The Griffin: The Greatest Untold Espionage Story of World War II* (Boston: Houghton Mifflin, 1986).

Kraus, Elisabeth, *Von der Uranspaltung zur Göttinger Erklärung: Otto Hahn, Werner Heisenberg, Carl Friedrich von Weizsäcker und die Verantwortung des Wissenschaftlers* (Würzburg: Königshausen & Neumann, 2001).

Lemmerich, Jost (ed.), *Der Luxus des Gewissens. Max Born James Franck Physiker in ihrer Zeit. Ausstellung der Staatsbibliothek Berlin* (Berlin: Stiftung Preußischer Kulturbesitz, 1982).

Bibliography 335

Lenard, Philipp, *Äther und Uräther*, 2nd Ed. (1922), in Schönbeck (2000), 36.

Lenard, Philipp, *Deutsche Physik*, 4 vols. (Munich: Lehmann, 1925).

Lenard, Philipp, "Ein großer Tag für die Naturforschung," *Völkischer Beobachter* (May 13, 1933).

Lenard, Philipp, und Johannes Stark, *"Hitlergeist und Wissenschaft," Großdeutsche Zeitung. Tageszeitung für nationale und soziale Politik und Wirtschaft* (May 8, 1924), 1–2, reprinted in *Nationalsozialistische Monatshefte*, 7/71 (February 1936), 110–111.

"Lights All Askew in the Heavens," *New York Times* (November 9, 1919).

Litten, Freddy, *Mechanik und Antisemitismus. Wilhelm Müller (1880–1968)* (Munich: Institut für Geschichte der Naturwissenschaften München, 2000).

Lorenz, Robert, *Protest der Physiker. Die "Göttinger Erklärung" von 1957* (Bielefeld: Transcript Verlag, 2011).

Ludwig, Karl-Heinz, *Technik und Ingenieure im Dritten Reich* (Königstein/Ts: Athenäum-Verlag, 1979).

Maier, Helmut, *Chemiker im "Dritten Reich": Die Deutsche Chemische Gesellschaft und der Verein Deutscher Chemiker im NS-Herrschaftsapparat* (Frankfurt: Wiley-VCH, 2015).

Maier, Helmut, *Forschung als Waffe. Rüstungsforschung in der Kaiser-Wilhelm-Gesellschaft und das Kaiser-Wilhelm Institut für Metallforschung 1900–1945/48, 2 Volumes* (Göttingen: Wallstein Verlag, 2007).

Maier, Helmut (ed.), *Gemeinschaftsforschung, Bevollmächtigte und der Wissentransfer. Die Rolle der Kaiser-Wilhelm-Gesellschaft im System kriegsrelevanter Forschung des Nationalsozialismus* (Göttingen: Wallstein Verlag, 2007).

Maier, Helmut (ed.), *Rüstungsforschung im Nationalsozialismus. Organisation, Mobilisierung und Entgrenzung der Technikwissenschaften* (Göttingen: Wallstein, 2002).

Martius, Ursula Maria, "Videant consules..." in Dieter Hoffmann und Mark Walker (eds.), *Physiker zwischen Autonomie und Anpassung. Die Deutsche Physikalische Gesellschaft im Dritten Reich* (Weinheim: Wiley-VCH, 2007), 636–640.

Mehrtens, Herbert, "Angewandte Mathematik und Anwendungen der Mathematik im nationalsozialistischen Deutschland," *Geschichte und Gesellschaft*, 12/3 (1986), 317–347.

Meitner, Lise, and Otto Frisch, "Disintegration of Uranium by Neutrons: A New Type of Nuclear Reaction," *Nature*, 143 (1939), 239–240.

Meldungen aus dem Reich. Die geheimen Lageberichte des Sicherheitsdienstes der SS 1938–1945, volumes 1–17 (Herrsching: Pawlak, 1984).

Menge, Wolfgang, *Ende der Unschuld: die Deutschen und ihre Atombombe* (Berlin: Volk und Welt, 1991).

Menzel, Willi, "Deutsche Physik und jüdische Physik," *Völkischer Beobachter*, 29, Ausgabe A, Norddeutsche Ausgabe (January 29, 1936).

Morrison, Philip, "Alsos: The Story of German Science," *Bulletin of the Atomic Scientists*, 3/12 (1947), 354, 365.

Morrison, Philip, "A Reply to Dr. von Laue," *Bulletin of the Atomic Scientists*, 4 (1948), 104.

Mott, Nevill, and Rudolf Peierls, "Werner Heisenberg. 5 December 1901–1 February 1976," *Biographical Memoirs of Fellows of the Royal Society*, 23/11 (1977), 212–251.

Nagel, Günter, *Atomversuche in Deutschland. Geheime Uranarbeiten in Gottow, Oranienburg und Stadtilm*, 2nd Ed. (Zella-Mehlis: Heinrich-Jung-Verlagsgesellschaft, 2003).

336 Bibliography

Nagel, Günter, *Das geheime deutsche Uranprojekt 1939–1945. Beute der Alliierten* (Zella-Mehlis: Heinrich-Jung-Verlagsgesellschaft, 2016).

Nier, Alfred, Eugene Booth, John Dunning, and Astrid von Grosse, "Nuclear Fission of Separated Uranium Isotopes," *Physical Review*, 57 (1940), 546.

Niethammer, Lutz, *Die Mitläuferfabrik: die Entnazifizierung am Beispiel Bayerns* (Berlin: Dietz, 1982).

Noakes, Jeremy, and Geoffrey Pridham (eds.), *Nazism: A History in Documents and Eyewitness Accounts, 1919–1945, Volume III* (Exeter: University of Exeter Press, 1988).

Noakes, Jeremy, and Geoffrey Pridham (eds.), *Nazism: A History in Documents and Eyewitness Accounts, 1919–1945, Volume IV* (Exeter: University of Exeter Press, 1998).

Nordmann, Charles, "Avec Einstein dans les régions dévastées," *L'Illustration*, 80/4128 (April 15, 1922), 328–331.

Osganian, Vanessa, "Rudolf Tomaschek: An Exponent of the 'Deutsche Physik' Movement," in Christian Forstner and Mark Walker (eds.), *Biographies in the History of Physics: Actors, Objects, Institutions* (Cham: Springer, 2020), 89–109.

Pegelow, Thomas, "Determining 'People of German Blood,' 'Jews' and 'Mischlinge': The Reich Kinship Office and the Competing Discourses and Powers of Nazism, 1941–1943," *Contemporary European History*, 15/1 (2006), 43–65.

Popp, Manfred, "Hitlers Atombombe. Störfall der Wissenschaftsgeschichte," *Spektrum der Wissenschaft*, 12/16 (2016), 12–21.

Popp, Manfred, "Misinterpreted Documents and Ignored Physical Facts: The History of 'Hitler's Atomic Bomb' Needs to Be Corrected," *Berichte zur Wissenschaftsgeschichte*, 39 (2016), 265–282.

Popp, Manfred, "Werner Heisenberg und das deutsche Uranprojekt im 'Dritten Reich': ein neuer Blick auf ein komplexes Kapitel der Wissenschaftsgeschichte," *Quanten: Schriftenreihe der Heisenberg-Gesellschaft*, 6 (2018), 9–67.

Popp, Manfred, "Why Hitler Did Not Have Atomic Bombs," *Journal of Nuclear Engineering*, 2 (2021), 9–27.

Popp, Manfred, and Piet de Klerk, "The Peculiarities of the German Uranium Project (1939–1945)," *Journal of Nuclear Engineering*, 4 (2023), 634–653.

Powers, Thomas, *Heisenberg's War: The Secret History of the German Bomb* (London: Jonathan Cape, 1993).

Rabinbach, Anson, and Sander L. Gilman (eds.), *The Third Reich Sourcebook* (Berkeley: University of California Press, 2013).

Rabinowitch, Eugene, "Comment by the Editor," *Bulletin of the Atomic Scientists*, 4 (1948), 104.

Rammer, Gerhard, "Allied Control of Physics and the Collegial Self-Denazification of the Physicists," in Helmuth Trischler and Mark Walker (eds.), *Physics and Politics: Research and Research Support in Twentieth Century Germany in International Perspective* (Stuttgart: Franz Steiner Verlag, 2010), 61–84.

Rammer, Gerhard, "'Cleanliness among Our Circle of Colleagues': The German Physical Society's Policy toward Its Past," in Dieter Hoffmann and Mark Walker (eds.), *The German Physical Society in the Third Reich: Physicists between Autonomy and Accommodation* (Cambridge: Cambridge University Press, 2012), 367–421.

Ramsauer, Carl, "Eingabe an Rust," *Physikalische Blätter*, 3 (1947), 43–44.

Bibliography 337

Reed, Cameron, "An Inter-Country Comparison of Nuclear Pile Development during World War II," *European Physical Journal H*, 46/1 (2021), 15.

Renneberg, Monika, and Mark Walker (eds.), *Science, Technology, and National Socialism* (Cambridge: Cambridge University Press, 1994).

Rhodes, Richard, *The Making of the Atomic Bomb* (New York: Simon & Schuster, 1986).

Rose, Paul Lawrence, *Heisenberg and the Nazi Atomic Bomb Project* (Berkeley: University of California Press, 1998).

Rowe, David, and Robert Schulman (eds.), *Einstein on Politics* (Princeton: Princeton University Press, 2007).

Rozental, Stefan (ed.), *Niels Bohr* (Amsterdam: North Holland, 1968).

Rozental, Stefan, *NB. Erindringer om Niels Bohr* (Copenhagen: Gyldendal, 1985).

Sachse, Carola (ed.), *Die Verbindung nach Auschwitz: Biowissenschaften und Menschenversuche an Kaiser-Wilhelm-Instituten* (Göttingen: Wallstein, 2003).

Sachse, Carola, "The Max Planck Society and Pugwash during the Cold War: An Uneasy Relationship," *Journal of Cold War Studies*, 20/1 (2018), 170–209.

Sachse, Carola, "'Persilscheinkultur'. Zum Umgang mit der NS-Vergangenheit in der Kaiser-Wilhelm/Max-Planck-Gesellschaft," in Bernd Weisbrod (ed.), *Akademische Vergangenheitspolitik. Beiträge zur Wissenschaftskultur der Nachkriegszeit* (Göttingen: Wallstein, 2002), 217–246.

Sachse, Carola, "'Whitewash Culture': How the Kaiser Wilhelm/Max Planck Society Dealt with the Nazi Past," in Susanne Heim, Carola Sachse, and Mark Walker (eds.), *The Kaiser Wilhelm Society under National Socialism* (Cambridge: Cambridge University Press, 2009), 373–399.

Sachse, Carola, *Wissenschaft und Diplomatie. Die Max-Planck-Gesellschaft im Feld der internationalen Politik (1945–2000)* (Göttingen: Vandenhoeck & Ruprecht, 2023).

Schirrmacher, Arne, "Physik und Politik in der frühen Bundesrepublik Deutschland. Max Born, Werner Heisenberg und Pascual Jordan als politische Grenzgänger," *Berichte zur Wissenschaftsgeschichte*, 30 (2007), 13–31.

Schmuhl, Hans-Walter, *The Kaiser Wilhelm Institute for Anthropology, Human Heredity, and Eugenics, 1927–1945: Crossing Boundaries* (Dordrecht: Springer, 2008).

Schmuhl, Hans-Walter (ed.), *Rassenforschung an Kaiser-Wilhelm-Instituten vor und nach 1933* (Göttingen: Wallstein, 2003).

Schönbeck, Charlotte, *Albert Einstein und Philipp Lenard. Antipoden im Spannungsfeld von Physik und Zeitgeschichte* (Heidelberg: Springer, 2000).

Schröder, Reinald, "Die 'schöne deutsche Physik' von Gustav Hertz und der 'weiße Jude' Heisenberg – Johannes Starks ideologischer Antisemitismus," in Helmuth Albrecht (ed.), *Naturwissenschaft und Technik in der Geschichte. 25 Jahre Lehrstuhl für Geschichte der Naturwissenschaft und Technik am Historischen Institut der Universität Stuttgart* (Stuttgart: GNT Verlag, 1993), 327–341.

Schüring, Michael, "Expulsion, Compensation, and the Legacy of the Kaiser Wilhelm Society," *Minerva*, 44/3 (2006), 307–324.

Schüring, Michael, *Minervas verstoßene Kinder. Vertriebene Wissenschaftler und die Vergangenheitspolitik der Max-Planck-Gesellschaft* (Göttingen: Wallstein, 2006).

Schwarz, Stephan, "The Occupation of Niels Bohr's Institute: December 6, 1943–February 3, 1944," *Physics in Perspective*, 23 (2021), 49–82.

338   Bibliography

Seelig, Carl (ed.), *Helle Zeit – Dunkle Zeit. In Memoriam Albert Einstein* (Zurich: Europa Verlag, 1955).

Serber, Robert, *The Los Alamos Primer: The First Lectures on How to Build an Atomic Bomb* (Berkeley: University of California Press, 1992).

Siegmund-Schultze, Reinhard, "Bartel Leendert van der Waerden (1903–1996) im Dritten Reich: Moderne Algebra im Dienste des Anti-Modernismus?" in Dieter Hoffmann and Mark Walker (eds.), *"Fremde" Wissenschaftler im Dritten Reich. Die Debye-Affäre im Kontext* (Göttingen: Wallstein, 2011), 200–229.

Sime, Ruth Lewin, "An Inconvenient History: The Nuclear-Fission Display in the Deutsches Museum," *Physics in Perspective*, 12 (2010), 190–218.

Sime, Ruth Lewin, *Lise Meitner. Ein Leben für die Physik* (Frankfurt: Insel Verlag, 2001).

Sime, Ruth Lewin, *Lise Meitner: A Life in Physics* (Berkeley: University of California Press, 1996).

Sime, Ruth Lewin, "The Politics of Forgetting: Otto Hahn and the German Nuclear-Fission Project in World War II," *Physics in Perspective*, 14 (2012), 59–94.

Sime, Ruth Lewin, "The Politics of Memory: Otto Hahn and the Third Reich," *Physics in Perspective*, 8 (2006), 3–51.

Sime, Ruth Lewin, "The Search for Transuranium Elements and the Discovery of Nuclear Fission," *Physics in Perspective*, 2 (2000), 48–62.

Smyth, Henry DeWolf, *Atomic Energy for Military Purposes: The Official Report on the Development of the Atomic Bomb under the Auspices of the United States Government, 1940–1945* (Princeton: Princeton University Press, 1945).

Speer, Albert, *Erinnerungen* (Berlin: Propyläen Verlag, 1969).

Speer, Albert, *Inside the Third Reich* (New York: Macmillan, 1970).

Stanley, Matthew, *Einstein's War* (New York: Dutton, 2019).

Stark, Johannes, *Die gegenwärtige Krisis in der deutschen Physik* (Leipzig: Barth, 1922).

Stark, Johannes, *Erinnerungen eines deutschen Naturforschers* (Mannhein: Bionomica Verlag, 1987).

Stark, Johannes, (letter to the editor) *Deutsche Tages Zeitung* (April 4, 1922) in Siegfried Grundmann (ed.), *Einsteins Akte*, 2nd Ed. (Berlin: Springer, 2004), 217.

Stark, Johannes, *Nationalsozialismus und Wissenschaft* (Munich: Zentralverlag der NSDAP, 1934).

Stark, Johannes, "Organisation der physikalischen Forschung," *Zeitschrift für technische Physik*, 14/11 (1933), 433–435.

Stark, Johannes, "Philipp Lenard als deutscher Naturforscher. Rede zur Einweihung des Philipp-Lenard-Instituts in Heidelberg am 13. Dezember 1935," *Nationalsozialistische Monatshefte*, 7/71 (February 1936), 106–111.

Stark, Johannes, "Stellungnahme von Prof. Dr. J. Stark," *Völkischer Beobachter*, Norddeutsche Ausgabe/Ausgabe A, Nr. 59 (February 28, 1936), 6.

Streit, Christian, *Keine Kameraden. Die Wehrmacht und die sowjetischen Kriegsgefangenen, 1941–1945* (Bonn: Dietz, 1991).

Stuewer, Roger, *The Age of Innocence: Nuclear Physics between the First and Second World Wars* (Oxford: Oxford University Press, 2018).

Tooze, Adam, *The Wages of Destruction: The Making and Breaking of the Nazi Economy* (New York: Viking, 2007).

Trischler, Helmuth, *Luft- und Raumfahrtforschung in Deutschland 1900–1970. Politische Geschichte einer Wissenschaft* (Frankfurt: Campus, 1992).

Bibliography

Trischler, Helmuth, "Self-mobilization or Resistance? Aeronautical Research and National Socialism," in Monika Renneberg and Mark Walker (eds.), *Science, Technology, and National Socialism* (Cambridge: Cambridge University Press, 1994), 72–88, 356–358.

Turner, Louis, "The Nonexistence of Transuranic Elements," *Physical Review*, 57 (1940), 157.

Turner, Louis, "Nuclear Fission," *Reviews of Modern Physics*, 12/1 (1940), 1–29.

"Und führe uns nicht in Versuchung. Vom gespaltenen Atom zu gespaltenen Gewissen – Die Geschichte einer menschheitsgefährdenden Waffe," *Der Spiegel* (May 8, 1957), 45–46, 48–53.

Vollnhals, Clemens, *Entnazifizierung: Politische Säuberung und Rehabilitierung in den vier Besatzungszonen 1945–1949* (Munich: Deutscher Taschenbuch Verlag, 1991).

von Ardenne, Manfred, *Die Erinnerungen* (München: Herbig, 1990).

von Halban, Hans, Frédéric Joliot, and Lew Kowarski, "Liberation of Neutrons in the Nuclear Explosion of Uranium," *Nature*, 143 (1939), 470–471.

von Halban, Hans, Frédéric Joliot, and Lew Kowarski, "Number of Neutrons Liberated in the Nuclear Fission of Uranium," *Nature*, 143 (1939), 680.

von Laue, Max, "Ansprache bei Eröffnung der Physikertagung in Würzburg am 18. September 1933," *Physikalische Zeitschrift*, 34 (1933), 889–890.

von Laue, Max, "Bemerkung zu der vorstehenden Veröffentlichung von J. Stark," *Physikalische Blätter*, 3 (1947), 272–273.

von Laue, Max, "The Wartime Activities of German Scientists," *Bulletin of the Atomic Scientists*, 4/4 (1948), 103.

von Weizsäcker, Carl Friedrich, "Angst vor der Bombe. Carl Friedrich von Weizsäcker über die neuen Dokumente und sein Treffen mit Bohr und Heisenberg," *Süddeutsche Zeitung* (February 8, 2002).

von Weizsäcker, Carl Friedrich, *Atomenergie und Atomzeitalter* (Frankfurt: Fischer, 1957).

von Weizsäcker, Carl Friedrich, *Bewusstseinswandel* (Munich: Hanser, 1988).

von Weizsäcker, Carl Friedrich, "Bohr hat Heisenberg nicht lange genug zugehört," *Die Welt* (February 8, 2002).

von Weizsäcker, Carl Friedrich, "Farm Hall und das deutsche Uranprojekt. Ein Gespräch," in Dieter Hoffmann (ed.), *Operation Epsilon. Die Farm-Hall-Protokolle erstmals vollständig, ergänzt um zeitgenössische Briefe und weitere Dokumente der 1945 in England internierten deutschen Atomforscher*, 2nd Ed. (Diepholz: GNT-Verlag, 2023), 519–549.

von Weizsäcker, Carl Friedrich, "Ich gebe zu, ich war verrückt' Carl Friedrich von Weizsäcker über die Chance der Deutschen im Zweiten Weltkrieg, die Atombombe zu bauen," *Der Spiegel*, 17 (1991), 227–238.

von Weizsäcker, Carl Friedrich, "Mit der Bombe leben (I)," *Die Zeit* (May 15, 1958).

von Weizsäcker, Carl Friedrich, "Mit der Bombe leben (II)," *Die Zeit* (May 22, 1958).

von Weizsäcker, Carl Friedrich, "Mit der Bombe leben (III)," *Die Zeit* (May 29, 1958).

von Weizsäcker, Carl Friedrich, "Mit der Bombe leben (IV)," *Die Zeit* (June 5, 1958).

Wagner, Patrick, *Notgemeinschaften der Wissenschaften. Die Deutsche Forschungsgemeinschaft (DFG) in drei politischen Systemen, 1920 bis 1973* (Stuttgart: Franz Steiner Verlag, 2021).

Walker, Mark, "Did Werner Heisenberg Understand How Atomic Bombs Worked?" *Berichte zur Wissenschaftsgeschichte*, 45 (2022), 219–244.

340   Bibliography

Walker, Mark, *Die Uranmaschine. Mythos und Wirklichkeit der deutschen Atombombe* (Berlin: Siedler Verlag, 1990).

Walker, Mark, *German National Socialism and the Quest for Nuclear Power, 1939–1949* (Cambridge: Cambridge University Press, 1989).

Walker, Mark, "Nuclear Weapons and Reactor Research at the Kaiser Wilhelm Institute for Physics," in Susanne Heim, Carola Sachse, and Mark Walker (eds.), *The Kaiser Wilhelm Society during National Socialism* (Cambridge: Cambridge University Press, 2009), 339–369.

Walker, Mark, "Physics, History, and the German Atomic Bomb," *Berichte zur Wissenschaftsgeschichte*, 40 (2017), 271–288.

Weart, Spencer, *The Rise of Nuclear Fear* (Cambridge, MA: Harvard University Press, 2012).

Weart, Spencer, *Scientists in Power* (Cambridge, MA: Harvard University Press, 1979).

"'Weiße Juden' in der Wissenschaft," *Das Schwarze Korps* (July 15, 1937).

Wellerstein, Alex, *Restricted Data: The History of Nuclear Secrecy in the United States* (Chicago: University of Chicago Press, 2021).

Wolff, Stefan, "Die Konstituierung eines Netzwerkes reaktionärer Physiker in der Weimarer Republik," *Berichte zur Wissenschaftsgeschichte*, 31 (2008), 372–392.

Wolff, Stefan, "Physicists in the 'Krieg der Geister': Wilhelm Wien's 'Proclamation,'" *Historical Studies in the Physical and Biological Sciences*, 33/2 (2003), 337–368.

Zierold, Kurt, *Forschungsförderung in drei Epochen* (Wiesbaden: Steiner Verlag, 1968).

Index

Abelson, Philip, 17, 40
Adenauer, Konrad, 230–236, 238–239
Alsos, 156–159
Alsos Mission, 116, 147–148, 171
Anschütz Company, 62, 80–82, 115–116
Ardenne, Manfred von, 41–42
Army Ordnance, 6, 23, 25–26, 29–30, 32–35,
    39, 42, 50–56, 59–62, 64, 69, 72, 83–84,
    88–89, 91–93, 95, 98, 116, 121, 125, 211,
    217, 260
Aryan Physics, 68, 175, 199, 209–213, 229, 257
Auer Society, 23, 34, 37, 50, 90–91, 98, 101,
    117, 120, 129

Baeumker, Adolf, 64
Bagge, Erich, 6–12, 23–24, 92, 105, 121,
    136, 151
Bamag Company, 114
Beams, Jesse, 61, 141
Belgium, 21, 35, 115, 256
Berg, Moe, 261
Beuthe, Hermann, 83, 203–204
Beyerle, Konrad, 80–81, 115–116, 126
Biermann, Ludwig, 244, 248
Blackett, Patrick, 7
Bøggild, Jørgen, 260
Bohr, Niels, 16–17, 21, 162, 169, 187, 198,
    220–222, 224, 226–229, 233, 240,
    243–249, 259–261, 263, 265–267
Bok, Bart, 177
Bonhoeffer, Dietrich, 131
Bonhoeffer, Karl-Friedrich, 30, 32, 43, 51, 59,
    79, 82, 118, 127, 131, 192
Borger, Gustav, 209, 257
Bormann, Martin, 133–134, 136
Born, Hedwig, 237–238
Born, Max, 216, 237
Borrmann, Gerhard, 119
Bosch, Carl, 18, 195, 217
Bothe, Walther, 23–24, 27–28, 35, 52, 54, 65,
    68, 81, 92–93, 95, 97–99, 101, 117, 148,
    154–155

Briggs, Asa, 42
Brighter than a Thousand Suns, 221, 226–227,
    233, 263, 272–273, 289
Brüche, Ernst, 154, 159
Bruno, Giordano, 186
Bulletin of the Atomic Scientists, 157, 159,
    166, 178
Bush, Vannevar, 71, 72, 107, 152, 169
Bütefisch, Heinrich, 60, 87, 111
Butenandt, Adolf, 218

Casimir, Hendrik, 255–256
Chadwick, James, 13
Clusius, Klaus, 25–26, 30, 32, 40, 54, 81,
    88–89, 97, 109, 113–114, 127–128
Coblitz, Wilhelm, 242, 258, 264
Conant, James, 72
concentration camps, 8, 104, 124, 126, 129–
    131, 133, 139, 152, 157–158, 170–174,
    194, 201, 204, 218–219, 225, 240, 242,
    253, 255–256, 258–259, 264
Coster, Dirk, 18, 171, 255
Cremer, Erica, 31
critical mass, 46–47, 53, 55–56, 66, 74–75,
    108, 142
Curie, Irène, 13–14
cyclotron, 17, 46, 66–67, 74, 107, 109, 148, 260

Dames, Wilhelm, 199–200
deBroglie, Louis, 187
Debye, Peter, 18, 54, 92, 187
Denmark, 21, 30, 220–221, 228, 240,
    243–249, 259–262, 264
Diebner, Kurt, 6–7, 11, 33–35, 41–42, 54,
    89, 93–95, 98–99, 101, 106, 117–118,
    120–121, 125–127, 137, 149, 154, 260
Dohnanyi, Hans von, 131
Döpel, Klara, 39, 63
Döpel, Robert, 37, 39, 63, 90, 97

Eddington, Arthur, 180
Eichmann, Adolf, 172

342   Index

Einstein, Albert, 20, 161, 169, 175, 179–185, 187, 189–191, 193–194, 198–203, 205–206, 209–214, 220
Eisenhower, General Dwight D., 85
Erbacher, Otto, 19
Esau, Abraham, 23, 54, 61, 80–82, 87–89, 91–95, 97–102, 109, 111, 115, 117, 132
Euler, Hans, 44
Euler-Chelpin, Hans von, 260

Faraday, Michael, 186
Farm Hall, 5–12, 23, 36, 55–56, 75, 132, 150–151, 156–157, 215, 219, 221
Fermi, Enrico, 13–14, 17, 20, 47, 107, 141–142, 165, 244
Finkelnburg, Wolfgang, 59, 209, 211
Fleischmann, Rudolf, 147–148, 157
Flügge, Siegfried, 16
France, 20–21, 35, 43, 147, 182, 189, 222, 253
Franck, James, 175–177, 216
Frank, Hans, 105, 242, 258–259, 264
Frank, Walter, 196
Franklin, Ursula Martius, 158
Freyer, Hans, 251–253, 264
Frick, Wilhelm, 192, 194
Frisch, Otto, 15–16, 18–19, 46, 215–216
Fromm, General Friedrich, 64–65, 211
Fünfer, Erwin, 101

Galilei, Galileo, 180, 186, 193
Gamow, George, 15, 175
Gehrcke, Ernst, 185
Geib, Karl-Hermann, 31, 113
Geiger, Hans, 24, 54
General Government, 257–259
Gerlach, Walther, 5, 7, 9, 11–12, 109–110, 112, 114–115, 117–121, 125, 132–134, 136, 148–149, 153, 204, 231–232, 303
German Academy for Aviation Research, 64, 80, 97–98, 257
German Chemical Society, 191
German Cultural Institute, 227, 240, 243–245, 247–249, 251–253, 259–261, 264
German Institute for Eastern Work, 242, 258–259
German Physical Society, 65, 181, 190–192, 210
German Research Council, 229–230
German Research Foundation, 194–197, 199, 230
   Emergency Foundation for German Science, 230
Gestapo, 41, 83–84, 128, 203, 224, 261–262
Glaser, Ludwig, 209
Glum, Friedrich, 217

Goebbels, Josef, 59, 77–79, 133, 135, 185, 194, 200, 258
Goerner, Johannes, 101, 132
Göring, Hermann, 7, 64, 94, 102, 132, 134, 205, 210
Görnnert, Fritz, 101
Göttingen Declaration, 229–235, 237–239
Goudsmit, Samuel, 147–150, 152–154, 156–157, 159–172, 174–179, 213–214, 220, 223, 233, 237–238, 255, 266, 284, 305
graphite, 24–25, 27–28, 32, 46, 52, 71–73, 106–107, 120, 122, 141–142
Great Britain, 21
Groth, Wilhelm, 23, 25, 61–62, 80–83, 115–116, 126, 141
Gürtner, Franz, 196

Haber, Fritz, 191–192
Haber Memorial, 192
Hahn, Otto, 5–7, 9–11, 13–19, 23, 35, 37, 39–40, 54–56, 59, 71, 92, 97, 105, 128–129, 132, 151, 157–158, 162, 168, 192, 215–219, 222, 231–232, 238–239
Haigerloch, 122–123, 135, 141
Halban, Hans von, 16
Hanle, Wilhelm, 23, 27–28, 52
Harnack House, 43, 68–70, 130
Harteck, Paul, 5–7, 9–11, 23, 25–27, 29–35, 37, 43, 48–49, 51, 54–56, 59–62, 79–84, 87–89, 92, 95, 97–98, 110–116, 118, 126–128, 131–132
Hartmann, Max, 218
heavy water, 6, 24–33, 37–40, 45–50, 52–53, 55–56, 58–63, 66, 70, 72–73, 81, 84–90, 92, 95–101, 106–107, 110–118, 120–123, 126, 133, 137, 140–141, 143, 149, 155, 159, 162, 226, 229
Hechingen, 8, 105, 118–121, 129–130, 134–137, 147, 149
Heisenberg, Elisabeth, 8, 22, 24, 35, 37, 39, 42–44, 63, 67, 69, 71, 102, 120–121, 128–131, 134–140, 149, 151–152, 172, 175, 203, 209, 216, 237, 241, 245–247, 249–252, 255–256, 258, 260, 266
Heisenberg, Erwin, 69
Heisenberg, Werner, 5–11, 12, 21–22, 24–25, 27–30, 33–40, 42–45, 48–51, 53–59, 61, 63–72, 75–76, 90–103, 105–106, 108–109, 111, 117–121, 123, 127–132, 134–140, 143, 147, 149–157, 159–176, 178–179, 198–214, 220–222, 224–231, 233, 238–267, 288
Hentschel, Klaus, 274
Herold, Paul, 30–31, 34, 60, 87, 114–115
Hertz, Gustav, 26

Index

Hess, Rudolf, 186, 197, 208, 214
Heuss, Theodor, 174
Heydrich, Reinhard, 8
Heymann, Ernst, 189
Himmler, Heinrich, 18, 61, 103–104, 133–134, 138, 157–158, 161, 171, 179, 186, 196, 202–208, 212–214, 229, 257, 264
Hindenburg, Otto von, 189, 191, 200
Hiroshima, 9–10, 55, 126, 142, 150–151, 156–157, 167, 215, 220, 229, 231
Hitler, Adolf, 7–9, 11, 18, 22, 35, 42, 45, 51, 64, 67, 69–70, 72, 77, 104–105, 107, 130–133, 136–139, 158, 164–165, 167–168, 172, 175–178, 184–186, 188–189, 192–197, 200–205, 207–208, 210, 214, 217, 219–221, 225–226, 258, 272–274, 307
Höcker, Karl-Heinz, 36, 51, 89, 94, 96, 98–100, 117, 147
Hoffmann, Dieter, 274
Höfler, Otto, 260–261, 264
Houtermans, Fritz, 41–42
Hungary, 251–253
Hutchins, Robert, 175–176

IG Farben, 25, 29–34, 60–61, 73, 84, 87–89, 112–114
Institute for Radium Research, 41
Irving, David, 65, 67, 69–70, 86, 140, 264
isotope enrichment, 6, 10, 17, 25, 27, 32–33, 41, 45–46, 48, 50, 52, 62, 72, 73–74, 83, 91, 97, 107–108, 140–142, 148
    separation tube, 25–27, 33, 84
    ultracentrifuge, 26, 61–62, 80–82, 115–116, 246
isotopes, 6, 13–15, 17, 25–26, 37, 48, 51–52, 61–62, 74, 107

Jensen, Johannes, 88, 229, 260
Jensen, Peter, 28
Joliot-Curie, Frédéric, 13–14, 16, 19–20, 29, 253
Joos, Georg, 22–23, 27
Jordan, Pascual, 232, 238
Juilfs, Johannes, 204, 207–208
Jungk, Robert, 221–228, 233–234, 239, 263, 272–274

Kaempffert, Waldemar, 159, 167, 170
Kaiser Wilhelm Institute for Anthropology, 218
Kaiser Wilhelm Institute for Brain Research, 218
Kaiser Wilhelm Institute for Chemistry, 14, 16, 18–19, 23, 37, 40, 105, 128–129, 217, 219

Kaiser Wilhelm Institute for Medical Research, 27
Kaiser Wilhelm Institute for Metals Research, 65, 195
Kaiser Wilhelm Institute for Physical Chemistry, 129, 191
Kaiser Wilhelm Institute for Physics, 6, 20, 23–24, 31, 34–35, 37–40, 49, 51, 54, 62, 70, 89, 91–93, 95, 98, 101–102, 105, 110, 113–114, 117–119, 121, 123, 128–130, 134, 136, 151, 179, 212, 257
Kaiser Wilhelm Institute for Psychiatry, 218
Kaiser Wilhelm Society, 18, 43, 53, 59, 64–65, 71, 77, 89, 91–92, 94, 100–101, 105, 109, 130, 132, 134, 151, 191–192, 194–195, 211, 216–219, 244, 251–252
Kaltenbrunner, Ernst, 8
Karlauf, Thomas, 272
Kepler, Johannes, 186, 190
Kienle, Hans, 244, 248
Koch, Peter Paul, 83–84
Korsching, Horst, 6, 151
Köster, Werner, 65
Kowarski, Lew, 16
Kramers, Hans, 254–257
Krauch, Carl, 87
Krupp Company, 62, 67
Kuiper, Gerard, 256
Kurchatov, I.V., 124

Ladenburg, Rudolf, 42, 220, 266
Langevin, Paul, 182
Laue, Max von, 5–11, 82, 92, 129, 136, 151, 157–159, 171, 175, 179, 190–194, 200–201, 204, 211
Laue, Theodore von, 9, 11, 158
Lawrence, Ernest O., 46
LeBon, Gustav, 185
Leeb, General Emil, 53–54, 211
Lenard, Philipp, 68, 175, 180–188, 192, 194–196, 198–200, 202–203, 206–207, 209, 211–212, 214, 257
Leopoldina Academy of Sciences, 273–274
Linde Society for Refrigeration, 33, 89, 113–114
Lüde Company, 118

Manhattan Project, 10–11, 76, 107–108, 141–142, 147, 157, 159, 162
Marshall, George C., 72
Mattauch, Josef, 23
Max Planck Institute for Physics, 151, 231
Max Planck Society, 151, 217–219, 239
McCloy, John, 174
McMillian, Edwin, 17, 40

344   Index

Meitner, Lise, 13–19, 23, 39, 170, 215–216, 219, 222, 248
Menge, Wolfgang, 273
Mengele, Josef, 218
Mentzel, Rudolf, 80, 91–92, 94, 97, 101, 109–110, 129, 133, 194–196, 199, 203, 208, 211, 242, 245
Mey, Karl, 193
Milch, General Field Marshall Erhard, 64–68, 97, 211
Montecatini Company, 88, 114
Morrison, Philipp, 157–159, 171
Müller, Paul, 36, 51, 89, 157
Müller, Wilhelm, 208–209

National Socialist German Workers Party, 7, 59, 64, 78–79, 103–105, 132–134, 136, 138, 172, 183, 185–186, 188, 194, 196–197, 202, 205–206, 208, 213, 217, 242, 245, 249–252, 257–258, 264
National Socialist University Lecturers League, 59, 209, 241, 257
Naturwissenschaften, Die, 15, 18, 160, 171
Netherlands, 21, 35, 170, 254–257, 259, 262
New York Times, 159, 167–168, 180
Newton, Isaac, 180, 186, 190
Nier, Alfred, 17, 61
Nobel Prize, 13, 183–184, 201, 215–216, 239, 251, 259
Norsk Hydro, 29–32, 48–49, 51, 55, 59–60, 73, 84–88, 110–113, 119, 286
Norway, 21, 28, 30, 32–33, 43, 49, 51, 59–60, 84–88, 110–112, 115, 117–118, 229, 248
nuclear reactor, 7, 10–11, 24, 40, 56, 71–73, 89, 106–107, 141–142, 168, 229, 231, 246
  uranium burner, 24, 28, 38–39, 41, 45, 49–50, 52–53, 62–63, 65, 70, 73, 98, 100, 118, 120
  uranium machine, 11, 16, 24–29, 31–39, 41, 45–46, 48–50, 52, 57–58, 62–63, 65, 70, 73, 90–95, 97–99, 106, 116–123, 141, 143, 148, 153, 155–157, 162, 165, 217

Operation Barbarossa, 44
Oppenheimer, J. Robert, 74–75, 108, 142, 165, 269
Osenberg, Werner, 115, 134
Ossietzky, Carl von, 201–202

Paschen, Friedrich, 193
Pash, Colonel Boris, 139–140, 147
Peierls, Rudolf, 46, 170, 305
People's Storm, 134, 136
Philipp, Kurt, 19

Physical Review, 244
Physikalische Blätter, 154, 159
Planck, Max, 43, 64, 179, 182–183, 187, 189–191, 193, 195, 212, 217, 219, 251–252
plutonium, 10, 42, 65, 69, 72–73, 75, 106–107, 141–142, 156–157, 162, 165–168, 217, 246, 274
  element 94, 17, 39–41, 46, 49, 52–53, 65–66, 75, 94
  transuranic element, 13–15, 17, 19, 39–40, 42, 45, 92, 157
Poland, 8, 21–22, 103, 105, 152, 216, 242, 249, 257, 259, 264
Pose, Heinz, 99
Prandtl, Ludwig, 205–207, 210, 213, 312
Prussian Academy of Sciences, 179–180, 189–190, 193, 213, 257
Pugwash, 236
  Federation of German Scientists, 239

Rabinowitch, Eugene, 159
Rajewsky, Boris, 218
Ramsauer, Carl, 65, 210, 213, 257
Rathenau, Walther, 182–183
Regional NSDAP leaders, 103
Reich Chemical-Technical Institute, 95, 98
Reich Kinship Office, 129–130
Reich Metals Office, 26
Reich Ministry of Armaments, 90, 92, 114, 125, 128, 257
Reich Ministry of Aviation, 205, 211
Reich Ministry of Foreign Affairs, 20, 172, 174, 243–245, 260
Reich Ministry of Science, Education, and Culture, 22, 64–65, 68, 175, 191, 194–196, 198–199, 202–204, 208, 211, 241–245, 249–251, 253–255, 257–258, 262
  Prussian Ministry of Culture, 191
Reich Ministry of the Interior, 18, 194
Reich Physical-Technical Institute, 91, 184, 192–193, 195–196, 203
Reich Research Council, 23, 53–54, 56, 59, 61, 64, 69–71, 91, 97, 109, 116, 119, 132–133, 157, 162, 194, 210, 230
Rein, Hermann, 218
Restoration of the Professional Civil Service, 190, 198
Rexer, Ernst, 99
Riehl, Nikolaus, 23, 34, 50, 91, 117, 129–130
Rittner, T. H., 5
Röntgen, Wilhelm, 183
Roosevelt, Franklin Delano, 20, 72
Rosenberg, Alfred, 185–186, 205, 257

Index

Ross, Colin, 138
Rust, Bernhard, 54, 65, 189, 191–192, 194–195, 200, 210, 244, 285
Rutherford, Ernest, 13

Sauter, Fritz, 211
Savitch, Paul, 14
Scherrer, Paul, 248
Schintlmeister, Josef, 41
Schrödinger, Erwin, 187, 190, 198
Schumann, Erich, 50–51, 54, 92, 95, 125, 194
Schwarze Korps, Das, 22, 200–203, 207–208
Siemens Company, 91
Slovakia, 253–254
Society for German Natural Scientists and Physicians, 181, 183
Sollinger, Karl, 196–197
Sommerfeld, Arnold, 128, 181–182, 184, 187, 197–201, 204, 208–209
Soviet Union, 22, 26, 40–41, 44–45, 50–51, 71, 77–79, 105, 113, 121, 124, 126–127, 151–152, 169, 210, 218, 230, 232, 235, 240, 246, 262, 265
Speer, Albert, 64–72, 90–92, 94–95, 97, 100–101, 103–105, 107, 109, 117, 119, 132–134, 154, 211, 223, 229, 257–258
Spiegel, Der, 233, 273–274
SS, 7–8, 18, 22, 35, 44, 61, 103–104, 115, 129, 133, 137–140, 149, 161, 172, 186, 194–195, 200, 202, 204–208, 212–214, 229, 247, 257, 260, 264, 293
    Security Service, 22, 79, 104, 196, 203–205
Stadtilm, 116–117, 121, 123, 137, 148
Stalingrad, 70, 77–79, 256, 262
Stark, Johannes, 68, 161, 175, 182, 184–188, 191–209, 211–214, 231
Starke, Kurt, 40
Stimson, Henry, 72
Strassmann, Fritz, 13–19, 35, 40, 162, 168, 217
Strauss, Franz Josef, 231, 233–234
Strömgren, Bengt, 244, 248
Strömgren, Elis, 248
Strong, General George V., 85
Suess, Hans, 29, 59, 84–85, 87, 112–115, 259
Suhr, Albert, 82–83
Swedish Academy of Sciences, 216
Switzerland, 250–251, 261–262
Szilard, Leo, 16, 19–20, 42, 47

Tailfingen, 8
Teller, Edward, 175–178, 223, 225, 234
Telschow, Ernst, 89, 92–95, 217–218, 251–252

Themistocles, 191
Thomson, J. J., 183
Thüring, Bruno, 209, 212
Todt, Fritz, 64
Tomaschek, Rudolf, 199, 209
Trinks, Walter, 125
Tronstad, Leif, 86
Turner, Louis, 17

United States, 5–6, 10–11, 16, 20–21, 23, 35, 45–47, 51, 53–55, 58, 62, 64–67, 71–76, 87, 97, 106–108, 139, 141–143, 149–157, 159–164, 168–169, 171, 175–178, 189, 198, 213–215, 217, 219, 221–223, 227, 229, 232, 235, 240, 243–244, 252, 259, 265–267
University of Berlin, 130, 193, 203, 218, 253, 257
University of Leipzig, 24, 164, 198, 202, 242, 250
University of Munich, 181, 198, 261, 264
Unsold, Albrecht, 244
uranium 235, 10, 17, 24–26, 28, 35, 39–41, 45–46, 51–53, 55–59, 61, 66, 72, 74–75, 80, 94, 97, 108, 124, 141–142, 156–157, 162, 217, 301
Urfeld, 102–103, 128, 130, 134–135, 137–140

Vahlen, Theodor, 195, 213
Verschuer, Otmar von, 218
Vögler, Albert, 53–54, 59, 64–65, 92–95, 101–102, 105, 109, 111, 117, 132, 134, 217, 252
Völkischer Beobachter, Der, 185, 192, 198–199, 201

Waerden, Bartel van der, 164–165, 220, 226
Wagner, Adolf, 196
Wallace, Henry A., 72
Watzlawek, Hugo, 41
Wednesday Society, 130
Weisskopf, Viktor, 166–167, 177–178, 235–236, 238
Weizsäcker, Carl Friedrich von, 6–8, 11, 20–21, 36, 40–42, 51, 58, 65, 71, 89, 93, 121, 131, 150–151, 157, 172, 174–179, 209, 211–212, 214, 220–229, 231–240, 243–245, 247–249, 251–253, 260–261, 265–266, 272–274
Weizsäcker, Ernst von, 69, 172, 174, 243, 245, 264
Wesch, Ludwig, 203–204, 209
Wheeler, John, 16–17, 162
Wiechert, Ernst, 194
Wigner, Eugene, 20

346 Index

Wildhagen, Eduard, 196
Wirtz, Karl, 6–8, 11, 31–32, 37, 39–40, 48,
　　59–60, 62, 84, 88, 100–101, 118–119,
　　121–123, 149, 151, 155, 236
Witzell, Admiral Karl, 65, 210–211

*Zeitschrift für die gesamte
　　Naturwissenschaft*, 206–207,
　　211, 214
Zimmer, Karl, 90, 117
Zinn, Howard, 16